SPANISH HORROR FILM

Traditions in World Cinema

General Editors
Linda Badley (Middle Tennessee State
    University)
R. Barton Palmer (Clemson University)

Founding Editor
Steven Jay Schneider (New York
    University)

www.euppublishing.com/series/tiwc

SPANISH HORROR FILM

Antonio Lázaro-Reboll

EDINBURGH
University Press

© Antonio Lázaro-Reboll, 2012, 2014

First published in hardback in 2012
This paperback edition 2014

Edinburgh University Press Ltd
The Tun – Holyrood Road
12 (2f) Jackson's Entry
Edinburgh EH8 8PJ
www.euppublishing.com

Typeset in 10/12.5pt Sabon
by Servis Filmsetting Ltd, Stockport, Cheshire, and
printed and bound in Great Britain by
CPI Group (UK) Ltd, Croydon CR0 4YY

A CIP record for this book is available from the British Library

ISBN 978 0 7486 3638 9 (hardback)
ISBN 978 0 7486 3639 6 (paperback)
ISBN 978 0 7486 3640 2 (webready PDF)
ISBN 978 0 7486 7062 8 (epub)

Grateful acknowledgement is made for permission to reproduce
material previously published elsewhere. Every effort has been
made to trace the copyright holders, but if any have been
inadvertently overlooked, the publisher will be pleased to make
the necessary arrangements at the first opportunity.

Arts & Humanities
Research Council

CONTENTS

ACKNOWLEDGEMENTS

This book would not have been possible without the funding of the Arts and Humanities Research Council and the British Academy. The Colyer Fergusson Fund at the University of Kent also financially supported the initial stages of this project. Colleagues at the University of Kent have been extremely generous with their support and encouragement throughout the completion of the book, in particular Karl Leydecker and Laurence Goldstein, who wholeheartedly supported applications for study leave in 2008 and 2010. Special thanks go to my colleague at Kent, Peter Stanfield, who has read and commented on every single chapter. Many ideas about film cycles and genres were informed by conversations with Peter over scrambled eggs and americanos. My thanks, too, to Jo Labanyi, who read and endorsed the original book proposal; this gratitude is extended to the anonymous Edinburgh University Press readers for their comments and suggestions; to Josetxo Cerdán and Miguel Fernández-Labayen, who had forced upon them the reading of some chapters; and to Andy Willis for his initial encouragement to write a book on Spanish horror film after our enjoyable collaboration on a co-edited volume on Spanish popular cinema a few years ago. The work of colleagues in Film Studies and Hispanic Studies on both sides of the Atlantic – Mark Jancovich, Tatjana Pavlović, Dolores Tierney and Núria Triana-Toribio – has been an influence on my own manuscript.

The initial gathering of archival material took place in the Filmoteca de Madrid and the Filmoteca de Zaragoza. Miguel Ángel, Alicia and Diego were terrific at locating primary resources in Madrid, while Teresa and Manolo went out of their way to track down material from the Archivo Rotellar in

Zaragoza. Manolo's memories of long-gone neighbourhood cinemas were wonderfully entertaining. I am also indebted to Katia Casariego at Filmax, Lucía Etxevarría at Telecinco, Mercedes González Barreiro and Diego Pajuelo Almodóvar at El Deseo, Carlos Plaza and Alfonso López at the San Sebastián Horror and Fantasy Film Festival for providing me with publicity and press material on contemporary Spanish horror production and genre festivals. Carlos Giménez (*Paracuellos*) and Miguel Ángel Martín (*Snuff 2000, Killer Barbys* and *La lengua asesina*) have been extremely kind in allowing me to reproduce their work, as have Jordi Costa and Darío Adanti (*Mis problemas con Amenábar*). Some material and factual information related to specialist genre publications, magazines and comics was promptly and generously made available to me by a number of people: Manuel Barrero, Director of tebeosfera.com, Antonio Guisado, Librarian of tercerafundacion.com, and Carlos Abraham at the 'Museo Iconográfico de la Literatura Popular' blog. A big thank you to Charles Young, technician at the School of European Culture and Languages, who scanned most of the illustrations used in this volume.

It was a pleasure to meet horrormeister Narciso Ibáñez Serrador – how did you pull that one out of the hat, Willis? Oh, yes. Chicho's daughter, Pepa Ibáñez, happened to be a student of yours at the University of Salford. Among the many other pleasures involved in this venture was exchanging e-mails with director Nacho Cerdà, whose generosity with press materials and illustrations is unparalleled – thank you for all the CDs. Manolo Valencia and his fanzine *2000maniacos* are to blame for some of my exquisite bad taste. Thanks for thirty years of psychotronic stuff and for sending all those front covers; they are gems. I am also grateful to many other *fanzinerosos* and cultural commentators, from different generations: Pierrot (also known as Antonio José Gracia, who sadly passed away in 2009, Luis Gasca, Carlos Águilar (*Morpho*), Jordi Costa (reviews, articles, books and so on), Pedro Calleja (*Serie B*), Carlos Díaz Maroto (*Sueño del Fevre*), Rubén Lardín (*ojalatemueras*), Borja Crespo (*Subterfuge*), Diego López (*El buque maldito*), David García (*Monster World*), and the many other fanzine and magazine editors mentioned in this book. My apologies if I fail to acknowledge anybody. José Manuel Serrano Cueto and Diego López were tremendously generous in sharing contact details and e-mail addresses with me. Hope we meet one day. Beyond Spain, I extend my thanks to Jo Botting (*Shivers*) and Ron McKenzie (*Rue Morgue*).

My heartfelt thanks to series editors Linda Badley and Robert E. Palmer for their belief in (and patience with) the project. Linda helped me to sharpen the original proposal. Gillian Leslie, my editor at Edinburgh University Press, has been tremendously supportive, tactful and patient. So were previous editors Sarah Edwards and Vicky Donald.

To my family I owe a lot. To my parents, Conchita and José Antonio, my education. My sister Patricia and my brother-in-law Roberto had to put up with me at their flat in Barcelona so that I could complete parts of the manuscript. Finally, all my love and gratitude have to go to my partner, Donna Fitzgerald; Donna read every single page and footnote, made suggestions and corrections, and proofread. She suffered my absences, preoccupations and silences, and looked after our daughter tirelessly. This book is dedicated to her.

FIGURE PERMISSIONS

Figures 1, 2, 4–8, 10, 12–13, 15–18, 20–22, 36: Used with permission from Filmoteca Española.
Figures 9 and 11: Used with permission from Arturo Marcos.
Figure 24: Used with permission from Enric Torres.
Figures 29 and 32: Used with permission from Manuel Valencia.
Figure 30: *Killer Barbys*. Used with permission from Miguel Ángel Martín.
Figure 31: *SNUFF 2000*. Used with permission from Borja Crespo.
Figures 33, 34 and 41: Used with permission from El Deseo.
Figure 35: Used with permission from Jordi Costa and Darío Adanti.
Figures 37 and 43: Used with permission from Telecinco Cinema.
Figures 38 and 39: Used with permission from Nacho Cerdà.
Figure 42: Used with permission from Carlos Giménez.
Figures 44 and 45: Used with permission from Filmax.

LIST OF ILLUSTRATIONS

TRADITIONS IN WORLD CINEMA

General editors: **Linda Badley and R. Barton Palmer**
Founding editor: **Steven Jay Schneider**

Traditions in World Cinema is a series of textbooks and monographs devoted to the analysis of currently popular and previously underexamined or undervalued film movements from around the globe. Also intended for general-interest readers, the textbooks in this series offer undergraduate- and graduate-level film students accessible and comprehensive introductions to diverse traditions in world cinema. The monographs open up for advanced academic study more specialised groups of films, including those that require theoretically-oriented approaches. Both textbooks and monographs provide thorough examinations of the industrial, cultural, and socio-historical conditions of production and reception.

The flagship textbook for the series includes chapters by noted scholars on traditions of acknowledged importance (the French New Wave, German Expressionism), recent and emergent traditions (New Iranian, post-Cinema Novo), and those whose rightful claim to recognition has yet to be established (the Israeli persecution film, global found footage cinema). Other volumes concentrate on individual national, regional or global cinema traditions. As the introductory chapter to each volume makes clear, the films under discussion form a coherent group on the basis of substantive and relatively transparent, if not always obvious, commonalities. These commonalities may be formal, stylistic or thematic, and the groupings may, although they need not, be popularly identified as genres, cycles or movements (Japanese horror, Chinese martial arts cinema, Italian Neorealism). Indeed, in cases in which a group of films is not already commonly identified as a tradition, one purpose of the volume is to establish its claim to importance and make it visible (East Central European Magical Realist cinema, Palestinian cinema).

Textbooks and monographs include:

- An introduction that clarifies the rationale for the grouping of films under examination
- A concise history of the regional, national, or transnational cinema in question
- A summary of previous published work on the tradition
- Contextual analysis of industrial, cultural and socio-historical conditions of production and reception
- Textual analysis of specific and notable films, with clear and judicious application of relevant film theoretical approaches
- Bibliograph(ies)/filmograph(ies)

Monographs may additionally include:

- Discussion of the dynamics of cross-cultural exchange in light of current research and thinking about cultural imperialism and globalisation, as well as issues of regional/national cinema or political/aesthetic movements (such as new waves, postmodernism, or identity politics)
- Interview(s) with key filmmakers working within the tradition.

INTRODUCTION

Contemporary contexts of horror, psychotronic and paracinema fandom in the US, UK and Spain have been crucial in the circulation and treatment of Spanish horror films past and present. As a fan, reader and consumer of American alternative publications such as *The Psychotronic Encyclopedia of Film* and *Video Watchdog* and of Spanish fanzine *2000maniacos* in the early 1990s, my own positioning, taste and subcultural capital in relation to Spanish and international horror cinematic traditions and, by extension, the wider cultural field of horror are informed by paracinema and psychotronic culture. In his fan publication *The Psychotronic Encyclopedia of Film* (1989), Weldon described psychotronic movies as exploitation films that have been 'treated with indifference or contempt' by critics but that have been sought after and celebrated by fans because of their bizarreness, unclassifiability or portrayal of 'violence, sex, noise, and often mindless escapism' (Weldon 1989: xii). A significant number of Spanish horror films produced in the heyday of European exploitation in the late 1960s and early 1970s are included in Weldon's global A to Z of psychotronic film, among them *La residencia / The Finishing School* (Narciso Ibáñez Serrador 1969), *La noche de Walpurgis / The Shadow of the Werewolf* (León Klimovsky 1970), *La noche del terror ciego / Tombs of the Blind Dead* (Amando de Ossorio 1972), *Pánico en el Transiberiano / Horror Express* (Eugenio Martín 1973), *No profanar el sueño de los muertos / The Living Dead at Manchester Morgue* (Jorge Grau 1974) and, above all, the films of the doyen of Spanish exploitation filmmaking, Jesús Franco (*El secreto del Dr Orloff / Dr Jekyll's Mistresses* (1964); *Drácula contra Frankenstein / The*

Screaming Dead (1971); *Las vampiras / Vampiros Lesbos* (1971)). Many of these films would also fit Sconce's critical category of 'paracinema', as articulated in his influential article '"Trashing" the Academy: Taste, Excess and an Emerging Politics of Cinematic Style' (1995). Here Sconce focuses on a cinematic subculture, of which *The Psychotronic Encyclopedia of Film* is a prime example, characterised by the valorisation of 'just about every other manifestation of exploitation cinema' through

> a particular reading protocol, a counter-aesthetic turned subcultural sensibility devoted to all manner of cultural detritus. In short, the explicit manifestation of paracinematic culture is to valorize all forms of paracinematic 'trash' whether such films have been either explicitly rejected or simply ignored by legitimate film culture. (1995: 372)

Sconce emphasises the role that paracinephiles play in their opposition to film theory and criticism within academia, for they introduce 'a dispute over *how* to approach cinema as much as a conflict over *what* cinema to approach' (1995: 380, author's emphases); more broadly, their opposition indicates that the differing reading strategies of fans and critics serve to expose and challenge the limits of film theory and historiography.

In Spain, the fanzine culture surrounding psychotronic cinema in all its elastic generic and subgeneric strands is typified by what is very possibly Europe's oldest fanzine publication, *2000maniacos* (1989 to the present). Contributors to *2000maniacos*, for example, would describe themselves as *cinéfagos* (cinéphages), where the suffix '-phage' is an indication of the way in which they engage with and, above all consume, films. Pedro Calleja, editor of Spanish fanzine *Serie B* in the early 1980s and a regular presence in *2000maniacos* for the last two decades, makes a distinction between 'cinéphiles' and 'cinéphages':

> All cinéphages have a cinéphile inside, but not all cinéphiles have a cinéphage inside. The term cinéphage started to be used in publications such as *Starfix* and *Mad Movies* in the late eighties, [which were] two of the most influential French magazines among lovers of cinéma fantastique and entertainment cinema. In Spain it was popularised through the film review sections of [popular film magazine] *Fotogramas*, the monthly [film specialist magazine] *Fantastic magazine* and the fanzine *2000maniacos*. A cinéphage is a cinéphile without prejudices. Somebody, as filmmaker John Waters once put it, with an exquisite bad taste. (2003b: 156)

Many contemporary North American and British genre magazines and fanzines (*Fangoria*, *Rue Morgue*, *Shivers*), mail-order catalogues and websites

(Sinister Cinema, European Trash Cinema, Something Weird Video, Anchor Bay), and internet forums (The Latarnia Forums, The Cinehound, Cult Laboratories Film and TV Forum) also affect and influence (re)configurations of Spanish horror film. For example, Spanish horror film is usually categorised and discussed as part of a wider 'Eurohorror' tradition, which more often than not intersects quite loosely and messily with the term (s)exploitation. These classificatory labels come together, for instance, in the work of Pete Tombs for Titan Books and for UK TV Channel 4. His work *Immoral Tales. Sex and Horror in Europe 1956–1984* (1995), co-authored with Cathal Tohill, contributed to the dissemination of European (s)exploitation traditions and gave prominence to the Spanish case. Similarly, his TV series *Eurotika!* (Channel 4, UK, 1999), created with Andy Starker, introduced British audiences to the horrific worlds of Paul Naschy, Amando de Ossorio, Jorge Grau and others, in the episode 'Blood and Sand'. Another episode was solely devoted to 'The Diabolical Mr. Franco'.[1] As the female voiceover seductively declares at the opening of 'Blood and Sand', 'Spain, the playground of Europe in the sixties, became a hotbed of horror in the seventies, turning out several hundred lurid shockers.' This initial contextualisation is then followed by a culinary metaphor pertaining to strong cinematic tastes: 'Spanish horror had a special flavour: it was earthy and primal.' This crude and visceral 'Spanish flavour' continues to captivate genre journalists and fans alike. *Fangoria*'s special 300th anniversary issue, devoted to the compilation of 'the mother of all horror-movie lists', selected *Horror Rises from the Tomb* (see Figure 1) and other Spanish titles for the 'earthy, innocent charm' viewed as characteristic of such 'messy or sleazy early-70s Spanish horror' (Alexander 2011: 43). A cursory look at internet forums devoted to the discussion of the international world of horror cinema reveals that Spanish horror film is frequently debated under the category or thread of 'Eurohorror', as in, for example, The Latarnia Forums (latarniaforums.yuku.com), which feature the popular and highly participatory message boards 'The Spanish Horror Film', 'The Paul Naschy Forum' and 'The Franco Lounge'.[2]

Over the last forty years, horror film has formed a significant part of Spain's local and transnational filmic production and is part and parcel of the international and global circulation, reception and consumption of horror cinema. It has produced its own auteurs, stars and cycles, which have reached the status of cult movies within contemporary contexts of horror fandom. Like any other traditions of horror cinema, it has contributed to the formulas, themes and motifs of a genre conventionally characterised by product differentiation and familiar patterns of reception and consumption. Certainly, any critical history of Spanish horror film must extend beyond histories of Spanish cinema and must be seen as part of transnational cultural flows and international traditions of horror cinema. Building on and establishing a dialogue with existing

Figure 1   Products such as *El espanto surge de la tumba* / *Horror Rises from the Tomb* (Carlos Aured 1973) have come to define Spanish horror film for many horror fans across the globe.

re-evaluations of the horror genre at an international level (Hawkins 2000; Schneider 2003; Schneider and Williams 2005; Hantke 2004; Jancovich 2002; Hills 2005; Hutchings 2008; Conrich 2010), *Spanish Horror Film* functions as a case-study for discussing current debates on how to think and write about a genre which has been excluded from dominant accounts of Spanish cinema. In relation to the academic field of Spanish film studies, one of the aims of the volume is therefore to reassess the place of the horror genre in dominant histories of Spanish cinema and reintegrate marginalised filmic and cultural practices into Spanish film history by considering and examining constructions of the field of Spanish horror film. Such a project inevitably forms part of the critical remapping of Spanish cinema history undertaken in recent studies on popular cinema and genre (Triana-Toribio 2003; Lázaro-Reboll and Willis 2004; Marsh 2006; Beck and Rodríguez-Ortega 2008). This critical history therefore examines Spanish horror film in relation to canonical histories of the genre and the role that specific cultural agents play in constructions of the canon and of Spanish film history, the shifting terrains of genre classification and taste, the impact of changing technologies in developments of the genre, and the ways in which different types of fandom write about Spanish horror film.

As Mark Jancovich argues in relation to the horror genre, 'different social groups construct it in different, competing ways as they seek to identify with or distance themselves from the term, and associate different texts with these constructions of horror' (2002: 159). Differing narrative histories of Spanish horror film, which act as cultural platforms for constructions of the genre and its canon, are bound up with cultural assumptions, tastes and values. In this respect, dominant critical frameworks for discussions of the genre have tended to focus on production and accord the individual author a central role in the development of Spanish horror film. While my study investigates key directors and films, *Spanish Horror Film* argues for a more inclusive cultural geography of horror which takes into account the institutions and technologies, genre users and consumers that shape and participate in the process of genre classification and (re)configuration.

For decades, horror has been the outcast genre of Spanish cinema. As Beck and Rodríguez-Ortega observe in *Contemporary Spanish Cinema and Genre*, 'the view of genre [in the case of Spanish film scholarship] has almost exclusively been constructed negatively' (2008: 5). The so-called 'horror boom' of the late 1960s and early 1970s was reviled by contemporary critics, film historians and scholars, who consigned horror titles to the margins of Spanish film history. Román Gubern's introductory remarks in the 'Foreword' to the first critical study devoted to genre cinema, *Cine español, cine de subgéneros* (1974), have held sway until very recently. The specific critical and ideological operations at stake in Gubern's writing are discussed in detail in Chapter

1. Briefly put, Gubern saw contemporaneous Spanish horror film as wholly derivative of authentic American and European horror traditions. 'This insubstantial Spanish filmic production', he prophesied, 'will never make it into histories of Spanish cinema, unless it is dealt with in a succinct footnote' (1974: 16). And yet Spanish horror film of this period, as I argue in the first five chapters of this volume, was a dominant and indeed crucial part of the film culture available during this period, intersecting in dynamic and productive ways with contiguous subgenres (fantasy, suspense, thrillers) and other media (comics, pulp and television). The crossover between genres, cross-media interaction or the synergies between cinema and television are aspects that are addressed at various stages in the book.

The opening lines of a recently edited collection of essays on international horror, *Horror Zone: The Cultural Experience of Contemporary Horror* (2010) – 'the horror film is arguably the most robust, pliable, and successful of genres within contemporary cinema' (Conrich 2010: 1) – are equally applicable to the Spanish horror context. The 1990s and the 2000s have witnessed the commercial, critical and cultural renaissance of the horror genre in Spain. For many commentators, this resurgence is associated with a new generation of filmmakers who have revitalised the genre and attracted mainstream audiences. It might be argued that the box-office and critical success of such films as *El día de la bestia / Day of the Beast* (Álex de la Iglesia 1995), *Tesis / Thesis* (Alejandro Amenábar 1996), *Los sin nombre / The Nameless* (Jaume Balagueró 1999), *El laberinto del fauno / Pan's Labyrinth* (Guillermo del Toro 2001) and *El orfanato / The Orphanage* (Juan Antonio Bayona 2007) has made the academic study of contemporary Spanish horror critically acceptable.[3] The vitality of the contemporary field of Spanish horror, however, cannot be accounted for solely in terms of changes in industrial and production practices and the work of individual directors. The fanzine scene, non-Spanish-language specialist genre publications, and the specialised film festival circuit in and beyond Spain have been the life force of the genre throughout the last two decades. As specific sites of cultural and taste formations, alternative publications and horror-themed film festivals play a significant role in acting as cultural and industrial platforms for the international, cross-generic and multifarious dimension of the genre. They also provide a key site for the social processes of classification of the horror and fantasy genres through the discursive activities of genre users.

Three well-informed and superbly illustrated histories of Spanish horror and fantasy film emerge out of this context: *Cine fantástico y de terror español. 1900–1983* (1999a), *Cine fantástico y de terror español. 1984–2004* (2005), both edited by genre critic and journalist Carlos Águilar in collaboration with the San Sebastián Horror and Fantasy Film Festival, and *Profanando el sueño de los muertos* (2010), written by critic and current Director of the Sitges

Festival, Ángel Sala. Águilar and Sala offer general readers and fans alike an invaluable catalogue of films, directors and actors, as well as information about trends associated with Spanish horror and fantasy throughout the last century. Above all, their edited collections demonstrate the vital role of festivals and fans in recording the twists and turns of a popular genre which had been overlooked and ostracised by mainstream critics and academic scholars.

Unlike the above anthologies, which take a much-needed encyclopedic approach to the subject, *Spanish Horror Film* proposes an archeology of the genre which draws upon recent theorisations of the horror genre within film studies, cultural studies, and historical and reception studies, to understand the larger cultural field of Spanish horror and its cultural experiences. In other words, the volume considers how the field of horror 'intersects with other fields, for example, journalism, academic subcultural production, literary, television and film production, and fan subcultural production' (Hills 2005: 168). Each chapter therefore integrates the discursive practices of genre journalism (specialist magazines) and fan writing (fanzines), the synergies between horror film and other forms of popular culture, and the significance of new technologies (video, digital technology and the internet) for genre production and consumption. In order to produce close readings of specific texts and figures, the volume brings promotion and advertising material (pressbooks, posters and trailers), multiple forms of reviewing (trade publications, critical reviews and fan writing) and legal documents (censorship files and film policies) into the analyses. These materials shape the analysis of the discursive structures through which Spanish horror film is produced, circulated and consumed – a critical, historical and methodological approach which has informed my work to date (2004, 2005, 2009, 2012).

As the chronological references in the chapter titles indicate, the volume is organised following a linear order. A glance at the table of contents reveals that more attention is given to the early period – the 1960s and 1970s era – than to the contemporary context. However, the rationale for structuring the volume in this manner reflects the fluctuations in the development of Spanish horror film, as well as wider industrial, cultural and socio-historical changes in the conditions of production and reception. Unquestionably, the highest point in production was the period 1968 to 1975. The production of horror in the late 1970s and during the 1980s decreases dramatically for several reasons: firstly, the boom in historical and political films during the early years of the democracy; secondly, the so-called Ley Miró (film legislation established by the Socialist government in 1983), which privileged the production of high-quality films, based mainly on literary or historical sources; and, thirdly, changing habits in the consumption of audiovisual material. It is not until the late 1990s and the early 2000s that Spanish horror reaches another production peak. Contextually, the examination of the historical period covered in the volume is firmly located in relation to broader shifts in recent Spanish history: namely, late Francoism, the end of the dictatorship with the death of Franco on 20 November 1975, the transition to democracy from the end of 1975 to the first democratic elections in June 1977 and the ensuing democratic period. The horror genre in the 1960s and 1970s provided, in common with other international counterparts, a barometer of the ideological, institutional and social contradictions and tensions of the times. While many horror films offered resistance to a repressive and homogenising mainstream, others presented reactionary themes, characters and narrative resolutions. Equally, some contemporary Spanish horror production continues to give voice to cultural anxieties at the turn of the twenty-first century: the role of the media in society and its representation of violence, as present in *Tesis* or the *[•REC]* franchise, or filmic representations of the Spanish Civil War and its legacy, such as Guillermo del Toro's *El espinazo del diablo / The Devil's Backbone* (2001) and *El laberinto del fauno*, which lend themselves to a more allegorical and political reading though their engagement with memories and histories that have been erased from official discourses on contemporary democratic Spain.

The volume is organised into seven chapters. Chapter 1 examines the so-called Spanish 'horror boom', the peak period in the production of Spanish horror films between 1968 and 1975. This commercially popular, yet critically derided, tradition is explored in relation to other contemporary popular genres and dominant aesthetics, as well as to institutional practices such as censorship and film legislation. The chapter addresses the diversity of production and the discrepancy between consumption and exhibition practices and praxes of critical reception in order to dispel homogenising views of the period and to provide a broad overview of the riches of the genre.

The following three chapters look at specific Spanish figures, films and horror creations. Chapter 2 provides a discussion of Dr Orloff, Jesús Franco's addition to the mad scientist movie tradition; the lycanthrope Waldemar Daninsky, the creation of actor, scriptwriter and director Jacinto Molina and his on-screen alter ego Paul Naschy; and the Knights Templar, the zombie-like medieval knights conceived by Amando de Ossorio. These horrific creatures serve as examples of the movement of transculturation inscribed in Spanish horror film, whereby Spanish filmmakers produced their own horror films following international genre products and established monster traditions populating movies, comics and pulp fiction while simultaneously translating them and imbuing them with a certain local flavour and relevance. Notwithstanding the popularity and cult status of the likes of Franco and Naschy among contemporary horror and psychotronic fans, the most culturally prominent image of horror in Spain from the mid-1960s to the mid-1970s was Narciso Ibáñez Serrador, due to his horror–suspense series *Historias para no dormir / Stories to Keep You Awake* (1966–8) on Spanish television. Chapter 3 provides a detailed analysis of Ibáñez Serrador's TV production, as well as his successful transition to the big screen with the films *La residencia / The Finishing School* and *¿Quién puede matar a un niño? / Who Can Kill a Child?* (1976). Ibáñez Serrador is a fascinating case which, on the one hand, enables us to delve into the creative, dynamic and productive cross-media relationships between pulp fiction, television, film and radio; on the other hand, it also raises questions about the cultural status of television and popular cinema and the vexed issues of quality TV and quality cinema. Chapter 4 also turns its attention to the work of a specific director, Eloy de la Iglesia, with particular emphasis on his body of work during the early 1970s, *El techo de cristal / The Glass Ceiling* (1971), *La semana del asesino / Cannibal Man* (1972), *Nadie oyó gritar / No One Heard the Scream* (1972) and *Una gota de sangre para morir amando / Murder in a Blue World* (1973). De la Iglesia's engagement with the horror genre and other related ones throws up remarkable questions of gender identity and representation, as well as genre and generic affiliations. His films are worthy of analysis for they speak to contemporary audiences about changing contexts of reception and authorship.

Chapter 5 moves away from a discussion of films to focus on the discursive activities of genre users and sites of fandom. Here I look at specialist genre publications and fanzine production from the early 1970s to the present day in order to provide a broader definition of the cultural field of Spanish horror. Two subcultural publications, *Terror Fantastic* (1971–3) and *2000maniacos* (1989–present), form the backbone of the chapter, although it places them in relation to their respective contemporary publishing scenes; *Terror Fantastic* was a genre magazine which specialised in horror and science fiction in the early 1970s, thus providing a prime site for the reception of national and international genre products, while *2000maniacos* is a fanzine covering the low end of the horror and porn markets, providing its niche readership with a wealth of archival and collector information on international psychotronic culture. Through an examination of these publications, the chapter discusses the cultural capital developing from and around horror cinema and the emergence of specific horror fan cultures in Spain from the early 1970s to the present. Furthermore, the broad historical coverage of publications devoted to the horror genre functions as a bridge between the two major periods covered in the volume.

The last two chapters examine contemporary Spanish horror production. Mirroring the contextual approach presented in the first chapter, Chapter 6 offers an overview of genre output from the 1980s to the 2000s, attending to the positioning of directors, films, trends and cycles in the local and international marketplace. While some products and filmmakers harked back to horror traditions embedded in the 1960s and 1970s, younger filmmakers respond to the new media landscape (for instance, the productive relationship between cinema and television with the arrival of private TV channels in the mid-1990s) and exploit long-established traditions and tropes in novel ways to accrue artistic credentials and auteur status, without relinquishing their aim to reach wider audiences.

The works of contemporary directors Nacho Cerdà, Jaume Balagueró and Guillermo del Toro reach a wide horror audience transnationally through their distinctive takes on the genre. Their horror auterism is the subject of the final chapter. The book concludes with a brief discussion of *[•REC]* as a further stage in the development of the transnational reach of Spanish horror film.

NOTES

1. The Franco episode was broadcast on 11 December 1999.
2. By the time this volume had gone to press, these forums listed over 2,000 topics and 25,000 messages.
3. Publications on Spanish horror film are limited to a few articles and chapters in books, among them Willis (2003, 2004), Pavlović (2003), Tierney (2002), Rodríguez-Ortega (2005), Jordan (2008) and Acevedo-Múñoz (2008).

1. THE SPANISH HORROR BOOM: 1968–75

In a résumé of Spanish cinematic activity in 1973, published in the film review yearbook *Cine para leer*, the country's filmic production was described with the following graphic visual image: 'There was a time when Spanish cinema was tinged with red ... bloody red' (1974: 21). It could well characterise the period 1968 to 1975, when the Spanish film industry went into horror overdrive, producing around 150 horror films, which accounted for more than a third of the national industry's output. 'Our producers, scriptwriters and filmmakers', the review reads, 'have released a whole "vile rabble" of sadists, traumatised victims, prostitutes, homosexuals, lesbians, werewolves, vampires, tramps, schizophrenics, fetishists, nymphomaniacs, necrophiles and people of dissolute life', populating our screens with the 'grossest depictions of physical, moral and sexual violence' in a 'maelstrom of crime, orgy and erotic morbidness' (1974: 21). Attempting to account for this ghoulish invasion and the sexual perversions generated by contemporary Spanish horror films, the reviewer wonders whether this horror boom is a desire on the part of the Spanish film industry to 'synchronise with a certain type of world cinema' or is simply a crude form of 'escapism, which unconsciously reveals the [repressive] social situation of the country' (1974: 22), concluding, in an explicit reference to Franco's dictatorial regime that, with the passing of time and with hindsight, this popular form of cinematic production might come to reflect 'an ideology of repression, terror and silence' (1974: 22).

Spanish horror film was certainly synchronous with a variety of horror products emerging from other national contexts, in particular Great Britain, Italy and the United States. Producers and distributors all over the world were interested in horror films, no matter where they came from. The changes occurring in European low-budget filmmaking during the 1960s and the 1970s allowed the production of horror films in Italy, France, Germany, Great Britain and Spain, as well as co-productions between the different countries. Equally valid is the reviewer's association of escapism with repression. The ideological interpretation of contemporary Spanish horror – 'an ideology of repression, terror and silence' – is a sign of the times and a statement informed by psychoanalytical and Marxist ideas about social repression and unconscious desires,[1] as a close examination of contemporary critical reception in the second section of this chapter shows. Spanish horror films provided, in common with the genre's counterpart in the Hollywood of the 1950s, a barometer of the decades' contradictorily overt conformism and latent dissent, a time when the repressed was on the verge of making a return, in monstrous form.

Spanish horror's extensive repertoire of monsters – and response to international traditions of horror cinema – is reflected both in the titles of many films and in the heterogeneity and variety of horror production. Although hardly scratching the surface of genre production, a partial overview of titles reveals takes on classic monsters (*La marca del hombre lobo* / *Frankenstein's Bloody Terror* (Enrique Eguíluz 1968), *El Conde Drácula* / *Count Dracula* (Jesús Franco 1969), *La maldición de Frankenstein* / *The Erotic Rites of Frankenstein* (Jesús Franco 1972)), as well as monstrous encounters which followed the tradition of Universal multi-monster narratives of the 1940s (*Los monstruos del terror* / *Assignment Terror* (Hugo Fregonese and Tulio Demicheli 1969), *Drácula contra Frankenstein* / *The Screaming Dead* (Jesús Franco 1971), *Dr Jekyll y el hombre lobo* / *Dr Jekyll and the Werewolf* (León Klimovsky 1972)). The exploitation of the latest international horror cycle success, such as the *Night of the Living Dead* (George Romero 1968) formula or *The Exorcist* (William Friedkin 1973) phenomenon, spawned Spanish offspring (for example, *No profanar el sueño de los muertos* / *The Living Dead at Manchester Morgue* (Jorge Grau 1974) or *Exorcismo* / *Exorcism* (Juan Bosch 1975)).[2] In true exploitative manner, some titles promised more titillation than they delivered (*La orgía nocturna de los vampiros* / *The Vampires' Night Orgy* (León Klimovsky 1972), *La orgía de los muertos* / *Terror of the Living Dead* (José Luis Merino 1973)). In fact, as a contemporary journalist claimed in the popular film magazine *Cine en 7 días*, 'in this genre once you have the title, the rest – the actual making of the film – is a cinch' (García 1973a: 16). And horror film was so commonplace by the early 1970s that it was prime fodder for spoofing, this same journalist suggesting a series of alternative titles based on topical news stories in his weekly column: 'Dracula at the United Nations', 'Frankenstein vs Moshe Dayan', 'Watergate Zombies' or 'The Mummy in the Europe of the Nine' (1973b: 10), to mention just a few. Many a sneering critic resorted to culinary analogies in the opening paragraphs of their reviews, reducing horror films to a list of ingredients which would allow almost anybody to concoct 'una de vampiros' (a colloquial expression in Spanish for a horror movie); as the opening lines of a less than favourable review for *La noche de Walpurgis* instructs, 'take an abandoned monastery, a werewolf, a devil countess, a stormy night, one or two skeletons, some fake fangs and a few litres of thick, red liquid . . .' (A. M. O. 1971).

Spanish horror film of the 1970s is commonly associated with filmmakers such as the prolific Jesús Franco, Argentinian-born León Klimovsky and Amando de Ossorio, among others. While most of their films were low-budget, having low production values and short shooting schedules, there is a general misconception that all Spanish horror films of this period were cheap and cheerful exploitation fare; Franco and Aured, for example, had respectable budgets to finance some of their films, *99 mujeres / 99 Women* (1969) in the case of the former and *El retorno de Walpurgis / Curse of the Devil* (1974) in the case of the latter. This presumed homogeneity is soon dispelled by looking at the middle-brow genre projects of directors as different as Narciso Ibáñez Serrador, whose films are the subject of Chapter 3, and Juan Antonio Bardem. Ibáñez Serrador, a household name in Spanish television, had 40 million pesetas at his disposal for his first feature film, *La residencia*, which spearheaded the 'boom', whereas Bardem, an established auteur associated with oppositional filmmaking throughout the 1950s and the 1960s, had more than 50 million pesetas and Spanish star Marisol to distinguish his *La corrupción de Chris Miller / The Corruption of Chris Miller* (1973) from contemporary low-brow horror. The period also offers the isolated incursions of up-and-coming art-house directors moving into commercial production, such as Vicente Aranda (*La novia ensangrentada / The Blood-Spattered Bride* (1972)), Claudio Guerín Hill (*La campana del infierno / Bell of Hell* (1973)) (see Figure 2) and Jorge Grau (*Ceremonia sangrienta / Bloody Ceremony* (1973) and *No profanar el sueño de los muertos*). Experimental filmmaker Javier Aguirre made commercial genre products *El gran amor del Conde Drácula / Count Dracula's Great Love* (1972) and *El jorobado de la morgue / Hunchback of the Morgue* (1973) in order to be able to finance his more radical, underground projects. There are also one-off, experimental reflections on the vampiric nature of filmmaking, such as *Vampir Cuadecuc* (Pere Portabella 1970), an experimental documentary shot in 16 mm during the making of Franco's *Count Dracula*, which combines disconcerting editing (scenes from the film, on-set footage, images of the cast and crew) and a dissonant soundtrack,[3] and collaborative projects like *Pastel de sangre* (1971), in which four young filmmakers offered their personal vision of the genre.[4] And, arguably, other films, *El bosque del lobo / The Ancine Woods* (Pedro Olea 1970) (see Figure 3) and *El espíritu de la colmena / The Spirit of the Beehive* (Víctor Erice 1973), which are not readily

Figure 2   *La campana del infierno* was directed by Claudio Guerín Hill, a director
with 'art-house' film credentials.

Figure 3   Spanish actor José Luis López Vázquez played a lycanthrope in *El bosque del lobo*, a story rooted in anthropological studies of the myth.

associated with the horror genre, form part of the same industrial and cultural milieu.

Spanish horror therefore came from different directions and was made in a variety of budgetary conditions. With the exception of Profilmes S. A. and some short-lived production companies, many producers financed one or two films and then disappeared from the market.[5] Such was the case with Eva Films (*El jorobado de la morgue*), Galaxia Films (*Odio mi cuerpo / I Hate My Body* (León Klimovsky 1974)) and Huracán Films S. A. (*El asesino de muñecas / Killing of the Dolls* (Miguel Madrid 1975)). There were a few companies whose names were linked to various horror projects. Plata Films was the name behind two commercial successes – *La noche de Walpurgis* (co-produced with the German Hi-Fi Stereo) and *La noche del terror ciego* (with Portuguese InterFilme P. C.); Maxper Producciones Cinematográficas produced two werewolf films – *La marca del hombre lobo* (co-production with the German Hi-Fi Stereo) and *La furia del hombre lobo / The Wolfman Never Sleeps* (José María Zabalza 1972) – and returned to the genre some years later with *El colegio de la muerte / School of Death* (Pedro Luis Ramírez 1975); Ancla Century Films were involved in the production of three Amando de Ossorio films (*El ataque de los muertos sin ojos* (1973), *El buque maldito / The Ghost Galleon* (1974) and *La noche de las gaviotas / Night of the Seagulls* (1975)), as well as a Paul Naschy project (*Inquisición / Inquisition* (1976)); Janus Films and Lotus Films also produced commercial vehicles for Paul Naschy – the former produced *El gran amor del Conde Drácula*, the latter *El retorno de Walpurgis* and *La venganza de la momia / Vengeance of the Mummy* (1973)). Established names in film production and distribution, like Arturo González, who specialised in comedies and spaghetti westerns,[6] also had a slice of the horror market, mainly through his distribution arm Regia Arturo González, selling commercial hits such as *La residencia*, *Dr Jekyll y el hombre lobo* and *Una gota de sangre para morir amando*. Co-productions with other European countries, mainly Italy, Germany and France, were the norm.[7] As for the distribution of horror films, there were no major players and the market was divided up into small companies (Belén Films, D. C. Films, Exclusivas Floralva, to name but a few) and established commercial firms (Hesperia Films, Mercurio, Hispamex) which exploited the horror film bonanza. This cursory overview of production and distribution companies reflects the fragmentation of the Spanish film industry in general and the lack of a sufficiently strong industrial infrastructure to create specialist genre companies.

The only attempt to develop and sustain a company with a profile in horror came from a Barcelona-based company called Profilmes, S. A., managed by Ricardo Múñoz Suay (1917–92), a figure well versed in the intricacies of the Spanish film industry,[8] and José Antonio Pérez Giner, in the capacity of executive producer. Múñoz Suay's commercial *savoir-faire*, his publicity skills and his connections within the industry were put at the service of genre filmmaking. With a capital of 100 million pesetas, Profilmes was a calculated commercial venture aimed at producing low-budget movies in a variety of genres, with an annual target of seven films. This chapter concludes with a detailed look at Profilmes' output and its international projection in pressbooks. At a time when Hammer House of Horrors was in decline and no longer a dominant force in the European horror market, Profilmes was one of a number of European production companies feeding the international demand for horror. Indeed, in industry magazines and in his writings for *Nuevo Fotogramas*, Múñoz Suay promoted and publicised the company as the 'Spanish Hammer'. Profilmes not only had the domestic market, mainly neighbourhood cinemas, in mind, but primarily intended its product for international distribution and consumption on specialised exploitation circuits as far away as the US or Hong Kong; as Múñoz Suay admitted, sales abroad amply recouped the production costs, and box-office takings in Spain were a welcome bonus. Between 1972 and 1975, Profilmes produced a significant number of horror, action and adventure movies. As we will see later on in this chapter when we examine

Profilmes' pressbooks, it is possible to argue for a Profilmes 'look', since there was some continuity in the production strategies and marketing tactics with the presence of recognisable national and foreign genre actors and actresses, the recycling of sets and locations, and the exploitation of successful commercial cycles of the early 1970s.

Profilmes horror films, like the bulk of the low- to medium-budget Spanish horror films, were the staple of the 'cines de barrio' (cheap neighbourhood cinemas), whose core audience was mainly a male, urban working class. Many horror films were released for double-bill programmes, Saturday matinees and the circuit of 'cines de verano' (summer cinemas), aimed mainly at a teen and youth audience. Films with considerable financial support, like *La residencia* and *La corrupción de Chris Miller*, on the other hand, were premiered in first-run and mainstream cinemas, and delivered well above the average Spanish commercial films at the box office: *La residencia* 104 million pesetas and 2,924,805 spectators and *La corrupción de Chris Miller* 62 million pesetas and 1,237,013 spectators. They were also widely promoted and distributed in Europe by Cinespaña. The vast majority of Spanish horror production regularly attracted audiences of 300,000 to 500,000 spectators, and averaged box-office takings of between 5 million and 13 million pesetas.[9] Bankable autochthonous horror stars like Paul Naschy proved to be commercially successful, with regular takings over the 13 million mark and reaching up to 40 million pesetas. As far as distribution abroad is concerned, Spanish horror films were not only fully exploited by the European co-producers and let loose on the European horror circuit, but also roamed the American exploitation circuit at the drive-in, where foreign distributors retitled them, dubbed them into English, added nudes and sexually suggestive scenes, cut scenes or reels for marketing purposes, and repackaged them as Euro-horror. Many 1960s and 1970s Spanish horror movies therefore form part of the global history of exploitation and sexploitation, and their distribution histories are common currency in genre magazines and fanzines, as well as DVD extra features.

The following pages focus on the national context of their production and reception. An initial look at the cinematic context in which Spanish horror film production emerged considers the circumstances that led to the proliferation of horror films in the late 1960s and early 1970s, a time which corresponds to crucial changes in Spanish society and culture – economic boom, consumerism and the last years of Francoism – and situates the genre in relation to other cinematic trends: namely, other popular genres and art-cinema. The first section of this chapter argues how Spanish horror film departs from the norms and ideals of contemporary Spanish cinema: on the one hand, from traditional forms of Spanish popular cinema production such as comedies, melodramas or folkloric films (known as *españoladas*), and, on the other, from the auteurist-led production philosophy promoted by the government, in particular what was to be labelled as 'Nuevo Cine Español' (New Spanish Cinema, NCE). A look at the industrial and cinema policies, led by José María García Escudero, Director General de Cinematografía, establishes how the production of horror films is shaped by a number of economic, legislative and aesthetic considerations affecting the film industry between the mid-1960s and the early 1970s. Like other international horror film traditions before (American and British), Spanish horror cinema had to contend with the institution of censorship, and filmmakers adopted a number of formal and stylistic strategies to avoid the censor's scissors. The second section of the chapter focuses on critical attitudes towards horror, which were profoundly influenced by the aesthetic and cultural views of figures such as García Escudero, pioneering critics such as Juan Manuel Company and Román Gubern, and mainstream review journalism. By judging horror according to their own standards and perceiving it as commercialising film culture, these critics not only neglected other rich areas of enquiry, such as how Spanish horror films of the period engaged with international examples of horror or how their consumption is linked to the development of a horror subculture; they also, more importantly, hampered the critical development of the genre in subsequent histories of Spanish cinema. While any critical study of Spanish horror film ought to consider the local context of production, the analysis must acknowledge the commercial realities of the genre, which are exploited at the level of marketing, publicity and consumption. The last section of the chapter turns to the examination of some of the cinematic riches of Spanish horror film of the period, relating marketing and publicity tactics to a long-standing tradition of exploitation and consumption practices of popular genre films.

Departing from the Norms and Ideals of Spanish Cinema

The arrival of José María García Escudero as Undersecretary of Cinema (1962–8)[10] at the 'Dirección General de Cinematografía y Teatro' (Secretariat of Cinema and Theatre) brought key changes to the Spanish film industry: namely, the restructuring of the economy of commercial cinema, the introduction of censorship norms and the promotion of the NCE, which aspired to compete aesthetically with other new European film waves of the 1960s. García Escudero's measures were directed against foreign film, the impact of television, and the declining audience numbers for national film in an attempt, on the one hand, to protect an ailing film industry and, on the other hand, to create the institutional conditions to improve the quality of Spanish cinema through the production of a 'cine de calidad' (quality cinema). Other policies involved the granting of 'Cine de Interés Especial' awards (Special Interest Films) to those films which offered sufficient quality in their inclusion of relevant moral, social, educative or political values, the regulation of co-productions, the introduction of box-office controls in 1966, the opening of

'Salas de Arte y Ensayo' (Experimental Arts Cinemas), and the promotion of the work of graduates from the 'Escuela Oficial de Cinematografía' (Official Film School, EOC).[11] In his own writings on Spanish cinema, in particular *El cine español* (1962), García Escudero 'lays out the critique of Spanish [popular] cinema which he had been expounding in contemporary articles and through his political decisions' (Triana-Toribio 2003: 66): namely, 'a market-driven production (the absence of good producers [. . .]), a deficient subsidy system (well meaning but inept [. . .]), and a bad audience in its majority' (2003: 67). The first two critiques would be addressed through a number of economic and legislative policies, whereas his views on popular audiences and tastes would influence the subsequent critical reception of horror films, as I demonstrate in the next section of this chapter. As Triana-Toribio has persuasively argued, 'García Escudero (and his followers) does not allow for any measure of agency in its public, nor for the pleasures these texts gave, and certainly not for the resistant readings that they might conjure up in their audiences' (2003: 69).[12]

The economic measures introduced in August 1964 encouraged the financial restructuring of the Spanish film industry:

> each Spanish film was granted one million pesetas in medium-termed credit from a Protection Fund which the Banco de Crédito Industrial could increase to up to 50 per cent of the production budget. All films received a grant equal to 15% of their box-office takings. 'Special Interest' films received 2 million pesetas credit, 30% of box-office takings, and counted as two normal Spanish films for the purpose of distribution and screen quotas. The State subsidy could be increased to 5 million pesetas (with a ceiling of 50% of a film's budget), only repayable from the 30% of box-office takings; and if commercial performance did not allow repayment, it was waived. (Hopewell 1986: 64)

This costly production system, however, led with the passing of time to delays in the payment of government subsidies to producers and exhibitors, leaving the administration with a debt of more than 250 million pesetas; this eventually provoked the dismissal of García Escudero from his role as Undersecretary of Cinema in 1968. The economic failure of the NCE and the impact of television in the country (in 1960, for instance, only 1% of households had a TV set, but by 1976 90% owned one), as well as the new position of cinema within the leisure industry, accentuated the crisis in film production and consumption. Between 1968 and 1975 the Spanish film industry – never very healthy – was witness to the closure of one-third of its total number screens (in 1968 there were 7,761 screens, by 1975 5,076) and a decrease in the sector's income.[13] By 1968, therefore, the Spanish film industry was in a critical state, the 'Dirección General de Cinematografía y Teatro' was replaced by the 'Dirección General de Cultura Popular y Espectáculos', and the NCE was practically defunct. As film historian John Hopewell has pointed out, 'only a few forms of film-life survived and festered in such an economic climate' (1986: 80). The survivors were the lowly 'genre' or 'subgeneric' films, the most commercially successful being the Iberian sex comedy and the horror film, which could easily recoup production costs and which consistently drew audiences to the cinemas. While the sex comedy was intended only for internal consumption, addressing as it did a series of issues related to the Spanish society of the late 1960s and early 1970s, the horror genre was intended for both internal and external markets and competed with other European productions. The Spanish audience continued to consume the squeaky-clean, censored versions of films whose more explicit originals were exported for international consumption, following a late 1950s policy whereby double versions were produced for home and overseas.

In addition to the economic and cultural changes engineered by the Dirección General de Cinematografía y Teatro, García Escudero also legislated on the ideological and moral values that would govern Spanish cinema until the end of the dictatorship by establishing official guidelines on film censorship. Although censorship had existed since the beginning of the dictatorship, the creation of the 'Junta de Clasificación y Censura' (Board of Classification and Censorship) in September 1962, the compulsory official examination of all film scripts from February 1963 onwards, and the establishment of a set of censorship rules established what was acceptable and what was not.[14] Modelled, to a certain extent, on the Hollywood production code, the thirty-seven norms covered a wide spectrum of subjects and situations, codifying the acceptable and the unacceptable, although in a very ambiguous and arbitrary manner, as we will see in the case of individual films. In theory, the 1963 norms codified the borders between the acceptable and the forbidden, the orthodox and the transgressive, and good and bad taste, but in practice some norms were ambiguous on paper and their application was highly inconsistent.

Keeping Spanish screens free from explicit political content was relatively easy. However, the limits put on sexual and violent images had to adjust constantly to more 'liberal' attitudes to sex across the Western world in the 1960s and 1970s and, above all, to the economic demands of the market. In the context of the later part of the Francoist regime, the realities of the dictatorship – political repression, strict control of sexuality through Catholic morality, strict control of cultural production through censorship – ran parallel to an intense process of socio-economic transformation, facilitated by tourism revenue, foreign investment and the influence of those Spanish emigrants who had witnessed change abroad, that begins to align Spain with Western consumer society and introduces a changed set of values in moral and religious attitudes. Horror participates in various ways in the representation of these complex and contradictory changes. In a film like *La noche del terror ciego*, for instance, as one reviewer observed, the film mixes 'bikinis and shrouds, monastic skeletons and curvaceous females, abbey ruins and ultramodern swimming-pools' (Anon. 1972c); tourism, eroticised bodies and the satisfactions of consumer society sit alongside traditional religious values and institutions. This film is analysed in Chapter 2.

The question is, how far did changes in social mores allow for the screening of violence, gore and deviations from the sexual norm, particularly in the case of a genre whose formal and stylistic conventions rely on graphic depictions of physical, moral and sexual violence? And, more generally, what were the institutional constraints faced by contemporary horror filmmakers? The general censorship norms announced official sensitivity towards the world of the film ('each film will be judged according to not only specific images or scenes but as a whole . . . in relation to the totality of its content') and the generic idiom ('each film will be judged . . . according to the characteristics of different genres and filmic styles'). With regard to the horror genre, the censorship norms made direct references to one of the genre's defining characteristics, the representation of evil ('mal') – a term which censors were obsessed with, for it was the main subject of norms 2, 4, 5 and 6. This conception of evil as wrongdoing evidently responded to a Christian dualistic view of the world. More explicitly related to the horror genre and other horror-related forms was the norm that prohibited 'images and scenes of brutality, of cruelty towards people and animals, and of horror presented in a morbid or unjustified manner'. As for the explicit references to sex, 'the representation of sexual perversions' and 'images and scenes that may lead to the arousal of base instincts in the normal spectator' were also prohibited. Still, a whole 'vile rabble' of sexual perverts and perversions found their way on to Spanish screens. As David J. Skal has observed with reference to horror films on 1930s American screens,

> censors, of course, were primarily interested in sex, and sex was fairly easy to contain, at least on screen. The rituals of erotic exorcism were, by then, firmly established. There were certain words, elements of costume, cleavage, the proximity of a bed – the danger signs were fully recognizable. (1993: 161)

Although Spanish censors were ready to cut scenes of a sexual nature, filmmakers and audiences were used to exerting self-censorship and reading sexual meanings into narrative ellipsis. Other tactics were regularly used by Spanish filmmakers in general, whereby sexuality and eroticism were traditionally inscribed in foreign female actresses. Like other Spanish film directors working under the institutional restraints of Francoism, horror filmmakers had to abide by the censor's rules, resorting thereby to their own formal and stylistic strategies, to their own 'aesthetics of censorship'. According to Aguilar:

Spanish horror took care of obvious geographical and narrative questions (the action was set outside Spain, the story-lines dealt with universal archetypes, the shooting locations were unusual) and deployed more subtle resources, mainly concerning the cast: the actors were dubbed (so that the regular filmgoer could not identify the voices of the actors with those of other Spanish film genres) and they used to be either foreign (Americans like Jack Taylor and Patty Shepard, French like Silvia Solar and Howard Vernon, Central European like Dyanik Zurakowska, Barta Barcy and Helga Liné, Argentinean like Alberto Dalbes, Rosanna Yanni and Perla Cristal) or Spanish who did not work – or hardly worked – outside the genre. (1999a: 24)

The coding of the source of horror as foreign, which was also typical of US horror films of the 1930s and 1940s set in mostly European settings, was a must. Nevertheless, universally understood locations, such as castles, abandoned houses, isolated villages or forests, came with the generic territory, while in other cases the international popular consumption of horror films demanded modern, cosmopolitan settings such as London or Paris. That said, specific elements did often connect the film with the Spanish landscape, for many locations are recognisably Spanish.

Cuts were always likely in the areas of politics, religion and sex. Horror films, whether Spanish or foreign, were censored on the grounds of their religious or sexual content. *Dracula – Prince of Darkness* (Terence Fisher 1965), which was not granted exhibition rights until 1972, suffered alterations at the stage of dubbing: 'suppress all specific allusions to "religion", "religiosity" or "Church" replacing them by terms such as "brotherhood" or "brethren",' read the censor's file; *The Exorcist*, according to the censors, was irreverent both towards the Virgin Mary, in the scene where a disfigured image of the saint appears briefly on screen, and towards Christian symbols ('suppress those sequences in which the crucifix is used as a weapon'). Some Spanish horror films were massacred: Eloy de la Iglesia's *La semana del asesino*, for instance, suffered sixty-four cuts (up to a hundred, according to other sources). The Francoist censorship board delayed its screening until 1974, and imposed a narrative closure whereby the assassin Marcos hands himself in to the police. The censors' imposed ending can be interpreted as an attempt to master the text. The authors of the script, de la Iglesia and Antonio Fos, were also obliged to include the following disclaimer: 'there is not the slightest sign of homosexuality in the character of Néstor' ('No hay un solo atisbo de homosexualidad en Nestor'). Disclaimers and all, the official film classification rated the film as 'severely dangerous' ('gravemente peligrosa'). *La semana del asesino* is discussed in detail in Chapter 4. Other films were dramatically shortened and the cuts demonstrated the existence of double standards in reference to the notorious double versions: the exhibition of Franco's *99 mujeres* was 'mutilated in twenty-four minutes', the dialogues were changed, and 'the ending differed from that in other countries' (Franco in Olano 1973: 10). Indeed, Franco's films were regularly subjected to the censors' scissors, as he himself acknowledged in numerous interviews of the period ('my most important films have not been exhibited in Spain or have been heavily cut' (Franco in Olano 1973: 10); *Las vampiras* (1971) was intended to be 'a re-reading, a refashioning of the myth of Dracula' but, in the director's own words, was left 'like a sieve. It was impossible to understand it' (Franco in Bassa and Freixas 1991b: 43). Provocation and sensationalism were at the centre of the planned marketing campaign for Aranda's *La novia ensangrentada*, but the question, 'the first sexual encounter: matrimonial consummation or rape?' ['el enfrentamiento con la primera experiencia carnal: ¿matrimonio o violación?'], splashed in red lettering across an image of a bride dressed in virginal white, was censored and removed from the final posters. The lurid title was kept but seventeen minutes were cut from the film. The censors neutralised the sexual and gender dynamics proposed by director Aranda, and in the end the imagery of the female vampire subgenre was to communicate the story of the film.[15]

Sexual perversions were duly dealt with, in particular lesbian intimations: in Franco's *99 mujeres*, scenes of a lesbian nature taking place in a prison hospital had to be removed, while Ibáñez Serrador's *La residencia* experienced similar cuts. Prospective viewers of the latter were also denied identification with a female character whose point of view might have triggered the arousal of inappropriate sexual urges (the censor's notes ordered the suppression of 'close ups of lascivious, wet lips when the character is thinking about the scene that took place in the shed between one of the inmates and the delivery man'). Cinemagoers, journalists and critics frequently noted the application of different standards, depending on the film under consideration and its potential impact on audiences. A reader in *Nuevo Fotogramas* entitles his letter to the editor '*99 mujeres* (Madame Censorship)':

> A date for history: 16 June 1969. The first decidedly pornographic film is released in Madrid: '99 mujeres'. Not even the cuts ordered by the censors have been able to lighten the complete treatise on sexual pathologies this film presents us with.

A catalogue of sexual pathologies follows (a sadist transvestite, a fetishist lesbian, several narcissists exhibiting their bodies, prostitutes, drug addicts and murderers) and the reader closes with a reference to the disconcerting ways of 'Madame Censorship':

while '99 mujeres', a typical example of how to exploit the most base instincts reaches our screens, 'Viridiana', 'Belle de jour', '¡Viva Maria!', 'Blow-Up', 'La dolce Vita' . . . and many other films by Godard, Bergman, Bellochio, Visconti, Rocha, to name but a few, sleep the sleep of the just.[16]

With reference to Pedro Olea's *El bosque del lobo*, film historian Gubern observed that, while the censors allowed the screening of graphic 'bloodsheds performed by British and Spanish Draculas', *El bosque del lobo* was made more palatable by severely softening the depiction of violence and brutality, therefore neutralising the critique contained in this 'study of criminal anthropology' (1981: 266) (see Figure 3). And, in a more tongue-in-cheek manner, critics recorded their awareness of the existence of a more explicit version made for the foreign market. A *Nuevo Fotogramas* reviewer is convinced that the Spanish version of *La noche de Walpurgis* is 'a light snack' (Picas 1971c: 41) in comparison to the more meaty German cut. Reviewing *La campana del infierno* for the newspaper *ABC*, the journalist takes it for granted that 'the complete version will be highly valued abroad' (López Sancho 1973). I return inevitably to the cuts and splices which shaped the films under analysis in the next three chapters, in order to appreciate how far and in what ways individual films were affected by the actions of the censors. But what is there to be said about the role of film critics in shaping contemporary (and future) attitudes towards the genre?

Critical Reception

In this section I focus on the critical reception of Spanish horror film, both in contemporary mainstream media reviews and original critical analyses of the genre. Although many popular films were not reviewed at national level or were not reviewed at all, added to the fact that some newspaper critics simply reproduced the promotional material included in the pressbooks, a look at this material gives us an idea of how these films were discussed and evaluated by mainstream critics,[17] sheds light on the reading protocols and critical tastes of the time,[18] and, more generally, places these critical responses in their wider historical and cultural context. These are documents that also, in some instances, describe cinemagoers' responses to individual films and the genre in general, information which would otherwise only be accessible through ethnographic research that has yet to be undertaken. We know, for instance, that during the screening of *La noche de Walpurgis* on 16 May 1971, at the Fuencarral cinema in Madrid, many spectators 'clapped spontaneously [in response to specific sequences] and at the end of the film' (Anon. 1971d) and that the few spectators who attended one of the screenings of Klimovsky's *Odio mi cuerpo* in that same venue on 10 June 1974 laughed a lot, particularly during those erotic scenes in which the image of the male character, whose brain had been transplanted on to the female character, is superimposed on to the image of the female protagonist resulting in bizarre moments of homosexuality. (Arroita-Jaúregui 1974)

It is possible to identify a series of recurrent themes surfacing in reviews. In the context of the endemic crisis of the Spanish film industry and the constraints imposed by the censorship board, references to economic and institutional matters were common. Many critics commented on the commercial and popular success of the genre, expressing their preoccupation with the subgeneric status of most horror products, while many others overtly condemned its pursuit of profit and its cheap mode of production. Engagement or lack of engagement with the textual features of the genre made for very different interpretations and judgements. But perhaps the most consistent interpretive frames were those which labelled horror films as mindless, repetitious fodder for the masses and explained horror narratives as reflections of social (read sexual) repression.

The initial reception of Spanish horror cinema in the industry magazines and the daily press was, to a certain extent, welcoming and encouraging as to the commercial and cultural possibilities of the genre, but individual films were heavily criticised for their slipshod mode of production and their exploitative aesthetics. *La marca del hombre lobo* was a 'frustrated film' on many narrative and stylistic levels, since it 'accumulates with some simplicity [. . .] all the primary elements of the horror genre' (Martialay 1971), wrote *El Alcázar*. However, Eguíluz's film suggested interesting thematic and generic possibilities embodied in the 'evident effeminate streak of the character played by actor Ugarte [vampire Janos Mikhelov]' (Martialay 1971), which added an original homoerotic undertone worthy of note. *La furia del hombre lobo* (José María Zabalza 1970), which was not released until 1972, admittedly suffered from visible budget and time constraints – 'low budget [. . .], a hasty shooting schedule [and] poor production values', although the reviewer conceded in a receptive mood that there was enough evidence of 'the necessary foundations for future projects', which, with better financial backing, 'would yield more satisfactory results' for the genre (Peláez 1973a). A year earlier, *La noche de terror ciego* had offered a 'completely new experience' to audiences and marked 'new directions' with the horrific creations of de Ossorio, the Knights Templar, whose slow-motion movements and ghastly look were described as 'accomplished moments of spectacle' (Anon. 1972c) by the *Pueblo* reviewer. The initial novelty of de Ossorio's characters and special effects soon wore off when three sequels appeared in the following years, so that, by the time that *La noche de las gaviotas* was exhibited in 1976, one critic summed up his views on the Knights Templar saga thus:

the truth is that the first film of the cycle captured our attention in its brilliant use and characterization of the cadaverous characters. But since then Amando de Ossorio has been resting on his laurels, repeating time and again the same effects. (Peláez 1976)

Innovation and repetition were two aspects addressed in many a horror film review. Trade journal *Cineinforme* acknowledged in its brief review of José Luis Merino's *La orgía de los muertos* that

it is true that make-up and special effects are getting more successful with every film. It is also true that there is a small variation, no matter how insignificant, from what we have seen the previous week. But all in all everything is a repetition. However, taking into account that there is a huge sector of the public who really enjoys this type of production, one has no other option than to admit that they are still commercially successful. After all, their main goal is to entertain. (Anon. 1975b)

While the journalist reluctantly showed a certain resignation regarding the popular success of the genre, his final comment revealed a dismissive attitude towards popular film as just entertainment. Yet it is precisely in the said 'small variation' that the interest lay for the horror film consumer, who already knew the plots and structures, was familiar with stock characters and images, and recognised patterns of meaning. What becomes important for many horror audiences and fans is how the film reworks and exceeds the textual features of the genre.

A clear example of the different meanings which films had for critics and audiences was the work of Paul Naschy, whose commercial success was hardly matched by critical acclaim; in fact, many Paul Naschy commercial vehicles were panned by reviewers. In his review of *Jack el destripador de Londres / Seven Murders for Scotland Yard* (José Luis Madrid 1973), Miguel Rubio wrote that 'any relation between this film (?) and cinema is pure coincidence [. . .] I can understand that this film was made but it is beyond my comprehension that it is being distributed and that some cinemas are prepared to exhibit it' (1972a); *La rebelión de las muertas / Vengeance of the Zombies* (León Klimovsky 1972) could only be described as 'puerile' and 'idiotic' fare (Anon. 1973b) by the *Pueblo* reviewer; *El espanto surge de la tumba* (Carlos Aured 1973) deserved 'no other comment than silence' (1973) for the *Arriba* reviewer; and after the release of *Exorcismo* one critic warned *La Vanguardia* readers that 'the Devil, conspiring with producers and distributors, will be among us for a long time' and closed his review with a 'God help us!' (1975).[19]

But the more hostile dismissals of Spanish horror films – and of subgeneric cinema in general – came from sources associated with oppositional politics and art-filmmaking practices: namely, the School of Barcelona. Two examples of such critical interventions will be considered here: firstly, journalist Jaume Picas reviewing a Jesús Franco film for *Nuevo Fotogramas*, and, secondly, media sociologist and film historian Román Gubern writing on Spanish sub-generic cinema in the preface to *Cine español, cine de subgéneros* (1974), co-authored by the Equipo 'Cartelera Turia' (Juan Manuel Company, Vicente Vergara, Juan de Mata Moncho and José Vanaclocha), a pioneering volume devoted to Spanish subgeneric film products such as the spaghetti western (or 'paella western'), the musical, the sexy Iberian comedy and the Spanish horror film.[20] The evaluations and reactions of critics can be seen as authentic, individual subjective responses to films; however, Picas and Gubern display a significant performative element with a specific agenda in mind.

> The reader will think that Jesús Franco's film [*El proceso de la brujas / Night of the Blood Monster* (1970)] is just an excuse to pose a series of grave issues affecting Spanish cinema. And my reply to the reader is affirmative,

confesses Picas in *Nuevo Fotogramas*. 'Where is the relevance in talking about a minor, ridiculous film, which lacks in interest and is nothing other than a grotesque product?', the critic continues. And, punning on the title of the film (literally, 'Trial of the Witches'), he claims that the real witch hunting is happening within the Spanish film industry because current film legislation makes 'the existence of auteur cinema an impossibility', as the failure of the NCE and the prohibition to exhibit many School of Barcelona films had demonstrated (1971a: 39). Picas's diatribe was a vehicle enabling him to articulate his views on the state of the Spanish film industry and the directions that Spanish cinema ought to take.

More damning for subsequent considerations of Spanish horror cinema were Gubern's introductory remarks on subgeneric production for the co-edited volume *Cine español, cine de subgéneros*, which was published in the heyday of horror filmmaking. The book examines Spanish popular genres 'through the filter of *subgéneros*, or sub-genres: a term used here to classify Spanish genre filmmaking as subpar to American and European genres' (Beck and Rodríguez-Ortega 2008: 5). Gubern's preface is followed by a chapter entitled 'El rito y la sangre. Aproximaciones al subterror hispano' (Company 1974: 17–76), the first 'study' of Spanish horror film. In the preface Gubern articulated his views on all forms of subgeneric cinema around the prefix 'sub-', which 'stands both for subgenre and a subnormal [person]' (1974: 12), the latter echoing García Escudero's description of popular film consumers as 'bad audiences'. Gubern's linguistic explanation was not limited to defining a mode of production and a type of audience, crudely marked as artistically and intellectually inferior, but also reached sites of exhibition and critical reception. For him this type of cinema is destined for 'specialist sub-cinemas, comparable to "porno-cinemas" (which do not yet exist in Spain)' (1974: 13), to be found in Pigalle in Paris, Soho in London and the flea-pits of 8th Avenue in New York. This preface to the volume encapsulated a series of critical discourses that were being rehearsed in contemporary mainstream criticism and that would become typical of subsequent academic histories of Spanish cinema. Gubern's prophesy – 'this insubstantial Spanish filmic production will never make it into histories of Spanish cinema, unless it is dealt with in a succinct footnote' (1974: 16) – held sway until very recently. The critical discourses at work in Gubern's observations had wide-ranging generic, thematic, ideological and sociological implications.

According to Gubern, Spanish horror films 'are mimetic and repetitive products in their imitation of previous models [German expressionism, Universal Pictures and Hammer films], which are also repetitive but have at least a genuine and autochthonous cultural character' (1974: 13). In his chapter 'El rito y la sangre', Company reiterated Gubern's interpretation by stating that, in Spanish horror films, 'the deterioration and trivialisation of the linguistic codes of the American genre cinemas has reached unimaginable heights or rather depths' (1974: 50). Unlike British horror cinema, which could claim 'a heritage of horror' – to use David Pirie's expression from his seminal 1973 study on British horror cinema, *A Heritage of Horror: The English Gothic Cinema 1946–1972* – steeped in Gothic literature, Spanish horror was rooted in neither an autochthonous literary tradition nor a local cinematic tradition. By not being associated with a literary tradition, the genre could not be artistically or aesthetically legitimated and attain respectability. Horror for Gubern and Company, therefore, was not peculiarly Spanish. Subsequently, some film historians have even categorised the horror genre as 'non-Spanish' (García Fernández 1992: 22). 'The Spanish disposition is fundamentally realist' (1971: 12), wrote Guarner in 'Spanish Speaking Terror . . .', a claim that would be seconded by Picas, Gubern and Company in their critical privileging of a realist aesthetic. If these cinematic forms had any relevance at all, its significance had to be consigned to the realm of 'sociological interest', thus Gubern's declaration that his real interest in subgeneric production came from his position as 'mass media sociologist' (1974: 11) and his distancing from consumers of subgeneric cinema ('I am a very occasional consumer' (1974: 12)). Spanish horror films are dismissed as disreputable commercial products and described as conformist and dupe entertainment for the popular masses, more specifically for male proletarian audiences, for the horror genre is a misogynist genre 'made by men and for men' (1974: 13). But the Spanish film industry as a whole could be described thus. Moreover, this male domination, or to use Gubern's words, '[films] made by men and for men', could arguably describe art-quality and experimental cinema, made by male directors and exhibited and consumed in the masculinised space of cine-clubs and art-house cinemas, which these very same critics frequented.

It is here that we return to the quotation with which we opened this chapter: Spanish horror films are a crude reflection of an 'escapism, which unconsciously reveals the [repressive] social situation of the country' (in *Cine para leer* 1974: 22). For Gubern, the representation and mythologisation of sex and power, which are at the centre of subgeneric products, are symptomatic of wider social issues like 'frustrated collective desires' or 'real lacks in the spectator' (Gubern 1974: 15). Company's study exemplifies these views in relation to horror films, which 'are just another example of the reactionary ideological chain that informs all our sub-cinema' (1974: 69). Whether the main protagonist is Dracula, a hunchback, a werewolf or the living dead, Company argued, the textual and ideological schema common to local horror production is repression. In order to illustrate his theoretical position, Company analyses the works of Naschy and de Ossorio. All Naschy characters respond to a self divided and torn between good and evil. The narrative pattern is simple: a beautiful and candid female character, who embodies values such as love, purity and goodness, falls irredeemably in love with the Naschy character. Their erotic encounter is never fulfilled, being displaced on to other objects and characters and sublimated into scenes of an S&M nature. Finally, their love is annihilated by a destructive force within the male character (1974: 51–61, 67). De Ossorio's films always present a confrontation between 'tradition' (the Knights Templar in *La noche del terror ciego*, Lorelei in *Las garras de Lorelei / The Lorelei's Grasp* (1974) or voodoo cults in *La noche de los brujos / Night of the Sorcerers* (1973)) and a series of 'modern elements' personified in heterosexual relationships (love affairs, eroticism, sexual perversions) which lead to violent punishments in the form of bloodshed or death. Chapter 2 explores this rift between the past and the present in a different manner. The consumption of these horror films, argued Company, acts as a sublimation of repressed and unsatisfied sexual needs, which has an exorcising and gratifying function. Spanish horror audiences, therefore, if the argument is to be followed to its logical conclusion, harboured basic repressions which needed gratifying. And Company, as critic turned sociologist and psychoanalyst, observes that the behavioural pattern of subgeneric audiences, whether they are watching a martial arts movie or a horror movie, responded to such sublimation:

> there is a general uproar because of the photogenic virtuosities of the film (the equivalent of Bruce Lee moves are the zombies marching to the rhythm of music [. . .] in *La rebelión de las muertas*) and everybody is holding their breath religiously when beheadings, gushes of blood and

eyes coming out of their sockets fill the screen. Sexual repression has been sublimated into aggression. (1974: 69)

These studies offer a valuable barometer of the critical landscape against which the genre was considered from certain academic and journalistic quarters. In the specific historical and political context of late Francoism, these critical acts have to be understood as political and ideological needs of the moment: an oppositional culture influenced by Marxism, critiques of mass culture, and contemporary understandings of reactionary and progressive texts. But this does not mean that their critical operations should not be questioned, for what is at stake here is an important aspect of Spanish popular culture, popular film, enjoyed and consumed by a large number of Spaniards. By condemning Spanish horror film for its commercial nature, they privileged the political (and cultural) economy sustaining 'legitimate' cinema; by staking out a bourgeois conception of cinema, they excluded genre and subgenre film production from accounts of Spanish national cinema; by signifying cultural hierarchies of aesthetic value, they established an aesthetic order that is deeply entrenched in narratives of Spanish film history; and, by positioning themselves as guardians of taste, they ignored other ways in which audiences used and made meanings from the commodities they consume.

Aesthetically and ideologically, therefore, the horror genre did not fit within established cinematic trends in Spain. Horror films did not form part of the more respectable art-cinema represented by the 'Nuevo Cine Español', which received official and critical support. Nor could it be easily related to the aesthetics prevalent in other forms of Spanish popular cinema (musicals, melodramas or comedies).[21] Both cinematic visions privileged a realist aesthetic mode which was promoted, as we have seen, by official institutions and the industry, and, in turn, policed by critics, and which came to represent 'the "national cinema" by their defenders and deemed non-representative of the nation by their detractors' (Triana-Toribio 2003: 71). Neither rooted in local cinematic traditions nor apt as a vehicle for the representation of real Spanish themes and concerns, Spanish horror film merely amounted to a mimetic relationship to its (superior) American and European counterparts and was systematically devalued by mainstream criticism. By not being peculiarly Spanish, the horror genre was far removed from the distinctive Spanish 'reality' portrayed in contemporary cinematic models and cast out from Spanish film historiography.

Yet Spanish horror film of this period established a dialogue with international horror traditions by engaging economically and generically with other horror commodities in the marketplace and sharing the modes of production and aesthetic attributes typical of exploitation and genre filmmaking. Sometimes this dialogue took the form of cheap, exploitative imitations; at other times, higher production values yielded films that made critics react with statements such as 'this doesn't look like a Spanish film.' Either way, Spanish horror films displayed thematic, generic and cultural specificities, which offered something different to national and international horror audiences. It is important, therefore, to recognise that Spanish horror films were as much the product of their context of production as the product of international market differentiation.

THE CINEMATIC RICHES OF HORROR

The exploitative richness of Spanish horror production has been untapped. Like any other popular genre, the commercial realities of horror are exploited in the processes of production, marketing, distribution and consumption. Indigenous horror films presented audiences not only with a familiar stock of horror iconography but also, in many cases, with the promise of 'taboo', 'shocking' or 'forbidden' subjects, which were duly exploited in the marketing of and publicity for the films. In the context of mid-1960s *apertura* (liberalisation), Spanish horror films did not differ radically from other film commodities in their representation of sexuality and sexual desires. Popular film genres – comedies and melodramas – and art-house films both exploited sexual imagery and various taboo subjects within the constraints imposed by censorship. Conceived as NCE 'quality cinema', *La tía Tula / Aunt Tula* (Miguel Picazo 1964) and *Nueve cartas a Berta / Nine Letters to Bertha* (Basilio Martín Patino 1965), for example, relied on the display of sexuality for their advertising campaigns. The photographic image of a woman in her lingerie studiously fastening her suspender and stocking was used as one of the publicity posters for *La tía Tula* to represent the main female protagonist Tula, a sexually repressed spinster in a provincial Spanish town;[22] other posters depict the image of Ramiro, Tula's brother-in-law, forcing himself upon her. *Nueve cartas a Berta* presented a young heterosexual couple kissing passionately, a de rigueur image in the publicity of many a European New Wave film, in particular French ones. The avant-garde film movement known as the Barcelona School used the bodies of actresses Serena Vergano, Romy (Carmen Romero) or Teresa Gimpera, whose physique responded to contemporary canons of beauty in the worlds of fashion and advertising, as marketing attractions for many of their projects. At the other end of the exploitative spectrum, the popular Iberian sex comedy traded in female imagery and sexual titillation, using cartoon-like representations as the predominant visual idiom. The promotional poster for *No desearás al vecino del quinto / Thou Shalt Not Covet Thy Fifth Floor Neighbour* (Ramón Fernández 1970), for example, depicts a caricature of a highly effeminate 'gay' dressmaker flanked by two female clients who have stripped down to their sexy underwear. *Lo verde empieza en los Pirineos* (Vicente Escrivá 1973) combined comedy and naughtiness in equal measure.

It ironically captured the real journeys of (male) Spaniards to France to watch films which were banned in Spain for their adult content. The publicity poster reproduced a map of the the Iberian peninsula shot through by caravans of cars and coaches heading towards the French border and three middle-aged males in the foreground running eagerly towards the Pyrenees, whose green and snowy peaks offer pleasurable rewards to the average male Spaniard: six attractive women hold signs to a world of adult entertainment (cabarets, night-clubs, sex shops, and two films banned from Spanish screens, *A Clockwork Orange* (Stanley Kubrick 1971) and *Last Tango in Paris* (Bernardo Bertolucci 1972)).

While Spanish horror films partake of the general permissiveness to reveal (parts of) the body and exploit the imaging of sexuality, the sale and marketing of 1970s horror must also be linked to a long-standing tradition of classical exploitation tactics[23] and consumption practices of popular genre films. As consumers of genre products, filmgoers were used to recognising conventions and interpreting familiar images and motifs, and expected a variety of emotional and physical pleasures. There is a wealth of advertising and promotional material that enables us to document the ways in which Spanish horror films were sold to Spanish audiences and the ways in which they circulated and were consumed. A more complex picture emerges away from home, where some Spanish horror films played at drive-in cinemas on the US exploitation circuit and many others led a more disreputable and sleazy life in adult and sexploitation cinema circuits in Europe and the US. Foreign distributors, in particular Italian, French and American, used more provocative and daring ads to sell these products on their respective exhibition circuits. Jesús Franco was the first Spanish filmmaker to break into these specialised international markets. One of the specialised exhibition markets he entered was the Times Square grindhouse circuit in New York. Here his *Succubus* (also known as *Necronomicón* (1967)) was hailed as 'THE sensual experience of '69', packaged as Eurosex and given an X rating. According to exploitation film historians Landis and Clifford, the film 'benefited enormously at the box office' from the fact that it was 'among the first [films] to be awarded X tags' and 'from its stylish ad campaign [. . .] designed and funded by the film's producer, Pier A. Caminnecci' (2002: 179–80), which simultaneously promised the bizarre and the sophisticated in a typical juxtaposition of exploitation and European art-house selling ploys: 'Because of the unusual nature of the title, we suggest you call . . . for the full meaning so that you will not be surprised by the sophisticated subject matter of the film.' In France the adult content was suggested visually by a sadomasochistic image of a dominant female character ready to crack a whip and the phrase 'de la perversion jusqu'au sadisme!'.[24]

Titles and print material have always been key ingredients in the sale of horror. Trailers usually completed the initial commercial campaign. Gimmicks and other classical exploitation tactics in exhibition sites such as ambulances parked outside the cinema door or first aid stretchers in the lobby were also used before and during the films' theatrical release. Throughout the 1960s there were some established Spanish distribution companies which promoted this latter aspect of film marketing and exhibition. Mercurio Films S. A. produced a lavish, detailed pressbook for *Miss Muerte / The Diabolical Dr Z* (Jesús Franco 1966), suggesting ways in which the film might lure audiences into the cinemas. Promotional campaigns covering various media and resorting to a variety of selling ploys, were hardly within the economic means of the average Spanish producer, distributor and exhibitor during the 'boom' period; instead, the sale of horror had to rely mainly on print material and pressbooks that producers sold or rented to distributors and exhibitors to back the advertising and publicity campaigns of films. The marketing material under analysis in this final section reflects the diversity of Spanish horror production and the contemporary international cinematic trends to which they relate. In order to include a wide range of marketing tactics deployed by producers, I look at the press materials used to advertise a number of Franco's films and the horror output of production company Profilmes S. A., grouping the material around three different manifestations of horror: firstly, those films which had a classic monster at the centre of their marketing campaigns, more specifically Dracula and Frankenstein as seen by Franco; secondly, those Franco products which exploited the sale of horror and sex; and, finally, a group of horror and horror-related films produced by Profilmes S. A., whose advertising strategies mobilised different generic features targeting different audiences. There is a common thread running through these visual materials: namely, the work of illustrator Jano (Francisco Fernández-Zarza Pérez (1922–92)), the creator of many horror film posters throughout this period. Jano's signature appears in the publicity material of the works to be analysed: *El Conde Drácula, Drácula contra Frankenstein, Bésame, monstruo / Kiss Me, Monster* (1969), *99 mujeres, Las vampiras, El espanto surge de la tumba* and *Los ojos azules de la muñeca rota / Blue Eyes of the Broken Doll* (Carlos Aured 1973).[25]

The pressbook for prospective Spanish distributors and exhibitors of Franco's *El Conde Drácula* will give the reader an idea of the publicity material on offer: for sale, 'one-sheet posters, two-sheet posters, leaflets, colour pressbooks'; for hire, 'colour trailer, colour blow-up stills, colour standard stills, press stills, press releases' and two types of print, '70 m/m. Super-Panorama' and '35 m/m. Cinemascope'. Apart from the visual material available for purchase or hire, the pressbook provided written information about the film in the form of plot synopsis, credit listings, news items ('gacetillas de prensa'), to be planted in local and national newspapers, and a selection of publicity slogans and stills for the marketing campaigns and for displays on cinema fronts and in lobbies. Ready-made slogans to be adapted to specific venues and playing dates were also available. Stock lines which have served to advertise horror films time and again all over the world found their Spanish equivalent in the pressbooks. Foreign and local products were put on the same marketing level and shared long-established advertising tactics, whether one was tempted by a foreign horror film like Terence Fisher's *The Curse of Frankenstein* (*La maldición de Frankenstein* in Spain), advertised as 'The most terrifying of all times', or contemporary Spanish horror products like Franco's *El Conde Drácula* – 'The culminating work of horror and suspense' – or Aured's *El espanto surge de la tumba* – 'Horror cinema has been surpassed in this most horrifying film.' Hyperbolic excess also reached extraordinary heights with some Spanish producers and distributors; *Drácula contra Frankenstein* was 'THE anthology of horror on cinema screens', the publicity for *Los ojos azules de la muñeca rota* advanced the proposal that 'The unexpected and the startling have finally arrived to the horror genre,' but perhaps the most preposterous cutline was that for *El buque maldito*, 'A film that has not been awarded an Oscar because it was not entered in the Academy Awards'.

Of course, Dracula, Frankenstein and the werewolf were internationally established brand names. Audiences around the world were familiar with these classic horror archetypes and knew more or less what to expect from the latest remake. The most obvious exploitation of the brand names in Spain is the foregrounding of the monsters' names. While Paul Naschy offered a distinctive take on the werewolf in his debut as Waldemar Daninsky in *La marca del hombre lobo*, establishing this character in a number of subsequent film episodes (see Chapter 2), the main two stars of the horror genre, Dracula and Frankenstein, were seldom treated by Spanish filmmakers. It was only Franco who tackled these two classical monsters in a horror cycle in the early 1970s, with *El Conde Drácula*, *Drácula contra Frankenstein* (1971) and *La maldición de Frankenstein* (1972). Franco's cycle established a visual dialogue with the classic monsters Dracula and Frankenstein. In *El Conde Drácula*, Franco and screenwriter Augusto Finocchi embarked upon the adaptation of Bram Stoker's novel. Producer and director proclaimed in the pressbook – and in the film's opening credits – that their Count Dracula was the first faithful 'adaptation of Bram Stoker's original *Count Dracula*', hence different from any previous Dracula film version. The announced literary respectability of this Spanish–German–Italian co-production would be endorsed by critics. In large part, cinematic respectability came in the form of Christopher Lee, who had become an established horror star since his success in Hammer's *Dracula* (Terence Fisher 1957).[26] A sense of loyalty to and love for Bram Stoker's original work came with Lee, whose collaboration was itself expressive of his much-publicised dissatisfaction (in trade journals, mainstream publications and monster-movie magazines throughout the 1960s) with the Hammer conception of the vampire and of his stated desire to take part in a filmic project that would faithfully resemble Bram Stoker's book. The producers' and Franco's claims to be true to the original were therefore embodied and confirmed in the figure of Lee, who lent the film authenticity, his powerfully erotic and predatory rendition of the Count polished in the Hammer Dracula series and, above all, guaranteeing international sales.[27] Lee was the main selling point, as his central position in posters told distributors, exhibitors and filmgoers.[28] The film's letter of introduction in the pressbook is a gentlemanly portrait of Lee, hoary-headed and moustached, his face illuminated by the candelabrum he holds aloft. The title 'El Conde Drácula', in Gothic lettering below his image, denotes his aristocratic status in the world of horror film. Contemporary reviews echoed the film's main selling assets, Christopher Lee and the various filmic reimaginings of the Count. One critic recommends the film to Dracula fans in general, 'those spectators who are familiar with Dracula and its different filmic versions' (Crespo 1973a), whereas another critic observes that the main attraction lies in the actor playing Dracula:

> Christopher Lee has proven his skills to play the character and many horror fans reckon that he is better than Lugosi. As we know, these competitions between vampires attract spectators, who remember the different actors and directors in *Dracula's Daughter* [Lambert Hyllier 1936], *The Return of the Vampire* [Lew Landers 1944], *House of Dracula* [Erle C. Kenton 1945], *The Brides of Dracula* [Terence Fisher 1960], and others. (de Obregón 1973)

If Lee's presence was not enough for contemporary male and female audiences, the poster artwork also reminded filmgoers of Franco's 'erotic' brand of horror by displaying a female figure whose nakedness is tantalisingly hidden (just) behind loosely held furs, perhaps a subtle visual reference to his 1969 *Venus in Furs* and the unnerving presence of Klaus Kinski, who had already collaborated with Franco in *Eugenie / Eugénie . . . The Story of Her Journey into Perversion* (1969), both films free adaptations of Leopold von Sacher-Masoch's novels (see Figure 4). None the less, the portrait of Lee becomes the focal point of all the posters, complemented by the recurrent Dracula imagery of coffins, stakes and incisions. Dracula fans were guaranteed the main ingredients of the myth ('An old castle . . . A flock of bats flying in the night . . . And Dracula transformed into a horrifying bat seeking the blood he needs to live on') and the affective qualities of horror ('Fear, shivers and terror! A fantastic and beguiling spectacle that will test if you can keep your nerve').

Producers and publicists have exploited the popular Dracula character, which, as Hutchings has argued, 'is a focus for cultural and economic activity as film-makers periodically seek to resurrect the vampire in a form that will be both interesting and profitable' (2004: 44).[29] For the second film in

Figure 4   Illustrator Jano brought together the key generic markers of horror in *El Conde Drácula*'s official poster.

the series, Franco resurrected and confronted two monsters, *Drácula contra Frankenstein*, and moved from the canon of Gothic literature to the pulp literature of kiosks. As an economic venture, the project was part of the film-maker's association with French producer Robert de Nesle from Comptoir Films to produce a numbers of films at low cost, using the same technical crew and cast (Howard Vernon, Alberto Dalbés, Britt Nichols, Anne Libert, Luis Barboo, Fernando Bilbao, Doris Thomas), and the same locations and sets, based around similar plots and stock characters. The distribution of cold and hot versions was a key production strategy, as the explicitness of some of the international titles attests: *Les Démons* / *The Sex Demons* / *She-Demons* (1973 as Clifford Brown),[30] *La maldición de Frankenstein* / *Les Expériences érotiques de Frankenstein* / *The Erotic Rites of Frankenstein* (1972) and *La hija de Drácula* / *La Fille de Dracula* / *Daughter of Dracula* (1972). Culturally, *Drácula contra Frankenstein* was a homage to the films of Lon Chaney, Boris Karloff and Bela Lugosi, and also to comics. Franco moves away from the literary exercise of retelling Stoker's novel and returns to the popular visual representations of the monster archetypes, as depicted in Universal films and comic magazines. As Franco himself acknowledged in the pressbook, the film was conceived as a 'comic-strip. A silent comic full of monsters'. And full of monsters it is. Besides the eponymous monsters of the title, there is a hoard of female vampires, a werewolf, and the deformed assistant to a scientist, Dr Steward, whose sole obsession is to see the world rid of monsters. Silent it is, too, since dialogues, in actual fact, were minimal – the script reduced merely to a couple of pages. *Drácula contra Frankenstein* is a strip of classic horror conventions, motifs, images and moments, and the comic idiom and the classic monster-movie imagery are captured in Jano's designs for the promotional material (see Figure 5). The film title follows the old-fashioned hand-lettered titling of classical horror films, while the monsters are depicted in all their Gothic splendour, as they appeared in Universal posters, or the pages of popular horror comics such as *Creepy* and popular horror movie magazines like *Famous Monsters of Filmland*. The drawing of Frankenstein conjures up the gigantic figure of Karloff in the Universal incarnations of the creature, whereas a close-up of Dracula, half-enveloped in shadows and surrounded by bats, peering menacingly, fangs ready for his next prey. The return of Dracula and Frankenstein, announced the pressbook, is a veritable 'anthology of horror cinema', thus placing the film in the tradition of Universal's 1940s monster rallies. Press releases emphasised how the film was working within this tradition, while at the same time it offered something different to what had gone before: Franco not only 'brings together a myriad of scenes from all the previous films featuring these two sinister characters' but also provides genre enthusiasts with 'new and hitherto unseen sequences'. Rather like the opening text-box in a comic, which is used to frame the action, the plot synopsis in

Figure 5   llustrator Jano's take on two classical monsters in Jesús Franco's *Drácula contra Frankenstein*.

the pressbook was preceded by a quotation (also used as a voiceover in the opening credits) attributed to a certain David H. Klunne:

> The vampire, sinister dweller of the night, was resting in his eternal sleep, when DOCTOR FRANKENSTEIN, attempted to take possession of him. A fight between these two Titans of Death broke out, awakened other monsters from their state of lethargy, like an other-worldly and devastating chorus.

David H. Klunne was none other than a pseudonym used by Franco. The pressbook for *Drácula contra Frankenstein* therefore draws very self-consciously on old mythologies, genre stereotypes, the history of horror cinema itself, and comic aesthetics. *Drácula contra Frankenstein* offered a multi-monster narrative, which, while drawing upon universally familiar characters, engaged in a process of product differentiation that exceeded the expectations of domestic and international audiences.

The advertising of Franco's *Bésame, monstruo* sends up classical monsters – 'Dracula . . . Frankenstein . . . the werewolf . . . How candid they are! Beautiful women are really terrible when it comes to taking possession of the perfect man' – and brings an altogether different type of 'monster' to the attention of Spanish audiences: beautiful women who use 'ALL sorts of weapons in their search for the magic formula to make the perfect man'. Released in Spain in 1970,[31] the film combined women detectives, mad scientists, deformed assistants and mutant supermen. 'Female monstrosity' was the speciality of Franco, whether in spoofs of the spy genre, female vampire films or women-in-prison movies. It would be disingenuous to deny Franco's commercial exploitation of images of female sexuality. And the label of 'pornographer' that was attached to Franco would never leave him. But it would be imperceptive to shut one's eyes to the ways in which his representations of female characters departed from conventional gender stereotypes in the context of contemporary Spanish cinema, as I discuss in Chapter 2. On the one hand, the spectacle of the female body must be related to the commercial exploitation of female sexuality (sexploitation); on the other hand, it can be read as a counterpoint to the dominant images of women within horror films, as mere love interests for the male protagonists[32] or as the passive victims of horror crimes. *Bésame, monstruo* also sent up the Bond girl stereotype and contemporary spy movies, and reinscribed the iconography of these popular genres into sites of female pleasure. The publicity material made the most of the statuesque bodies of Janine Reynaud and Rosana Yanni, and was meant to function as 'eye stoppers'.[33] The one-sheet poster designed by Jano showed pop-art representations of two young women in short mini-skirts and low-cut tops, sporting weapons in a very Bond-girl pose (see Figure 6). Other posters playfully subverted exploitative

Figure 6　'Eye-stoppers' at work in Jano's poster for *Bésame, monstruo*.

female imagery; depicting the film's male zombie mutants as beefy bodybuild-ers, almost like replicas of magazine advertisements promising the perfect male body, the male body is objectified since the dwarfed, scantily clad male model is easy prey for the female detectives.

Franco and Jano were consummate connoisseurs of popular filmic tradi-tions, contemporary subgenre production cycles and pulp fiction imagery. *Las vampiras* and *99 mujeres* drew on the openly exploitative nature of horror for their marketing campaigns. The exploitative aspects of *99 mujeres* were already built into the title. The advertising offered the promise of multiple women on display, playing with imagery from the subgenre of women-in-prison films – the attractive and probably wrongfully imprisoned young woman, the sadistic, menacing warden, and the no less menacing, aggressive inmates. Some press releases and taglines moved away from erotic adventuring, sadomasochistic scenarios and hints of lesbianism, and promoted the film as a drama in which the prison acts as a backdrop against which human relationships are explored; by framing the film in melodramatic terms ('99 women, each and every one of them with their dramatic past, and nothing but a tragic future'), a broader audience could be reached. In the early 1970s, a time when female vampires were getting their commercial teeth into audiences across Europe, Franco con-tributed to the female vampire exploitation cycle with *Las vampiras*, which was not released theatrically in Spain until May 1974.[34] Franco shifted the emphasis to the feminine with a narrative loosely inspired by Bram Stoker's short story *Draculas's Guest*. The advertising material played up the direc-tor's fame as pornographer and traded on the sadomasochistic iconography. The one-sheet poster for *Las vampiras* depicted a Gothic 'necro-tableau': the ecstatic face of a female vampire in the foreground alongside the body of a young woman lying (in implicit post-coital languor) on a slab (see Figure 7). This *mise-en-scène* of desire and death alludes to forbidden sexual practices and promises sophisticated adult entertainment since the scenario might also be read as an erotic show.[35] The all-female Gothic scenario invited the male heterosexual viewer to pleasures – voyeurism, fetishism and S&M –other than the ones usually associated with vampire films. The publicity taglines, on the other hand, played up the mysteriousness and sinisterness of vampirism ('The black curtains of mystery are drawn back, laying bare the sinister image of vampirism') and focused on predatory relationships ('Like the innocent but-terfly she was trapped in the web of the scorpion'). Critics, however, focused neither on atmospherics nor on the libidinal dynamics of the film. In *Las vampiras*, Franco '[is] bordering on the pornographic' and 'responding to the demands of a certain international market not particularly bothered about aesthetic standards' (Peláez 1974b).

Takes on classic monsters and low-budget or semi-art horror variants of the female vampire subgenre, as well as other manifestations of horror, were just

Figure 7   Jano captured Jesús Franco's distinctive brand of horror and erotica in *Las vampiras*.

part of the cinematic offering dished up for Spanish audiences. In this competitive milieu, producers and distributors had to differentiate their products
from other horror films. By offering a range of generic pleasures, Profilmes
S. A. sought to find a niche in the horror marketplace. In order to appeal to
a broad cross-section of cinematic tastes, Profilmes' marketing campaigns
for individual films evoked different generic categories. Most of their output
shared a number of production and advertising strategies destined to attract
different segments of the audience. Such is the case with a group of films in
which Múñoz Suay and Pérez Giner joined forces with up-and-coming Spanish
horror star Jacinto Molina: *La rebelión de las muertas*, *El espanto surge de
la tumba*, *Los ojos azules de la muñeca rota*, *Una libélula para cada muerto
/ A Dragonfly for Each Corpse* (León Klimovsky 1973) and *Exorcismo*.[36] All
these films featured Jacinto Molina both as scriptwriter and protagonist under
his artistic name Paul Naschy. They were all set in international locations,
offered reworkings of successful horror cycles, and presented narratives and
stock characters that were highly recognisable for domestic and international
audiences. Profilmes promoted these production strategies in their pressbooks
and posters by presenting a variety of modes of address to which domestic
audiences could easily respond. Audiences, in turn, could consider these films
in relation to each other and in relation to other contemporary Naschy products.[37] Moreover, when the movies were read alongside each other, audiences
could also place them in relation to different international horror cycles of the
1960s and early 1970s, like the *gialli*, the living dead genre or *The Exorcist*
phenomenon, and consume them in an intertextual way.

Naschy's mere appearance designated the horror genre, even though he
appeared in roles that were different from his werewolf trademark: a double
act in *La rebelión de las muertas*, in which he plays Krisna, a London-based
Hindu guru, and his raving mad, disfigured brother; another double act in *El
espanto surge de la tumba*, where he embodies both a resurrected fifteenth-cen-
tury French knight (Alaric), sentenced to death because of his hideous crimes
and seeking revenge for his family in contemporary France, and a Parisian professional (Hugo), who is a direct descendant of the knight; in *Los ojos azules
de la muñeca rota*, ex-con Gilles imprisoned because of a rape attempt and
looking to start a new life in the idyllic French countryside; the tough Milanese
police inspector Paolo Saaporella in *Una libélula para cada muerto*; and, in
Exorcismo, an English priest fighting against demonic forces in contemporary London. Apart from signifying the horror genre, the producers pointed
towards other generic markers in the titles and the publicity material. While
La rebelión de las muertas and *El espanto surge de la tumba* positioned themselves in relation to the living dead / zombie subgenre, the titles *Los ojos azules
de la muñeca rota* and *Una libélula para cada muerto* were clearly reminiscent
of the contemporary Italian *giallo*. *Exorcismo* announced itself as the Spanish

Exorcist, even though Friedkin's film had not yet arrived on Spanish screens due to censorship. Spanish audiences saw the imitation before the original.

In the international pressbooks, the image of Paul Naschy made way for photographic stills of the film. Spanish and English plot synopses destined for the Latin American and American markets, respectively, occupied the central pages. The front cover for *El espanto surge de la tumba* featured a medium close-up of a blank-eyed member of the living dead against a dark background, positing a direct relationship between the film and the post-*Night of the Living Dead* cycle so that international distributors and exhibitors could capitalise on this successful commercial subgenre (see Figure 1). The back cover captured a specific filmic moment where the knight Alaric, in his medieval attire, is strangling one of his victims, dressed in contemporary clothes. Similarly, the front cover for *Exorcismo* referred to the *Exorcist* phenomenon as a way of driving the point home for international buyers: the tagline read, 'A theme that has thrilled audiences all over the world, now terrifyingly set forth'; in the foreground, there is a demonic male face and a photograph of a possessed female character. This and other stills reproduce key 'exorcist' moments like the possession of the sick young girl or the priest performing the exorcism. But, for the Spanish market, Paul Naschy was the main selling point. For *El espanto surge de la tumba*, the upper section of the Spanish one-sheet poster depicted a female zombie about to claim her female victim, and a further two female zombies in the sleep-walking postures typical of the subgenre to which the film belonged. The cast combined female beauty and sophistication with the participation of Romy, the muse of the Barcelona School, and Mirta Miller, while the names of male actors Paul Naschy and Vic Winner (also known as Víctor Alcázar) were readily associated with male-oriented genres, the horror genre and the spaghetti western, respectively. The publicity lines supplied by the producers – a total of twenty-three – mobilised a range of genre expectations and pleasures. The exotic and the erotic, the ancient and the modern were brought together in this tagline: 'The ancient rites of African voodoo and the secrets of Indian magic, with all their morbidness and eroticism, meet in contemporary London.' Horror and a constellation of terms associated with horror were invoked in various taglines: 'Horror cinema through the paths of black magic' or 'Once they were dead they were revived as monstrous devils.' Other publicity taglines framed the film as a revenge plot – 'A revenge that trespasses the limits of life and uses black magic to commit horrific crimes' – whereas on other occasions the murderer is gender-specific, a misogynistic psycho-killer ('He promised his revenge on all women' or 'He murdered women in order to use them after their death').

Los ojos azules de la muñeca rota is a whodunnit with a twist, set in contemporary rural France. The arrival of Gilles (Paul Naschy), an ex-con convicted of rape, in the region of Angers coincides with a spate of brutal murders which terrorise the area. All the victims are blonde, blue-eyed young females – the recurrent woman-as-doll cliché of the horror tradition. The murderer slits the victims' throats and gouges out their eyes. Giles finds work as an odd-job man in an isolated countryside house inhabited by three sisters: the sexually repressed older sister Claude (Diana Lorys), the sexually insatiable Nicole (Eva León) and Yvette (Maria Perschy), who has been wheelchair-bound since she suffered a traumatic accident. Their only contact with the outside world is a doctor (Eduardo Calvo), who visits Yvette and Gilles, the presence of the latter heightening the tensions between the sisters. When Nicole is murdered, the local gendarmerie turn their attention to Gilles, hunting him down and killing him. But when the dead body of Yvette is subsequently found, the gendarmerie's investigations lead them to the doctor, who has been hypnotising Yvette and inducing her to commit the murders. His motive: his visually impaired, blonde, blue-eyed daughter had died in an operation due to the negligence of a nurse. Most of the publicity for *Los ojos azules de la muñeca rota* revolved around the genre's association with 'eyes watching horror' (Clover 1992: 185). In the pressbook, characters, locations, situations and mood were explicitly linked to the 'THE EYES . . .'. 'Three women tormented by their past and always watched over by "THE EYES . . ."', read one tagline in reference to the sisters. 'When [the killer] looked at "THE EYES . . .", her / his sick mind was transformed into that of a murderer thirsty for death' described to audiences the killer's uncontrollable urges. The house, too, acquired human qualities – 'Death looked through "THE EYES . . ." from the dark corners of this gloomy house.' The pressbook generically defined the film as horror cinema ('Horror film has found a new approach, horrific, horrendous and macabre'), yet the whodunnit structure is emphasised via references to the detective genre ('The police were unable to put an end to the perverse spate of crimes and discover the motive behind them'). The desire to find the murderer and disclose the motive for the murders was transferred to the filmgoer in a series of open questions that acted as publicity slogans: 'Why were the victims blonde, blue-eyed girls?' or 'What was the dreadful motive behind the perverse criminal wanting the blue eyes of the victims?' Critics responded to the generic classification deployed by Profilmes in their promotional material, defining the film as yet another 'Spanish horror film' or classifying it more specifically as 'psychological horror'. But they also positioned the film in relation to the foreign cinematic tradition of the *gialli*, a generic classification that was not addressed textually in the pressbook. Santos Fontenla opened his review in *Informaciones* thus: 'With a title *à la* Italian, this is a new horror film *à la* Spanish,' (1974: n.p.) and Peláez admitted that, as an average Spanish genre product, *Los ojos . . .* 'is superior to the vast majority of overtly pretentious and sensationalist Italian *gialli*' (1974: n.p.). The visual material designed by Jano, however, did mobilise the iconography of the *giallo* format. The posters draw our attention to the

Figure 8   Title and imagery *à la giallo* in this Naschy vehicle, *Los ojos azules de la muñeca rota*.

female cast (rather than to Naschy) and to the representation of multiple eyes piercing the darkness, although it is ambivalent whether these are 'THE EYES . . .' of the all-seeing murderer, the eyes of the female victims, or a combination of both – or those of the audience. In his artwork for the one-sheet poster, Jano combined drawings and photography. The drawings occupy the right-hand side of the poster and feature a blonde, doll-like figure freefalling among four pairs of eyes. Photographs of reaction shots of the three female characters ran along the left-hand side: a scared Claude looking into the eyes of her attacker, a traumatised-looking Yvette and a disdainful-looking Nicole. These reaction shots convey the victimised female imagery characteristic of the Italian *gialli* cycle, together with the lurking presence of a sadistic killer in the form of a black-gloved hand clenching a knife in the bottom left-hand corner of the poster, which subtly marked a threat coming from the outside (see Figure 8).

Profilmes, in association with local horror star Paul Naschy and the dexterous hand of illustrator Jano, drew upon established iconography and generic markers which catered for the expectations and tastes of domestic and international audiences alike. The riches of Spanish horror film advertising reveal the cultural interaction between the different traditions of horror cinema and the international nature of horror production, reception and consumption.

Notes

1. The association between horror film and repression has come to define an influential critical approach to horror film, which was theorised by Robin Wood in 'An Introduction to the American Horror Film' (1979) and 'The American Nightmare: Horror in the 70s' (1986). Here Wood argued that horror monsters are expressions of social and psychological repression that can reveal the truth about the political and social structures in which we live.
2. There is a whole plethora of titles for Grau's *Let Sleeping Corpses Lie: Don't Open the Window* or *Breakfast at the Manchester Morgue*.
3. The film was never released theatrically. It was shown, however, on the cine-club circuit. More recently, the film has been shown in festivals and film institutes, acquiring a cult status.
4. The participants were José María Vallés (*Tarota*), Emilio Martínez Lázaro (*Víctor Frankenstein*), Francesc Bellmunt (*Terror entre cristianos*) and Jaime Chavarri (*La danza*).
5. This is not exclusive of the horror genre and can be applied to Spanish cinema in general.
6. Arturo González was brother of Cesáreo González, one of the great producers in the Spanish film industry from the mid-1940s until the late 1960s.
7. Co-productions with Italy occurred regularly throughout the 1960s and 1970s: in the early 1960s, straight black-and-white Gothic horror *Horror / The Blancheville Monster* (Alberto de Martino 1963) and *La maldición de los Karnstein / Crypt of the Vampires* (Camillo Mastrocinque 1964), which featured Christopher Lee; in the late 1960s, a series of films influenced by the comic format (*fumetti*), featuring fantastic characters Kriminal (*La máscara de Kriminal / Kriminal* (Umberto Lenzi 1966) and its sequel *Il marchio di Kriminal* (Fernando Cerchio 1968)), Satanik

(*Satanik* (Piero Vivarelli 1968)) and Superargo (*Superargo, el hombre enmascarado / Superargo Versus Diabolicus* (Nick Nostro 1966) and its sequel *Superargo, el gigante / Superargo* (Paolo Biancha 1968)); and, in the early 1970s, following the success of the *gialli* genre, *Una lagartija con piel de mujer / Una lucertola con la pelle di donna / Lizard in a Woman's Skin* (Lucio Fulci 1971), *Días de angustia / Le foto proibite di una signora per bene / Forbidden Photos of a Lady Above Suspicion* (Luciano Ercoli 1970) and *La muerte camina con tacón alto / La morte cammina con i tacchi alti / Death Walks on High Heels* (Luciano Ercoli 1971).

8. Critic, scriptwriter, producer and distributor, Múñoz Suay's name has been linked to the industry from the 1930s until his death in 1997. In the 1950s and early 1960s, he was associated with UNINCI, the production company supported by the Spanish Communist Party while in exile, which co-produced, among other nuevo films, Buñuel's *Viridiana* (1961). In the late 1960s, via his weekly column in *Fotogramas*, Múñoz Suay manufactured and sponsored, the cinematic label 'Escuela de Barcelona' (Barcelona School) in response to the Madrid-based 'New Spanish Cinema'; it was modelled on contemporary European New Wave cinemas, bringing together a number of avant-garde and politically committed filmmakers (Jacinto Esteva, Joaquín Jordá, Carlos Durán, Gonzalo Suárez, Jorge Grau, Vicente Aranda, Jaime Camino) under a coherent cultural label. He was not only the main publicist of the Barcelona School but also the executive producer of many of their films between 1965 and 1970 through production company Filmscontacto. Thus, by the time Profilmes S. A. was created, Múñoz Suay's knowledge of the industry, as well as his expertise in art-house, avant-garde and mainstream practices, had been translated into commercial genre filmmaking.

9. These figures are taken from the Spanish Ministry of Culture database (www.mcu.es).

10. García Escudero had already held the post from July 1951 to March 1952. His second term commenced in July 1962 and ended in November 1968.

11. For further detail on García Escudero's policies and the NCE, see Caparrós Lera (1983: 41–59) and Triana-Toribio (2003: 70–4).

12. For a detailed discussion of 'García Escudero's judgments of taste', see Triana-Toribio (2003: 65–9).

13. See 'Evolución de la Exhibición Cinematográfica en España, 1968–1995', in Fernández Blanco (1998: 19).

14. Ministerial Order 9/02/1963.

15. The US title for the American exploitation market, *Till Death Do US Part*, certainly retained the marriage theme, although the film suffered cuts of another nature.

16. Miguel Ángel Diez (Madrid), '*99 mujeres* (Madame Censura)', *Fotogramas*, 11 July 1969.

17. Among the critics whose names are recurrent in the reviewing of horror films in the daily press, one finds Pascual Cebollada (*Ya*), Marcelo Arroita-Jaúregui (*Arriba*) and Pedro Crespo (*Arriba*) – all of them members of the censorship board as well. Other journalist regulars were Miguel Rubio (*Nuevo Diario* and *El Alcázar*), Félix Martialay (*El Alcázar*), Jesús Peláez (*El Alzácar*), Lorenzo López Sancho (*ABC*), Pedro Rodrigo (*Madrid* and *Pueblo*) and Tomás García de la Puerta (*Pueblo*). There is a second group of critics – Jaume Picas, Román Gubern, José Luis Guarner and Juan M. Company – identified with the leftist, anti-Franco opposition and intellectually and culturally linked to art-filmmaking, who mediated between texts and audiences with their reviews and articles on the genre from the pages of *Nuevo Fotogramas* and other publications. A final group of contributors to the field of horror came from the pages of genre magazine *Terror Fantastic*, whose role in

contemporary horror film cultures is examined in detail in Chapter 5.

18. With the exception of a handful of films produced in the first years of the boom, horror films were not reviewed in the serious specialist film magazines of the period. *Film Ideal* (1960–70), close to a moderate Catholicism, could be described as *cahier*-ist in its agenda, whereas *Nuestro Cine* (1965–71) followed a materialist critique of cinema as it was closer to the Spanish Communist Party.

19. The reviewer was right. Around the same time there was a spate of films which dealt with exorcism, demonology and spiritism (*El juego del diablo* (Jorge Darnell 1975), *El espiritista* (Augusto Fernando 1974) and *La endemoniada / The Possessed* (Amando de Ossorio 1975)).

20. A regular contributor to *Nuevo Fotogramas* since the mid-1960s, Picas had appeared in some of the Barcelona School films and championed the movement's cinema from his position as critic (see Riambau and Torreiro (1999: 108–9)). Before becoming a full-time academic, Gubern had co-directed *Brillante porvenir* (1964) with Vicente Aranda, was also an active member of the so-called School of Barcelona and was a regular contributor to the specialist film magazines *Nuestro Cine* and *Positif*. He was also a member of the PCE (Spanish Communist Party) and the PSUC (the Unified Socialist Party of Catalonia). Around the time that he was working on the preface to *Cine español, cine de subgéneros*, he was writing a number of works on the interpretation of mass media from a Marxist perspective (*Mensajes icónicos en la cultura de masas* (1974), *Comunicación y cultura de masas* (1977)).

21. And yet audiences were drawn to horror films. A detailed look at audience figures for comedies and 'New Spanish Cinema' films makes interesting reading since, generally speaking, horror films are on a par with popular comedies and are above auteur films.

22. The publishers of *Los 'Nuevos Cines' en España. Ilusiones y desencantos de los años sesenta*, a volume devoted to the analysis of the filmic production of both the 'New Spanish Cinema' group and the School of Barcelona used an image of *La tía Tula* on the front cover, while the back cover features a photograph of Romi, one of the muses of the Barcelona School, on the set of *Cada vez que . . .* (Carlos Durán 1967).

23. In *Bold!, Daring!, Shocking!, True!*, Eric Schaefer analyses the 'singular attributes and unique history' (1999: 2) of classical exploitation cinema, examining its production, distribution, marketing and exhibition. For Schaefer, the term exploitation derives from 'the practice of exploitation advertising or promotional techniques that went over and above typical posters, trailers and newspaper ads' (1999: 4). 'During the 1960s and 1970s', he argues, 'the term was modified to indicate the subject that was being exploited, such as "sexploitation" and "blaxploitation" movies' (1999: 4).

24. There are many examples of the exploitation of Spanish horror films on European and American specialised circuits. For example, the ad campaigns for the Italian version of *Ceremonia sangrienta*, which was retitled *Le vergini cavalcano la morte*, openly used sexploitative artwork in its foregrounding of female sexuality, in contrast to the more restrained Spanish poster.

25. Many Spanish producers and distributors used the talents of Francisco Fernández-Zarza Pérez (1922–92), artistically known as Jano. Associated with distribution companies such as Hispamex, Chamartín or Mercurio Films, his signature appears in the publicity material of hundreds of films. See www.cinejano.com for a selection of his work.

26. *Dracula* was distributed by Hispanomexicana Films S. A. in Spain and exhibited in 1960 (72,860 spectators and takings of 13,574.19 euros). Interestingly, *Dracula*

Has Risen from the Grave (Freddie Francis 1968) was distributed in 1971 by Warner Española S. A. (872,439 spectators and takings of 130,375.71 euros) before *Dracula Prince of Darkness* (Terence Fisher 1965), which would not reach Spanish screens until 1972 (742,590 spectators and takings of 128,108.14 euros). As we can see, Spanish horror movies were effectively competing with international horror in the early 1970s.

27. Lee also worked on other Franco projects around this time. *Fu Manchu y el beso de la muerte* (1968), which had its theatrical release on 16 March 1970 in Barcelona and on 26 October 1970 in Madrid, was followed by the release of *El Conde Drácula* in Barcelona later on that year, 16 November 1970, and in early 1971 in Madrid. The exhibition of these films was followed by *El castillo de Fu Manchu* (1969) on 18 September 1972 in Barcelona and *Drácula contra Frankenstein* (1972) on 18 November 1972; Madrid would have to wait until 1973. Lee's appearances in the Spanish horror of the early 1970s also stretched to other commercial co-productions, such as *El proceso de las brujas* (Franco 1970) and *Pánico en el Transiberiano* (Eugenio Martín 1973), and avant-garde projects *Vampir Cuadecuc* and *Umbracle* (1972), both by Pere Portabella, which were outside traditional circuits of film production and exhibition.

28. British producer Harry Alan Towers brought Christopher Lee into the project.

29. See Hutchings' section on the 'Prince of Darkness' for a number of possible explanations 'for the ceaseless popularity of Dracula' in film (2004: 48).

30. Some critics regard this film as a sequel to *El proceso de las brujas*.

31. German producers Karl-Heinz Mannchen and Adrian Hoven helped to produce *Necronomicon* in 1967. After the success of the film in Germany and the US, they decided to cash in with two other Franco films the following year, *Kiss Me, Monster* and *Sadiserotica*. According to Tohill and Tombs, the success of *Necronomicon* in the US can be explained thus: 'It was pitched at the audience who'd been wowed by *La dolce vita* and *Boccaccio '70* and the trailers and promotional material emphasised the daring and sophisticated naughtiness of the film' (1995: 94).

32. Even in the more sophisticated films of the NCE, women 'were mere "love interests" and sometimes not even given a proper name in the credits' (Triana-Toribio 2003: 73).

33. Here I follow Eric Schaefer's use of the term, originally coined by Vance Packard in *The Hidden Persuaders* (1957), in his article 'Pandering to the "Goon Trade": Framing the Sexploitation Audience through Advertising' (2007: 19–46). 'Eye stoppers' are 'those sexy images [used in film advertising] that can arrest the eye' (2007: 21).

34. The film was financed by German producer Arthur Brauner, introduced to Franco by Karl-Heinz Mannchen. Brauner also produced *She Killed in Ecstasy / Sie Tötete in Ekstase / Mrs Hyde* (1970).

35. Franco's 1960s horror production regularly featured night-clubs and strip clubs where female singers' performances and striptease acts, reminiscent of American post-war burlesque films, functioned as moments of spectacle. Around the time that the film was produced, Karl-Heinz Mannchen was Franco's 'regular companion in out on the town [visits to Berlin's] strip clubs and sex shows. They'd see striptease acts featuring lesbian numbers, or pseudo lesbian numbers' (Tohill and Tombs 1995: 98).

36. Other films which featured Paul Naschy were: *El mariscal del infierno / Devil's Possessed* (León Klimovsky 1974) and *La maldición de la bestia / The Werewolf and the Yeti* (Miguel Iglesias Bonns 1975). Amando de Ossorio was also on the company's books with *Las garras de Lorelei*, *La noche de los brujos* and *La noche de las gaviotas*. The horror production of Profilmes is completed with *El refugio del*

miedo / Refuge of Fear (José Ulloa 1974). Among the cycle of adventure films, the company produced the following: *Tarzán y el misterio de la selva* (Miguel Iglesias 1973), *Tarzán y el tesoro de Kawana* (José Truchado 1974), *La diosa salvaje* (Miguel Iglesias 1974) and *Kilma, Reina de las Amazonas* (Miguel Iglesias 1975).

37. Naschy's contribution to Profilmes overlaps chronologically with the films of his werewolf cycle, as well as with other films.

2. SPANISH HALL OF MONSTERS IN THE 1960s AND EARLY 1970s

The crimes, obsessions and ghoulish activities of Dr Orloff, lycanthrope Waldemar Daninsky and the macabre Knights Templar form the focus of our attention in this chapter. These are the select 'vile rabble' that entered the Spanish Hall of Monsters: a sadistic mad doctor, a werewolf and the Blind Dead, who terrorised, captivated and entertained local and international horror audiences in the 1960s and 1970s. And these days, they have an international reputation among horror fans all over the world. Chronologically speaking, Dr Orloff is the avant-gardist of the rabble. His first appearance in *Gritos en la noche / The Awful Dr Orloff* (Jesús Franco 1962 was followed by nominal references in *El secreto del Dr Orloff* (Jesús Franco 1964) and *Miss Muerte* (Jesús Franco 1966), all of them black-and-white films which were variations on the tradition of the mad-scientist movie.[1] Waldemar Daninsky, the werewolf, was the creation of scriptwriter Jacinto Molina and his on-screen alter ego Paul Naschy, whose particular conception of the werewolf myth was mainly based on cinematographic adaptations, in particular the second Universal cycle of horror films of the 1940s. The iconography invented to accompany Waldemar Daninsky and his characterisation of the werewolf ensured that Molina left an indelible mark on the werewolf subgenre, what has come to be known as the *sello Naschy* – the Naschy hallmark. With *La noche del terror ciego* (1972), audiences were introduced to the horror world of the Blind Dead, a group of zombie-like, skeletal creatures from the medieval order of the Knights Templar. Their forays into the world of the living spawned three consecutive sequels (*El ataque de los muertos sin ojos* (1973), *El buque maldito* (1974) and *La noche de las gaviotas* (1975).

Whilst both Jacinto Molina (1934–2009) and Amando de Ossorio (1918–2001) exploited their monstrous creatures in distinctive cycles that featured the same monster and shared similar narrative and stylistic traits after their original commercial successes, the tracing of Dr Orloff's family tree and monstrous legacy poses a number of problems relating to its commercial lines of descent. While this chapter discusses these three distinct cycles in separate sections, it also argues for a number of interconnected strands running through the films of Franco, Molina and de Ossorio. Firstly, their films must be considered within the parameters of industrialised popular culture and of commercial production. All these cycles were influenced by mass culture forms – from pulp novels and movies to genre filmmaking and Spanish popular cinema traditions to comics and pop culture – which contribute to their formal and stylistic look. They were produced and marketed as repetitions and variations of successful narrative and generic formulas. Each section discusses the marked pulp quality and mechanics of these individual cycles: namely, the intensity of their production and the time constraints imposed by demanding production schedules, the repetition of limited story plots and the interchangeable use of stock characters and devices, and the rhetorical excess and inclusion of shock elements. But the works of Franco, Molina and de Ossorio are also imaginative reworkings of established horror film traditions or individual commercial successes. This is the second interconnecting strand of the chapter: in other words, how these groups of films deviate from the formula and how they use formulaic horror traits. Working within and departing from previous cinematic traditions, producers and filmmakers positioned their films through their press materials and narratives as part of an international horror film culture whilst offering a distinctive take on familiar mythologies, stories, tropes and styles. A third point of connection focuses on the different ways in which these cycles engaged with genre and gender stereotypes in relation to Spanish cinematic traditions. Whereas Franco reinscribes horror conventions and iconography with sites of female pleasure and exploits the limitations of his male characters, the representation of male characterisation in Molina and de Ossorio will take me to a discussion of certain versions of Spanish masculinity. Finally, as key figures in the development of Spanish horror, Franco and Molina have been strategically seeking to establish themselves in the pantheon of national and international horror by creating and promoting a series of discourses – even constructing their own mythology – around their work and artistic personas that deserve consideration. De Ossorio, on the other hand, had long been forgotten before fan publications in the 1990s and 2000s turned their attention to and revived his filmic production.

The One and Only . . . Dr Orloff

Considered by many as the first Spanish 'horror' film, *Gritos en la noche* broke with Spanish cinematic conventions of the time by moving away from realist aesthetics and into the terrain of mystery, fear and terror. The film combined horrific ingredients – a sinister doctor, his creepy assistant, an atmospheric Gothic *mise-en-scène* – with a police investigation and a romantic subplot, whose protagonists, Conrado San Martín (Inspector Tanner) and Diana Lorys (Wanda Bronsky in the role of Tanner's fiancée) were stars with established images.[2] It offered audiences 'romance', 'mystery', 'suspense' and 'shocks', as well as taboo subjects (sex crimes, sexually oriented material) and risqué scenarios (cabarets) – elements that were not part of the cinematic staple of Spanish filmgoers. Franco's film also undermined prevailing representations of women in genre cinema as mere love interest and damsels in distress, since Wanda becomes a modern heroine who drives the narrative forward, at the same time poking fun at the male hero embodied in the figure of Inspector Tanner as representative of the established authority. Playing with gender expectations and combining different genres, Franco produced a film that was an anomaly in the context of Spanish cinematic production, whether in the form of commercial genre filmmaking or an incipient neorealist tradition. For the director, *Gritos en la noche* initiated a long-lasting affair with the horror genre, brought his work to the attention of the international horror market,[3] and acted as a letter of intent as to the horror characters he was able to create. His pulp elements would certainly resonate through the works of Molina, de Ossorio and other Spanish horror filmmakers.

Gritos en la noche saw the introduction of Dr Orloff to Spanish and international audiences. It was also his exit – at least as far as the 1961 storyline and characterisation were concerned, since Dr Orloff is killed at the end of the film. Although the horrific deeds of Dr Orloff end with *Gritos en la noche*, his name and scientific legacy are perpetuated in *El secreto del Dr Orloff* and *Miss Muerte*. Franco returns to his creation in the 1980s with *El siniestro Dr Orloff* (1982) and *Faceless* (1988). The invocation of Dr Orloff in *El secreto del Dr Orloff* and *Miss Muerte* was more a production, marketing and distribution ploy than a return to the original storyline. In both films, Dr Orloff is mentioned as the prestigious scientist whose knowledge and groundbreaking experiments on mind control have been passed on to his disciples, Dr Fisherman in *El secreto del Dr Orloff*, and Dr Zimmer and his daughter, Irma Zimmer, in *Miss Muerte*. Any narrative continuation of the life and times of Dr Orloff lies in the tale of criminality and its horrors which provides the narrative impetus of the three films. Apart from the use of a group of essential conceptual elements recurrent throughout the films, their consideration as a cycle lies elsewhere: firstly, it is built into Franco's specific mode of production,

Figure 9   Dr Orloff (Howard Vernon) in full mind-control of his assistant Morpho (Ricardo Valle) in *Gritos en la noche*.

which aligns his films with exploitation production strategies and pulp cultural production; secondly, it is visible in the exploitation of the Orloff iconography and universe in the advertising of *El secreto del Dr Orloff* and *Miss Muerte*; and, thirdly, it can be traced in the history of distribution and exhibition for local and international markets at the time and in the repackaging of the Orloff myth for video and DVD consumption subsequently.

Gritos en la noche has been mainly associated with the activities of a mad doctor, whose skin-graft transplants could be related to those of Dr Génessier in Georges Franju's *Les Yeux sans visage* (1959), thus positioning the film as part of a spate of films that followed the tradition of the mad surgeon. In fact, the basic plot of *Gritos en la noche* does not differ much from that of Franju's film.[4] In *Les Yeux sans visage*, plastic surgeon Dr Génessier (Pierre Brasseur), with the assistance of his nurse and mistress Louise (Alida Valli), kidnaps and murders beautiful young women in 1950s Paris to procure skin grafts for his daughter, whose face was disfigured after a car accident. Set in 1912, *Gritos en la noche* tells the story of a mad doctor, Dr Orloff (Howard Vernon), who, aided by his monstrous assistant Morpho (Ricardo Valle) (see Figure 9), kidnaps young women and removes the skin from their faces in order to graft them on to the disfigured face of his daughter after a fire destroyed his laboratory. Both

Génessier and Orloff fail in operation after operation, and both are killed. Like *Les Yeux sans visage*, which was inspired by the homonymous novel of Jean Redon, *Gritos en la noche* is based upon a literary source, a novel of the same title by David Khune, whose existence (or not) I go on to discuss in the next paragraphs. Both films contain conventional, unoriginal ingredients borrowed from the mad-scientist narrative template but their engagement with this international horror tradition is different. Dr Génessier's and Dr Orloff's actions are driven out of love for their daughters, but whereas the former is presented as a contemporary plastic surgeon exploring new surgical techniques and research on how to perform successful skin grafts in a modern clinical environment, the latter is a more traditional mad doctor placed in a Gothic setting of underground laboratories and torture chambers. Franco's distinctive treatment of the transplant surgery theme mixed horror, medical science fiction and doses of sex. By playing up some sexual elements in the film (the burlesque aspects of the cabaret scenes, the sadoerotic moments during the abduction of the female victims and the operations performed in the operating room), Franco changed, for many, 'the face of Euro horror for the next twenty years' (Tohill and Tombs 1995: 77), for he not only took Hammer's showing of blood, viscera and flesh to further morbid and erotic explicitness but also incorporated into his films (s) exploitation tactics that injected new life into conventional horror narratives. Franco himself cites the viewing of Terence Fisher's *The Brides of Dracula* (1960) as the catalyst for convincing his sceptical producers Sergio Newman and Marius Lesœur from the Eurociné company to open their eyes to the commercial possibilities of the horror genre.[5] But *Gritos en la noche*, as well as *El secreto del Dr Orloff* and *Miss Muerte*, exceed the genre and its aesthetics, and announce Franco's plural relationship to cinematic genre and to pulp cultural production since they also work as moments that show Franco's cinephilia and popular culture connoisseurship.

Two types of pulp fiction – the horror story and the detective story – form the backbone of *Gritos en la noche*. Its pulp and generic plurality is established in the pressbook, as well as in the opening sequences. According to the pressbook, the film tells the story of 'A mystery that startled the world in 1912. Five women went missing in strange circumstances.' And it continues by saying, 'Among scenes of horror, fear and suspense you will meet: Orloff – Doctor in Surgery; Morpho – a monstrous man created by Orloff; Taniver [sic] – Police Inspector in charge of the case; Beautiful young women – target of the criminal machinations of the killer.' Generic markers of horror films, detective stories and pulp crime fiction are brought together to maximise their appeal to different audiences. The film was therefore not strictly classified as a horror film. However, the conventions and iconography of horror are efficiently set up, both visually and aurally, in the opening scene. This sensory immediacy is achieved through inspired cinematography, lighting, camera work and music score: the Gothic period setting, dimly lit back streets and expressionist shadows; a jittery, unnerving bebop jazz score (at odds with the period setting) and sounds of horror; a disturbing-looking man with a very distinctive facial disfigurement and bulging eyes abducting a young female victim; and the visualisation of fear and horror through reaction shots showing some neighbours. The opening of the film immediately delivers the promises of its title when a night-time scene and (female) screams draw the audience into a world of horror in a very self-conscious manner. The story of the police investigation and the romantic subplot are personified in Wanda Bronsky, a ballet dancer, and Edgar Tanner, a police inspector, who have just returned from a fortnight's holiday and are madly in love with each other. As soon as Inspector Tanner arrives at the police station, he is assigned to a complex case: women of 'doubtful reputation' have been disappearing under identical circumstances over the last three months and the only clues available point to a 'creepy-looking man' with a peculiar walk. But this 'creepy-looking' man is not Dr Orloff.

Like villains in expressionist and classic horror movies, Dr Orloff is first introduced as a shadow, a shadowy figure in cape and top hat. And from the shadows he guides a humanoid monster, tapping his cane through the deserted streets of Holfen. His second appearance is a close-up which focuses on the strange fixity of his gaze – intense, almost hypnotic – while he avidly observes a female singer in a cabaret club. Orloff's first appearances display an alternate personality, a mixture of sinister mad doctor operating in the shadows and a respectable gentlemanly figure enjoying a performance in a cabaret. While his elegant dress and distinguished demeanour insinuate an aristocratic air (cabaret singer Dani, for instance, believes he is a duke), his wild eyes suggest a malevolent, perverse side, which is confirmed with the first words he utters when addressing Dani at his table: 'I'm so fascinated by your skin. It's perfect, so soft and fresh.' She is abducted and becomes another victim of Orloff's cruel machinations to reconstruct his daughter's face. Played by Swiss actor Howard Vernon, who would become a fetish actor in subsequent Franco films, Dr Orloff simultaneously acquires a gentlemanly yet creepy screen image in this first scene of seduction. Vernon here bestows upon Orloff quietness and poise, charm and charisma, insiduousness and insanity in equal measure. Orloff is a man of few words, whose monomaniacal obsession is transferred to Vernon's mesmeric gaze. In Vernon's performance there is a hint of vampirism and the alluring powers of a Dracula when he charmingly preys upon young women and seduces them into spending the night with him. Outside the cabaret hall, Dr Orloff becomes a sinister villain again. His *modus operandi* is presented to the audience in a montage of Gothic and expressionistic aesthetics. Canted frames, sharp angles, eerie lights and shadows convey the doctor's state of mind and emphasise the horrors to come. The victims are taken to an abandoned boathouse, transported by boat down the river and finally carried by cart to his isolated mansion. With every new victim ready to go under his knife in his operating theatre-cum-crypt, Orloff assures his daughter Melissa, who is enclosed in a glass sarcophagus, that he will make her as beautiful as she once was. The young women are murdered, their faces skinned and their bodies disposed of.

But Dr Orloff is more than a 'Doctor in Surgery', as the pressbook announced. Franco's original concoction presents the audience with a figure who shares the vampiric qualities of Dracula, the creative powers of Doctor Frankenstein and the monomaniacal traits of mad surgeons. Moreover, the string of kidnaps and murders expose Orloff as a callous and ruthless criminal. His monstrous assistant Morpho carries out Orloff's horrific orders. And as his past as a prison doctor is disclosed by Inspector Tanner, it is patent that his illegal activities have been going on for a while, placing him far beyond society's laws and morals. We learn from the police that Orloff is an ex-prison doctor, who falsified the death certificates of a female convict named Armée and of Morpho Lautner, a dangerous psychotic murderer who had been imprisoned for the murder of his father and had been killed in 1905 before the authorities could execute him. But is Dr Orloff a monster? If Orloff is a monster figure at all, as Hawkins has observed, 'his monstrosity predates his obsessive need to repair his daughter's damaged face' (2000: 101). Admittedly, his crimes are motivated by desperation and love for his daughter, rather than genuine medical interest in the science of skin-grafting. But this prototypical obsessed scientist hides a dark past; 'his mad-science mania is linked in the film to the darker sides of law enforcement – incarceration, institutional medicine, experimentation on prisoners', in other words, to 'the dark side of the legal and penal system' (Hawkins 2000: 102). And Morpho, the product of Orloff's medical experiments on mind control, was created to become the doctor's own personal killing machine. The legacy of Dr Orloff on mind control, in particular the creation of monstrous humanoid assistants for criminal purposes, is retained and adapted to the narratives of *El secreto del Dr Orloff* and *Miss Muerte*, where the worlds of science and criminality are juxtaposed once again in variations on the familiar mad-doctor narratives.

Although Franco had killed Orloff at the conclusion of *Gritos en la noche*, *El secreto del Dr Orloff* and *Miss Muerte* present a series of recurrent formal and stylistic features. Stylistically, they play off German expressionism and French-style thriller aesthetics, as well as the Gothicism of Corman and Hammer horror productions, in their use of settings, lighting and cinematography. Orloff's iconographic legacy was imprinted on the advertising process, as well as on the films' use of *mise-en-scène* – in fact, connections with the original Orloff character in *El secreto del Dr Orloff* and *Miss Muerte* are tentative within the narrative world of the film. Like *Gritos en la noche*, both narratives bring the female figures to the fore, as they drive the action forward. In a similar vein, the monstrous assistants in *El secreto del Dr Orloff* (Andros) (see Figure 10) and *Miss Muerte* (Miss Muerte) (see Figure 11) take centre-stage in the publicity material. *El secreto del Dr Orloff* would exploit unashamedly the name of the mad doctor in its title and its plot synopsis by establishing the relationship between Orloff and the film's protagonist in these terms: 'Dr Fisherman has succeed in bringing Andros back to life thanks to the secret entrusted to him by his friend and teacher Dr Orloff.' Franco, reads the pressbook, has created a 'new monster', perhaps 'not as repulsive as previous monsters but whose brutal acts, cold and soulless, terrorise a whole region'. The publicity privileges the creation of the mad scientist and the relationship between the scientist and his creature, Andros, a mute assistant, whom Dr Fisherman utilises to murder women of dubious character. In the promotional posters, Andros is alternatively portrayed as a Frankenstein-like figure strangling a young female or attacking his creator. The cutlines also stressed the murderous nature of the monster – 'There was only one purpose in his life: to kill, to kill without respite' – and his lifeless attributes – 'cold, lifeless hands, created to kill', nothing more than 'a lifeless body animated only before the presence of his victims'.

Apart from the mind and body control operations, *Miss Muerte* also features some elements of brain surgery and skin-grafting, which make it difficult viewing for the faint-hearted. *Miss Muerte* 'is twenty-five years ahead of the most audacious advances in science', announced the pressbook. The film, which is clearly marketed around affect, deals with science-fiction topics whose effect on the audience could be fatal (see Figure 12):

> if you are not a brave person, refrain from watching this film [. . .] More than ever we are obliged to guide the fan to protect her health. In all sincerity, not everybody can view it. This film is forbidden to the neurotic, to those suffering from heart complaints, to those whose nervous system cannot deal with strong emotions.

But 'it is recommended to all those that profess loyal admiration for this type of horror film'. There is no reference to Orloff in the publicity material for *Miss Muerte* or in the plot synopsis. The opening sequences of the film, however, summarily introduce Orloff into the film's narrative world when Dr Zimmer (Antonio Jiménez Escribano) makes a passionate speech in front of the medical establishment in a conference on neurology, defending the scientific legacy of Dr Orloff for the goodness of human kind. Following Dr Orloff's research and teachings on neurophysiological theories relating the location of good and evil in the brain, Dr Zimmer has developed a technique to control people through electronic impulses. But the scientific establishment accuses him of performing

Figure 10   Yet another female victim for Dr Orloff.

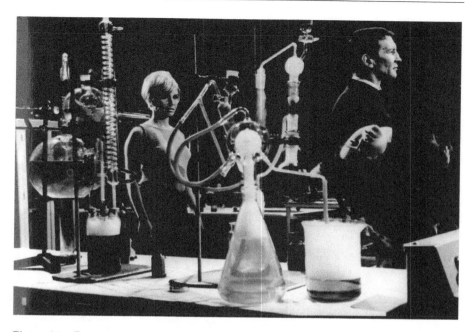

Figure 11   Franco's twist on the mad-scientist genre in *Miss Muerte* where a female
mad-doctor continues the family tradition.

illegal experiments and being an old fool. Such rejection and exclusion provoke
his death. His daughter Irma (Mabel Karr) promises to avenge her father and
exact brutal revenge on the men that derided and, ultimately, killed her father.
Her revenge is conducted through another 'new monster': 'A girl of flesh and
blood. A beauty to seduce and destroy those I wish', an exotic night-club
dancer Nadia, artistically known as 'Miss Muerte' (Estella Blain), whom she
abducts and controls. This monster is described in the pressbook as 'A beautiful and sculptural woman, who has created a strange and suggestive dance for
the stage [. . .] and will become, thanks to the most audacious operation, a
merciless priestess of crime'. No wonder, then, that this beautiful and deadly
monster steals the limelight on the promotional posters. The poster, which
reproduces a still from the film, is marked as an erotic moment of visual spectacle. The viewer is invited to look at a powerful and highly sexualised image
of exotic dancer Miss Muerte, framed in medium shot, in a daring costume
that emphasises her voluptuous figure and performing some sort of sensual
(and sexual) dance in front of a male mannequin. With its night-club setting
and stagy arrangement, the image suggestively plays with the performance of
gender identity: a real woman taking an active role and a passive male mannequin. The poster blatantly promises a dangerous and exciting world (for
male heterosexual spectators). The last film in the cycle therefore refocuses the

Figure 12   The pleasures of horror in *Miss Muerte*: Fear! Fear! Fear! Fear!

gender dynamics of *Gritos en la noche* and *El secreto del Dr Orloff*, since the killing machine in *Miss Muerte* is a woman and her creator is a female mad doctor seeking revenge for the death of her father. And the victims this time are not young women but three middle-aged professors (Professor Vicas (Howard Vernon), Professor Moroni (Marcelo Arroita-Jaúregui) and Professor Kallman (Chris Huerta)).[6]

In this cycle of films, Franco shrewdly engaged with genre and gender sterotypes from different film horror traditions. Moreover, the horror genre enabled him to undermine conventional gender norms through excess, parody and spectacle and to challenge the stereotypical representation of women in (Spanish) subgeneric cinema as inferior, introducing female subjectivity to genre filmmaking. It could be argued, on the other hand, that there are certain elements in these films that reinstate a more conventional reading: for example, the father–daughter relationships running through these narratives, whereby these young women are still in the service of men – that is, their fathers; or the reunion of the heterosexual couple at the end of the film. Let me explain these differing – but not necessarily exclusive – readings. In *Gritos en la noche*, Wanda becomes the prototypical female heroine. Attributes such as activeness, ratiocination and self-assertiveness are associated with Wanda. As representatives of the male world, the ex-prison doctor turned obsessed criminal and the clueless Inspector do not fare well in comparison with Wanda. Franco draws parallels between the two male characters and brings their narrative trajectories together through editing devices; while Dr Orloff is unsuccessful in his skin-graft operations, Inspector Tanner struggles with his enquiries. It is Wanda who points her fiancée Tanner in the right direction by suggesting a more methodical and logical approach to the investigation, comparing the different descriptions and looking at them as pieces of a puzzle waiting to be joined together so that a 'real' picture of the criminal(s) may be formed. And when she decides to take a more investigative approach herself, she becomes the main point of identification in the narrative and is the character who eventually ensnares the awful doctor with her plan. Masquerading as a 'shameless hussy', to use her own words, Wanda goes to the club where the last missing girl worked in the belief that the murderer might return there for a new victim. At the night-club, Orloff's and Wanda's eyes make contact and the doctor is transfixed by Wanda's resemblance to Melissa (Melissa and Wanda are played by the same actress). But Wanda's attempts to alert Tanner to the criminal's true identity go briefly, suspensefully awry, and by the time that Tanner finally arrives at the mansion, Morpho has taken Wanda to the castle's tower. Tanner shoots him and kills him. The close of the film parodically reinstates the male inspector as the brains behind the solving of the mystery. Tanner addresses Wanda with a 'We were right, weren't we, dear?', to which she candidily and proudly replies, 'You're the best detective in the world.' As the camera shows a close-up of the reunited couple, Tanner acknowledges, 'You're my right-hand woman from now on.' The other female character in the film, on the other hand, represents, to a certain extent, the damsel-in-distress formula typical of horror movies, for she is waiting to be released from captivity and from her predicament. The horrible Dr Orloff becomes, in a perverse sort of way, the 'hero' who will come to the rescue of his disfigured daughter, Melissa, but ironically her 'release' would only be possible through entrapment and finally death.

Melissa (Agnès Spaak) is also the name of the orphan protagonist of *El secreto del Dr Orloff*. When she visits her uncle, Professor Conrad Fisherman (Marcelo Arroita-Jaúregui), and her aunt Ingrid (Luisa Sala) in their old village house, her inquisitiveness triggers the unravelling of a family secret: her father's death. Melissa's father was murdered by her uncle after he found out that his wife and his brother were having an affair. Melissa also discovers that his uncle then performed a horrific operation on her father, transforming him into the monstrous creature – Andros (Hugo Blanco) – that is terrorising the region. Finally, Fisherman is murdered by his own monstrous creation, and the monstrous Andros is killed by his own daughter, Melissa, and her fiancé, Juan Manuel. Her purpose and *raison d'être* throughout the narrative, like Irma in *Miss Muerte*, are to justify the father.

The attraction of Orloff for many fans lies in his afterlife. Franco's Dr Orloff is a perfect example of the distribution, advertising and exhibition of exploitation cinema. Producers Marius and Daniel Lesœur managed to obtain worldwide distribution for *Gritos en la noche*, which was shown in France, the US, and Latin American territories such as Mexico and Argentina. The initial distribution of *Gritos en la noche* for international markets foregrounded the name of the mad doctor, making the film more recognisable as fitting into a generic category. French audiences were invited to view the universe of *L'Horrible Docteur Orloff*, perhaps following the contemporary Italian success, *Orribile segreto del Dr Hichcock* (Riccardo Freda 1962). Similarly, American audiences were invited to enjoy the cruel tortures of *The Awful Dr Orloff* ('You haven't had so much fun since they shut down the torture chambers of the Spanish Inquisition'). When it was exhibited at the Palace Theatre in New York in 1964, the film was double-billed with Freda's film. For the Italian market, Dr Orloff is not just a monster but acquires devilish qualities in *Il diabolico Dott. Satana*; this French–Spanish co-production was marketed as an American product, in which Franco became Walter Alexander and the names of the cast were Anglicised. The Mexican distributors portrayed Orloff as a vampiric figure in the promotional material and exhibited the film under the title *El Doctor Demonio*. As for the other films in the cycle, *El secreto del Dr Orloff* becomes the more sexually suggestive *Les Maîtresses du Dr*

Jekyll for the French market due to the commercial success of Hammer's *Les Maîtresses de Dracula*, whereas the US market privileges the original Orloff brand in *Dr Orloff's Monster*. *Miss Muerte* was retitled *Dans les griffes du manique* and *The Diabolical Dr Z*, responding to the different audience expectations in France and the US, respectively. By the mid-1960s and the early 1970s, Orloff's name was used as a commercial hook in the distribution of films which had nothing to do with Franco's original doctor. Thus the Spanish horror film *El enigma del ataúd* (Santos Alcocer 1967) became *Les Orgies du Dr Orloff* in France. And other directors, such as Frenchman Pierre Chevalier, reappropriated the character and the mythology of Orloff – and even the actor Howard Vernon – in *Orloff y el hombre invisible* (1971).[7] As for Franco himself, Orloff disappears (officially) from his production between 1961 and 1984. But Franco recycles his own stories in *La venganza del Dr Mabuse* (1972), in which Dr Mabuse's assistant kidnaps young women in order to turn them into robotic zombies. In *Los ojos siniestros del Dr Orloff / The Sinister Eyes of Dr Orloff* (1973, Franco transforms the original surgeon into a psychiatrist. Other films that rehearse similar storylines are *Al otro lado del espejo / The Obscene Mirror* (1973) and *Cartas boca arriba / Cartes sur table* (1966). It is not until 1982 that Franco returns to the Orloff brand with *El siniestro Dr Orloff* (1984). With the Orloff series, Franco achieved a number of variations on the mad doctor theme. More recently, Orloff and the consideration of Franco's films as a cycle respond to the repackaging of the original films for the DVD market, together with other Franco reformulations of the Orloff story in the 1970s and 1980s, the Orloff Collection being a prime example.

Gritos en la noche, *El secreto del Dr Orloff* and *Miss Muerte* are all adaptations for the screen from 'novels' by Franco's pulp fiction alter ego, David Khune. Throughout the last four decades, Jesús Franco has claimed that, under the pseudonym David Khune, he wrote an enormous number of pulp novels (detective fiction, westerns and horror), which he sold to popular literature publishers on a weekly basis in the 1950s, earning himself a comfortable living. Such claims have been readily accepted by most interviewers, critics and fans. Thus Tohill and Tombs state in their chapter devoted to the films of Franco that

> he supported himself by writing pulp novels under various pseudonyms [. . .] These youthful pulps were crazed, fantastic creations. Many of their plots and strange scenarios were later to provide inspiration for his films. He wrote over a hundred crime thrillers and horror stories and was paid around $20 per title. (1995: 80)

A more recent piece on Franco replicates more or less the same information:

during his student years in Madrid, he earned extra money by writing horror stories and Western serials under the pseudonym David Khune (a name he would continue to use throughout his film career). These student writings already envisioned the world of eccentric and unconventional characters that would later become his characteristically outlandish cinematic milieu. (Pavlović 2003: 108)

No individual pulp titles are mentioned in either case. Scholarship on Spanish popular fiction which features detailed catalogues of pulp literature publishers, series and writers does not include the name David Khune. Nor do fan websites, run by collectors and completists devoted to pulp writing produced by Spanish authors.[8] Franco's claims fly in the face of the evidence. Any research on the novelistic production of David Khune yields no traces of this 'enormous number of pulp novels', sending the Franco aficionado on a wild goose chase which leaves one wondering whether these novels actually existed in the first place. Yet references to a pulp past are regularly mobilised by the director himself in multiple interviews and more recently in his autobiography *Memorias del tío Jess* (2004), and have been picked up by journalists, critics and fans. It is worth dwelling upon Franco's fictional pulp past and considering the cultural implications behind his creative strategy.

An obvious one is that a foreign name like David Khune lent the films a certain degree of authenticity. But why would Jesús Franco invent this writer of non-existent novels? What would be the purpose behind this autobiographical move? And how does this fictional pulp past affect the reading of these films?[9] Franco inserts himself into a popular film tradition harking back to the Fantômas series of Louis Feuillade in the early 1910s, the Dr Mabuse saga adapted for cinema by German Fritz Lang in the 1920s and 1930s, and the Fu Manchu films made in the USA during the 1930s and 1940s, which translated on to the screen the pulp fiction works of Pierre Souvestre and Marcel Allain, Norbert Jacques and Sax Rohmer, respectively.[10] At the same time he is acknowledging the reciprocal influence of these mass culture forms, pulp movies and pulp novels, in his filmmaking. His relationship with pulp writing and pulp movies is undeniable when viewing *Gritos en la noche*:

> in some ways the material of Franco's film was familiar – many of the dark motifs and visceral icons were plucked from the pulp fictions of Edgar Wallace, or were reworked staples of the popular horror film. (Tohill and Tombs 1995: 77)

Thus the name Orloff was used by Edgar Wallace in *The Dark Eyes of London*, where a Dr Feodor Orloff is an insurance agent who kills single men in order to inherit their money through insurance scams (in the film of the same title by Walter Summers in 1940, also known as *The Human Monster*, the role was interpreted by Bela Lugosi). Yet Franco claims that the Orloff character was one of his pulp creations. Similarly, Inspector Edgar Tanner, the police detective in *Gritos en la noche* whose name reappears in *Miss Muerte* (this time played by Franco himself), was a character created by Wallace for *The Case of the Frightened Lady* (a role played by George Merritt in the film adaptation directed by George King in 1940).[11] One can only speculate on the genealogy of these names and admire their enchanting quality. But notwithstanding the importance of trivia as a form of cultural capital within fan discourses, my interest in Franco's own construction of his pulp past lies in the fact that Franco is lending himself and his films a pulp status, granting his filmic production a (sub)cultural value which aligns him with American and European pulp fiction and pulp movie traditions. Such status is reflected, as I have shown, in the mode of production and style of his films, where one can recognise a marked pulp quality and mechanics in his filmmaking.

A Wolf Like Me

Although Paul Naschy has played 'more monsters in films than any other actor' (Regal 1984: 10), his generic popularity is due to his role as Waldemar Daninsky, the werewolf, Naschy's own interpretation of the werewolf legend inspired by the Universal horror classic *Frankenstein Meets the Wolfman* (Roy William Neill 1943), in which Lon Chaney Junior plays Larry Talbot. From its first incarnation in *La marca del hombre lobo* to more recent ones such as *The Unliving* (Fred Olen Ray 2003), the Waldemar Daninsky saga comprises a total of twelve films spanning more than three decades. The Spanish 'hombre lobo' was a persistent and disturbing presence in the late 1960s and early 1970s (*Las noches del hombre lobo* / *Nights of the Werewolf* (René Govar 1968), *Los monstruos del terror* / *Assignment Terror* (Tulio Demichelli and Hugo Fregonese 1969), *La furia del hombre lobo* / *The Wolfman Never Sleeps* (José María Zabalza 1972), *La noche de Walpurgis*, *Dr Jekyll y el hombre lobo*, *El retorno de Walpurgis*), returned to haunt the screens in the 1980s under Naschy's real name as director, Jacinto Molina (*El retorno del hombre lobo* / *Night of the Werewolf* (1980), *La bestia y la espada mágica* / *The Beast and the Magic Sword* (1983), *El aullido del diablo* / *Howl of the Devil* (1988)), and had an outing in the 1990s (*Licántropo. El asesino de la luna llena* / *Lycanthropus. The Moonlight Murders* (Rafael Rodríguez Gordillo 1996)). More recently, the return of Jacinto Molina to the contemporary horror scene, both in Spain and abroad, was witnessed in the work of young Spanish filmmakers who repackaged Naschy for young audiences and revitalised his career with films such as *School Killer* (Carlos Gil 2001) and *Rojo Sangre* (Christian Molina 2004). Naschy's contemporary production is covered in Chapter 6. In this section, I focus on Naschy's films of the late 1960s and early 1970s, charting Molina's creation of nobleman-turned-werewolf Waldemar Daninsky; looking in detail at *La marca del hombre lobo*, which set Naschy up in the serial role of Daninsky and established the narrative template for the cycle; examining whether his treatment of the werewolf has left its mark on the subgenre; and, finally, discussing Molina's very self-conscious construction and promotion of his horror star story in interviews and writings.

According to Molina, the source of inspiration behind his first script harks back to his viewing of *Frankenstein Meets the Wolfman* in his childhood and his memories of cinema-going in 1940s Spain. Naschy talks enthusiastically about his first encounter with the Universal classics when watching *Frankenstein Meets the Wolfman* in 1946, thanks to the efforts of an usher who allowed him to sneak into the neighbourhood cinema.[12] 'I had the opportunity to watch it when it was shown as part of a double-bill programme in a neighbourhood cinema near my house' (as Paul Naschy 1997: 38), writes Molina in his autobiography, *Memorias de un hombre lobo*:

> The magic started: the lights came off, and, all of a sudden, I was immersed in a fascinating story which culminated with a delirious scene in which the tormented lycanthrope and Doctor Frankenstein's monstrous creature came face to face in a spectacular fight – it was almost surrealist. (1997: 38)

Once he stepped out into the street, Molina describes his state of mind as a 'semitrance'; he replayed in his head 'the formidable transformations on screen', acted out sequences from the movie, and immortalised that spectacular 'monster rally' in a drawing, as if to reinforce his movie-going experience. 'Larry Talbot became from then on my hero' (1997: 38), Molina proudly acknowledges. It might be easy to forget the effect of these classic Universal monsters on post-war Spanish audiences and the context in which his viewing experience was taking place, but some Universal films such as *The Wolf Man* (George Waggner 1941) had been banned by the authorities.[13] Molina is, at the same time, celebrating his own film-going experience when he reminisces about frequenting, with his mother, those neighbourhood cinemas which played double-bills of 1940s serials, such as *Los tambores de Fu-Manchú / Drums of Fu Manchu*, *El misterioso Doctor Satán / Mysterious Dr Satan* or *Las aventuras del Capitán Maravillas / The Adventures of Captain Marvel*, whose cliff-hanger endings left him 'waiting for the next episode, after days of tension and impatience' (1997: 37); he also saw pulp westerns, repeated viewing of which, on the same day or later on in the week, was not uncommon among avid consumers of popular films. In his autobiography, Molina also confesses to wolfing down the comic adventures of Spanish heroes Juan Centella, El guerrero del Antifaz ('The Masked Warrior') and Roberto Alcázar y Pedrín, whose fascist aesthetics and ideology shaped the bodies and minds of post-war Spanish males, as well as stories featuring international characters such as Tarzan and El Hombre Enmascarado ('The Masked Man'), who offered heroic versions of masculinity. It is clear that the pulp education of the young Molina, like that of Jesús Franco, was steeped in mass culture commercial traditions, the conventions of pulp fiction, film serials and comic strips, and, as it will be argued later on, the spectacle of the male body in action.

Such familiarity with the conventions of plot, narrative, character and aesthetics of serial, horror films and comics will be put to work by Molina in the creation of his werewolf scripts. Unlike those of Jesús Franco, Jacinto Molina's claims to pulp writing are authentic; under the pseudonym Jack Mills he wrote four pulp westerns published between 1960 and 1961.[14] The mechanics of pulp writing are transferred to the episodic construction of the werewolf series and the less than meticulous development of plots and characterisation, which on many occasions are done under great pressures of time. The metamorphosing of storylines, one the one hand, and the seriality and mobility of characters, on the other, are fundamental in the conception and continuation of the Waldemar Daninsky saga. As an attempt to move beyond the simple reversal of the good and bad dichotomy in werewolf stories, Molina is drawn to the character's humanity and doomed fate, and introduces the romantic (and feminine) element lacking in the Universal cycle narratives, seeing his hero as a tragic character redeemed by love rather than as a mythical creature. The balance of seriality and metamorphosis would give the cycle its formulaic distinctiveness.

Before it reached the screen, the genetic make-up of the Spanish werewolf suffered a number of modifications during the various stages of film production and distribution. Molina had initially intended the wolf man of his original script, entitled 'El licántropo', to be a certain José Huidobro and the setting to be the Spanish region of Asturias. But the original character's nationality and the film's geographical location had to be changed to pass the requirements of the censorship board – there were no werewolves in Spain and lycanthropy and other superstitious beliefs were against Catholic doctrine, declared the censors. From Polish lands came Waldemar Daninsky, named after an Edgar Allan Poe character ('The Facts in the Case of M. Valdemar' (1845)) and a Polish weightlifting world champion, Waldemar Baszanowsky. The name brought together two of Molina's passions – horror stories and weightlifting – which permeated some fundamental aspects of the film. The project's commercial viability was enhanced by a more traditional and popular title, which established a direct relationship with the Universal horror cycles. As a proof of the commercial ambition of the German producers HI-FI 70,[15] Lon Chaney Junior's agent was contacted but the American actor was in no shape – old, sick and overweight

– to accept the role. Out of luck with the casting of the male protagonist and running out of time, the producers suggested that Molina himself could take the role. The screen tests reflected the key generic elements that the producers had in mind since Molina was asked to act as both *galán* (heart-throb) and monster. Not only did the protagonist of Molina's script become foreign but Molina himself also had to acquire a foreign nationality in order to find a name that could resonate with international audiences and thus attract international distribution. The more exotic Paul Naschy was born. In Molina's own words, this was done in a matter of hours and with the help of some newspapers which were lying around on his kitchen table; a headline featuring Pope Paul VI, along with the name of Hungarian weightlifter and fellow competitor Paul Nagy, which was Germanised, resulted in Paul Naschy.[16] The film's distribution, therefore, was marked by the commercial demands of the international horror market beyond the German and Spanish territories. Technical developments and novelties were highlighted in the posters, not only with the inclusion of the phrases "EN RELIEVE" (3D) and 'HI-FI', capitalised below the title, but also through the representation of a magnified werewolf's face and claws leaping off the poster; the intense, rich colours of Eastman Colour were transferred by illustrator Jano to the vivid palette of the poster to enhance the spectacle on offer. A Dracula figure casting his cape across the prone body of his blonde female prey evoked recognisable scenes from vampire films. Jano's inclusion of various generic features signified other thrills directed at different segments of the audience (see Figure 13). The conventions of the werewolf myth were observed, in order to pander to genre purists, by including recognisable narrative elements and props in the posters (the visual representation of the werewolf), and the story was economically summed up in appropriately succinct taglines ('The curse of the pentagonal mark will transform him into a werewolf on full moon nights', 'The death with silver bullets was the price to be paid to save his beloved'). Audiences were offered the promise of an unforgettable filmic experience: 'The horrific story of the werewolf with the attraction of colour and stereoscopic sound'. If the werewolf was not enough to attract audiences, the publicity offered a multi-monster narrative: 'For the first time in the history of horror film two werewolves fight two vampires to death.' During the summer of 1968, Spanish audiences, some of whom had seen Universal Studios' werewolf in black and white, were being offered something different: an updated version of the werewolf, the new colours and sounds of horror, and a multi-monster narrative. And some spectators did love it, albeit for reasons not directly related to fear, as this letter sent to *Nuevo Fotogramas* by a certain Lizito Tayloro – a camp rewriting of Liz Taylor – illustrates:

> *La marca del hombre lobo* is the horror film that has made me laugh most in my entire life. I have never seen a horror film with so much sadism,

Figure 13   Werewolf Waldemar Daninsky is born in *La marca del hombre lobo*.

like for example in the scene where Dracula is biting [the actress] Dianik Zurakowska, Dracula's wife is biting [actor] Manuel Galiana, and the two werewolves are destroying each other. In the cinema once the film finished there were more claps than in a Conchita Piquer concert [a famous Spanish folkloric singer]. (*Nuevo Fotogramas* 1971a: 8)

Whether laughable or just plain scary, *La marca del hombre lobo* set up Paul Naschy, no longer Jacinto Molina, in the serial role of Waldemar Daninsky the werewolf, and, as his reputation with Spanish and international horror audiences grew, his name and his trademark werewolf characterisation were explicitly exploited in the advertising material for the werewolf cycle.

The beginnings of the cycle with *La marca del hombre lobo* introduce us to the tragic character of Waldemar Daninsky and announced the narrative template for his future wanderings. Cutting across time, the only connecting thread between the films is our monstrous hero, since all the films that make up the cycle follow a similar narrative pattern: the state of lycanthropy gnaws at Waldemar Daninsky, and death by a bullet or cross forged of silver, the sole cure, can only be administered by a woman who comes into his life and falls fatally in love with him. At some point in the plot, his beloved is threatened by a monstrous creature whom our 'hombre lobo' is forced to destroy in order to save her and, in turn, secure his own death. Hero and victim: that is the sempiternally doomed nature of Naschy's character.

Incoherence of time, space and character after this first instalment do not matter. Daninsky dies at the end of each film, only to reappear as a new Daninsky in the next instalment.[17] The source of Daninsky's lycanthropy varies. In *La marca del hombre lobo*, Waldemar is bitten by his ancestor, Count Imre Wolfstein, the last of the dynasty; he, in turn, had been resurrected by two gypsies, who had profaned the Count's tomb and removed a silver cross from his dead body. In *La noche de Walpurgis*, two pathologists carrying out an autopsy on the corpse of a man suspected of being a werewolf extract a silver bullet from his heart, reviving the dead werewolf. Daninsky's family is cursed by Elizabeth Bathory de Nadasdy in *El retorno de Walpurgis* and he is transformed into a werewolf by a group of devil-worshipping gypsies. *La furia del hombre lobo* stages a mad-scientist scenario whereby an evil female scientist manages to control the mind of university professor Waldemar Daninsky and unleashes the beast inside him. Even the werewolf lore changes early on in the series when, in *El retorno del hombre lobo*, a dagger fashioned with a silver cross is used as the weapon to destroy the werewolf, replacing the original silver bullet of the first few scripts. The flexibility and adaptability of Molina's creation to different periods and settings are remarkable. His character cuts across time and space, moves from one mythical tradition to another, and faces every famous monster in filmland. Thus *La marca del hombre lobo* brings together lycanthropy and vampirism, whereas in *Dr Jekyll y el hombre lobo* Molina's script links lycanthropy with the Jekyll and Hyde formula, moving between the Transylvanian mountains and modern London. *La maldición de la bestia* makes the Count join an expedition to the Himalayas and ends up with Daninsky confronting the Abominable Snowman, while, in the Spanish–Japanese co-production *La bestia y la espada mágica*, Daninsky is initially placed in sixteenth-century Japan before travelling back to a geographically indeterminate medieval Europe and then to Renaissance Spain. For Molina, the possibilities of the werewolf character were endless, unlike those of other classic monsters whose spatiotemporal co-ordinates were more limiting. 'The werewolf', as Molina often puts it, 'could have a family, children. He could get a mortgage, buy a car, walk down the street and no one knows he is a werewolf. Only when the full moon rises, he will be transformed into a werewolf.'[18] At times, Molina modernises the myth; at others, he locates it in a more traditional setting and period. For many commentators, however, his mixture of myths is sacrilegious and shows scant regard for generic conventions.

Molina's distinctiveness, not necessarily a mark of excellence, lies, firstly, in this ever-shifting process of displacement within a limited narrative framework; secondly, in his creation of an iconography for Waldemar Daninsky, which draws upon different mythologies, legends and film horror traditions; and, thirdly, in Paul Naschy's performance style as both normal human character and monster. Among the main borrowings from the second Universal cycle, Molina adopts Larry Talbot's tragic fate, a certain sympathy for the monster and the staginess of the 'monster rally' to provide a cheap and cheerful finale. As for Daninsky's unique werewolfry, Molina immersed his character in a mythology without frontiers and cutting across time. The Nazis' fetishism for the wolf and their search for the Holy Grail in the French region of Mayenne gave him the idea of naming the silver cross associated with Daninsky, Mayenza; Central European gypsy folklore added age-old curses to the Daninsky story; an ancient Japanese legend about the liberation of death and love through sacrifice provided him with a basic narrative running through his scripts – a woman who is able to give her life for the tragic, lonely hero; esoteric symbolism contributed to one of the defining attributes of the werewolf – the sign of the pentagram; and the scripts were peppered with Christian imagery – crosses and holy water stoups.

Let us focus on *La marca del hombre lobo* as the representative microcosm of the Waldemar Daninsky series, in order to delve into the Daninsky legend, iconography and characterisation and to explore Naschy's nobleman-turned-werewolf performance. The opening sequences are organised around a series of encounters and interplays between the enigmatic Daninsky and the female protagonist, Janice von Aarenberg (Dianik Zurakowska). His sudden appearance at Janice's masked ball and birthday party announces the arrival of an outsider

to the narrative world and sets the romantic storyline in motion. Daninsky dramatically enters the stage, dressed in a bright red devil costume; he introduces
himself to the eighteen-year-old as a 'satanic majesty' and interrupts her dance
with her boyfriend, Rudolph Weissmann (Manuel Manzaneque). His unexpected appearance also attracts the attention of their fathers, who describe
him as a stranger. In the couple's second encounter, in an antique shop, we
learn that this devilishly irresistible stranger is a very respectable and wealthy
aristocrat who owns Wolfstein Castle. Their next meeting takes place in a
church, when their hands touch over the holy water stoup; their desire for each
other is visibly sacrilegious. Their fourth encounter occurs at Daninsky's own
Gothic property, when the young couple stumble upon it on an outing. It is in
this Gothic location that Daninsky's past begins to unravel and the horror narrative starts to unfold. Daninsky relates the tragedy of his nineteenth-century
Polish ancestor, Imre Wolfstein, who, according to legend, was attacked by a
wolf man during a trip to the Far East. After he recovered from the attack, a
series of horrible murders took place in the region and the local people decided
to kill Wolfstein, driving a silver cross through his heart. He can only rest in
peace if he is saved by a woman who is in love with him. Following the conventions of horror storytelling, Janice and Rudolph reinstate the main elements of
the legend when they leave in their sports car, reintroducing the viewer into the
modern world. But, soon, recognisable cinematic moments from the Universal
series take us back to a Gothic context, preparing the audience for the arrival
of the monster. Imre Wolfstein's tomb is profaned by two gypsies, who remove
the silver cross from his dead body, bringing the werewolf back to life. During
the ensuing hunting-down of Imre the wolf man – modelled visually on the
famous *Frankenstein* episode – Waldemar is bitten and the curse passed on to
him. Through an old book and a letter from 1927, found in the subterranean
vaults of the castle, Waldemar learns that his ancestor Wladimir Wolfstein fell
under the spell of an evil vampire in the fifteenth century and that a certain Dr
Mikhelov possesses the cure for lycanthropy, a silver bullet. But the arrival of
Dr Mikhelov's ancestor, Janos, and his wife Wandessa, brings with it the vampiric forces that aim to destroy Daninsky rather than cure him.

The actual metamorphoses of Waldemar Daninsky are a major set piece of
the film, and, by extension, the cycle, since they announce the lurid moments
of spectacle and violence.[19] The transformation of Daninsky into werewolf is
gradually anticipated through *mise-en-scène* devices and editing before the first
physical symptoms take effect, for Imre Wolfstein and Waldemar Daninsky
inhabit the same spaces – the castle, the crypt and the forest. The context
within which Waldemar's transformations occur is the castle, the first in the
domestic space of his own bedroom and subsequent ones in the dungeon. When
Waldemar recognises the visible signs of lycanthropy – the pentacle branded
on his chest – in the mirror, denoting the split identity of the character, he is

Figure 14   The moment of lupine spectacle in *La maldición de la bestia*.

locked in his bedroom. Rudolph, whose life was saved by Waldemar in the hunt for the wolf man, attempts to help Waldemar by chaining him up. But Waldemar's animal strength allows him to break free from the chains and the transformation at full moon is irremediable. Technically, the bright, hazy lighting, the red colour filters and a repetitive score highlight the hallucinatory atmosphere of the scene, whereas the use of Vaseline on the camera produces a blurry optical effect which craftily disguises the transformation. An extreme close-up of the werewolf's face emphasises the distinctiveness of Waldemar Daninsky's lupine alter ego. The make-up effects convey a creature far more bestial than the Universal werewolf: fangs in the upper part of the mouth, as well as the lower, and an excessive hairy guise (see Figure 14). Other man-into-werewolf episodes occur when Waldemar is caged in the castle dungeon and dramatise it through shadows or bodily contorsions.

Naschy's transformations on screen are certainly moments of spectacle, not just providing the awaited horrific element of the film but also exhibiting the spectacle of the male body in action. In a wolf parade, Naschy's Waldemar Daninsky would definitely stand out. As a weightlifting competitor in the 1950s and 1960s, Naschy had developed an athletic and muscular body which he proudly displayed in his first role as Waldemar Daninsky, whether he was wearing tight T-shirts or other garments which accentuated his musculature and strength, or showing his naked torso. Such displays of the muscular male body were uncommon in Spanish cinema, setting him apart from representations of the average male Spaniard in other popular film traditions. In his dual role as nobleman and werewolf, Naschy's robust sporting physique and his energetic performances conveyed (physical and sexual) prowess and virility. In his performances, Naschy favours his character's physicality. He smashes through windows, leaps around, snarls and growls, launches bestial attacks and rips out jugulars. In contrast to Chaney Junior's static and inexpressive performances, Naschy's animal-like movements and actions are more brutal and vicious. On screen, Naschy is a blood-spattered werewolf. But he also conveys the monstrous pathos of the Universal werewolf, manifesting the 'loss of bodily control and a physical subjection to forces more powerful than oneself' (Hutchings 2004: 164). As for his *galán* performance, Daninsky's masculinity and sexuality in *La marca del hombre lobo* are contrasted with those of Rudolph, whose adolescent, well-groomed appearance functions as a counterpoint to Daninsky, the real man. Likewise, in his encounters with Janice, Daninsky's masculinity is defined in relation to female characters: commanding and manly, gallant and passionate.

On the one hand, therefore, Waldemar Daninsky embodies a traditional, mythic form of masculinity readily associated with a Don Juan: his aristocratic status, his powers of seduction and his virile, confident presence. On the other hand, the character's metamorphosis into a werewolf enables Naschy to show his muscular talent in action through aggression, violence and fighting in a display characteristic of male genre films and macho heroes. Daninsky is a serial seducer, a wolf, but a passionate, sensitive and vulnerable wolf. One could even argue that this Spanish werewolf of the 1970s reflects both the traditional attributes of the (Spanish) macho and the desirable qualities of the new man, as portrayed in the publicity images fed to the average male Spaniard during that decade. My point is not to ascribe to Naschy the embodiment of a certain Spanish masculinity but to account for the ways in which he acts out various versions of masculinity and embodies certain traditions of representation in popular film, which do not necessarily depend on psychological depth and motivation.

Hailed by the Spanish press as 'the Spanish werewolf for European cinema' (headline in the newspaper *Madrid* on 28 January 1971), Naschy's diverse monstrous outings were recognised by his contemporaries in genre festivals and genre magazines. The 4th International Week of Fantasy and Horror Movies, held in Sitges in 1971, acknowledged his role in promoting Spanish fantasy cinema. His international reputation was enhanced two years later by the Georges Meliès Best Actor Award at the International Convention of Fantastic and Science-Fiction Cinema, celebrated in Paris, for his interpretation of hunchback Wolfgang Gotho in *El jorobado de la morgue*. Both his screenwriting production and his acting achieved prominence in Spanish genre magazine *Terror Fantastic*, which granted Waldemar Daninsky the werewolf the whole of the front cover for their special issue on the werewolf genre (January 1972) and bestowed on him the honorary title of 'Man of Fantasy' (August 1973), sharing iconic status with the likes of Boris Karloff, James Whale, Terence Fisher, Roger Corman, Lon Chaney, Iroshimo Homan or Ricardo Fredda. Paul Naschy had become not just a Spanish werewolf for Europe but an international horror star.[20] And certainly, he revitalised the long-forgotten myth of the werewolf for the screens, dared to tackle a number of monsters on the screen, and, above all, was seen at home and abroad as the driving force behind the Spanish horror boom. Paul Naschy acquired mythical status. Ángel Falquina and Juan José Porto described him as 'a myth, an Iberian myth' (1974: 116) in their volume *Cine de Terror y Paul Naschy*,[21] while Luis Vigil introduced him to the readers of *Famosos Monsters del Cine* as 'Paul Naschy, el mito nacional' (1975). The Daninsky character even crossed over to another medium, comics, appearing in a series of strips in the Basque newspaper *El Correo Español – El Pueblo Vasco*.[22]

A consecrated local horror star by the early 1970s, Naschy was interviewed habitually in popular film publications to give his views on the genre and often collaborated in genre publications, showing his connoisseurship and commenting on his particular intervention in the werewolf subgenre. Naschy compared his creation Waldemar Daninsky and his performing style to those of previous actors who had played the monstrous creature, inserting himself in the tradition of Lon Chaney Junior, Oliver Reed (*The Curse of the Werewolf* (Terence Fisher 1961)) and Michael Landon (*I Was a Teenage Werewolf* (Gene Fowler Junior 1957)). As Molina himself puts it,

> goodbye to the tormented tenderness of Lawrence Talbot (Lon Chaney, Junior), goodbye to the romantic candour of Leon Carido (Oliver Reed). Times are changing for werewolves, too, and this is the time for Waldemar Daninsky, the Hispanic and universal lycanthrope. (1976: 23)

And, despite his admiration and respect for Chaney Junior, he has never hesitated in declaring that his Waldemar Daninsky is far superior to Larry Talbot, not only in terms of werewolf folklore but also in his exploitation of the monster's narrative possibilities,[23] characterisation and portrayal of monstrosity. Molina concedes, however, the superiority of the Universal werewolf in two aspects: the quality of the directors and the wizardry of make-up artist Jack Pierce.

Beyond the fiery defence of his creation, Naschy advocated for a dignification of Spanish horror film, whereby the people involved in the making of the films had to produce 'worthy works' ('obras dignas') (Naschy in Yoldi 1971:

51) and lamented the critical dismissal of the genre and the 'lack of specialist genre criticism' (Naschy in Company 1974: 35). His views were supported in the pages of *Terror Fantastic*. If anybody can change Spanish horror film, a genre critic observed, elevating them from

> banal productions to quality films, with form and content, with intentionality, with a real investigation of the historical and legendary material being dealt with [. . .] that is Naschy, the actor recognized internationally, the person who has [the] popular approval [of Spanish audiences] and at the same time [has proven to be] a financial hit for producers. (Camín 1973: 40)

Yet Naschy had to raise his standards, too, evolving in his double facet of screenwriter and actor. As a producer of scripts, the only way of 'elevating the quality of Spanish fantastique cinema' is to move away from clichés; as a performer, Naschy 'has to stop doing repetitive roles, has to get more into the characters he interprets and has to pay special attention to his acting [stiff and affected] when he is not hiding behind the make-up' (Camín 1973: 40).

In the 1980s and 1990s, a more canny (read, art-conscious and media-savvy) Molina would begin to emerge. From the early 1980s onwards, Molina develops a more sophisticated discourse around his films and assiduously vindicates his place within the history of Spanish horror cinema, reaching its most significant moment with the publication of his autobiography *Memorias de un hombre lobo*.[24] His reputation was enhanced in these decades in two ways: on the one hand, his careful cultivation of fandom, and, on the other, the iconic status the man with a thousand faces had for specific audiences in the early 1970s. The retelling of Molina's own creative influences and legendary status starts with Belgian fanzine *Fantoom* at the turn of the 1980s. The views of *Fantoom* editor, Gilbert Verschooten, act as turning point in Molina's auteurist construction of his own horror star story. The second turning point, I argue, is Molina's direction of documentaries about the Prado Museum and its art holdings for Japanese producer Horikikaku Seisaku, which enabled him to articulate an aesthetic discourse around his earlier work.[25] According to Verschooten,

> Naschy is pure autodidact essence, wise and profound as popular culture itself. With his peculiar aesthetics (Goya, Solana, El Bosco, Vermeer de Delft or Brueghel the Old) as well as his peculiar literary vision (Gustavo Adolfo Bécquer, Guy de Maupassant, Edgar Allan Poe, M. R. James, Bram Stoker, Arthur Rimbaud or Spanish picaresque novel), Naschy creates a wholly fantastic world, which, nonetheless, cuts our gaze like a real knife. (Verschooten in de Cuenca 1999: 261)

And now, Molina's artistic and literary influences are exposed in – and reappropriated for – his autobiography: 'my lycanthrope moves aesthetically in the visual palette of [painters such as] Vermeer de Delft, Peter Brueghel the Elder, or Hieronymus Bosch El Bosco' (as Naschy 1997: 232); among his major literary influences, he cites the literary worlds of Gustavo Adolfo Bécquer, Edgar Allan Poe, Victor Hugo or H. P. Lovecraft.[26] The transition from encounters with mass-culture experiences and artefacts to canonical frames of reference is also carried out at the autobiographical level, for 'art' had always run in the family. Uncle Jacinto had introduced him to the writings of Romantic writer Gustavo Adolfo Bécquer; uncle Emilio, a painter and sculptor, was a friend of José Gutiérrez Solana and used to take the young Molina to the artist's studio. While Jesús Franco was strategically seeking pulp status with his mad-doctor cycle and has since remained in the realms of exploitation, Molina has been incorporating artistic references to explicate his filmic production. Such invocation of artistic sources attaches some form of dignity and cultural value to his work and elevates it from the realms of popular culture.

It is difficult to disentangle Molina's early views on his filmic creation and his own position as a popular culture producer within the Spanish film industry in the early 1970s from the discourses that critics, fans and Molina himself have been mobilising around horror icon Paul Naschy throughout the last few decades. Although Naschy tended to vainglory and self-mythologisation when he talked and wrote about his films,[27] Waldemar Daninsky was the product of one person's vision, Jacinto Molina, who self-consciously took genre conventions, stereotypes and old mythologies to create a distinctive werewolf and a character that could travel beyond Spain. His prolific output, with more than thirty credits altogether between 1968 and 1975, and his passionate – and for many amateurish – performances as a werewolf deserve a place in the histories of Spanish cinema and of international horror. As Fernando Savater has observed, Naschy is 'not the authentic and artistic wolf man, but rather the amateur lycanthrope that the fans of the genre would have liked to interpret at least once' (1998). Perhaps his amateurish and autodidactic approach accounts for the success of Naschy and is the reason why his performances have struck a chord with audiences.

THE SPANISH KNIGHTS OF TERROR

In the highly commercial and competitive business of 1970s horror film production, new products had to offer something distinctive. Scriptwriter and director Amando de Ossorio brought the Knights Templar to Spanish screens, an idiosyncratic approach to the zombie tradition which offered a generic, thematic and cultural take on a well-established subgenre. After the box-office success of the first instalment, *La noche del terror ciego*, which had attracted

789,579 spectators and box-office takings of 163,324.38 euros, the Templars were revived in three consecutive films between 1972 and 1975 (*El ataque de los muertos sin ojos* premiered a year and a half later (29 October 1973), managing 409,070 spectators and 82,597.11 euros; *El buque maldito* (15 September 1975) was less successful, with 330,040 spectators and 74,766.97 euros; and *La noche de las gaviotas* brought the cycle to an end with 156,336 spectators and 53,212 euros). Ossorio's formula, which combined Gothic horror ingredients, adult themes and saleable scenes of sex and violence, relocated horror in a recognisable present-day world and responded to contemporary takes on the genre initiated internationally with Romero's *Night of the Living Dead*.

At that point, zombie movies were in the offing, so it was just a matter of time before a Spanish horror filmmaker clued into the trend and made a zombie film. As Kim Newman observes, in his *Nightmare Movies*, 'Living Dead imitations soon became popular' in Spain (1988: 7). The zombie craze was spearheaded by Ossorio's Templars, *La rebelión de las muertas*, *La orgía de los muertos* and *No profanar el sueño de los muertos*, the latter 'Spain's most blatant reworking of the Romero formula' (1988: 7). For Newman the 'living characters' in Ossorio's films 'are uniformly tiresome – it seems as if everybody in Spanish horror film is compelled to wear Carnaby street dresses, polo-neck pullovers or macho man medallions', although he concedes that his 'marauding band of zombie crusaders on skeletal horses dash[ing] about Portuguese plains in slow motion [. . .] prove striking enough to continue their rampages in a clutch of sequels' (1988: 7). Weldon's *Psychotronic Encyclopaedia of Film* describes Ossorio's knights of terror as both 'mummified bloodthirsty skeletons on horseback' (1989: 66) and 'the Spanish zombies' (1989: 332). Although Ossorio's fictional creations noticeably form part of the zombie subgenre, the director is at pains to distinguish his monsters from zombies – 'mummies on horseback, not zombies', 'entirely different from zombies or any other kind of living dead creature' – in a clear attempt to move away from *Night of the Living Dead* and subsequent spin-offs:

> 1) The Templars are mummies on horseback, not zombies. A displacement in the relationship Time/Space (sic) slackens their motions. 2) The Templars come out of their tombs every night to search for victims and blood, which makes them closely related to the vampires of myth. 3) The Templars have studied occult sciences and continue to sacrifice human victims to the cruel and blood-lusting being that keeps them alive. 4) The Templars are blind and guided by sound alone. All of this makes them entirely different from zombies or any other kind of living dead creature without soul or reason. (de Ossorio in Burrell 2005: 4)

For de Ossorio the Knights Templar share the attributes of two different monster myths, mummies and vampires. Like the vampire, they return from the dead at night seeking blood. Like the mummy, they come from a distant past and irrupt into the modern world of the narrative, therefore deploying a relationship between the old and the new, the past and the present, which is explored in this section. Other mummy-like features are their slow movements and their general physiognomical depiction (cadaverous presence, wrapped in decaying clothes). As for the fraternity's links with the occult, the Knights Templar are associated with necromancy and perform sacrificial ceremonies offered to an evil supernatural force to gain immortal life. While the monstrous status of the Knights of Terror seems to be a point of contention and distinctiveness, what is undeniable is that Ossorio created a monster with a unique physiognomy, which arguably belongs to the zombie subgenre.

The composite nature and characterisation of the Knights Templar thus conflated the attributes of different types of monsters – mummy, vampire, ghost, zombie – and incorporated ingredients from well-established horror narratives. While the various myths and legends surrounding the Order of the Knights Templar form the backbone of the cycle, Ossorio drew upon a number of artistic sources of influence: on the one hand, contemporary international horror traditions, and, on the other hand, local Spanish sources which ranged from the Romantic legends of Spanish writer and poet Gustavo Adolfo Bécquer (1836–70), in particular 'El monte de las ánimas' and 'El miserere', to iconic visual images associated with General Franco's authoritarian regime. By paying attention to these representational traditions, I consider not only the international pulp credentials of the cycle but also the latent local political critique inscribed in it, since these monsters might be said to represent specific ideas, institutions and values pertaining to Francoist ideology. Thus, while the Templars' unique physiognomy forms part of international horror traditions such as the visual style of American horror anthology series, EC comics, their look is very Spanish (and Christian) in custom and appearance, evoking the conflation of the militaristic and the religious so deeply ingrained in Spanish history from the Middle Ages through to Franco's dictatorship.

The Templars had never been portrayed as horror figures before. At first, producer José Antonio Pérez Giner resisted financing Ossorio's project because the monstrous characters he had created had no cinematic precedent and the story surrounding their historical as well as mythical existence was the stuff of legends. Spanish and international audiences, argued the producers, were only familiar with the classic monsters. How did Ossorio, then, persuade the producers to invest in a 'new' monster? And how were the Knights Templar sold to distributors and exhibitors first and introduced to Spanish audiences later? Ossorio created his own art-horror work to show them the horrific potential of the undead Templars. Designs and illustrations, such as the medieval prints which feature in *La noche del terror ciego* as an explanation of the historical existence of the Templars, masks and props – together with the script – finally swayed the producers, who invested 10 million pesetas in the film. The foray into new monster territory was counterbalanced with appropriate exploitative strategies, such as the producers' resolve to add the phrase 'la noche' (night) to the original title, 'Terror ciego' (blind terror), to capitalise on the domestic success of Klimovsky's *La noche de Walpurgis* and the international reputation of *Night of the Living Dead*, as well as the plethora of generic markers displayed in the publicity material.

The pressbook and contemporary reviews of *La noche de terror ciego* are my first points of entry into the world of the Knights Templar. The pressbook introduced the new characters thus:

> Bells that do not exist ring in the empty belfry. Their pealing makes the ground tremble. Graves open and tombs turn over. Cadaverous, skeletal hands emerge from beneath the marble slabs and the mummified corpses of the old Knights Templar who inhabited the abbey centuries ago come to the surface. Their monk and warrior vestments have been ruined by time.

Graveyards and ruins are the habitat of these living dead, whose return from the grave is signalled by ghostly sounds. While the original script names the monstrous creatures as Knights Templar and the pressbook dwells upon their monk–warrior condition, the publicity taglines refer to them simply as monsters, a simple marketing strategy to induce curiosity about their appearance and attributes. One tagline warned audiences: 'Monsters emerging from tombs whose sole presence paralyzes men'; another tempted audiences with some of the traditional pleasures and thrills of horror: 'Three desiring, ambitious and brave women in stark contrast to abominable, nightmarish monsters'. Love interest and loss of emotional control were also used to pull in audiences: 'Jealousy pushed her to live a horrifying adventure.' But perhaps the constant theme that is established in relation to the film's plot is the monsters' link to the past and to their violent acts: 'In *La noche del terror ciego* medieval tombs open to give way to the most terrifying massacre,' or 'They return from the Middle Ages, blind and thirsty for innocent blood.'

Visually, the artwork of director Ossorio and illustrator Jano for the pressbook borrowed from the pulp cover artwork and the comic book imagery of the American EC series of the early 1950s, in particular *The Crypt of Terror*, which had been in international circulation. The publicity material depicted the Knights' hybrid monstrosity and their recognisable iconographic wardrobe. The film posters responded to cultural and generic expectations of male monstrosity and female victimisation by presenting the ghastly beings attacking a horror-stricken young woman or about to perform a sacrificial ritual. The main poster for *La noche del terror ciego*, for instance, shows four Knights frontally, surrounding their female victim, two of them in the foreground clutching at her body with their cadaverous hands, and two other magnified figures in the background revealing, through the opening of their rotten hooded cloaks, their mummified, hollow-socket faces. The large hilt of a sword, which visibly doubles up as a cross, is firmly grasped by one of the Knights to convey not only their religious provenance and violent nature but also their sexual threat (see Figure 15). I will return to the fusion of the cross and the sword later on, but suffice to say at this juncture that what this element underlines is the characters' background as military and religious figures. By blatantly incorporating the promise of fear and sexuality, the prospective viewer was invited to buy a ticket on these two basic bodily premises. And the moments leading to the first aural and visual appearance of the Knights of Terror on screen delivered on both fronts. The narrative of *La noche del terror ciego* situates one of its main female characters lost at night among the ruins of an abandoned monastery, disturbing the sacred silence of the cemetery with modern music blasting out of her radio. Her noisy music awakens the dead. Slabs open, skeletal hands emerge from the graves, and the mummified monk–warriors step out from the underworld. Guided by the sound of the living and mounting their ghostly horses, they search for their first victim. Slow-motion shots and the unnerving choral Gregorian-style score augment the eeriness of their first apparition.[28]

Spanish genre magazine *Terror Fantastic* commended Ossorio's desire to renew the genre and his search for new forms of fantasy. For the magazine, one word encapsulated the director's efforts with *La noche del terror ciego* (and its sequel, *El ataque de los muertos sin ojos*): 'NOVEDAD' ('novelty') (Cervera 1973: 50). And any comparison to Romero's film was laid to rest since *La noche del terror ciego* emphatically 'shares NO connection or similarity' with it (Cervera 1973: 50). The source of inspiration for the Knights Templar, according to Cervera, was not to be found in American popular culture or in the filmic medium, but rather in Spanish and European history – the real existence of the medieval order – and in painting – the apocalyptic aesthetics of Pieter Brueghel the Elder's 'The Triumph of Death' (1973: 50), to be found in Madrid's Prado museum. The initial critical reception in the mainstream press, after the film's release on 10 April 1972, was positive overall and also applauded the innovative aspects of de Ossorio's first film, in particular the fact that it opened up new directions in contemporary Spanish horror production and displayed stylistic accomplishments worthy of note. For the *Pueblo* reviewer, 'mixing bikinis and shrouds, monastic skeletons and sculptural women, abbey ruins and ultramodern swimming pools is an unheard-of formula in horror cinema' (Anon. 1972c). The reviewer went on to say that Ossorio had created a 'tale for adults' and marked 'new directions in what is usually a trite genre'.[29] For

Figure 15   EC comics, damsels in distress and nights of blind terror in Amando de Ossorio's successful *La noche del terror ciego*.

the *Arriba* journalist, the film's 'suggestive argument' was 'full of expressive horror possibilities' (Anon. 1972b). And, similarly, he welcomed the film's stylistic choices, in particular the Knights' slow-motion cavalry raids, which were a very interesting device. Critics varied in their categorisation of the monsters. For some, they embodied a 'new type of "vampirism" with a twist, which is most certainly modelled on the cavalry order of the Knights Templar', as stated in *Arriba*; for others, they were merely nightmarish apparitions typical of ghost stories ('skeletal ghosts') (Martialay 1972). And while some were torn by the Knights' hybrid nature, others would allow no categorical hesitation: 'in fact, they are descendents of Count Dracula' (Rubio 1972b). The novelty soon wore off, and although in subsequent features the director placed the Knights in different situations and contexts (in a ghost ship at sea in *El buque maldito* and in a coastal village in *La noche de las gaviotas*), critics argued that the formula had been exhausted.[30] Furthermore, as the last two sequels came out, Ossorio's cycle was seen to epitomise the 'systematic degradation of the genre which has reached the most appalling instances of [Spanish] sub-cultural nudie production' (Company 1974: 61)[31] and was held to belong to the ideologically reactionary subgeneric cinema whose sole purpose was the sublimation of repressed and unsatisfied sexual needs (Company 1974: 61).

This subcultural (and pulp) identity, however, was central to the cycle. Ossorio's scripts were plotted very much like pulp stories and were infused with pulp attributes. Depictions of gore, sexuality, sadism and excessive violence – major selling points of the pulps – are draped around a basic storyline and presented within the framing devices typical of horror stories and the self-referential qualities of the genre. The Gothic horror of churches, abbeys, graveyards and steam trains is combined with adult themes and recognisable modern settings (swimming pools and workshops making mannequins in *La noche de terror ciego* or yacht clubs in *El buque maldito*). The narrative template for the series features a series of transposable elements: a love triangle, erotic scenes, isolated and enclosed settings, a siege situation, and a flashback to a past time which functions as an explanatory note to the Templars' actions. With only shoestring budgets at his disposal and shooting schedules of no more than five weeks (or just over two weeks in the case of *El buque maldito*), due to the producers' demands on him to churn out films at a rapid pace, Ossorio resorted to exploitation production strategies, formulaic plots and shock value throughout the cycle. Thus exploitation practices in *La noche del terror ciego* ranged from the use of a relatively unknown cast[32] to the film's open ending, which had to be resolved with screams off screen and a freeze frame to save time and money; nevertheless, this functioned as a shrewd device to build into the story the possibility of a further episode. The most notorious recycling strategy of the cycle, however, was the reuse of footage, more specifically the reuse of what was to become Ossorio's trademark scene

– the resurrection in *El ataque de los muertos sin ojos*, as well as in *La noche de las gaviotas*, of the slow-moving monsters initially seen in the abbey in *La noche del terror ciego*.[33]

Let us focus in detail on the narrative of *La noche del terror ciego* to assess its pulp horror identity. Two old schoolfriends, Virginia (María Elena Arpón), a model, and Betty (Lone Fleming), a mannequin designer, meet by chance in a tourist resort in Portugal. Virginia is there on holiday with her boyfriend César (Roger Whelan). The three arrange to go on a train excursion to the mountains but when Virginia feels jealous about Betty's and Roger's flirtations – a flashback informs the audience of the two women's lesbian relationship in the past – she jumps off the train. Virginia finds an abandoned village and an abbey, where she decides to spend the night, thus trespassing on the sacred space of the cemetery. The next morning she is dead. When Betty and César ask about the village in the holiday resort, their questions are met by suspicion and fear by the local waiters, who can barely articulate a response ('we are forbidden to talk about that because it scares tourists away'). According to local legends, the village of Berzano belonged to the Knights, who worshipped the Devil. A few days later, Roger visits Betty in her mannequin workshop, where her assistant Nina (Verónica Llimera), a Berzano local, informs them that strange stories about the Templars are told in her village. Meanwhile, in the morgue next door, Virginia rises from the slab and attacks the attendant. While the police believe that the main suspect is Pedro (Joseph Thelman), a local smuggler, Betty and Roger decide to take matters into their own hands and enlist Pedro and his girlfriend María (María Silva) to help them. Roger and Betty learn from librarian and local historian Professor Cantell (Francisco Sanz), who happens to be the father of the wayward Pedro, that the abandoned village of Berzano was the ancient capital of the Knights Templar, a group of monk–warriors who were excommunicated and executed by the Inquisition in medieval times for their satanic practices and sacrificial rituals. According to Cantell, who supports his scholarly explanations with visual evidence of their historical existence, shown by way of medieval prints, the locals killed the monks and hanged them so that ravens would peck their eyes out. In the mean time, Nina is attacked by Virginia, now one of the living dead, but manages to destroy her with fire. As soon as the group arrives at the abbey, individual desires break the members' unity. When the bells strike midnight, the tombs in the cemetery open up and the blind dead rise, besieging and killing Roger, Pedro and María. Betty manages to escape by getting on to the train. But the Knights Templar assault the train, swarming aboard and massacring the passengers. When the train arrives at the station, a crazed Betty appears to be the only survivor. But a freeze frame of Betty screaming and the mummified hand of one of the Knights Templar suggest otherwise.[34]

Ossorio maximised the basic narrative template of his original *La noche de terror ciego* and deployed similar framing devices typical of the horror genre in the three subsequent instalments, while at the same time introducing some variations by placing his monstrous protagonists in different contexts. References to the legend and folklore of the Knights Templar also suffered alterations throughout the cycle, in the same way that Jesús Franco and Jacinto Molina were inconsistent in the use of the mythology surrounding Dr Orloff and Waldemar Daninsky in their respective cycles. In *La noche del terror ciego* the framing devices function thus: firstly, through the oral elements of a local legend and superstitions connecting the place with some mysterious deaths, as related by the local waiters at the hotel complex and confirmed by Nina later on at the mannequin shop, which captures the imagination of the outsiders; secondly, with the introduction of a scholar, Professor Cantell, who provides the historical framework and a voice of authority;[35] and, thirdly, through the actions of the monsters themselves, which provide the shocking and sensationalist murders. These framing devices, whose narrative function is to state and restate the plot for the audience, similarly structure *El ataque de los muertos sin ojos*, *El buque maldito* and *La noche de las gaviotas*.

The first sequel, *El ataque de los muertos sin ojos*, opens in summary style, refamiliarising the viewer with the legend and introducing new audiences to the history of the Knights Templar. It offers only a slightly different version of the legend. While, in *La noche del terror ciego*, the local scholar explains that, in the thirteenth century, the local people of Berzano had killed the monks and hanged them so that ravens would peck their eyes out, the pre-credit sequence of *El ataque de los muertos sin ojos* is set in the past, when the local population of Bouzano executed the monks before burning them at the stake. The rest of the action moves to the present time, when the villagers are celebrating the pagan festival which commemorates the defeat of the monks. The mayor of the village, Duncan (Fernando Sancho), who has employed an American pyrotechnic expert, Jack Marlowe (Tony Kendall), for the occasion, is unaware that his fiancée Vivian (Esperanza Roy) and Jack have had a relationship in the past, which rekindles as soon as they take a walk around the abbey ruins. This time, the Knights Templar come to life when an embittered hunchback cripple named Murdo (José Canalejas) murders a girl, whose fresh virgin's blood, together with the noise of the fireworks, wakes them up. Soon after, they attack the village and massacre the villagers. The survivors barricade themselves in the local church against the monsters but the relentless, gory siege of the Knights and the flaws demonstrated by the group lead to bloodshed. One violent death follows another. Only Jack, Vivian and an orphaned girl manage to walk out into the dying day to an uncertain future. In *El buque maldito*, the setting is moved to the sea, and the habitat of the Knights Templars is a lost galleon, wandering the seas in its own time zone (see Figure 16). In similar vein to *La noche del terror ciego*, *El buque maldito* mixes the

Figure 16   *El buque maldito*, the last and least successful of the Knight Templars' cycle.

glamorous present-day setting of a yacht club with the old and decrepit ghostly galleon of the wandering Knights. Fashion models Kathy (Blanca Estrada) and Lorena (Margarita Merino) disappear during a publicity stunt to launch a boat, which goes horribly wrong. Kathy's flatmate and lover Noemi (Barbara Rey), the director of the modelling agency, Lillian (Maria Perschy), business-man Howard Tucker (Jack Taylor), his henchman Sergio (Manuel de Blas) and scientist Professor Grübber (Carlos Lemos) form a rescue party, who, like the models who have disappeared, end up entering the twilight zone of the galleon. A logbook found in the ship by the Professor situates the Knights Templar back in the sixteenth century as part of the mysterious cargo of the Dutch galleon: a group of excommunicated devil worshippers in wooden sarcophagi and a priceless treasure. In this third instalment, the inability of the group to fight off the bloodthirsty ghouls ends in the death of all the rescue party. The final part of the cycle, *La noche de las gaviotas*, returns to the mainland and to the familiar historical explanation of the Knights as told in the first two films. Here, in the pre-credit sequence, the monk–warriors sacrifice a young woman, drink her blood and offer her corpse to an age-old amphibian deity, adding a Lovecraftian touch to the Knights' mythology. This arcane sacrificial ritual is still being performed in the twentieth century by the superstitious vil-lagers of a remote coastal village, who, for seven nights of every year, sacrifice seven young girls to the deity and the Knights. When the new doctor, Henry Stein (Victor Petit), and his wife, Joan (María Kosti), arrive in the community, they witness the macabre ritual. Their attempts to protect other victims are met with suspicion and then by violence, finally unleashing the anger of the Knights, who murder the villagers and lay siege to the heroic couple who are hiding in the castle. *La noche de las gaviotas* is the only film in the cycle which concludes with the defeat of the monsters, who perish once their idol has been destroyed by the doctor.

While Jesús Franco was producing a cinema removed from oppositional filmmaking, and, similarly, Paul Naschy's werewolf cycle lacked any political commentary, critics have identified a veiled critique of Francoist ideas and beliefs in Ossorio's cycle. For some contemporary reviewers, such as Company (1974: 64), for example, the films represented a confrontation between tra-dition and a series of modern elements: namely, the new patterns of sexual behaviour emerging in the changing social context of late 1960s and early 1970s Spain. The Templars mercilessly punished any signs of sexual liber-alisation demonstrated by young couples and sexually independent women, functioning therefore as superego figures and reaffirming, through murder and violent reprisals, the mechanics of repression so necessary for a patriarchal society and a dictatorial regime. Three decades later, Burrell and Sala read the Templars along similar lines. For Burrell, the appearance of the Templars sym-bolises 'the rising of Old Spain against the permissive generation, the repressive fascism of the Franco regime versus the youth of the day', while he nevertheless points out that 'a knowledge of that (possible) subtext isn't necessary in order to enjoy the film' (2005: 11–12). Sala argues that, through their attacks on 'all that signifies eroticism and physical provocation', the Templars function as 'an allegory of Francoist religious repressive forces' (1999: 315). Such readings of the film's allegorical significance tend to focus primarily on the narrative action and interpret the films almost as morality plays, the moral being 'have sex and die'. However, there is a much more distinctive and scathing ideological and political commentary running through the cycle, which lies not only in the violence embedded in the narrative but also in Ossorio's symbolically charged use of *mise-en-scène*, iconography and editing; there is also his subversive invocation of a filmic tradition associated with the Francoist regime in its first decade in power: namely, the 'cine de cruzada' of the 1940s.[36]

Interpretations of Ossorio's cycle have overlooked the fact that the director had attempted to question forms of ideological and propagandistic representation through the use of subversive imagery with his first feature film, *La bandera negra*, in 1956. This film was censored, heavily fined and never distributed because it dealt with the theme of capital punishment and grappled with some of its political, legal and religious ramifications, a taboo subject in the context of the dictatorship. Based on an adaptation of a text by playwright Horacio Ruiz de la Fuente,[37] the film followed the vicissitudes of a middle-aged man awaiting his son's execution. In the context of our discussion of Ossorio's cycle, it is worth retrieving the director's use of iconography in his début film, in particular the court scenes, in which the official representatives of the judiciary and the military are not represented by real actors but rather metonymically, by specific items of clothing such as the gowns of the judge and the public prosecutor and the uniforms and *tricornios* (three-cornered hats) of the Spanish Civil Guard which are suspended in mid-air. By stripping down his characters to their institutional attire, Ossorio denounces the conflation of the sanctioning and repressive forces implementing Francoist laws. In fact, the director's filmic career was curtailed by this first encounter with the forces of censorship. Afterwards, Ossorio worked for Spanish radio and television, which was controlled by the state, and in film advertising, also seeking 'refuge in commercial filmmaking' (Borau 1998: 648) with westerns (*La tumba del pistolero* (1964)), musicals (*Pasto de fieras* (1966) and *La niña del patio* (1967)), and horror films such as *Malenka, la sobrina del vampiro / Fangs of the Living Dead* (1969). Broadly speaking, therefore, Ossorio was well acquainted with official Francoist cultural institutions and their corollary discourses and representational strategies. More than twenty-five years later, he returns to his initial critique of Francoism, this time reinscribing it in the unique physiognomy of his Spanish Knights of Terror. Although *La noche del terror ciego* was also affected by censorship, it could be argued that, this time,

Ossorio outmanœuvred the censors with a series of production and aesthetic choices. Overall, the commercial vessel of a popular genre such as horror and an iconography associated with fictional characters did not pose too many problems for the censorship board. The producers were denied permission to film in Spain and were obliged to abandon the original idea of setting the narrative in Galicia, as the Ministry of Information and Tourism, under the direction of Manuel Fraga Iribarne, believed that the appearance of monsters in Spanish locations would scare tourists away. Spain's neighbour, Portugal, entered the project as co-producer and provided Ossorio with a location that had remarkably similar socio-political connotations: Portuguese tourist locations clearly stood for other similar Spanish tourist spots, and, more importantly, Portugal was at the time also under the authoritarian regime of dictator General Salazar (1932–68). The editing of the first twenty minutes of the film evokes the most recent history of Spain by juxtaposing images of decay and devastation with the glamorous and affluent world of tourism. The recent past of the Spanish Civil War is conjured up in the opening credits by the still images of a destroyed and abandoned village; it is in this crumbling setting that the medieval Templars emerge out of their tombs, irrupt in the present world of the narrative and re-enact scenarios of crimes and masacres. Subsequently, the opening sequence introduces the viewer to the modern tourist resort, where the protagonists are enjoying the pleasures and commodities of modern capitalist society, unaware of the horrific reality they are about to unearth.

But it is the presence of the monstrous Knights Templar and their monk–warrior uniform which provide continuity in the critique of specific Francoist institutions and values. Although the appearance of these zombie crusaders in modern settings is hauntingly anachronistic, they summon up a very recent past, threatening to return at a time when the Francoist state was disintegrating. The army of zombie monk–soldiers become Ossorio's representation of a grotesque and horrific version of the Fascist masculine ideal of the 'monje-soldado' (monk–warrior) associated with the Fascist rhetoric that pervaded Nationalist propagandist texts during the late 1930s and throughout the 1940s. The 'monje–soldado' was in a constant state of war against anything anti-Spanish, shedding blood and sacrificing his life for the cause. By extension, the Knights Templar hark back to the Francoist propaganda machinery of the 'cruzada de liberación', which shaped the essence of Spanish National-Catholicism during and after the Civil War period, when the Nationalist forces lead by Franco defeated the Republican army. In official Francoist narratives, the 'cruzada de liberación' was linked to the wider medieval mythical and heroic tradition of the Christian crusaders, as well as the local Christian reconquest of the peninsula from the Moors, which spanned almost seven centuries and culminated in 1492. Franco constructed himself as a military man with a religious mission, etching this message in Spaniards' imagination through iconic visual images which portrayed him as a heroic military figure. The regime's rhetoric granted him appellatives such as 'general–sacerdote' ('general–priest') or 'espada del Altísimo' ('Sword of the Highest') – thus fusing religious and military – and described the dictator as an otherworldly being ('Captain of the vessel'). In the medium of cinema, the narrative of the crusade was represented and legitimated through the subgenre of 'cine de cruzada', which celebrated 'the crusade (the Spanish Civil War), its participants, and the resultant militarist state' (Triana-Toribio 2003: 44) and inculcated 'particular views of Spanishness' (Triana-Toribio 2003: 44). Films such as *Sin novedad en el Alcázar* (Augusto Genina 1940), *Raza* (José Luis Saénz de Heredia 1941), *¡A mi la legión!* (Juan de Orduña 1942) and *Los últimos de Filipinas* (Antonio Román 1945) depicted militarist values, Fascist aesthetics and the ideological force of the Catholic Church, and structured their narratives around the metaphor of 'Spanishness under siege' (Triana-Toribio 2003: 44). The siege, as it has been argued, is a key structuring element in Ossorio's cycle.

Although Ossorio has acknowledged in interviews that he 'had no pretensions to innovate the genre' (Ossorio in Sala 1999: 355), his was not only a conscious effort at product differentiation and an original contribution to the international hall of monsters, but also an incisive critique of Franco's regime through the codes and conventions of horror. Perhaps initial comparison with and distinction from *Night of the Living Dead* reach beyond the low-budget horror movie model of generic traits and exploitative elements; Ossorio's cycle must be also considered as subversive as Romero's work through critical recuperation. Romero's film, after all, has been, and still is, read as a critical commentary on the American society of the 1960s. The violence and destruction inscribed in the *mise-en-scène* of Ossorio's cycle are a far cry from contemporary Francoist official discourses about Spain being a 'peaceful forest' and Franco being the 'artificer of peace', or carefully devised propagandistic representations of the sanitised world of tourism and affluence, as advertised by the Ministry of Information and Tourism. The iconographic wardrobe of these zombie crusaders – military–religious uniforms, avenging swords – and their violent attacks from horseback act as a reminder of the forces which created and maintained an authoritarian regime based on terror and death. Furthermore, these Knights of Terror are the literal embodiment of death, whose resurrection conjures up a history of death and institutional violence.

Making a total of nine horror films between 1969 and 1975, de Ossorio was much less prolific than Jesús Franco and Paul Naschy, and for much of the 1980s and 1990s he remained inactive.[38] Unlike Franco and Naschy, he has not been particularly vocal about his work and has not written any memoirs, remaining relatively anonymous outside horror film fandom until very recently. However, his monstrous creations have acquired a cult status with the passing of time, as shown by the successful DVD editions of his work for the European and American market by Anchor Bay – the collector's edition of *The Blind Dead Collection* (2005) – and for the Spanish market and then in Spain by Divisa Ediciones.

NOTES

1. *La mano de un hombre muerto* (1962), produced the same year as *Gritos en la noche*, is not a variation on the mad-scientist narrative formula, so it will not be considered here as part of the cycle.
2. Some Spanish film posters sold the film on the established 1950s male sex-symbol Conrado San Martín, whose face occupies a central position. His image is flanked by two smaller ones: a Frankenstein-like figure on the right-hand side and a young female leaning forward and looking at us. A second poster features a victimised female character screaming as a monstrous man approaches her, while a second, elegantly dressed character lurks in the background.
3. Accounts of Franco's life and work can be found in Águilar (1991, 1999a, 1999b), Balbo (1993) and Tohill and Tombs (1995), as well as in the director's auto-biography (2004). Franco had already made *Tenemos 18 años* (1960), *Labios rojos* (1960), *La reina del Tabarín* (1960) and *La muerte silba un blues* (1964). Throughout the 1950s he had also gained some experience in the industry, working for Eduardo Manzanos (Union Films), Joaquín Romero Marchent (UNINCI) and Klimovsky (in *Miedo*).
4. For Tim Lucas, Franco's film is 'often fatuously compared to Georges Franju's *Les yeux sans visage*' but its 'more authentic point of comparison is Alfred Vohrer's *Die Tolen Augen von London* (Dark Eyes of London 1961)', as part of the adaptation of Edgar Wallace's novel (Lucas 2010: 32).
5. Both producers had already worked with Franco on *La reina del Tabarín* (1960) and *Vampiresas 1930* (1961). They were all working on a new script entitled *The Rebellion of the Hanged*, based on German enigmatic writer and anarchist revolutionary Bernhard Traven Torsvan (also known as B. Traven), which was prohibited by the censors.
6. The first two had played roles in the previous films: Howard Vernon in *Gritos en la noche* and Marcelo Arroita-Jaúregui, replacing the unavailable Vernon for the role of Fisherman, in *El secreto del Dr Orloff*. There is a certain perverse irony in their deaths, almost as if Franco was telling us that Orloff is well and truly dead.
7. With reference to Chevalier's film, an Internet Movie Database (IMDb) reviewer comments,

> I always assumed that it was Jess Franco who had a monopoly on this type of cinema, namely: the routine euro-exploitation flicks with an always-returning villain (Dr Orloff), absurd storylines (invisible ape-creatures??), truckloads of sleaze and absolutely no logic at all. Every small detail in *Orloff Against the Invisible Man* has got Franco's name written all over it, so it was quite a surprise to find out that he actually hasn't got anything to do with it. (Coventry from the Draconian Swamp of Unholy Souls, 21 October 2005)

See 'Typical Jess Franco Film . . . only NOT by Jess Franco'.
8. See *Literatura y cultura de masas* (Díez Borque 1972) or *La novela popular en España* (V. A. 2000) and encontretuslibros.blogspot.com/search/label/terror, respectively.
9. In the mid-1950s, Franco had worked with Spanish western director Joaquín

Romero Marchent on the adaptation of the pulp western character 'El Coyote', created by José Mallorquí for two films, *El Coyote* and *La justicia del Coyote*.

10. In interviews, Franco associates Orloff with Fantômas: 'When I see *Gritos en la noche* I feel I'm watching an old movie, like Feuillade's *Fantômas*. I have to watch it with a historical eye' (Franco in Costa 1999: 153). Franco also made films based on Mabuse and Fu Manchu.

11. The fiction of Edgar Wallace was published in the series 'Novelas de intriga, misterio, y de terror de Edgar Wallace'. Franco has acknowledged the influence of the popular crime fiction of writers such as Edgar Wallace and his admiration for British directors such as Walter Forde, who adapted Wallace's pulp novels for the screen.

12. The film was first screened in the Capitol cinema in Madrid.

13. As Jo Botting (2003) has rightly observed, 1940s Spanish audiences saw a censored and dubbed version of *Frankenstein Meets the Werewolf* when it was first screened in 1946. Furthermore, the films that were part of this Universal cycle were not shown in the order in which they were produced, with all the implications that this release pattern might have had for Molina's understanding of the Universal approach to the myth of the werewolf.

14. *Dale la mano al diablo* (1960), *La muerte te acompaña* (1960) and *¡Yo sé que ganarás!* (1961), all published by Editorial Rollán for the series 'Colección Oeste' and 'Colección Extra-Oeste'. Molina also designed sleeves for Columbia Records, among them ones for releases by Elvis Presley, Frankie Lane and Bill Haley. His pop credentials extend to the creation of a comic character called 'Snake Black', whose adventures were published in a Barcelona newspaper.

15. The German Hi-Fi Stereo 70 originally entered the production process as part of the company's brief to develop and test the new technologies available in the image and sound market: namely, 3D systems and high-fidelity sound reproduction. These technologies were therefore an important selling point from the project's inception.

16. For its American distribution *La marca del hombre lobo* suffered further exploitation and adaptation for the overseas market. The film was retitled *Frankenstein's Bloody Terror* because Sam Sherman, head of Independent International Pictures, which picked up the film for distribution on the American exploitation circuit,

> had promised a number of theatres playdates for a new Frankenstein movie and had to deliver fast [. . .] Since the story already had a character with the surname 'Wolfstein' in it, a prologue was added explaining the situation and the film [. . .] was called *Frankenstein's Bloody Terror*.

The film was also Americanised: fifteen minutes of the opening footage from the Spanish original were cut in order to introduce the monster action more quickly, names were Anglicised in the credits (director Enrique Eguíluz is called Henry L. Egan; actress Rosanna Yanni becomes Rosemary Winters), and, overall, in Sherman's words, there was a move to 'place the film in a more neutral place'. For a more detailed history of the film's distribution in the US, see the Shriek Show DVD sleeve for *Frankenstein's Bloody Terror* and the commentary feature.

17. The only exception to his series of tragic endings was in *The Werewolf and the Yeti*, where he does not die but is cured and walks off into the sunset with the girl he loves.

18. Molina in an interview in the 'Blood and Sand' episode on Spanish horror film, included as part of the Channel 4's series *Eurotika* (11 December 1999, Andy Starke and Pete Tombs).

19. Naschy describes the make-up process for *La marca del hombre lobo* as long and

arduous, submitted as he was to six hours of make-up application. The werewolf transformation was done hair by hair by make-up artist José Luis Ruiz, and no pieces or prosthetics were used.

20. Key overseas genre magazines of the period, which turned their attention at some point or other to Paul Naschy, include *Mad Movies* and *Vampirella* in France, and *Monsters of the Movies* in the US.

21. When the first general publications on Spanish horror film came out in the mid-1970s, the genre became synonymous with the name Paul Naschy, as this title attests. In actual fact, the authors offered a very general overview of the horror genre and a brief section on Paul Naschy. *Cine español, cine de subgéneros*, mentioned above, devotes more space to Naschy, with a long interview (Equipo 'Cartelera Turia' 1974: 33–9) and an analysis of 'el infortunado Waldemar Daninsky' (Equipo 'Cartelera Turia' 1974: 51–6). Two decades later, the trend continued, with a doctoral thesis by Adolfo Camilo Díaz, who approaches the genre in Spain via Naschy's films (*El cine fantaterrorífico español. Una aproximación al género fantaterrorífico a través del cine de Paul Naschy* (1993)).

22. People as diverse as philosopher Fernando Savater, writer Juan Manuel de Prada and poet and politician Luis Alberto de Cuenca fondly recall their film-going experiences and vividly remember Paul Naschy, as I describe in Chapter 6.

23. While Talbot is 'constantly fighting against the same monsters', Molina writes, Daninsky's stories are 'totally independent from each other' (1976: 27).

24. *Memoirs of a Wolfman* was translated into English and published in 2001 by Midnight Marquee Press, an American publisher that focuses on the horror genre.

25. 'El Museo del Prado: Genios de la Pintura Española y Universal' (1980) is an eight-hour documentary shown in Japan as a TV series and in Spain as two feature films in 1982.

26. 'Like Lovecraft, I invented my own mythology, my own *necronomicón*', Molina writes in 'El hombre lobo español' for the cultural supplement *El País de las tentaciones* (29 May 1998).

27. All these quotations have been extracted from the interview carried out by Juan Antonio Molina Foix (1999): 'I had no references. To my surprise I found out that there were movies that used several different monsters in a single story'; 'the idea of mixing it up with vampires and other things was my innovation, my idea'; 'there is a certain euphemism [sic] that Franco was the pioneer of Spanish *fantastique* cinema, but I started before. He had made similar things, but not fantastic'; 'I was the one who tackled the big myths' (Naschy in Molina Foix 1999: 291).

28. Composer Antón García Abril's unique score, which evoked Gregorian chants, would later be adopted in *The Omen* and a number of Italian horror films.

29. Other critics begged to differ, emphasising that *La noche de terror ciego* repeats 'extremely well-known situations' (Rubio 1972b) and is just a padded and inane film whose only aim is to satisfy the viewer's base appetite (Martialay 1972).

30. Profilmes toyed with the idea of bringing Amando de Ossorio's creations and Paul Naschy together in what would have been a fourth sequel, provisionally entitled 'El necronomicón de los Templarios', where a doctor who is trying to find a cure for lycanthropy learns that in an abbey owned by the Templars lies their great secret, the Necronomicon, and in it the secret of lycanthropy. But the project was never realised.

31. Ossorio's films amount to 'repeated female exhibitionism [. . .] in which the anatomies of Barbara Rey, Blanca Estrada, Maria Kosti and Lorena Tower compete with each other' (Company 1974: 63).

32. None of the actors was professional, according to de Ossorio, who added that he 'chose cheap actors who hadn't done feature films [. . .] the female lead was in a

soap advertisement. The two male leads hadn't been seen in any other film.' This was to change with the commercial success of the film, however. For *El ataque de los muertos sin ojos* he had at his disposal known genre actors such as Tony Kendall, Fernando Sancho and Esperanza Roy, all of whom were recognisable faces.

33. De Ossorio's films were also exploited – and they still are – at the level of distribution, since titles were changed, individual films repackaged and nude scenes added or censored depending on the markets. There are, for example, multiple titles for *La noche de terror ciego* (*Crypt of the Blind Dead* / *Night of the Blind Dead* / *The Blind Dead* / *The Night of the Blind Terror* / *Tombs of the Blind Dead* / *Mark of the Devil 4: Return of the Blind Dead* / *Revenge from Planet Ape*), *El ataque de los muertos sin ojos* (*Attack of the Blind Dead* / *Return of the Blind Dead* / *Return of the Evil Dead*), *El buque maldito* (*Ghost Ships of the Blind Dead* / *The Blind Dead 3* / *The Ghost Galleon* / *The Damned Ship* / *Horror of the Zombies* / *Ship of the Zombies* / *Zombie Flesh Eater*) and *La noche de las gaviotas* (*Night of the Seagulls* / *Night of the Blood Cult* / *Night of the Death Cult* / *Don't Go Out at Night* / *Terror Beach*).

34. In interviews, Ossorio acknowledges that this ending was a response to financial constraints, as he had originally planned to shoot the train arriving at the station, the passengers getting on to the train and screams in the distance. However, the freeze frame built into the ending the possibility of a sequel.

35. The distributors of the American version of *La noche de terror ciego* positioned the historical explanation of the Templars' origins as a prologue to the present narrative action.

36. Crusade films, which were also known as epic or heroic films, celebrated the Civil War (the crusade), the Nationalist victors and the ensuing Francoist state.

37. 'La bandera negra (1956)', in Julio Pérez Perucha (ed.) (1997), *Antología crítica del cine español 1906–1995*, Madrid: Cátedra-Filmoteca Española, pp. 407–9.

38. Apart from the Knights Templar quartet, De Ossorio directed *Malenka, la sobrina del vampiro*, *Las garras de Lorelei*, *La noche de los brujos* and *La endemoniada*. After that, he only directed one other monster movie, *Serpiente de mar*.

3. NARCISO IBÁÑEZ SERRADOR, HORRORMEISTER: *HISTORIAS PARA NO DORMIR* (1966–8), *LA RESIDENCIA* (1969) AND *¿QUIÉN PUEDE MATAR A UN NIÑO?* (1976)

Narciso Ibáñez Serrador was the most culturally prominent image of horror in Spain in the late 1960s due to his horror–suspense TV series *Historias para no dormir / Stories to Keep You Awake* (1966–8). This chapter provides a detailed analysis of Ibáñez Serrador's horror production made for television and his two forays into film, *La residencia / The Finishing School* and *¿Quién puede matar a un niño?*,[1] and appraises how the director's work legitimated a popular taste in horror which was formative for generations of Spanish television audiences. While journalistic approaches to the work of Ibáñez Serrador have offered a general overview of his television career and cinematic output (Torres 1999), recent academic publications have addressed his key role in the history of Spanish horror film by describing how he set up the right conditions for the horror boom of the late 1960s and early 1970s, and the part he played in the history of Spanish television, his work being an essential part of a shared experience of Spanish popular culture (Lázaro-Reboll (2004), Cascajosa (2011), Cerdán et al. (forthcoming)). Three major threads run throughout this chapter: firstly, a discussion of the relationship of Ibáñez Serrador's horror genre production for television and film vis-à-vis international horror traditions; secondly, a discussion of how the director's work becomes a pretext for critics to address wider issues around the cultural status and the quality of Spanish television and cinema, leading me to critical notions such as quality TV and quality cinema, cultural esteem and respectability, and taste and distaste in relation to industrial production, institutional policies, and film and television criticism; and, thirdly, a consideration of how the master of suspense *par excellence*, Alfred Hitchcock, becomes a model through which Ibáñez Serrador presented himself to Spanish television and film audiences and the critical yardstick by which critics reviewed his filmic work.

HISTORIAS PARA NO DORMIR

Ibáñez Serrador's connection with the horror genre lies in Argentina, but his life started on the other side of Río de la Plata, in Montevideo, Uruguay, in 1935; both his parents, Narciso Ibáñez Menta (1912–2004) and Pepita Serrador (1913–64), belonged to the Spanish theatre groups that toured around Spain and Latin America. Like the Isbert or Bardem family, the Serradors have an artistic familial pedigree that is characteristic of Spanish show business, in particular the world of theatre and cinema. The boy's father, Narciso, was a child prodigy *à la* Shirley Temple or Freddy Bartholomew; as a teenager, tired of his repertoire and life as a child star, he went to Hollywood and the story goes that he ended up carrying Lon Chaney's make-up case. From the master of disguise he must have learned not only make-up and interpretation techniques but also how Lon Chaney characterised his monsters: Dr Jekyll and Mr Hyde, the Hunchback of Notre-Dame, the Phantom of the Opera, and so on. From child prodigy to monster, Ibáñez Menta adapted popular horror classics (Edgar Allan Poe, Bram Stoker, H. P. Lovecraft) for the theatre during the 1940s and 1950s. When he and Pepita Serrador divorced in 1947, Chicho (as the young Narciso was nicknamed), who was four, stayed with his mother while she was on tour and eventually moved back to Spain, where he stayed during his adolescence, learning the ropes in the theatrical world. It was not until the late 1950s that Chicho arrived in Argentina with the intention of persuading his father to adapt for television the repertoire that had proved so successful on stage. By the time that *Historias para no dormir* reached Spanish television sets in 1966, the father–son tandem had drawn upon an established genre repertoire which had appeared in pulp publications and genre magazines, staged in theatres and shown on television in both the US and Argentina. Ibáñez Serrador's rich and wry knowledge of the traditions in which he was rooted – literary, theatrical, radiophonic, cinematic and televisual – and his knowledge of the specificities of the new medium were put into practice in *Historias para no dormir*.

By August 1959, father and son had created *Obras maestras del terror* (Masterworks of Horror) for Canal 7, Argentina's only TV channel at the time, based on a number of tales by Poe ('The Tell-Tale Heart', 'The Facts in the Case of M. Valdemar', 'Ligeia', 'Berenice' and 'The Cask of the Amontillado') and Robert Louis Stevenson ('The Strange Case of Dr Jekyll and Mr Hyde'). Argentinean audiences were familiar not only with Ibáñez Menta's successful stage adaptations of horror classics but also with their popularisation in pulp anthologies such as *Narraciones terroríficas* (1939–52, Editorial

Molino Argentina), which shamelessly drew upon American pulp magazines *Weird Tales, Horror Stories* and *Terror Tales*.[2] While the father stamped his work with his inimitable and recognisable acting style and took charge of the *mise-en-scène*, the son scripted the episodes under the literary pseudonym of Luis Peñafiel.[3] So popularly successful was the series that Argentinean production company Sono Films produced a film with the same title, *Obras maestras del terror* (Enrique Carreras 1960), exploiting the father–son tandem in their capacities as leading actor and scriptwriter, respectively.[4] The second TV series of *Obras maestras del terror* was aired between July and November 1960 and followed the same production method: that is, free adaptations of popular horror and mystery tales written by Luis Peñafiel and interpreted by Ibáñez Menta, although this time the newly created private channel Canal 9 bought the rights. The line-up was: 'El fantasma de la opera' / 'The Phantom of the Opera' (Gaston Leroux), 'Al caer la noche' / 'Night Must Fall' (Emlyn Williams), 'El hombre que cambió de nombre' / 'The Man Who Changed His Name' (Ibáñez Serrador), 'La mano' / 'The Hand' (Guy de Maupassant), 'La carreta fantasma' / 'The Phantom Carriage' (Selma Lagerlof), 'La figura de cera' / 'The Waxwork' (A. M. Burrage), 'El hacha de oro' / 'The Golden Axe' (Gaston Leroux), 'Dónde está marcada la cruz' / 'Where the Cross is Made' (Eugene O'Neill) and the serialised '¿Es usted el asesino?' / 'Are You the Murderer?' (Fernand Crommelynck). The third and last series sees the return of the Serradors to Canal 7 in 1962 with the serialisation of Gaston Leroux's 'La Poupée sanglante' (also known as 'La Machine à assassiner') under the title 'El muñeco maldito', as well as an adaptation of W. W. Jacobs's 'The Monkey's Paw' / 'La pata de mono', a short story by Argentinean Agustín Caballero entitled 'Las huellas del diablo', and two scripts by Luis Peñafiel himself, 'Un hombre encantador: las aventuras de Landrú' and 'El hombre que comía los pecados'. That same year, father and son moved into neighbouring generic territory with *Mañana puede ser verdad* (It May Come True Tomorrow), a science-fiction series which was Canal 7's modest answer to the highly successful America series *The Twilight Zone* (CBS, 1959–64). Again, the scripts written by Luis Peñafiel are mainly adaptations from Ray Bradbury's tales, such as 'The Fox and the Forest' and 'The Third Expedition', but perhaps the most successful was Peñafiel's original, 'Los bulbos'. Many of these pre-existing horror and science-fiction plots, as well as the original scripts by Luis Peñafiel, would be subsequently imported into Spanish television during the second half the 1960s.

It was the world of theatre and the stage relationship of mother and son, however, that brought Ibáñez Serrador back to Spain in 1963. Pepita Serrador and Ibáñez Serrador had attained huge success in Buenos Aires for four consecutive years with a comedy of manners entitled *Aprobado en castidad* ('A Pass in Chastity'). Play and personnel crossed the Atlantic after the Spanish censorship board had approved its staging with a new title *Aprobado en ino-cencia* ('A Pass in Innocence'), and it proved to be a resounding triumph in the Teatro Lara in Madrid. Tucked under his arm, Ibáñez Serrador had also brought his television portfolio, with the idea of offering his knowledge of the medium to the then incipient Televisión de España (TVE), which had just been founded in 1956 as a public-service television channel controlled by the Francoist regime.[5] Episodes of *Obras maestras del terror* and *Mañana puede ser verdad* persuaded José Luis Colina, Director of TVE, to invest in the creative potential of a young author whose work would play a key role in Francoist government attempts to sell a culturally liberal image of Spain in the European arena. The Spanish authorities had sought to join the European television network as soon as TVE started broadcasting. Strategic financial and political investments, such as the inauguration of the new studios in Prado del Rey in 1964 and the increase in production and resources, were geared towards the support and promotion of television products that could win awards at prestigious international festivals. The so-called 'Operación Premios TV' ('Operation TV Awards') (Palacio 2001: 148–150), led by Manuel Fraga Iribarne from the Ministry of Information and Tourism, incorporated professionals like Ibáñez Serrador who could contribute to the modernisation and internationalisation of Spanish television.[6]

Ibáñez Serrador debuted on Spanish television with contributions to the programme *Estudio 3* (1963–5), where he participated not only as director and scriptwriter but also as actor on many occasions.[7] This programme featured both original and adapted teleplays and presented Spanish audiences with a variety of genre stories (comedy, romance, suspense, biography, detective tales and fantasy), either in one episode or in serialised format. While he was still making *Estudio 3*, TVE offered Ibáñez Serrador the chance of doing a remake of *Mañana puede ser verdad*, in which he repurposed the same science-fiction material that he had previously adapted for Argentinean TV screens and for which he reunited with his father.[8] The success of *Mañana puede ser verdad* in the 1964/5 season would be followed by two seasons of *Historias para no dormir* in 1966/7 and 1967/8, via which Ibáñez Serrador introduced into many Spanish homes some of the best tales from the international Gothic and science-fiction repertoire, marking a shift in the history of Spanish television. In fact, Spanish audiences had hardly seen any science fiction or horror on their screens before 1966; 'in those days', as Savater notes, 'the fantastic genre, horror and science-fiction seemed to be luxuries that only Anglo-Saxon spectators could afford' (1999: 31). It is worth reminding ourselves here that the only Spanish horror available at the time was the films of Jesús Franco produced in the first half of the 1960s and other isolated instances.

Before I move on to a discussion of the *Historias para no dormir* series and Ibáñez Serrador's growing status as *horrormeister*, it is necessary to highlight more generally the role played by the director in the landscape of Spanish television as it developed, as well as the cultural impact of his TV output which goes beyond the field of horror. His arrival coincides with the growth of TV as a cultural industry,[9] which he duly exploited with his understanding of the experiences and tastes of mass audiences across the Atlantic. He aligned Spanish TVE with other international developments in programming and scheduling, thereby modernising what it could offer. And, above all, he delivered quality popular entertainment. Both *Mañana puede ser verdad* and *Historias para no dormir* followed the tradition of revered American TV series of the 1950s and 1960s featuring sci-fi, horror, mystery or suspense, such as *Alfred Hitchcock Presents* (CBS, 1955) *The Twilight Zone* or *The Outer Limits* (ABC-TV, 1963–5), which had been exported overseas and would be emulated in other European countries, including Great Britain (*Armchair Mystery Theatre* (ABC, UK, 1960–5); *Out of the Unknown* (BBC, 1965–71); *Mystery and Imagination* (ABC / Thames, UK 1966–70)). As Wheatley has argued in reference to British television production of these series,

> the development of the Gothic anthology series in the 1960s and 1970s [. . .] fulfilled a dual remit for popular entertaining television which would, it was hoped, attract a large and dedicated audience, and for respectable, culturally valued television drama, often adapted from the Gothic 'classics' (M.R. James, J.S. Le Fanu, Mary Shelley, Bram Stoker, etc.) which would appeal to television regulators as well as its viewers. (2006: 27)

Similarly, Ibáñez Serrador's production fulfilled this 'dual remit': it achieved enormous popularity with TV audiences while still retaining a cultural cachet. In fact, some of his work was considered by television critic Enrique del Corral to have an 'artistic' sensibility which elevated horror, suspense and science-fiction stories to the status of quality TV.

In stark contrast to the dramatic output of Spanish television, Ibáñez Serrador moved away, on the one hand, from a *costumbrista* aesthetics – the popular cultural tradition of *sainete* (farce) and *zarzuela* (Spanish operetta) – and, on the other, from the theatricality of some contemporary television drama that was characterised by an anti-illusionist mode; he thus provided something different from what was on offer on Spanish television – in this instance, a window on to the international and imaginary topography of horror, suspense and science fiction. This innovation in aesthetic and visual language was accompanied by the possibility of experimenting with the form of television drama and by a technical know-how he learnt under the supervision of American and Dutch technicians while working at different Argentinean TV channels.[10] Apart from the close collaboration with his father, Narciso Ibáñez

Menta, in terms of producing, directing, screenwriting, adapting and acting, Ibáñez Serrador had at his disposal skilful professionals from the new medium and established actors from the world of theatre who contributed to the delivery of both novel and entertaining horror production made for television, and quality television drama. Among the stable of creative and technical personnel, there are professionals such as Fernando Saénz and Jaime Queralt (sets), César Fraile, Enrique Romay and Mariano Ruiz Capillas (lighting) and Waldo de los Ríos (sound); among the actors, Fernando Delgado, Teresa Hurtado, Gemma Cuervo and Manuel Galiana, to name but a few. Although most episodes retained features of the popular story (that is, the predominance of dialogue over description) and the theatre (highly staged dramatisations), the series introduced a distinctive Gothic vision to Spanish television audiences.

What is undeniable is that *Historias para no dormir* had spectators glued to their television sets for two seasons. Like his previous work on *Obras maestras del terror*, the stories were mainly adaptations from supernatural and Gothic classics such as Poe ('El Pacto' / 'The Facts in the Case of M. Valdemar', 'El Tonel' / 'The Cask of Amontillado', 'La promesa'/ 'The Premature Burial' and 'El trapero' / 'Berenice'), Henry James ('El muñeco') and W. W. Jacobs ('La zarpa' / 'The Monkey's Paw') and from the science-fiction worlds of his contemporary Ray Bradbury ('El doble' / 'Marionettes, Inc.', 'La bodega' / 'Boys! Raise Giant Mushrooms in Your Cellar (Come into My Cellar'), 'La sonrisa' / 'The Smile', 'El cohete' / 'The Rocket' and 'La espera' / 'The Long Years'); other scripts were written by Luis Peñafiel ('La alarma' / 'The Alarm' (two parts), 'La oferta' / 'The Offer', 'La pesadilla' / 'The Nightmare', 'NN23', 'El cuervo' / 'The Raven', 'El transplante' / 'The Transplant'), and some episodes were adapted from stories originally conceived by new Spanish horror and science-fiction writers, such as Carlos Buiza ('El asfalto' / 'The Asphalt') and Juan Tébar ('El vidente' / 'The Séance' and 'La casa' / 'The House'). The duration of the episodes varied between the short 'El cumpleaños' / 'The Birthday Party', which lasts 18 minutes, to half an hour in 'La oferta' or 'La cabaña' / 'The Hut', to an hour, as in the case of 'El pacto' or 'El tonel'. The first episode of the series, 'El cumpleaños', appeared on Spanish TV sets in black and white at 11.15 on the night of 4 February 1966 and was rated with two diamonds or rhombuses ('dos rombos'), TVE's distinctive sign of classification warning contemporary audiences about the (pernicious) contents of a programme. Ibáñez Serrador's on-screen introduction set the scene for the objectives of the series, the mode and tone of what was to follow, and the visual prologue for each week's programme.[11] This weekly on-screen introduction actively promoted a Hitchcockian association, which I examine later on in this chapter to account for the successful establishment of Ibáñez Serrador's public persona by the end of the decade.

Following the tradition of American TV genre series which were introduced by a charismatic host (*Alfred Hitchcock Presents, The Twilight Zone* or *The Outer Limits*), as well as that of the crypt keeper and master of ceremonies in the EC horror comics, Ibáñez Serrador would advance the thematic skeleton of the tale to be told, sometimes with a humoristic touch, other times in a more thoughtful mode. The opening confronted Spanish viewers with the staple audiovisual of a creaking door slowly opening to reveal a superimposed and capitalised 'NARCISO IBÁÑEZ SERRADOR' against the streaming white light. The first name and surname of the director, punctuated by fierce drumming, was followed by 'presenta' and the title 'Historias para no dormir'. The token scream followed, the creaking door closed and the horror would begin.

Ibáñez Serrador's first on-screen introduction self-consciously sets up a quality profile for the series by connecting it with an established Gothic literary tradition and aesthetically aligns it with American and British suspense, mystery and horror TV anthologies. Spanish audiences were introduced to a conventional Gothic space – cobwebs, candelabra and skulls – through a slow panning which eventually focuses and lingers on the book spines of a library composed of respectable authors from Gothic literature – namely, Maupassant, Leroux, James, Poe and Stevenson – while the voice of Ibáñez Serrador solemnly declares that they all 'wrote immortal tales. Tales that mixed horror, madness, evil. Tales which more often than not disturbed the sleep of those who read them.' A close-up of a huge fake spider and the dramatic swelling of non-diegetic music start to lay bare the technical devices at work in the studio; this is confirmed by Ibáñez Serrador's voice, as he despairs about these special effects and their ineffectiveness in scaring people. Then the master of ceremonies appears on screen moving around the studio, showing the audience the artificiality of the settings, until he comfortably leans against part of the décor to address viewers directly:

> Indeed, the important men of letters I have just mentioned wrote the stories which we are going to show you. The bad news is that we will be responsible for adapting and presenting their works to you for the small screen. Today it is the beginning of a new programme [. . .] And what is the title of this new series of scripts? *Historias para no dormir*. What are these stories about? They are tales of suspense, horror, adaptations of classics or original scripts; we will also include some science-fiction tales to satisfy the fans of this genre. In most cases, like today's show, the programme has been made in [the TVE studios of] Prado del Rey; in other instances, we will offer a selection of American, British or German telefilms. [. . .] Every Friday you will be able to watch a story that will keep you awake. [. . .] Stories which differ from each other but which have something in common: our purpose is to cleanse, or attempt to cleanse, the horror and suspense genre of its clichés, its commonplaces

[. . .] Put simply, our aim is to translate on to the small screen a suspense series whose main aspiration is not to achieve shocking, horrific impacts but rather to offer small doses of quality.

Here Ibáñez Serrador places his series within an established literary and audiovisual tradition, brings to Spanish TV audiences a new and diverse genre portfolio, and introduces himself as a self-conscious practitioner of the art of televisual suspense.

In this context, Ibáñez Serrador's first episode does not come as a surprise: 'El cumpleaños' is based on one of Fredric Brown's pulp crime stories, 'Nightmare in Yellow' (1961). Under his alter ego Luis Peñafiel, Ibáñez Serrador adapts a pulp author renowned for his playful engagement with popular genre conventions, his artistry in the creation of suspense and surprise, and his use of humour. More widely, the episode engages with the narrative and stylistic procedures of other master practitioners of the art of horror–suspense, whether in literature (Poe and O. Henry) or in film and television (Hitchcock), and deploys a number of Hitchockian effects. The story throws us into the psychological world of its male lead, Roberto (Rafael Navarro), from the opening frame by focusing on an extreme close-up of his closed eye and listening to his first-person narration, which gives us unrestricted access to his thoughts. 'It is already daytime. Saturday 22 January 1966. Today I am fifty. Yes, today at 10.32 I will start my new life, a life of freedom.' As he looks to his right, we are introduced to his wife (Josefina de la Torre) in these terms: 'she always sleeps soundly. She doesn't wake up. She doesn't dream. Even when she is sleeping, she is vulgar.' He detests not only her vulgarity but also her role as the perfect housewife, in particular her orderliness. Close-ups of his wife's appearance ('look at her in her robe and rollers') and mouth ('she talks and talks and talks') visually reinforce his loathing for her. Likewise, his blunt comments are heightened with close-ups of the kitchen knife, his weapon of choice to carry out the murder. Every little detail has been worked out. An establishing shot of the married couple having breakfast in the kitchen and then Roberto leaving the flat provide some respite for the audience by resituating the action in a more conventional domestic atmosphere. Roberto lovingly reminds his wife of their evening out and the need to be back on time to watch something on television. From here onwards, the audience is drawn again into the subjective point of view of Roberto, following him to collect a plane ticket, to the bank where he works as a clerk, to the restaurant where he meets his wife and back to the flat, where he consummates his crime as she is about to open the door. As Roberto drags her corpse inside the flat and turns the lights on, a group of friends surprises him with a birthday party. The final shots capture the shock in his face, while the camera zooms into an extreme close-up of his eye closing, thus returning the audience to the same image that frames the entire narrative.

The twist in the plot structure of 'El cumpleaños' is typical of many of episodes of *Historias para no dormir*. 'El cumpleaños' builds up to a twist at the end, after forcefully placing the audience in the mind of the murderer and unrelentingly engaging them in the meticulous yet unsettling plan he is about to put into action. Plotting devices and stylistic choices guide our emotions and fears, heightening the generation of tension. While the domestic environment and the presence of a stereotypically middle-class married couple are fairly conventional and traditional – in fact, the closing credits refer to the characters as 'the man' and 'the woman' – the treatment of the subject matter is certainly contemporary and unconventional. Roberto voices his motives for murdering his wife, his desire to break free from his marriage and daily job, and to commence a new life abroad. The precision with which he explains how he is going to commit the perfect murder and the intensity of the workings of his mind present him as an absorbed and cold-blooded character. As the compressed plot progresses, the mood of dread and foreboding intensifies. Cinematography, editing and sound convey stylistically the psychological effects of his hatred of his wife and, by extension, the shackles that marriage has placed on him. On the one hand, Roberto is portrayed as an ordinary, charming and refined man, yet, on the other hand, the *noir* mood created by cinematographer Alfonso Nieva plunges the viewer into the dark side of his mind. The black-and-white film stock, the high-contrast lighting which partially obscures Roberto's face, and the use of shadows in the build-up to the murder scene emphasise the story's doom-laden and ominous mood. Similarly, tight framing and close-ups of the protagonist indicate his sense of entrapment and the intensity of his emotions, whilst extreme close-ups and zooms focus on the objects that are key to the execution of his perfect plan: the knife, clocks and watches, and the door-lock. Camera angles and framing persistently engage the audience with Roberto's subjective point of view. Editors Mercedes Alonso and Pedro Baldie also effectively pace the generation of tension and suspense by interlocking the everyday normality of the married couple with moments of unease, thus piecing together the workings of Roberto's obsessive mind in the final hours leading to the murder of his wife. Finally, the last sequence – that is, the twist in the tail – captures Roberto's reaction in a dramatic succession of shot / reverse shots between him and the group of people celebrating his birthday until three different close-ups close in on his face and eye. Tension, foreboding, surprise and shock are also produced through sound: from the obvious identification with the murderer's voice through his first-person narration to the silencing of his wife, the screeching sound effects *à la* Hitchcock and the jazzy notes anticipating the impending murder.

Aurally and visually, therefore, 'El cumpleaños' plays knowingly with the mechanics of suspense and surprise in the tradition of American practitioners such as Brown and Hitchcock. In the Spanish context, the disruption of an essentially realist text arguably exceeds the social and political conservatism of its milieu. Moreover, its contemporary setting and its unconventional addressing of the institution of marriage would have surprised and shocked Spanish TV audiences, and, most probably, would have kept them awake. Other episodes devoted to suspense and horror stories were closer to the Gothic tradition, in particular to the mechanical aspects of Poe's stories and the traits of Gothic TV. 'El pacto', part of the first series (27 March 1966), and 'La pesadilla', part of the second series (20 October 1967), correspond to more traditional Gothic stories.

In 'El pacto', Ibáñez Serrador adopts aspects of 'The Facts in the Case of M. Valdemar' (1845) and revisits familiar territory, since he had already adapted Poe's tale for television and for the cinema in Argentina. The story is set in the mid-nineteenth century in a recognisably Gothic mansion; Frederick Extron (Narciso Ibáñez Menta) is a doctor whose expertise in the pseudoscience of mesmerism and hypnotism caused him problems with the medical profession after one of his sessions went wrong and a female patient committed suicide. One of Extron's disciples, Enrique Valdemar (Manuel Galiana), who is suffering a terminal illness, believes in the powers of his master and the theory whereby his soul will remain alive if he is mesmerised at the point of death. On his deathbed, Valdemar is induced into a suspended hypnotic state. His voice from beyond the grave claims 'I am dead.' Several months after Valdemar's death, his corpse has not deteriorated at all. But one day Extron decides to wake him up from this state. On the count of three, Valdemar's body becomes a decaying and putrescent corpse.

'La pesadilla', penned by Luis Peñafiel, tells a traditional vampire tale with a twist. In a village situated in the Carpathians, six young women have been murdered. All of them have mysterious marks on their necks. The local inhabitants believe that the deaths have coincided with the arrival in the village of a foreigner, Yolati (Fernando Guillen), who only leaves his house at night. The opening sequence in the tavern sets up conventional framing devices like the confrontation between the village doctor (Tomás Blanco), man of science and friend of Yolati, and the locals, who believe in vampires and are prepared to kill Yolati. Stock figures and symbols populate the tale, and death and love drive the narrative forward. Catalina (Gemma Cuervo), the doctor's daughter, is madly in love with Yolati. Her love not being returned, she decides to blackmail him, saying that she possesses the belongings of the mysteriously murdered women, which could incriminate him. As part of her plan, she fakes being attacked by Yolati and makes everybody believe he is the vampire. But, as the title indicates, the story is structured around a nightmare suffered by one its characters. In a twist at the end, which subverts conventional vampire stories, the nightmare turns out to be that of Yolati, the vampire.

The critical reception of these two episodes allows us to gauge the significance of *Historias para no dormir* for those few critics who were writing about the relatively new medium of television in Spain. *ABC* critic Enrique del Corral wrote brief yet meaty reviews of many of the episodes shown. When reading them, the cultural historian can discern a number of critical issues which seem to concern del Corral: namely, the specificity of the medium, the production of quality television drama and the cultural status of television. His reviews of 'El pacto' and 'La pesadilla' certainly address these issues in the context of Ibáñez Serrador's horror and suspense series. Ibáñez Serrador 'must be praised unreservedly for his honesty in being true [. . .] to the techniques of the medium, without resorting to any of the specific devices of cinema, which are overwhelming in previous programmes directed by him' (del Corral 1966c: 117), as was the case with 'La bodega' ('a detailed narrative full of filmic prejudices' (1966d: 91)) or 'La broma' ('some directors are obsessed with expressing themselves "in filmic language" rather than '"talking" the language of television' (1966a: 119)). In 'La pesadilla', writes del Corral, Ibáñez Serrador demonstrates 'his accomplished use of the television medium as [a form of] art and a technique, and of "suspense" as a literary and visual practice' (1967: 105). In sum, Ibáñez Serrador tells horror–suspense stories specifically for the medium. As Matt Hills has observed in relation to horror on television, 'those producing, publicizing and writing about television can also produce cultural distinctions, suggesting that "Gothic TV" is superior to devalued (or culturally inappropriate) TV horror' (2005: 119). Del Corral certainly expresses his tastes and distastes, and advocates middle-brow quality and respectability. In its most extreme form, his distaste is expressed in his review of 'La sonrisa', which is entitled 'Unnecessary repugnance / revulsion' (1966e: 119). As for 'El pacto', despite its unquestionable quality at the level of direction and production values, the episode 'becomes repugnant' and 'recreates itself unnecessarily in completely irrelevant gruesome details', such as the graphic sequence of the 'toad cut open with the sole purpose of showing the blood', which does not advance the development of the plot nor contribute to the mood (1966c: 117). Del Corral comes to the conclusion that Ibáñez Serrador is obsessed with 'accumulating horror' (1966c: 117). The critic favours a more restrained form of supernatural horror, like the one Ibáñez Serrador deploys in 'La pesadilla' ('*mise-en-scène* and characterization [. . .] dialogue and composition of shots are superbly academic' (1967: 105)), and, by implication, a more acceptable adaptation of Gothic literary classics. Arguably, though, Ibáñez Serrador is closer to the original Poe, whose tales of suspense and horror provided abundant instances of gore, disgust and shock, than to the more middle-brow respectability of TV adaptations of Poe for the small screen.

Del Corral's favourite work by Ibáñez Serrador comes with episodes like 'NN23', 'El asfalto' or 'El transplante', which were originally conceived as individual projects with a didactic dimension that could be entered in international television festivals in the context of so-called 'Operación Premios TV',[12] but which made their way into the series. Ibáñez Serrador himself described these episodes as 'Stories to Make You Think', fulfilling a dual remit in their appeal to TVE regulators and in their function as culturally valued television drama. 'El asfalto' certainly appealed to the cultural value and pedagogic mission this television critic ascribed to the medium in his writings. In del Corral's words, this programme is one 'hundred per cent television; hundred per cent current. It is a gripping drama. Full of anguish. But it is also resolved with humour, good taste, and talent. Talent at the service of television as an art of expression, as a cultural vehicle with a message' for a society which is 'so alienated, so uncharitable, so selfish' (1966b: 111). 'El asfalto' follows the tragic fate of its main character, a middle-aged man in a plaster cast (Narciso Ibáñez Menta), who, while crossing the road on a very hot day, gets stuck in the melting tarmac and begins to sink. Passers-by are oblivious to his pleas for help; members of public bodies, such as the firemen, put bureaucracy ahead of assistance and are impervious to his predicament. As the episode develops, the man sinks unrelentingly until his body is finally swallowed by the asphalt. Theatrical in its staging, dramatic in its mood, and with a Kafkaesque treatment of its subject matter, the nightmarish horror of 'El asfalto' lies in the anonymity of its character and his relationship with a dehumanised environment. To a certain extent, therefore, 'El asfalto' is also a Gothic fiction, albeit in a form which addresses contemporary social fears about the alienation of the individual, bureaucratisation or dehumanisation.

By the time the second series reached Spanish television screens in 1968, Ibáñez Serrador was 'without any doubt the most important man working for Spanish TVE' since its beginnings (Garci 1968: 22), and *Historias para no dormir* 'the best quality programme' in its schedule (Garci 1968: 23). From the pages of film journal *Cinestudio*, critic José Luis Garci regards Ibáñez Serrador as a 'man of cinema' and is of the view that, if some of episodes were to be translated into film, they could easily exceed the works of Bava or Marghiretti. Ibáñez Serrador owed his successful transition from household TV to the big screen to his established image as a TV entertainer. In *Hitchcock: The Making of a Reputation*, Robert E. Kapsis describes how 'a close analysis of the opening sequence of each programme vividly conveys the probable impact that the opening had on audiences and suggests the force of Hitchcock's image on the viewer' (1992: 35), enabling him to be 'the first Hollywood director to become a bonafide TV star' (1992: 26). Any comparison between Hitchcock and Ibáñez Serrador is unsustainable in terms of context and œuvre; what interests me here is the self-conscious promotion-by-association of Ibáñez Serrador's name with the by then acknowledged master of suspense. Moreover, by the time *La residencia* was released in 1969, the name Narciso Ibáñez Serrador was readily connected in the public's mind with the horror genre. In the Spain of the 1960s, Chicho's pioneering transition from television to cinema was a unique phenomenon understandable only in terms of the institution of the author, of authorial reputation. The Hitchcockian link, for instance, would in fact be played up – or down – by contemporary reviewers; Hitchcock's cinematic 'influence' would be a common source of outrage and derision among specialist film journalists, whereas trade journals and daily press reviews would emphasise the TV persona link. In the same way that Hitchcock 'had been able to establish a generic contract with his TV audience' via his TV shows (Kapsis 1992: 42), Chicho drafted his own contract and honoured it by catering to audience needs and expectations. The popularity of *Historias para no dormir* led to the publication of two periodicals with the same title in 1966. One was published in Madrid by Julio García Peri and was edited by Ibáñez Serrador. Classics of horror and science fiction, together with stories based on his scripts for television as Luis Peñafiel, were introduced by Ibáñez Serrador, his familiar face in the top corner, and the Master's ceremonial words on the back – 'the most scary stories of the past, the present and the future, horror that scares some, amuses others, entertains others, but that bores nobody' – in a marketing operation reminiscent of Alfred Hitchcock's *Mystery Magazine*, as well as other anthologies. A second one, published in Barcelona by Semic Española de Ediciones, presented itself as 'graphic novels for adults'. The interest and financial performance of the collections were constructed around the 'Chicho' figurehead.

Ibáñez Serrador paved the way for other horror and science-fiction publications in the late 1960s and early 1970s which were looking to find their own niche in the market: anthologies like *Narraciones genéricas de terror* (1968) and *Relatos de terror y espanto* (1972), the science-fiction magazine *Nueva dimensión* (1972), edited by Domingo Santos, horror publications such as *Terror Extra* (1969) and specialist genre magazine *Terror Fantastic*, to which I will return in Chapter 5. The proliferation of comics, fanzines and magazines devoted to the genre attests not only to its growing commercial importance, but also to the significance of horror in the popular culture of the period. By the end of the 1960s, 'Chicho' had become the most culturally prominent image of horror in Spain, a 'monstruo sagrado' (Anon. 1969: 12), as film magazine *Nuevo Fotogramas* described him.

LA RESIDENCIA

Ibáñez Serrador's popular standing among audiences was equal only to an almost uniform critical devaluation of *La residencia* as a horror genre product with Hitchcockian aspirations in specialist film journal reviews of the period (*Cinestudio*, *Film Ideal*, *Nuestro Cine* or *Reseña*); however, the polarised critical response to *La residencia* needs to be considered within a broader discussion of the cultural politics that underpinned popular genres in Spanish cinema and the historical context of an industry in crisis, issues which were addressed in Chapter 1. Many film reviewers criticised Ibáñez Serrador's production on the grounds of the director's formative years in television and the tastelessly excessive budget made available to him – more than 50 million pesetas, unheard of in the history of the Spanish film industry; how, when the industry was in dire financial debt, could a first-time director have such a considerable sum at his disposal? The discrepancy between *La residencia*'s spectacular success and the critical response surrounding the film calls for analysis. Given Chicho's already firmly established persona as a brand name for horror and suspense among audiences, it is arguably this very association that underlies the critical prejudices of the 'serious' film reviewers against a (dis)reputable generic figure within horror.

'Annabel Films S.A. presents *The Finishing School* (*La residencia*). The film that breaks all public and box-office records,' read an advertisement in trade journal *Cineinforme* (Anon. 1970a: 31). The advertisement provided some figures relating to the takings in four major cities (Madrid, Barcelona, Zaragoza and Valencia): an overall 44,879,482 pesetas in the first 6 months since its opening day on 12 January 1970. The October issue of the same year presents a double-page advertisement that reads: 'the first Spanish boom in the world's box-office [. . .] 916.732$ USA in the first 8½ months (in only 25 cities). Pic is due for release in 27 more cities in the country'. Under the heading '*La residencia*. A New Spanish Cinema?', *Cineinforme* proudly announces a welcome, though unforeseen, event: 'a home production occupies first place over the last few months' (Anon. 1970a: 31). The deliberately polemical question that opens the news piece is matched by the probing closing lines: 'will this example be followed?' (Anon. 1970a: 32). Such framing raises questions about the ongoing debate around the 'New Spanish Cinema' promoted by García Escudero between 1962 and 1967. Figures show that *La residencia* is the most commercially successful film of all time – certainly since box-office control was introduced in 1966 – and further enthuses, unabashedly, that we are probably facing 'one of the most important films in the cinematography of the world' (Anon. 1970a: 31). As the director stated in the pressbook, producers and distributors had in mind the exportability of the film: *La residencia* was conceived as 'a stepping stone from which we can break into the international market'.[13] Strategic decisions were taken at the production level to facilitate the placing of the film in international territories: the first Spanish picture to be shot in English, an international cast led by the internationally renowned German actress Lily Palmer, exceptional production values, a French setting (although it was filmed in Spain) and a generic dialogue with international horror traditions.

La residencia was routinely advertised as 'the first Spanish horror and suspense film'. The marketing novelty was relied on the familiarity of Spanish audiences with Ibáñez Serrador's horror–suspense TV series. Audiences and critics, however, as Ibáñez Serrador wrote in the pressbook, were also expecting some degree of innovation:

> Many expect to find in *La residencia* 'new forms', 'unconformity', 'the breaking of old moulds' . . . I am sorry to disappoint them. There is none of that in my film. I wanted to tell the story in the right way, in a classic manner.

The academicism of Ibáñez Serrador's first filmic project, which echoes his introductory words in the first episode of *Historias para no dormir*, might be said to model itself on a spate of respectable horror made during the early 1960s in Great Britain – *The Innocents* (Jack Clayton 1961), adapted from William Archibald's play of the same title, based on Henry James's *Turn of the Screw*, and starring Deborah Kerr, and *The Haunting* (Robert Wise 1963), based on Shirley Jackson's *The Haunting of Hill House*, starring Claire Bloom and Julie Harris – or even the American *What Ever Happened to Baby Jane?* (Robert Aldrich 1962), with Bette Davis and Joan Crawford. These literary adaptations, made in the early 1960s, were a legitimate attempt by the genre to clean up its act, and in most cases resuscitated the careers of their ageing lead actresses. *La residencia* presents aesthetic and narrative similarities with this cycle of films: period settings, canonical Gothic *mise-en-scène*, stories centred around the figure of a governess, and restrained performances. Therefore, in its formal qualities, Ibáñez Serrador's film appears to be a modern Gothic thriller with a classical style of filmmaking. But *La residencia* also displays an awareness of developments in the genre and plays off other international horror: namely, Hammer in its flaunting of horror, sex and violence, Americal International Pictures (AIP) in its Gothic visualisation of the settings, and Hitchcock's *Psycho* (1960) in its generation of visual and narrative suspense and in the setting up of a repressive mother–son relationship. Made at the end of a decade in which the genre had undergone remarkable aesthetic and thematic changes, *La residencia* thus straddles both classical and contemporary influences.

Based on a story written by Juan Tébar, who had scripted episodes of *Historias para no dormir*,[14] and adapted by the director under his pseudonym Luis Peñafiel, *La residencia* is set in a French boarding school for difficult girls at the end of the nineteenth century. As the headmistress Madame Fourneau (Lily Palmer) explains to the tutor of Teresa (Cristina Galbó), the latest boarder to arrive, the institution aims to 'return young women who have gone astray to the correct path by treating them with utmost rigour and discipline'. Her treatment of the boarders is ruthlessly authoritarian. Madame Fourneau exerts the same power and repressive control over her adolescent son Luis (John Moulder Brown), whom she forbids to have any contact with her pupils – none of them being quite good enough for her boy, as she constantly reminds him. When a series of mysterious disappearances and murders take place, including that of Teresa and Madame Fourneau's right-hand girl Irene (Mary Maude), Fourneau decides to investigate. Her investigations lead her to the author of the crimes in the final sequence: up in the attic Luis has been dismembering his victims in order to stitch together his 'ideal' woman. Addressing his mother, Luis justifies his actions:

> Look, there she is, only the hands were missing. Irene had the same hands as you, slim but strong. Look, I took the dress from you some time ago. I decided to make a girl like you; a girl for me. Now she's got everything: blonde hair like yours, the same eyes . . . you always said I'd have a girl like you when you were young and now I've got her.

The film closes with Luis locking up his mother alongside his monstrous creation and repeating the words of advice his mother had drummed into him: 'Now you must teach her to take care of me the way you do and love me as you've always loved me. Talk to her, mother, talk to her.'

The authoritarian experiences of Francoism can be read on the narrative level, mainly through Madame Fourneau's ruthless rule over the school, her domination of the lives of the boarders and her obstructionism towards Luis, as well as through *mise-en-scène*. In true Gothic tradition, the school is a repressive institution; the sense of confinement and entrapment is explicitly conveyed in the credit sequence and sustained by a claustrophobic ambience and a number of motifs throughout the narrative (the isolation chamber, shadows of bars, secret rooms). Confinement and entrapment are conveyed as soon as the carriage bringing the new boarder enters the school grounds and slowly makes its way to the building located deep in the forest. The credit sequence ends with a close-up of the groundsman's hand closing the gate, aurally reinforced by the loud noise of the bolt. As the girls disappear, Fourneau locks and bolts all the doors and windows of the school so that nobody can leave the building. As an authoritarian headmistress, Fourneau, whose costume is reminiscent of Fascist uniforms (military shirt and black tie), tolerates no active rebellion, as the first classroom scene with her pupils makes clear. While she is dictating from a novel, one of the pupils silently defies Fourneau by not following the passage. This act of defiance is immediately punished, with the rebel being taken away to a solitary confinement cell where she is tied up and whipped by Fourneau's right-hand assistants, unbeknown to the rest of the pupils. But the film deals mainly with the effects of repression and generational conflict in the mother–son relationship.

Luis, like Norman Bates in Hitchcock's *Psycho*, is also the product of an overprotective, obstructionist, devouring mother. As Tébar acknowledged in a *Nuevo Fotogramas* interview, the main theme of the film is 'maternal vampirism, the excessive love of a mother towards her son; one could even say that her own sexual frustrations are compensated through her maternal love' (Anon. 1969: 12). Some publicity material foregrounded this (suggestively overprotective) mother–son relationship, while other posters insinuated and exploited the sadistic and lesbian streaks in the film (see Figure 17). While Fourneau voices the reasons why her son should not have a relationship with the boarding-school girls, the lack of a man in her own life and the repression of her sexual nature are left unexplained; for example, the scene where she patrols the showers suggests lesbian intimations. The first scene between mother and son reveals simultaneously a controlling, oppressive mother and a loving, caring mother, establishing the thematic and stylistic threads repeated in subsequent encounters. Aware of Luis's illicit acts of voyeurism after unsettling the newcomer Teresa, Fourneau storms into her son's room and forbids him to spy on the girls. Framing and camera angles establish relations of power and define the nature of their relationship: initially Fourneau stands authoritatively in control of Luis, who is sitting on the floor and who denies any wrongdoing while fidgeting with a musical box, and then she moves behind him to embrace him and lay down firmly yet affectionately what she wishes for him: 'what you need is a woman like me, who takes care of you, loves you and protects you.' As the scene unfolds, both the main non-diegetic musical theme of the film and the diegetic sound of the music box acquire an eerie tone which underscores their relationship and symbolically anticipates the murder sequences. The first murder reworks this scene aurally and visually. Held from behind, the victim, Isabel, who has furtively befriended Luis, is repeatedly stabbed; the main music theme is now adapted to match the thrusts of the knife, and, as the victim stops struggling, the distorted sound of a musical box winding down conveys her death. The three murders committed by the psychologically unstable Luis represent his vindictive turn on his mother, who has been repressing his sexual awakening and denying him what he desperately wishes for.

As I have already argued, trade journals emphasised the possibility of *La residencia* being the incarnation of 'A New Spanish Cinema'. The daily press also echoed this view: 'if Spanish cinema produced more "Residencias", it is possible that it could produce the odd "Milky Way" or "Strada"' (1970: 3), wrote Joaquín Aranda in *Heraldo de Aragón*. The critical elite did not award such high praise; *Cinestudio*, *Nuestro Cine*, *Film Ideal* and *Reseña* rehearsed the typical criticism of the horror genre, but, more importantly, they framed their discussions of the film within wider considerations of the state of the national film industry and the directions that Spanish cinema ought to be taking. As Ángel Pérez Gómez acknowledged in *Reseña*, the release of *La residencia* had

Figure 17   The mother-son relationship and women-in-prison iconography come to the fore in Ibáñez Serrador's *La residencia*.

been 'surrounded by a tense atmosphere that has had a notable influence on critical assessment' (1970: 172) of the film, and added that critical opinion was polarised – the film 'has been the object of either furious or enthusiastic assessments' (1970: 174). Whether explicitly or implicitly, several points act as structuring elements in the reviews under consideration: the politics of production, the institution of censorship, the generic choice (as part of a wider debate on the cultural status of film) and the figure of the director. Symptomatic of such readings is Antonio Pelayo's review in *Cinestudio*. Pelayo drew attention to the unprecedented financial and institutional support at the service of the film, a 'Trojan horse' in the Euro-American market since, to quote the press-book, 'the production values and the censors' standards have reached an enviable European "standard"' (1970: 39). Pelayo questioned the need for such an exorbitant budget at such a critical moment in the Spanish film industry; other Spanish filmmakers – no names given – could have produced 'at least two films of the same technical standard' (1970: 40). As for the censors, he expressed his dissatisfaction with double standards: 'a censor should be able to discriminate between pornography, box-office appeal and expressive needs' (1970: 39). On a more positive note, Pérez Gómez in *Reseña* considered the significance of *La residencia* in the context of contemporary Spanish cinema: valuing the uniqueness of Ibáñez Serrador's project in the country's cinematic production and his ability to draw audiences, Pérez Gómez described the film as 'respectable commercial cinema' (1970: 175) and concluded that the film is an example of what can be achieved at the level of production, but 'not an example of an artistic formula or the way forward for a cinematography' (1970: 175). Interestingly, this same issue of *Reseña* addressed the crisis in Spanish cinema in its editorial statement, demanding a 'complete restructuring of the Spanish film industry' (1970: 171) in all sectors, in particular those involved in the economic infrastructure – producers and exhibitors – and the end – or, at least, the 'democratisation' – of censorship.

Watching over the 'interests' of Spanish cinema, as well as those of Spanish audiences, were Miguel Marías, contributor to *Nuestro Cine*, and José María Latorre, writing for *Film Ideal*. For Marías, Ibáñez Serrador's film was disrespectful both to the institution of cinema and to audiences; the audiences' financial support for films that 'insult them and consider them a retard whose bad taste and subnormality needs to be fed' (1970: 73) was inexplicable. Marías, as well as Latorre, set himself up as a custodian of taste, protecting a retarded industry (and a retarded viewer) from the perils of *La residencia*; he even called into question the value judgements of the mainstream critics who approved of the film. Cultural distinctions are made not only between critic and filmgoer but also between a critical elite and mainstream journalism, thus reproducing a hierarchy of taste in film criticism.

On a formal and stylistic level, specialist film journal reviewers refuse to engage with the horror genre by displaying a series of conventional arguments against it. Firstly, their approach to this generic form as a 'formula' film responded to mass culture and auteurist theories of popular cinema; secondly, this type of criticism rejected popular forms on aesthetic grounds. *La residencia* was formulaic and predictable: 'a purely formulaic film', which featured a 'panoply of commonplaces' (Latorre 1970: 72); nothing more than 'a collection of typical generic effects' (Pelayo 1970: 40). The ideological underpinnings of auteurism seep through to their treatment of the figure of Ibáñez Serrador. Latorre and Marías accused the director of being merely derivative of Hitchcock, while Pelayo summed up the film as 'badly assimilated Hitchcock' (1970: 40), attributing the final product to a group of 'specialistas' – that is, craftsmen. The conclusion of these claims is to deny Ibáñez Serrador the category of 'auteur' even before a filmography is established. 'There is not a "world-view", one cannot even trace a particular personal vision' in *La residencia*, wrote Pérez Gómez (1970: 173). The film was a flight from reality and, by extension, lacked any contemporary socio-political significance – 'the world begins and ends behind the walls of "la residencia"' (Latorre 1970: 483) – or any definable moral stance since 'the panorama of values is bleak' (Pérez Gómez 1970: 173). Lacking realism and moral fibre and devoid of political intentions, *La residencia* offers none of the major appeals of 'New Spanish Cinema': that is, an ideological stand.

Despite performing solidly at the box office and proving popular with audiences – or even because of it – *La residencia* experienced a corresponding loss of credibility among 'serious' critics, and not always for reasons of artistic merit. The consensus among audiences was that *La residencia* looked nothing like a Spanish film, breaking stylistically and qualitatively as it did with cinematic forms of the period.

Ibáñez Serrador would direct one other movie in 1976, *¿Quién puede matar a un niño?* The film appeared at a time when the director's popularity was linked to his new television venture, the game show *Un, dos, tres. . ., responda otra vez* (One, two, three . . ., respond again), which, like *Historias para no dormir*, would be formative for generations of Spanish spectators from 1972 onwards and a familiar landmark in the history of Spanish television, running almost continuously for a period of twenty years. Between the first (1972–3) and second (1976–8) seasons of this family-oriented programme, Ibáñez Serrador shocked audiences with *¿Quién puede matar a un niño?*

¿QUIÉN PUEDE MATAR A UN NIÑO?

Based on the science-fiction novel *El juego de los niños* (Children's Game) (1976), written by Spanish author Juan José Plans,[15] and with a script initially entitled 'El polen' (Polen), 'Los niños' (The Children) and 'La noche que empezaron a jugar' (The Night They Started Playing), *¿Quién puede matar a un niño?* was the second – and final – film made by Ibáñez Serrador (see Figure 18). The film opens with a black-and-white still of a helpless, frightened child, arms raised, and the title *¿Quién . . .?* superimposed in red lettering. This is followed by a prologue composed of a black-and-white montage of photographs and real news footage of twentieth-century wars and genocide (death camps in Auschwitz, the Indo-Pakistan conflict, wars in Korea and Vietnam, civil war in Biafra). The narrative voiceovers inform the viewer that the main victims of these man-made tragedies are always the children – some hard-hitting figures relating to the death toll amongst children that results from the horrors of war runs across the screen, underlining the message still further. A dissolve to a blonde child playing on a beach packed with tourists introduces the fictional narrative. The momentary tourist postcard atmosphere is interrupted when a body washes up on the shore; police car and ambulance sirens replace the carefree bustle of the holidaymakers. Unaware of this event, Tom (Lewis Fiander) and Evelyn (Prunella Ransome), a middle-class English couple, have just arrived in Benavís on the Spanish Mediterranean coast in the middle of the local festival, as a bemused local passerby informs them as they get off the coach – Ibáñez Serrador himself in a cameo, playfully introducing the characters and the audience to his tale of horror. Tom and Evelyn are on their way to the quaint, remote island village of Almanzora, which Tom had already visited a decade earlier and now wants to take his wife to for a belated honeymoon. They have two children, who have stayed at home, and Evelyn is expecting a third. Before they set off for Almanzora, the audience sees the village through the eyes of the foreign couple in a typical tourist itinerary: the colours and noises of the local 'fiestas', a hotel, the information centre, the tobacconist's, the guest house where they stay for the night, and the night-life. The following day, the two embark on a small boat to their remote destination, four hours away from the mainland.[16] As they walk through the streets of the village, they realise that the only villagers they have come across are children. Almanzora is like a ghost village and its inhabitants behave very strangely. While Tom explores the village, Evelyn waits in an empty bar, where she is approached by a girl who is drawn to her pregnant stomach, feeling it in an eerie manner. Not having come across any adults, Tom seems to believe that they are all somewhere in the vicinity celebrating a local festival. When he witnesses a girl bludgeoning an old man to death and the macabre game the children play with the corpse, used as a *piñata* until it is decapitated off screen, he does not tell his wife. Other violent acts of murder, and the full realisation that the adults have been killed off by the children, make Tom change his mind. He fights for his life and that of his wife and future child. Soon the children lay siege to the couple, who have sought refuge in the police station jail. Here Tom is forced to kill a child who was about to shoot them dead. The siege stops for the night,

Figure 18   Who Can Kill a Child?

slowing down the action before the film approaches its extremely brutal finale. When morning breaks, Evelyn begins to feel violently ill, screaming 'It's killing me.' Her own unborn child attacks her from inside and kills her. In the end, Tom – and the audience – is faced once again with the titular question when he finds himself cornered by the children in the village square. Shooting his way out to the boat with a machine gun, he kills more children. Surrounded, he fights the children off with an oar. A coastal police patrol approaching the harbour witnesses the vicious fight and shoots him down. The policemen disembark on the island and are massacred by the children. The closing scene sees a group of children taking to the sea and heading for mainland.

¿Quién . . . ? presented many similarities with *La residencia* at the level of production. It was also made with the international market in mind: shot in English, with an international cast in the lead roles (British actors Lewis Fiander and Prunella Ransome),[17] and establishing a dialogue with international horror traditions. But Ibáñez Serrador's second film reached Spanish screens in a very different historical context to that of *La residencia*. When ¿Quién . . . ? was released in April 1976, the country was going through a period of social and political uncertainty. General Franco had died on 20 November 1975 and Spain had entered a period of transition before the first democratic elections, which were held in June 1977. And yet contemporary reviews hardly related the film's subject matter to its immediate historical reality, the end of Francoism. For many reviewers, any allegorical value was understood in relation to the future and not the present, and through the lens of a science-fiction tale which contained a universal lesson; as *La vanguardia española* critic Martínez put it, the film was 'a parable to meditate on what may happen in the future in the world' (1976: n.p.). However, the film's prologue and its taboo subject matter – children murdering adults and adults murdering children – proved to be controversial and shocking among cultural commentators and the mainstream press. The director and the distributors had to handle the controversies generated by the film in interviews and promotional material by explaining the message it contained. When asked about it, Ibáñez Serrador invariably answered along the same lines:

> I don't like talking about the message of a film but I think [in the case of my film] this is easy to understand. If the children are cruel and they rebel against the adults, they are not to blame; we are to blame [. . .] Children are the recipients of our cruelties, our indifference, our coldness. (Ibáñez Serrador in Masó 1976: 51)

He would claim that 'the film is a defence of children [. . .] Adults sow cruelty and violence in children' (Ibáñez Serrador in Castilla 1976: 14). Distributors published one-page advertisements in the press with the following announcement in capital letters, 'A FILM IN DEFENCE OF THE CHILDREN OF THE WORLD', below the portrait of the director and the customary favourable review snippets.[18] A final instance of the extent of the hullabaloo surrounding the film came in the form of a two-page debate on children and violence entitled 'Are we educating our children to be violent?' (Anon. 1976a: 41–2), published in the cultural weekend supplement of the daily *ABC* newspaper, *Blanco y Negro*; six experts (a doctor, a sociologist, a psychiatrist, a psychologist, a pedagogue and a paediatrician) answered two questions, 'do you think that our society is to be held responsible for stimulating violence in children?' and 'what are the solutions society should be adopting to resolve this type of behaviour?' The debate is framed via a reference to Ibáñez Serrador's film:

> *¿Quién puede matar a un niño?* This is the title of Narciso Ibáñez Serrador's latest film which has stirred up so much controversy [. . .] Even though this is just a fictional film, the spectator leaves the cinema with a nasty taste in the mouth because behind the images, behind the fiction, lurks a distressing and unpleasant reality. (Anon. 1976a: 41)

This is not 'moral panic' over the content of a popular film, for none of the experts mentioned the film in their responses, but rather a pretext to address a larger contemporary topical concern which Ibáñez Serrador's film seemed to tap into, the loss of traditional norms and values at a time when Spain was undergoing a process of change.

Critical reception of *¿Quién . . .?* was polarised. Many commentators disliked the film, rebuffing the whole project; others read it through Ibáñez Serrador's previous body of work, in particular his TV series *Mañana puede ser verdad* and *Historias para no dormir*. Probably the most scathing words were those of critic Luciano González Egido in the newspaper *Pueblo*. For Egido 'the film is a pastiche' and commits 'a triple immorality': firstly, it is a plagiarism of Hitchcock's *The Birds*; secondly, 'the genre apparatus is degraded' in its handling of generic conventions; and, thirdly, the film's 'gross manipulation of historical footage reduces Nazi concentration camps, famine in Biafra, the bombing of Vietnam, etc. to a simple fight between men and children: the former to be blamed, the latter the victims' (1976). Most reviewers focused their negative criticisms on the film's prologue, questioning its narrative and thematic function, as well as its content. Marcelo Arroita-Jaúregui in *Arriba* described the opening as a 'useless preamble' which denies 'the film any possibility of suspense' and the spectator any participation in the narrative process (1976). *Nuevo Diario*'s reviewer reiterated this point – 'an absurd prologue' – and added that the message of the film was 'confused and moralistic' (Anon. 1976c). Fernando Lara, in political and cultural weekly magazine *Triunfo*, dismissed the film as 'a cheap humanist pretext' without any 'psychological or parabolic depth' (1976: 62) and the director as 'the amauterish translator of a certain type of popular literature', whose only dubious achievement had been to popularise for 'mass audiences stories that other authors created before him' (1976: 62). Bronce, in satiric magazine *La codorniz*, defined the film as a 'pro-childhood plea riddled with incoherence' and contemptuously renamed the director 'Hitchcock Ibradbury Serrador' (1976). Other critics, on the other hand, understood the film in relation to the director's previous trajectory, linking the subject matter to the 'what if' premise central to much science-fiction literature. In stark contrast to González Egido's scathing review, another *Pueblo* reviewer enthusiastically lauded the film in '¿*Quién puede matar a un niño?* A film to make you think' (Anon. 1976d), in an explicit reference to those episodes in *Historias para no dormir* which Ibáñez Serrador described as 'Historias para pensar' ('Stories to Make You Think'): for instance, 'El asfalto'. This is a film, reads the review, which poses a 'bold hypothesis' and affectively and effectively exposes the cruelties of the real world ('the prologue sends a shiver down the spine' (Anon. 1976d)); Ibáñez Serrador 'is fully aware [. . .] of a controversial subject matter [. . .] which would be duly exploited in the marketplace' (Anon. 1976d). Lorenzo López Sancho in *ABC* also connected the film to the generic status of *Historias para no dormir*: ¿*Quién* . . .? is a 'vigorous tale' which convincingly 'straddles horror and science fiction' and which successfully generates narrative suspense 'akin to the one that Hitchcock creates in *The Birds*' (1976: 58). Referring to the artistic merit and commercial value of the film, *ABC* critic Antonio Colón welcomed it because it opened 'new horizons' for a Spanish cinema which tended to oscillate between 'the utmost vulgar products and an obscure and undecipherable intellectualism' (1976: 65). The critical reception of ¿*Quién* . . .? and *La residencia* shared similar agendas and arguments, among them questions of taste and distaste around the horror genre,[19] questions of artistic and cultural quality, and references to Hitchcock.

A discussion of the impact of and controversy surrounding ¿*Quién* . . .? and, by extension, its director, from the point of view of critical reception, allow us to understand the cultural and historical positioning of contemporary audiences in relation to Ibáñez Serrador and his popular genre production. Certainly, in many instances, the director himself and his work were the subjects of disapproval and derision; for many commentators the unsettling subject matter proposed in the film title and the prologue proved problematic and polemic and the film was all artifice, lacking meaning. For others, the relationship between prologue and narrative was intelligible, and the director simply wanted to make a statement about the violence that characterised twentieth-century civilisation. A consideration of the pressbook and the trailer enables us to tell a slightly different story concerning the marketing and promotion of the film, for they mobilised the pleasures of horror through generic markers associated with the director's generic repertoire and affirmed the contract that director and audiences had established from the mid-1960s onwards. In the trailer, modelled on the familiar trademark on-screen introductions to *Historias para no dormir*, Ibáñez Serrador explains the aims of his new project: *¿Quién . . .?* is 'a horror film free from topics. There are no sombre manor houses, no storms, no monsters, no vampires with long fangs. This is horror in broad daylight.' And to this conscious departure from the 'classic' horror formula I will turn shortly. Adopting an ironic tone, he then introduces prospective audiences to different horror-cliché situations in the film, only to deny them playfully a full sequence of any of the fragments shown. And, finally, Ibáñez Serrador invites the audience to watch his film because 'you will have a very, very, very . . . bad time'. The pressbook also rehearsed the familiar territory of horror, science fiction and suspense, as laid out a decade earlier in *Mañana puede ser verdad* and *Historias para no dormir*. In the taglines included in the pressbook, distributors explicitly reminded exhibitors and audiences of the director's landmark TV series *Mañana puede ser verdad* and *Historias para no dormir*, from the simple and generically overarching 'Suspense, horror and science fiction' and 'A film where horror becomes ANGUISH', to a reminder of the television title indelibly etched on the audience's memories, 'A story that may come true tomorrow' to the more suggestive 'A horror tale in broad daylight', which, like the trailer, announced the film's departure from previous horror conventions. As a way of examining how Ibáñez Serrador built on his previous work and was influenced by other contemporary international horror traditions, let us focus on the film's commonality with those episodes qualified as 'Stories To Make You Think' by examining some of the production values and thematic concerns, as well as the ways in which the film works within and against horror traditions.

Episodes such as 'El asfalto', 'NN23' or 'El transplante' offered a critique of society's dehumanisation in the tradition of Bradbury's science-fiction stories. The prologue in *¿Quién . . .?* seems to tread a similar thematic path by shaking viewers up and placing them in thoughtful mode. The prologue functions, firstly, as a meta-narrative preface, whose traditional expository function in science fiction is to take the viewer from the familiar world to the unfamiliar, and, secondly, as a device to demand from the viewer an intellectual and affective engagement with the images – in other words, to make the viewer think. The explicit title is challenging, for indeed, who can kill a child? In terms of character identification, the challenge for the audience is the question of which characters we should feel for, the children or the tourist couple; in terms of narrative suspense, the when, how and why of who can kill a child are at work from the very beginning. The children's lullaby and laughter, which disturbingly and disconcertingly punctuate the prologue sequence, also manipulate the viewer into a state of direct suspense by warning of future narrative events. The creation of cinematic suspense in *¿Quién . . .?* is another aspect shared with the television series and continued here through the long-term collaboration between Ibáñez Serrador and Argentinean musician Waldo de los Ríos, whose scores were the perfect aural complement to the suspenseful, frightful and disquieting moods created by Ibáñez Serrador in *Mañana puede ser verdad* and *Historias para no dormir* – and for the film *La residencia*.

¿Quién . . .? is a horror tale told in broad daylight. From the moment when a corpse appears on the sunny beach of Benavís to the closing scene where the murderous children embark for the mainland, violence is bathed in sunshine. One critic in *Actualidad* even labelled the film as a promising example of 'terror mediterráneo' (Mediterranean horror) (Anon. 1976b). Although some of the exterior location scenes were filmed on the Mediterranean coast, set designer Ramiro Gómez successfully transformed a Castillian village into a typical Mediterranean one flooded with light, which contrasted markedly with the bloody presentation of horror.[20] Cinematographer José Luis Alcaine conveyed the steady build-up of tension and the escalating physical ordeal of Tom and Evelyn through tight framing; the explosive violence of the final segment is constructed by using a combination of wide shots and very tight shots reminiscent of spaghetti westerns.

Ibáñez Serrador's claim that *¿Quién . . .?* was a horror film 'free from topics' needs further qualification – notwithstanding that it was a commercial ploy like any other. For example, the prologue introduces a defamiliarising effect, the traditional character identification of horror films is problematised and the stylistic presentation of horror in broad daylight goes against the dark grain of the genre. However, other strategic imitations of narrative and aesthetic devices from successful horror films and trends of the 1960s and early 1970s come into the open: the science-fiction narratives of *Village of the Damned* (Wolf Rilla 1960) and *Children of the Damned* (Anton M. Leader 1963)[21]; *Night of the Living Dead*, in the final siege and shooting of the protagonist by his potential rescuers; and, as already discussed, the customary association with – for many, imitation of – a Hitchcock film, in this case *The Birds*. The children in Ibáñez Serrador's film possess the extraordinary psychic powers and telepathic bond of the possessed children in *Village of the Damned* and, like them, act as a group. The pressbook synopsis indicates that the children have suffered some sort of mysterious genetic mutation that induces them to annihilate the adults, but the narrative gives no natural, supernatural or pathological reason to explain the children's murderous actions. (In the novel the cause of their behaviour is linked to a yellow powder that fell over the village; hence one of the possible working titles for the script.) Structurally, therefore, *¿Quién . . .?* emulates the unexplained, violent attacks of the birds in Hitchcock's film, and is constructed around a typical Hitchcockian narrative strategy, the so-called

'MacGuffin effect': why do the children murder the adults? Other plot devices, such as the setting (a coastal town), the mood (daylight horror) and the unsettling open ending, are also reminiscent of *The Birds*.

Perhaps the interlocking of horror, science fiction, suspense and social commentaries confounded contemporary critics and audiences alike. Its dual modes of representation – documentary and fiction – were certainly difficult to reconcile. As Ibáñez Serrador has acknowledged in some recent interviews, the prologue is a misplaced 'lecture' about violence. What is undeniable is that the film generated – and still lends itself to – literal, generic, cult, topical and symbolic readings.[22]

Ibáñez Serrador wholly embraced the genre and its traditions. *Historias para no dormir* offered a fascinating confluence of representational heritages – literary, theatrical, radiophonic and cinematic. *La residencia* and *¿Quién . . .?* connected with contemporary international horror traditions. His television and film output overcame the distinction between popular genre and auteurism, and illustrated the struggle over the meaning of film at a crucial time within the Spanish film industry. As this chapter has shown, screening out what did not fit the aesthetic standards of television reviewers and specialist film journals, there were a number of critical operations to safeguard the interests of these media and of Spanish audiences from the horrors of the genre. Even though his horror production did not achieve an acceptable cultural status at the time, *Historias para no dormir*, *La residencia* and *¿Quién . . .?* have sustained cult status in Spain and abroad. *Historias para no dormir* would be resuscitated in 1982 and Ibáñez Serrador would return to his horrormeister role in a number of programmes such as *Mis terrores favoritos*. And the twenty-first century would see him collaborating in *6 Películas para no dormir* with contemporary Spanish horror filmmakers Jaume Balagueró, Alex de la Iglesia, Mateo Gil, Paco Plaza and Enrique Urbizu with the financial backing of Filmax (see Chapter 6).

NOTES

1. Other titles are *Who Can Kill a Child?*, *Would You Kill a Child?*, *Island of the Damned*, *Death is Child's Play* and *Island of Death*.
2. I am indebted to Carlos Enrique Abraham and his wonderful website 'Museo Iconográfico de la Literatura Popular' (museodeliteraturapopular.blogspot.com) for details about the Argentinean pulp magazine *Narraciones Terroríficas*.
3. Episodes were directed by Martha Reguera.
4. The three Poe stories on which the film is based had appeared in *Narraciones Terroríficas*: 'The Facts in the Case of M. Valdemar' in issue 5, 'The Cask of Amontillado' in issue 11 and 'The Tell-Tale Heart' in issue 12. The film was released in the US as *Master of Horror*, as Weldon observes in *The Psychotronic Encyclopedia of Film*: 'A trilogy of Poe's stories, including two Corman filmed as Tales of Terror a year later. The third segment, "The Tell-Tale Heart", was deleted from this dubbed feature presented by [producer] Jack Harris. It was released as *Master of Terror* (aka *The 4-D Man*)' (1983: 465).

5. It was also in 1956 that Spain was admitted to the United Nations.
6. In 1968 he became Director de Programas para el Exterior de TV Española and in 1972 he was Director of Programming, the same year in which he started 'Un, dos, tres . . .'.
7. 'Muerte bajo el sol' on 9 December 1963, 'El extraño caso del señor Kellerman' on 12 April 1964 and 'Obsesión' on 15 June 1964.
8. In *Mañana puede ser verdad*, 'El hombre y la bestia', for example, was serialised in four parts during February and March. 'NN23' was shown in April, 'El zorro y el bosque' / 'The Fox and the Forest' in May, 'La tercera expedición' / 'The Third Expedition' in June, and 'Los bulbos' / 'The Bulbs' in two parts in November. Dates are based on the schedules published by newspaper *ABC*.
9. According to Palacio, there were around 600 TV sets in the Madrid area in 1956 but 3 to 4 million by the end of the 1960s.
10. Companies like Phillips sent their technicians to developing countries in order to train future television directors and technicians following the demands of a fast-changing market.
11. A reconstruction of the number of episodes and their original scheduling is well nigh impossible because the survival of television programmes from this period leaves historians, critics and fans with a lack of primary information due to the fact that the recording of programmes was not common practice at TVE. This is further complicated by the director's inclusion of stories already used in *Mañana puede ser verdad*, *Tras la puerta cerrada* and *Historias para no dormir*, either with the same title, as in the case of 'El cohete', or with a different one ('El pacto' becomes 'El extraño caso del señor Valdemar'), or even some originally conceived as independent teleplays, as in the case of 'El asfalto' or 'NN23'. Ibáñez Serrador himself, for example, noted that eighteen episodes were broadcast (Ibáñez Serrador in Serrats Ollé (1971: 52)), whereas subsequently critics have diverged substantially on the total number of episodes (for instance, Baget Herms (1993) lists fifteen, García Serrano (1996) twenty-four, and Águilar nineteen (1999a)).
12. 'NN23' was awarded second prize at the Festival of Berlin in 1965, 'El asfalto' the Golden Ninfa at the Festival of Montecarlo in 1967, and 'El transplante' the best script in Prague in 1968.
13. Unfortunately, the film was a failure on the international front since American International Pictures' promotion and distribution failed to reach contemporary American audiences. The film was released for the drive-in circuit as a 'screen shocker' and a 'suspenseful mystery', as part of a double-bill feature with *The Incredible Two-Headed Transplant* (Anthony M. Lanza 1971). Nowadays, *The House that Screamed* is a classic of Euro-horror fare and has been labelled a proto-slasher.
14. In an interview with Juan Tébar, 'Dickens, Hitchcock y . . . Juan Tébar', published in *Nuevo Fotogramas*, the author said that it was originally conceived as a 'tale written for the series *Historias para no dormir*. Chicho thought it was an interesting project that could lend itself to the cinema' (Anon. 1969: 12).
15. The plot of the novel shares similarities with Ray Bradbury's short story 'Zero Ground', published in the collection *The Illustrated Man* (1951). In 'Zero Ground', a group of children play at invasion until the adults realise it is not a game.
16. Appositely, Tom and Evelyn hire the boat from Enrique, who is played by Luis Ciges, a regular in horror films of the period. Like Ibáñez Serrador's cameo, Ciges's presence acts as a harbinger of horrors to come.
17. Fiander's name was associated with Hammer through *Dr Jekyll and Sister Hyde* (Roy Ward Baker 1971) and *Dr Phibes Rises Again* (Robert Fuest 1972).
18. See, for example, the Seville edition of the newspaper *ABC*, 2 May 1976, p. 4.

19. When the film was rereleased in 1983, *El país* film critic Diego Galán argued that it was not successful for two reasons: firstly, because 'it was distant from the tense polemics that marked the last years of Francoism'; and secondly, because it committed an outrage against bourgeois taste: 'watching a group of murderous children does not correspond to the conventions of good bourgeois taste which still mythologizes childhood as a period of innocence' (1983).
20. The locations on the coast were Sitges, Almuñécar and Menorca. Ciruelos, situated in inland Toledo, was used as the main location for the scenes that take place in the fictional Almanzora.
21. These two films were also literary adaptations: *Village of the Damned* is based on John Wyndam's *The Midwich Cuckoos* (1957) and *The Birds* on Daphne du Maurier's novella of the same name written in 1952.
22. See, for instance, 'Franco's Kids: Geopolitics and Post-dictatorship in *¿Quién puede matar a un niño?*' (Steinberg 2006).

4. THE HORROR CYCLE OF ELOY DE LA IGLESIA (1971–3)

An approach to Eloy de la Iglesia's horror cycle of 1971–3 began to form itself during the course of a research visit to the Spanish Film Institute in Madrid, and arose from what I now relate in the form of two anecdotes: the first is based on a brief exchange I had with one of the archivists in the Archivo Gráfico unit when I requested the pressbooks for the films *El techo de cristal, La semana del asesino, Nadie oyó gritar* and *Una gota de sangre para morir amando*; the second comes in the form of a cartoon published in the popular film magazine *Nuevo Fotogramas* in October 1971 by Perich (Jaume Perich Escala (1941–95)). When I requested the pressbooks, I described these films as horror. I was promptly taken to task by the archivist, who corrected my generic labelling with a stern: 'No. Look, sonny, these are thrillers.' Apart from the generational difference, her reply revealed different experiences of watching and consuming de la Iglesia's films. Of course, the films in question are (psychological) thrillers; but they are not limited to the thriller format. For the archivist, they were still firmly located in their original context of production and reception as thrillers, whose main features were considered to be intrigue, suspense and crime, whereas my first experience of a de la Iglesia film, *La semana del asesino*, had been mediated through its reputation as a 'video nastie' in the 1980s and, subsequently, as a cult classic of European horror. In fact, a consideration of the reception of de la Iglesia's films in different periods and beyond Spain reveals fascinating reconfigurations in the understanding of their fluid generic status and their circulation from the early 1970s to the present, where *La semana del asesino* and *Una gota de sangre para morir*

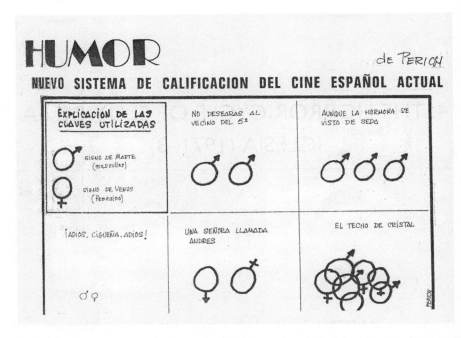

Figure 19   Cartoonist Perich coming to grips with the new Spanish rating system and getting in a muddle when trying to account for Eloy de la Iglesia's *El techo de cristal*.

amando are packaged as cult Euro-horror. The second anecdote began in the Film Institute's reading room, when I was scouring *Nuevo Fotogramas* for the period 1971 to 1974 and came across a cartoon which satirised Spain's system of film classification (see Figure 19). Cartoonist Perich proposes a new rating system based on two categories: the male sign ♂ and the female sign ♀. The cartoon is certainly a good barometer of the filmic production of those years; this is the time of changing attitudes toward sex and its cinematic representation, with phenomena such as 'destape' and 'landismo',[1] as well as of the now-legendary journeys undertaken by Spanish filmgoers to Perpignan, over the border in France, to watch censored films. In Perich's rating system, the comedies *No desearás al vecino del quinto / Thou Shall Not Covet Thy Fifth Floor Neighbour* (Ramón Fernández 1970) and *Aunque la hormona se vista de seda / No Matter What the Hormone Dresses In* (Vicente Escrivá 1971) qualify as excessively masculine film products (♂♂ male signs and ♂♂♂ male signs, respectively), whilst the rating of *¡Adiós cigüeña, adiós! / Bye-bye, Stork* (Manuel Summers 1971) points to the film's teenage protagonists, who have to deal with a teenage pregnancy (♂♀). The title *Una señora llamada Andrés / A Lady Called Andrés* (Julio Buch 1970) speaks for itself – a simple inversion of signs. Finally, de la Iglesia's 1971 *El techo de cristal* presents a confusing picture: a disorderly cluster of male and female signs suggesting an orgy of sexual desire and relationships. Perich's comic image is symptomatic of the critical responses to de la Iglesia's filmic production of the late Francoist period, since many critics found his cinema confused and confusing in its deviation from contemporary filmic production and from the heterosexual norm through its engagement with the cinematic possibility of sexual relationships that escape mainstream representations of sexuality. Archivist and cartoon(ist) had both pointed up the difficulty of neatly classifying de la Iglesia's cinema, either in terms of its generic affiliations – the focus of the first half of this chapter – or its gender representations – the focus of the latter half.

De la Iglesia's treatment of sexual experiences and relationships, and of violence, upset the Spanish censors, who found his films gratuitous and unpalatable. Indisputably, his 'gross depictions of physical, moral and sexual violence' linked him to the 'vile rabble' of genre filmmakers whose low-brow wares were condemned by censors and mainstream critics alike as a 'maelstrom of crime and erotic morbidity' (*Cine para leer* 1974: 21), to refer back to the official evaluation of Spanish horror production with which we opened Chapter 1. Contemporary coverage of the director's work was invariably accompanied by the terms sex and violence: cultural magazine *Triunfo* published an interview with the title 'Eloy de la Iglesia y la violencia' (Lara et al. 1973), while Gubern and Font framed their interview with de la Iglesia with the title 'Erotismo enfermizo' ('Morbid eroticism') in their book *Un cine para el cadalso. 40 años de censura cinematográfica en España* (1975). As Paul Julian Smith states in his seminal analysis of 'Eloy de la Iglesia's Cinema of Transition' (1992: 129–62), which focuses on the director's post-1975 films,[2] 'the central paradox of the director's work' is 'the curious combination of mass technique (sex and violence) and personal, indeed idiosyncratic, obsessions' (1992: 136). While de la Iglesia's films of the mid-1970s and early 1980s have been the subject of a number of critical studies over the last two decades,[3] in particular his representation of homosexuality and his use of the generic codes and conventions of popular genres, especially that of melodrama in such films as *Los placeres ocultos* ('Hidden Pleasures' 1976), *El diputado* ('MP' 1978) and *El pico* ('The Shoot' 1983), the films under discussion in this chapter have been largely overlooked and no attempts have been made to establish links between his pre- and post-1975 production. As Smith rightly observed in relation to de la Iglesia's Cinema of Transition, 'critical abuse of de la Iglesia has been [. . .] motivated by an inability to '"read" his use of genre' (1992: 130). As an affiliated member of the illegal Spanish Communist Party (PCE) and a homosexual director, de la Iglesia's political and sexual orientations were clearly outside of official Francoist discourse. In the highly politicised context of the periods of Transition and early democracy, de la Iglesia was able to produce an explicitly 'homophile cinema', to use Mira's term (2004: 223). But in the late Francoist period he could only intimate and articulate it through the vehicle of the horror and the thriller genres. Andrew Willis has recently discussed de la Iglesia's use of the horror genre in *La semana del asesino* as a means of articulating 'challenges to the dominant ideas and beliefs' (2005: 167) of Francoist institutions: in other words, as a vessel for policitised ideas and social critiques of contemporary issues such as sexuality and class.[4]

De la Iglesias's trademark use of shock, terror, horror and other exploitative pleasures gave his films a graphic and visceral style which contemporary censors and mainstream critics found difficult to reconcile (and stomach). As the director himself observed in the *Triunfo* interview 'Eloy de la Iglesia y la violencia', 'Cinema is the manifestation of a state of mind which can sometimes be horny [. . .], other times transcendental, and at other times bad humoured' and 'I express myself "a lo bestia"' (de la Iglesia in Lara et al. 1973: 63). This emphatic 'a lo bestia', translated as 'crudely' or 'vulgarly', certainly describes a cinematic style which lacks proper aesthetic distance. De la Iglesia's films display moments of visual excess in their eroticisation of the male body and male sexuality which not only defy the conventions and reading protocols of contemporary Spanish mainstream cinema but also pose interesting questions around representations of the male body and the production of masculine identity in popular culture during the late Francoist period. The excessive – almost belligerent – presentation of masculine flesh 'as a source of both considerable pleasure and considerable anxiety' (Shapiro 1993: 158) is the focus of the second half of this chapter, which pays particular attention to the ways in which de la Iglesia inscribes a 'homosexual affect' (Smith 1992: 138) through the use of *mise-en-scène*, cinematography and casting. In specific episodes of *La semana del asesino*, *Nadie oyó gritar* and *Una gota de sangre para morir amando*, the films display moments of visual excess in the eroticisation and shocking treatment of the male body. The cinematic bodies and affective moments present in de la Iglesia's pre-1975 films articulate a homosexual discourse whose direct treatment would have been unthinkable within contemporary Francoist structures of censorship and domination. By traversing the registers of text, genre, star image and cinematic traditions, it will be possible to examine the workings of the homosexual diegesis (for instance, the homosexually motivated voyeurism inscribed in certain scenes) and those moments that allow us to think otherwise about these films and their gay male (sub)cultural value in the context of late Francoism.

GENERIC AFFILIATIONS

El techo de cristal, La semana del asesino, Nadie oyó gritar and *Una gota de sangre para morir amando* offered audiences a range of different generic features evoking various pleasures and emotions: mystery, horror, fear, shock, romance. This range can be demonstrated by considering the ways in which the films were sold to audiences in pressbooks, as well as the ways in which they were understood by two types of audience and institutions – namely, censors and mainstream film critics – by drawing on censorship files and film reviews, respectively. The generic understanding of *La semana del asesino* and *Una gota de sangre para morir amando* has changed in different periods as these films have been variously (re)classified.

Conceived, produced and released within a period of three years, these four films demonstrate similar production values – notwithstanding the fact that different production companies were involved in the projects – and shared narrative, stylistic and generic features. Their production, distribution and exhibition ran into serious censorship difficulties which constrained and shaped their reception. The distribution and exhibition patterns of *La semana del asesino*, *Nadie oyó gritar* and *Una gota de sangre para morir amando*, for instance, were badly affected by the censors; the release of *La semana del asesino* suffered a delay of more than two years, while *Una gota de sangre para morir amando* and *Nadie oyó gritar*, which were produced and shot in 1972, were not exhibited until 22 August and 27 August 1973, respectively (this double release – and in the middle of a Spanish summer – makes little sense in marketing terms, and also constitutes a type of censorship). Budgets and shooting schedules varied from 7,870,450 pesetas and forty-two days for *El techo de cristal* to the sizeable 24,500,000 pesetas and eight weeks for *Una gota de sangre para morir amando*, an international co-production from Spanish José Frade Producciones Internacionales and French Intercontinental Productions.[5] For three of these films, de la Iglesia and his producers joined forces with two Spanish popular film stars and veterans of the Spanish screen, Carmen Sevilla (1930–) and Vicente Parra (1931–97), then in their early forties, who saw their participation as an opportunity to move away from their previous roles; Sevilla had been the protagonist of folkloric musicals and comedies and Parra a matinee idol in period costume films. Even though they were cast against type (and perhaps because of this), their star cachet was a selling point for distributors and exhibitors, the subject of gossip and press coverage, and a potential source of spectatorial pleasure derived from their erotic charge.[6] Carmen Sevilla was the female lead in *El techo de cristal*, Vicente Parra was the male lead in *La semana del asesino* – as well as its producer – and both were paired in *Nadie oyó gritar*. Despite the films bringing Sevilla and Parra together, the controversies surrounding the extensive cuts to and delayed release of *La semana del asesino* and the accusations of plagiarism thrown at *Una gota de sangre para morir amando* meant that their box-office performances were limited. *Nadie oyó gritar* frankly underperformed (334,030 spectators and 65,034.59 euros) and, when compared to the popular success of *El techo de cristal* (1,053,574 spectators and 186,290.48 euros) and *Una gota de sangre para morir amando* (618,265 spectators and 151,445.41 euros), *La semana del asesino* (334,827 spectators and 57,696.77 euros) was a relative commercial failure.

The 'crude look' of de la Iglesia's films was created and maintained by a fairly consistent team of technicians, whose names frequently appear in the credits of popular genre products of the 1970s and early 1980s. As director of photography, Francisco Fraile can be credited for the sense of suffocating horror that pervades *El techo de cristal* and *Nadie oyó gritar*, and successfully conveyed a futuristic atmosphere in *Una gota de sangre para morir amando*, while Raul Artigot's cinematography was responsible for communicating the sense of alienation and mounting despair of the main character Marcos in *La semana del asesino*. Concurrent with their collaboration with de la Iglesia, both Fraile and Artigot were involved in the production of other Spanish horror films (Fraile in *Dr Jekyll y el hombre lobo* (1972) and *Trágica ceremonia en Villa Alexander* (Riccardo Freda 1972), and Artigot in *La maldición de Frankenstein* (1972)). José Luis Matesanz in *La semana del asesino* and *Una gota de sangre para morir amando* began what would prove to be a long-standing collaboration with de la Iglesia throughout the 1970s and 1980s. But continuity in terms of the films' formal and thematic concerns lay in the screenwriting, and here the creative partnership of de la Iglesia and Antonio Fos was pivotal in creating a sense of cohesion across the four films in this suspenseful horror cycle through recurring plotlines, the deployment of genre formulas and the re-presentation of key motifs and themes. (The only exception is the multi-authored script of *Una gota de sangre para morir amando*.)[7] The common threads and motivations running through the films are acknowledged by the director in an interview:

> these stories can be reduced to one: a story about death, love, and a peculiar 'voyeurism' where characters constantly pursue each other, watch each other. I tell my obsessions through a prism of repression: my own repression, my way of expressing myself in life, and an institutionalized repression related to my surroundings, which can be seen in the ways we communicate with each other [. . .] I am conscious that I live in a society full of repressed people, and that – within this society – I belong to an elite which is even more repressed. [In my films] this repression manifests itself in an aggressive manner. (de la Iglesia in Lara et al. 1973: 62)

Repression and marginalisation, more specifically 'the social processes by which certain groups are marginalized' (Smith 1992: 141), cut across de la Iglesia's body of work.

Let us now look at the plotlines created by de la Iglesia and Fos to familiarise ourselves with their narrative scenarios before examining the promotional material created and distributed by the producers to market the films. In *El techo de cristal* Marta (Carmen Sevilla), a lonely housewife living in an isolated house in the countryside, becomes suspicious of and obsessed with the noises in the flat above her where Julia (Patty Shepard) and her sick husband live. She decides to investigate. Marta shares her suspicions with the owner of the house, Ricardo (Dean Selmier), a young sculptor and photographer who has a studio on the ground floor, with whom she soon becomes intimate. But Ricardo watches and desires both Marta and Julia, keeping a photographic record of the plot's various love triangles and infidelities, and masterminding their tragic outcomes. In *Nadie oyó gritar* Elisa (Carmen Sevilla) witnesses her next-door neighbour Miguel (Vicente Parra) disposing of his mistress's body down a lift shaft; rather than kill her, Miguel decides to kidnap Elisa and forces her to assist him in moving the corpse and dumping it in a lake. *La semana del asesino* (see Figure 20) and *Una gota de sangre para morir amando* (see Figure 21) present us with two serial-killer narratives, male and female, respectively. *La semana del asesino* follows the tragic events surrounding Marcos (Vicente Parra), a factory worker who lives with his brother Esteban in a shack in the suburbs of Madrid. One night, on the way back home with his girlfriend Paula (Emma Cohen), he has a row with a taxi driver, to whom he delivers a fatal blow. He then embarks on a number of brutal killings in order to avoid detection by the police and to cover his previous crimes. Moving away from the realistic contemporary settings of the other films, *Una gota de sangre para morir amando* is set in a violent near-future world where leather-clad, whip-wielding sadist gangs rule the streets and the medical authorities conduct secret mind-control experiments; against this dystopian background, a beautiful nurse (Sue Lyon) seduces young men, takes them back to her apartment and kills them. How were these narratives of murder and violence sold to Spanish audiences? And how were they understood and received by the official institutions of censorship and mainstream film criticism?

Official posters for *El techo de cristal* focused on the erotic appeal of its Spanish female star, Carmen Sevilla, pictured in seductive semi-nude poses caressing a cat (see Figure 22), or pitted against the other female lead, Patty Shepard, who at the time was mainly known to Spanish audiences for her modelling work. However, the pressbook and trade publications such as *Cine-Asesor* underlined the film's generic affiliations and advised distributors and exhibitors to sell it as a 'mystery drama' and a 'suspense film'. In its commercial assessment of the film, *Cine-Asesor* predicted that the film would yield a 'GOOD BOX-OFFICE PERFORMANCE' in cinemas frequented by 'mystery and suspense aficionados' and informed prospective buyers that the film delivered on two fronts: firstly, as an 'exemplary achievement of a cinema of consumption well above what is usually produced in our country', and, secondly, as a successful 'cinema of imitation where there are influences of Hitchcock

Figure 20   The divided self of Marcos, main protagonist and serial killer in *La semana del asesino*.

Figure 21   The female avenger and serial killer in *Una gota de sangre para morir amando*.

Figure 22   Spanish female star Carmen Sevilla venturing into thrilling territory in *El techo de cristal*.

and other directors of the [suspense] genre' (*Cine-Asesor* 1971: 102). It was precisely the film's commercialism, as well as the formulaic nature of popular genres, that the censors condemned. Dismissed as but another example of an overly commercial film culture, de la Iglesia's project was deemed unworthy of official financial support: namely, the 'Interés Especial' (Special Interest) award. The censors' report (1970) described *El techo de cristal* as 'a story of suspense peppered with some notes of lab-designed eroticism and a few crimes', concluding that it was just 'an ordinary horror and murder mystery film'. Contemporary reviewers also read the film through its affiliative strategies, although many devoted a significant part of their reviews to Carmen Sevilla's forceful performance. The *El Alcázar* and *ABC* critics stressed the director's creation of mystery and suspense, whereas those in *Arriba*, *Nuevo Diario* and *Ya* extended the film's generic affiliations and pleasures: the film is 'premised on eroticism and horror' (Anon. 1971b); it 'belongs to the genre of suspense but with ingredients borrowed from horror cinema and a diffuse and timid eroticism' (Anon. 1971d); and the denouement of the plot brings together 'elements from horror and crime films' (Cebollada 1971). Critics routinely referenced individual films (*Gaslight* (George Cukor 1944)) and suspense auteurs (Clouzot and Hitchcock), as well as contemporary Spanish films which had mixed crime horror and suspense effectively (*La residencia*, *Las crueles / The Exquisite Cadaver* (Vicente Aranda 1969) and *Marta* (José Antonio Nieves Conde 1971)), to stake out the generic contours of *El techo de cristal*. With de la Iglesia having just two previous features under his belt (*Algo amargo en la boca* (1969) and *Cuadrilatero* (1970)), magazine *Nuevo Fotogramas* considered that this third film placed the director among 'the European specialists of [a cinema of] cruelty' (Picas 1971b: 41) – whether the journalist was here drawing an explicit parallel with Artaud's theatre of cruelty and its transformative function, or whether he saw de la Iglesia's use of violence and shocking imagery as just as unsettling as that of Buñuel, Clouzot or Hitchcock remains unexplained. If we read the pressbook for clues to determine its generic pedigree, strategies of suspense and cruelty and specific thematic concerns are flagged up in the synopsis and notes. The setting proposes a classic country house whodunnit scenario, and a victimised female protagonist links Marta to the classic 'paranoid woman' film of the 1940s; complicitous relationships, sexual intrigues, voyeuristic activities and a shocking ending, which, according to the pressbook synopsis, 'is the culminating point of a diabolical and cruel plot', align *El techo de cristal* with elements of the plot structure of Clouzot's *Les Diaboliques* (1955) and the voyeuristic portrayals of photographer L. B. Jeffries in Hitchcock's *Rear Window* (1954), as well as aspiring filmmaker Mark Lewis in Michael Powell's *Peeping Tom* (1960).

'Have you ever heard of voyeurism?' Ricardo asks Marta in one of the central scenes of *El techo de cristal*. His definition is simple: 'Voyeurs are people who get a kick out of spying on the most intimate, the most personal secrets of other people.' He further expands his views on the term by suggesting that nearly everybody has this voyeur instinct:

> if not, what do you think is the object of cinema, of photography [. . .] ? Someone once said that photography is truth twenty-four times a second. It is a pretty phrase but I think it's false. It's simply a release, an escape valve for this voyeur instinct.

Perhaps Roberto's – and, by extension, de la Iglesia's – meditations on looking and the qualities of the medium as a voyeuristic practice lack the subtleties of Hitchcock or Powell. The scene just described in *El techo de cristal* is somewhat heavy-handed. But it is nevertheless indicative of de la Iglesia's exploitation of the physical and objectifying qualities of the medium, from the spectatorial pleasure derived from watching the star–protagonist to his exploration of different cinematic looks and camera voyeurism, or the morbid urge to gaze, through the codes and conventions of horror. 'Eyes watching horror' (1992: 185), to borrow Carol J. Clover's expression, is a recurrent theme in the cycle of de la Iglesia, reflected in the director's manipulation of the spectator's viewing positions. In *La semana del asesino*, for example, voyeurism is homosexually motivated and therefore transgressive of conventional heterosexual scenarios and generic conventions, offering a challenge to institutional censorship.

    La semana del asesino was a controversial film from various moral and artistic angles, provoking much debate among censors, critics and journalists concerning issues of censorship, quality and taste. *Una gota de sangre para morir amando* would prove to be equally polemical. When the original script for *La semana del asesino* was submitted to the Spanish censorship board under the title 'Auténtico caldo de cultivo' ('Genuine Meat Broth'), de la Iglesia's project was rejected on the grounds that it was 'an accumulation of gruesomeness' (18 August 1971). The censors' reports recommended that, in order for the film to be viable, the following aspects had to be changed: the fact that 'the murderer goes unpunished at the end'; the role of Néstor, who is 'a character with a marked homosexual personality'; and the film's bad taste, in particular and in an obvious reference to the title, the inclusion of scenes where the murderer disposes of body parts in the slaughterhouse where he works and these make their way into the production line for the broth, ready for public consumption. The initial censorship file classified the film as 'horror' because of its 'accumulation of crimes and blood'. A revised script submitted a month later and entitled *La semana del asesino* was also rejected (15 September 1971) on the grounds that the plotline was 'too gruesome', the 'dialogues and situations are too risqué' and in general many scenes 'are of vile taste'; there is a recommendation that the producers suppress the scenes of 'bad taste and *tremendismo*'[8] and tone down the 'signs of eroticism'. Another censor's report conceded that the violence included in the film was justified in terms of the conventions of the genre to which the film belonged but that the 'sexually ambiguous Néstor' was unacceptable. The project was still refused a release certificate. The final script contained a disclaimer in which screenwriters de la Iglesia and Fos affirmed that 'There is not the slightest sign of homosexuality in Néstor' ('No hay un sólo atisbo de homosexualidad en Néstor'). Moreover, they wanted to avoid any confusion that Néstor might cause: 'even though we believe that Néstor as a character is perfectly defined in the script, we are adding this note to avoid any possible confusion and misrepresentations concerning the behaviour of said character.' And the note concludes:

> Néstor's curiosity and interest in approaching and becoming intimate with Marcos is purely and simply motivated by being involved in the most exciting game a character of a certain intellectual level can find himself in: a murder intrigue; he can talk, walk alongside, ask and get to know a man who has killed without him suspecting that he who seems like a friend knows all along that he is a murderer. There is no other interest in their relationship whatsoever.

Disclaimers and all, the film was given an official (4) classification and defined as 'gravemente peligrosa' ('severely dangerous'). Enmeshed in controversy for two years, *La semana del asesino* was not released nationwide until 1974; the Francoist censorship mutilated the film with sixty-two cuts (up to a hundred, according to other sources) and imposed a narrative closure whereby the murderer hands himself in to the police. As the synopsis in the pressbook reads, 'Marcos, disgusted with himself, DOES NOT WANT TO KILL ANY MORE! He feels cornered by his own crimes. He goes to a phone box, dials 091, says his name, and confesses his crimes, begging the police to detain him.' De la Iglesia protested about the fate of his character and of his film in interviews: 'to be forced to make this man call the police is to betray him as a character. It is ultimately an imposed betrayal' (de la Iglesia in Olano 1972: 7).

Whereas the title *La semana del asesino* and the synopsis alike frame Marcos as a serial killer, the promotional campaign cued different pleasures to appeal to different audiences.[9] Taglines offered a range of pleasures, emotions and affiliative strategies. Many stressed the effect of the film on audiences, warning about its affective power: 'A film totally forbidden to those sensitive to brutality'; 'Sadistic in its subject matter, brutal in its form. Don't watch this film if you are impressionable,' and 'A macabre week of events. You will never forget this film.' One of the main marketing ploys suggested in the pressbook was to drum up interest in the tradition of masters of suspense Clouzot and Hitchcock by allowing no one into the cinema once the film had begun: 'Strict punctuality is required. Violence starts off from the very beginning.' Other taglines connected the on-screen content with reality and truthfulness, whether in the form of a question – 'Could what you are going to see in *La semana del asesino* happen in real life?' – or the juxtaposition of certain horror effects with the veneer of realist representation – 'Brutal, chilling, but truthful'. The protagonist, Marcos, was likened to the archetypal symbol of fratricide – 'Marcos: A contemporary Cain' – lending the story both universal appeal and a local inflection, since the Cain reference invoked a Spanish literary tradition which used the biblical story as a symbol for recent Spanish history. The fluid generic legibility of the film was also mobilised by the director in promotional interviews, where he defined his production as 'a commercial and popular film. First of all, it is a film with humour. It is also a bloody film, and, above all, a love story' (Anon. 1972a: 13). The love story alluded to refers to that between the two male protagonists, Marcos and Néstor, and was furtively presented in the tagline 'What type of relationship united Marcos and Néstor?' The film's violence and its notorious relationship with censorship was an aspect exploited in full-page advertisements in trade journals and the daily press: 'Perhaps one of the most violent films ever made in Spain' and 'Finally, the most polemic film in the history of Spanish cinema is put on release.' The very same affective qualities underlined by the producers were brandished by *Cine-Asesor* with clear warnings about the nature of the film with the ultimate aim of deterring exhibitors from programming the film, clearly another type of censorship: 'This film is definitely gruesome. It does not avoid bloody effects [. . .] Due to its excesses, the film is even unpleasant, especially for sensitive spectators' (*Cine-Asesor* 1974: 82).

Contemporary reviewers read the film through different generic and aesthetic lenses. While the mainstream daily press view it in relation to the realist frameworks associated with Spanish literary traditions and works such as *La familia de Pascual Duarte* ('its "tremendismo" and the desolation of the main protagonists remind us of a type of Spanish literature rooted in our tradition' (Rubio 1974)), publications such as *Nuevo Fotogramas* and specialist film magazine *Terror Fantastic* read it through the lens of horror. The former described the film as a 'Grand Guignol', which reflected in a graphic manner 'the impotence and isolation of the proletariat' (1972d: 70) in order to link the film to contemporary social issues and the director's ideological association with Marxism; the latter criticised the director's use of the horror genre because *La semana del asesino* fell between two stools: on the one hand, 'intellectual horror (through the possible reasons to account for Marcos' uncontrollable murderous conduct) and, on the other hand, pure gore-horror (preferably bloody red)' (Montaner 1972d: 55).

Together with de la Iglesia's perceived moral and sexual sordidness, his crude, visceral style gripped and exasperated critics in equal measure. Some recognised that his brutish and sensationalist subject matter demanded an aggressive and primitive filmic language, or, in other words, an aesthetic counter to the bourgeois cultural values characteristic of official film culture. 'De la Iglesia has invented a "poor cinema" gushing with content. A vulgar cinema for a vulgar world' (1972d: 70), declared one *Nuevo Fotogramas* journalist. In *La semana del asesino*, he captures 'fear, disgust, the stench of body decomposition' and 'the impotence and loneliness of the proletariat [. . .], of a man mocked, despised, disregarded, exploited' (1972d: 70). In contrast, his detractors disparaged his 'wearisome obsession with the use of extreme close-ups in the most inappropriate moments' and his editing technique, which at best denoted a 'lack of rigour in the coordination of scenes' (Peláez 1974a), and at worst was synaesthetically described as 'screeching' (Rubio 1974). Notwithstanding the role played by the censors in the final edited product, de la Iglesia's use of this aspect of the cinematic medium calls attention to larger thematic and aesthetic concerns, which are addressed in my analysis of *La semana del asesino* and *Una gota de sangre para morir amando* later on in this chapter.

Una gota de sangre para morir amando suffered less than *La semana del asesino* at the hands of the censors. But it was savagely attacked by some critics on account of what they considered to be a mendacious relationship between de la Iglesia's film and Stanley Kubrick's *A Clockwork Orange* (1971), to the point that de la Iglesia had to send a letter to *ABC* newspaper to defend himself against accusations of plagiarism; this letter was followed by an interview with the director in an obvious attempt to clear his name.[10] But let us not get ahead of ourselves in the chronology of events and all the communications pertaining de la Iglesia's controversial film. When the first script for *Una gota de sangre para morir amando* (entitled 'La agonía del siglo XX' (The Death Throes of the 20th Century)) was submitted to the censorship board, the Ministry of Information and Tourism informed producer José Frade that the film was authorised with the proviso that the director showed more restraint 'as far as sadism, violence, homosexuality and eroticism' were concerned. Specific scenes were singled out: the amorous rapture of nurse Ana and Tony the gigolo, the filming of the TV-spot in which the effeminate advertising director directs the poses of a scantily clad male model whose crotch is foregrounded in a slow zoom, and the episode at a club where a homosexual couple are getting too close for the censors' comfort. Regardless of the film's catalogue of perversions and graphic depiction of violence, the producers applied for the 'Special Interest' award, claiming that 'La agonía del siglo XX' 'contained virtuous social and educational values for this is a work that takes a look at the pernicious results of irrational and anti-social behaviour' and suggested that its generic affiliation – that is, the codes and conventions of the science-fiction genre – ought to be read as a 'didactic warning for the younger generation'.

SPANISH HORROR FILM

Needless to say, the authorities did not see the moral and artistic merit of this admonitory fable nor did they seem to believe in the transformative power of the genre, so no award was given.

For many cultural commentators, *Una gota de sangre para morir amando* was a 'vulgar imitation' of *A Clockwork Orange* (1971) (Donald 1973: 72), a 'shameless and opportunistic' product (Peláez 1973b), 'an underdeveloped version of the type of cinema that is made elsewhere' and nothing less than 'a poor substitute for the forbidden product' (Briz 1973: 51). Imitation in these reviews begins to acquire the (pejorative) status of a distinct genre – Briz's review in *Cinestudio* is entitled '*Una gota de sangre para morir amando*: Cine de imitación'. For others it was blatant plagiarism of Kubrick's film, 'a spin-off of Kubrick's film', which could only be described with disapproving terms such as 'indigestible, leaden and gloomy' (Crespo 1973b). The film came to be popularly known in the industry and among audiences as 'la mandarina mecánica' (the clockwork tangerine), a scornful tag used in almost every review and that has since become a celebrated part of the cult fandom trivia surrounding the film. Many critics were also aggravated by the double standards of the censors, who had banned the release of Kubrick's film in Spain but had eventually sanctioned *Una gota de sangre para morir amando*. De la Iglesia's alleged rip-off of *A Clockwork Orange* was at the heart of many a review, although narrative and aesthetic similarities were not always substantiated with evidence beyond general references to the futuristic setting, the ultraviolent youth gang or the overall 'message' of Kubrick's film. Critics agreed that elements of *A Clockwork Orange* were grafted on to the crime story of a psychologically disturbed female nurse who becomes a serial killer of young men. Thus Crespo wrote in *Arriba* that 'a clockwork tangerine has been interpolated into a traditional and foolish intrigue about a female killer who murders her occasional lovers' (1973b), while Garcival in *ABC* explains it in terms of an axial and a coaxial relationship, 'an axial topic where a paranoid woman (Suy Lyon [sic]) is a female variant of Bluebeard' and 'a coaxial topic concerning a youth gang acting violently' (1973). However, this insertion, grafting or imitation can be read in terms of a strategic imitation and reworking of specific narrative and stylistic aspects of *A Clockwork Orange* which enabled de la Iglesia to inscribe a homosexual subtext and expose the treatment of homosexuals in contemporary scientific and contemporary discourses, as I will go on to argue in the second section of this chapter.

As has already been noted, de la Iglesia defended himself against accusations of plagiarism in the press. Questioned about the film's production history, the director explained that

> the first draft of the script was written with [co-screenwriter] Antonio Artero towards the end of 1970; earlier, I think, than the release of *A*

Clockwork Orange anywhere in the world, at least much earlier than me watching the film in London. When I first watched *A Clockwork Orange* I realized there were some possible lines of connection, especially at the level of style in relation to the futuristic atmosphere of the film. When we were writing the final version of the script, we included this futuristic atmosphere. (de la Iglesia in Flores 1973: 132)

Any other relation to the Kubrick film, de la Iglesia argued, was intended as a parodic homage: for example, 'the sequence in *A Clockwork Orange* where Kubrick himself can be seen on a television screen' (1973: 132). In *Una gota de sangre para morir amando* this takes the ironic form of a TV newsreader announcing the broadcasting of *A Clockwork Orange* and is evident in the clear intertextual reference to Kubrick's *Lolita* via de la Iglesia's casting of Sue Lyon, who had played Lolita in Kubrick's film; this connection is driven home in the episode where Lyon as Ana is reading Nabokov's *Lolita*. 'I am afraid', de la Iglesia continued, 'that those critics who have written that my film is plagiarism have not seen *A Clockwork Orange*, or if they have seen it, they have not understood it, and, consequently, have not understood mine' (1973: 132). When probed on his own understanding of and creative engagement with Kubrick's film, he conceded that the two films shared a similar thesis: namely, the analysis 'within the context of an immediate future of the decadence of the society we live in' (1973: 133). And the interview pushed de la Iglesia to elaborate on his thesis in relation to the immediate Spanish political and cultural context, to which he replied that his film explored 'the ideological decadence towards which today's youth is heading' and 'the violence of a society where consumerism, repression and the role of science are instruments to control man's freedom' (1973: 133).

Reading the contemporary reviews, one can grasp the difficulties critics and audiences had in pinning down the film's generic affiliations. *ABC*'s Garcival (1973) opened his review with a series of questions: 'What did the director intend to do when he undertook this project? [. . .] Is it a parody of *A Clockwork Orange*? [Is it] a statement against elemental brutality which can be found in literary and filmic science-fiction arguments?' Briz used the term 'pamphlet' – 'a vain and gratuitous pamphlet' (1973) – to define the film.[11] Unsympathetic reviewers aligned the film to 'the pathological trend typical of the latest Italian whodunit products reaching our screens' (Peláez 1973b) or 'those "thrillers" made in Italy' (Crespo 1973b). Readers sending their views to *Nuevo Fotogramas* seemed to be more sensitive to the film's conflation of genres. One particular reader takes pleasure in what is characterised as 'a crazy collage of diverse genres, from comedy to science-fiction, as well as drama, romance and suspense' (La pantera rosa 1973: 8). According to this same reader, audiences' reactions to the film were varied:

Some think it is an 'odd comedy' and laugh every now and again. Others are there expecting intrigue and are disappointed because there is none, and leave the cinema slightly annoyed. Something similar happens to those who were expecting morbidity for the film is generally chaste. And those of us who wanted to see a repetition of *A Clockwork Orange* – like myself – had to resign ourselves to watching a pale reflection of some aspects of Kubrick's film. (1973: 8)

A second reader provides us with another account of the effect of de la Iglesia's film on some audiences:

at the end of the showing there was the most memorable hiss I have ever heard [. . .] Patrons were agitated, angry, hysterical. [Their reaction made me realise that] the cinema of Eloy de la Iglesia was the most revolutionary thing [a director had] spat in my face. Violently revolutionary, viciously revolutionary. (Un gorila que no es Morgan disfrazado 1973: 13)

The Marxist vocabulary invoked by this reader bestows upon de la Iglesia's crude and violent cinema a transformative power which some leftist critics would also acknowledge during the Transition period. Thus, in the pages of *Triunfo*, Galán wrote that de la Iglesia's cinema was sexually revolutionary because it was 'an invitation to de-repress our most sophisticated sexual needs' (1976: 66).

More recently, the shock and horror elements at work in *Una gota de sangre para morir amando* and *La semana del asesino* have displaced some of the aesthetic, generic and thematic features identified by critics and audiences in their original context of reception and consumption. Neither *La semana del asesino* nor *Una gota de sangre para morir amando* was marketed solely as horror, as I have shown. Nor were these films identified solely as horror by contemporary critics. In the US, however, *La semana del asesino* was distributed by Hallmark Releasing as *The Apartment on the 13th Floor* and circulated on a double-bill with Jorge Grau's *Don't Open the Window* (a retitling of *The Living Dead at Manchester Morgue*) (1974) for the US drive-in circuit and the grindhouse cinemas of New York's Times Square, assuring from thereon its cultural afterlife in the American and British circuits of reception and consumption. Once VHS and DVD copies of *La semana del asesino* and *Una gota de sangre para morir amando* became available in the 1980s and 1990s, the films entered the canon of cult horror.

In the early 1980s, British censors slaughtered *La semana del asesino* for similar moral and aesthetic reasons to the Spanish censorship board. The film was released uncut on video by Intervision in November 1981 under the title

Cannibal Man for the American and European markets. Two years later it was included in the inventory of horror titles known as 'video nasties' and in July 1983 the film was banned. Under the 1984 Video Recordings Act, all videotapes for the home-video market had to be approved and classified by the British Board of Film Censors (BBFC) prior to release. Despite its retitling, there are no scenes of cannibalism in *Cannibal Man*. The reputation acquired by the 'video nasties' has made de la Iglesia's film a must-have cult movie among horror fans and collectors in the last twenty-five years, spurring a search for and consumption of other films made by the director at that time: namely, *El techo de cristal*, *Nadie oyó gritar* and *Una gota de sangre para morir amando*, which by association are viewed as low-budget Spanish horror. According to one of several websites devoted to the 'video nasties' phenomenon, the film 'stayed on the list throughout the panic and became one of the collectable DPP39s': that is to say, the 39 films, of a total of 74, withdrawn from the shops and successfully prosecuted by the Director of Public Prosecutions.[12] *La semana del asesino* highlights the relevance of cultural mediation and media consumption in constructions of the field of Spanish horror. The reception and consumption of films like *La semana del asesino*, as well as many other Spanish (and international) horror films, from the second half of the 1980s onwards are mediated through fandom culture, when video stores and mail order catalogues made inaccessible and unobtainable films available to Spanish and international viewers and fans alike. As Kendrick has argued in relation to the British market, American distributors flooded the British (and the Spanish) video market with low-budget films on video, heralding 'a new form of transnationalism emerging from the introduction of a new media technology: the VCR' (Kendrick 2004: 156).

The recent release by Anchor Bay and Blue Underground (November 2007) of an uncut and uncensored VHS and DVD copy of *Cannibal Man* flagged up the film's inclusion in the infamous UK video nasties dossier and played on its notoriety in the DVD trailer: 'The Cannibal Man, living in today's jungle, kills for his freedom' and invites the intrepid viewer to 'discover his unique ways of disposing of bodies'. Although *Cannibal Man* is invariably reviewed as horror on cult horror film websites, the film's generic classification is still fluid. Thus, while the Latarnia and horrordvds forums place the film and, by extension, de la Iglesia's cycle squarely in the horror genre ('a unique horror film to emerge from Spain' from 'director Iglesia's [sic] who made several films in the fantasy/horror/terror genres' (thelatarniaforums.yuku.com); 'Gore fiends may be satisfied with this one given it has a fair amount of bloody scenes' (horrordvds.com)), the reviewers at classic-horror.com go beyond the boundaries of horror and into the porous categories of exploitation and horror / thriller, describing it as 'a brutal, bloody exploitation film' which offers 'a violent study of madness and a shrewd social satire'. Elsewhere, 'it is not the gut-munching splatterfest you might expect. Instead it's a truthful, intelligent and deliberately paved study of one man's descent into madness [. . .] It's not really a crime film and not really a horror film' (eccentric-cinema.com). Similarly, *Una gota de sangre para morir amando* is associated with various genre categories on cult horror film websites. Video and DVD outlets have exploited the resemblance between de la Iglesia's and Kubrick's films; Empire Video, for example, released the film as *Clockwork Terror* in the American market and attempted to sell it almost as a sequel to *A Clockwork Orange* ('After Clockwork Orange Comes Clockwork Terror. Brutal Savagery in a Future World!'). In 2004, Pagan / Hanzibar Films released the British cut in a 98–minute DVD version under the title *Murder in a Blue World* and featured a bloody Sue Lyon on the box cover. More recently, DVD label Substance has commercialised it as a 'controversial shocker' and aligned it visually with the mad-doctor subgenre, whereas Cinema Sewer Collection markets the film as part of a package of varied European exploitation fare (*The Vampire's Night Orgy* (León Klimovsky 1972), *The Coming of Sin* (José Larraz 1977) and *Rectuma* (Mark Pirro 2004)), referring to it as a 'low-budget Spanish sci-fi thriller'.

Homosexual Intimations

As I explained when discussing the problems de la Iglesia had with the censors during the filming of *La semana del asesino*, he and co-screenwriter Fos were pressed to include a disclaimer concerning the representation of Néstor's sexuality: 'There is not the slightest sign of homosexuality in Néstor.' The last section of this chapter examines the ways in which de la Iglesia inscribes a homosexual subtext on both formal and stylistic levels in *La semana del asesino*, *Una gota de sangre para morir amando* and *Nadie oyó gritar*. The implicit and explicit inclusion of the homosexual subtext is achieved through a number of strategies: the acknowledgement of the homosexual gaze and homosexually motivated voyeurism through point of view and framing, the casting of specific actors who were either homosexual or read as camp, as in the case of Vicente Parra, the stylistic irruption through *mise-en-scène*, cinematography and editing of alternative meanings associated with gay male subculture, and oblique references to contemporary legal and medical discourses on homosexuality. Returning to the example of *La semana del asesino*, the imposition of a neat denouement whereby the murderer hands himself over to the police can be interpreted as an attempt to master the text by closing off its narrative possibilities. And yet, an analysis of *La semana del asesino* and *Una gota de sangre para morir amando* reveals aesthetic and political tensions that remain unresolved.

How does the homosexual diegesis work in *La semana del asesino*, then? Cinematography, editing, *mise-en-scène* and dialogue intimate a homosexuality that cannot be openly conveyed. Marcos and Néstor are characters thrown together by the proximity of their dwellings, as we learn in the opening sequence. The start of the film proposes a scenario of classic scopophilic lures conveyed through voyeuristic point-of-view shots. Half-naked, Marcos walks around his house while he is listening to the radio (a piece of news on Torcuato Fernández Miranda, who was Secretario Nacional del Movimiento[13] between 1969 and 1973) and smoking a cigarette. The camera focuses on a series of objects: a sofa, photographs of female pin-ups covering the wall, which are very like the images one would find in contemporary popular film magazines such as *Cine en 7 días* and *Nuevo Fotogramas*, and a set of tools. Restless, Marcos decides to lie down on the sofa and focuses his gaze on the pin-ups. A cut to the exterior is followed by a tilting plane showing the high-rise tenement block, crudely suggesting Marcos's erection. From his balcony Néstor witnesses Marcos's sexual stimulation through his binoculars, focusing (and zooming in) on Marcos's agitated and sweaty face as he reaches climax – extreme close-ups of his eyes, mouth, forehead and hair show Néstor's sexual interest as well as voyeuristic pleasure. The heterosexual visual economy proposed at the beginning of the opening sequence, therefore, is immediately disrupted by the sexually suggestive quality of editing – the editing in of homosexual desire – which turns our attention to the desire of Néstor. The blatantly fetishistic and voyeuristic first moments subvert a traditional heterosexual mode of narration and complicate gendered patterns of audience identification. The demarcation of a heterosexual or homosexual desire is produced by the camera and the formal manipulation of editing devices.

The relationship between Marcos and Néstor develops through a series of encounters. The ambiguous nature of that relationship is underscored by one of the publicity taglines suggested in the pressbook: 'What type of friendship did Marcos and Néstor have?' De la Iglesia described the film as 'an impossible love story' (de la Iglesia in Olano 1972: 7). Given that many contemporary critics questioned the plausibility of the characters' friendship, it is hardly surprising that reviews made no reference to their relationship in terms of romantic 'love'. For example, Peláez in *El Alcázar* expressed his views in a very dogmatic manner: the film contains 'unbelievable dialogues and implausible scenarios between the worker [the physical Marcos] and the ambiguous student [the intellectual Néstor]' (1974a: n.p.). *Terror Fantastic*'s critic Montaner argued that characterisation and motivation were unrealistic: 'if it is necessary to tell the story of an introvert sexual psychopath and with homosexual tendencies, let's do it in a serious manner' (1972d: 55), alluding implicitly to the stereotypical notion that homosexuals have a special affinity with psychotic killers; Montaner also resorted to humour (and exclamation marks) to dismiss the characters' relationship: 'It seems that love (!) redeemed [Marcos]' (1972d: 55).

We can certainly speculate about the nuances of Marcos's and Néstor's relationship by focusing on the dialogue and settings. Their encounters take place at night in the fields next to the blocks of flats and shanty houses when Néstor is walking his dog. Their encounters are accompanied by romantic music. As they become acquainted in these nightly encounters, they agree that they have more in common than they initially thought. 'I think that we are two peculiar guys' ('dos tipos raros'), confesses Néstor while he explains to Marcos his theory about what society expects from them:

> I should be with people of my own age, dancing in discos, on holiday and driving at 140 miles per hour along the highway. And you should be married, with a couple of kids, worrying about the next bill for the washing machine, and with the hope that someday you will be able to buy a small car.

Apart from their value as generational, social and cultural snippets of a modernising yet conventionally traditional Spain of the early 1970s, what is interesting here is Marcos's agreement and identification with Néstor: 'You are right: we are two peculiar guys.' This 'raro' (or 'rarito', 'bicho raro') carries similar connotations to terms such as 'marica' or 'loca', which in Spanish are derogative words for gay.

In the pressbook Néstor is described as 'a mysterious young man' whereas Marcos is a 'rareza', a term which emphasises his peculiarities. Marcos's sexuality is ambiguous throughout the film and this ambiguity is accentuated by the publicity material. The official poster portrays Marcos as a divided man, his face split in two (see Figure 20). This split can be considered in light of the scene in which Marcos shops for eau de toilette and air freshener in order to rid the house of the stench of the dead bodies heaped on his bed. After spraying the house and its contents (television, image of the virgin, family photos, posters on the wall, sports bag – all acting as icons of Francoist institutions), he goes into the chamber of horrors to cut up yet another body. Having worked up an appetite, he goes for dinner. The composition of shots in the local chemist, where we are presented with a triptych of mirrored images, is particularly telling in its construction of gender positions. On the left hand of the frame we see Marcos's reflection; on the right side of the frame we view the reflected image of a conventionally feminine woman in a cosmetics advertisement (matching hat, silk scarf and make-up). The trio of images is completed by the effeminate shop assistant (the 'marica' stereotype, typical of 1970s comedies) who takes centre frame. The heterosexual ideal is undone by a number of lures: the images we see are merely reflections; the female figure is a construction of mainstream advertising (twice removed, then, from a real woman) and Marcos no less so, as the shop assistant makes all manner of assumptions regarding his sexuality and his masculinity ('no woman can resist this eau-de-Cologne'), and even his marital status ('your wife will love it').

The brutal murders, to which Néstor bears witness, reflect Marcos's growing confusion and increased sense of isolation, entrapment and desperation. The second and third victims, Paula and Esteban, who are closest to him, try to persuade Marcos to give himself in. Their insistence that he go to the police unsettles the twitchy Marcos, yet his continuous repetition of 'No, I will not go to prison' suggests that there is something more to his anxiety than at first appears. The presence of the police later on in the film while he is having a drink on a terrace late at night in the company of Néstor triggers a traumatic physical response (cold sweat, fear, panic), conveyed cinematographically by fast editing between Marcos's face and the police weapons and symbols. Such emotional and physical reactions may well suggest that Marcos has been in prison or has had some experience with the enforcers of the law. The fourth of August 1970 saw the institutionalisation of the 'Ley de Peligrosidad y Rehabilitación Social' (The Social Order and Rehabilitation Law) in Spain, which came to replace the 'Ley de Vagos y Maleantes' (Law of Idlers and Delinquents) of 1954 and which was enforced until 19 January 1979, whereby the so-called enemies of society, among them homosexuals, could be interned for a period of no less than six months to five years in a centre for re-education.[14] *Una gota de sangre para morir amando* makes implicit references to contemporary discourses on homosexuality as a crime, as I will argue.

The same evening that Marcos attempts to cover over the vile reek of decaying bodies, Néstor invites him (appropriately enough) to a swimming club. It is the first time in the film that Marcos is seen relaxed and smiling, and such is the feeling of well-being that he even manages to fall asleep in Néstor's car as they return to their neighbourhood. For Marcos and the spectator, the presence of Néstor offers a necessary respite from the spree of killings and is a calming force in the narrative. Néstor corresponds to what Smith has called 'the good homosexual' (1992) ('el buen homosexual'): a non-stereotypical homosexual character who, we might argue, is the real subject of de la Iglesia's film. As the director argued in an interview twenty-five years later, 'the homosexual subtext of the film was inextricably linked to [. . .] the character that looks. His prominence [in the film] vindicates this key aspect' (de la Iglesia in Águilar et al. 1996: 110).

Thus far I have examined how the relationship between the two male characters, specific narrative episodes and filmic techniques intimate the film's homosexual subtext. A reference to casting closes my analysis of *La semana del asesino*. Vicente Parra was a well-known actor whose roles shaped specific constructions of contemporary ideas of the masculine in the second half of the 1950s and during the 1960s, in particular the figure of the 'galán' (or matinee idol) in melodramas, musicals and plays. For Spanish audiences he became the embodiment of the populist King Alfonso XII in *¿Dónde vas Alfonso XII?* (Luis César Amadori 1958). With *La semana del asesino*, in which he participated as co-producer, Parra attempted to move away from his previous roles and his public persona in the popular press, which constantly associated him with camp performances and a certain type of romantic cinema: 'I hope that those audiences who have seen me in romantic stories accept my natural artistic development' (*Cine en 7 días* 1972: 6). Both the pressbook and the publicity materials were at pains to emphasise his 'consecration as a dramatic actor'. Parra's masculinity and (hetero)sexuality throughout the 1950s and 1960s were clearly cinematic. While his participation in *La semana del asesino* (as well as in *Nadie oyó gritar*) gave him the artistic challenge and kudos he was seeking, his performance as Alfonso XII remained inscribed in the popular imaginary, which in a way enabled him to protect his private life. His casting in the role of Marcos, however, can be seen as a radical departure from his male star status and what he had come to represent. The script knowingly plays up his constructed masculinity and self-consciously offers an ironic, distanced, critical account of the cinematic and social construction of the actor's normative masculinity. The heterosexual behaviour expected of him in the mainstream popular press ('Vicente's single status is starting to arouse our readers' curiosity, and everybody wants to see him married' (*Nuevo Fotogramas* 1971b: 26) is referenced ironically in his conversations with Rosa the barmaid ('when are you going to find a woman to marry?') and his fiancée Paula ('sometimes I feel we will never get married; you never talk about it'). Both Rosa and Paula will be murdered.[15]

Nadie oyó gritar and *Una gota de sangre para morir amando* also hint at homosexual imagery. In the case of *Nadie oyó gritar*, the fascinating introduction of a secondary young male character called Tony offers a moment of spectacle that can be appropriated by heterosexual and homosexual viewers alike. Played by Tony Isbert, who makes his film début in de la Iglesia's movie, an Adonis-like Tony breaks into the fame riding a motorbike, flicking his hair, showing his chest, taking his shirt off and, finally, striking a camp and playful pose in a tight swimsuit. The storyline is suspended as the spectator is given time to dwell on this image of masculine beauty. Tony's appearances in the film are studiously staged as a series of intensely and exploitatively erotic scenarios which exalt his looks, his virility, and the splendour of his youth. But the way in which the camera suggestively frames Isbert's body is also evocative of the 'beefcake picture', typical of body building magazines published in the US after the Second World War, which circulated and were consumed in Spain. Two aspects of this evocation of the figure of the 'beefcake' are of interest: firstly, these were images or photographic portraits which, in their original context of production, were disguised as an artistic representation of sport. A parallel could be drawn here with the Spanish context, particularly in a period when censorship was tight: de la Iglesia draws on the conventions of the 'beefcake picture' circulating in international gay subculture. Secondly, and also highlighting the parallel between the US and the Spanish context, Isbert is like those young models who arrived in Hollywood in pursuit of stardom: photographed in the film like a young model, this is his presentation portfolio. With these visual strategies, de la Iglesia's cinema engages with gay male subcultures through the filmic display of male flesh. In *Una gota de sangre para morir amando*, to which we shall now turn, he engages not only with the popular cultural stereotyping of homosexuals but also with scientific stereotyping.

The narrative establishes quite explicit references to medical discourses on homosexuality, at the time considered to be 'revolutionary' and 'progressive'. I am referring here to what came to be known as 'aversion therapy', which was first developed in the US and some Western European countries before it arrived in Spain in the 1960s, when it was used by psychiatrists who believed that lobotomy could offer a cure for homosexuality. Patients were shown images of naked or half-naked men while receiving electroshocks. This technique had its artistic semblance in Kubrick's *A Clockwork Orange*, where it takes the name of the 'Ludovico technique', a fictitious drug-assisted aversion therapy whose guiding principle is the psychological phenomenon known as classical conditioning (Pavlov's dog being the classic example). In *A Clockwork Orange*, Alex's criminal behaviour is treated with ultra-violent images and electroshocks. In *Una gota de sangre para morir amando*, a sadistic gang roams the city at night terrorising law-abiding citizens. In a top-secret laboratory sanctioned by the official authorities, mind-control experiments are being conducted on juvenile delinquents, the purpose of which is to make these young criminals useful to the state. It is in this context that de la Iglesia's strategic imitation of *A Clockwork Orange* acquires a new meaning. An analysis of the opening moments of the film, from the pre-credits sequence to the point where Kubrick's film is mentioned explicitly as part of the diegesis of *Una gota de sangre para morir amando* – that is, those specific episodes which many critics cited as plagiarised – shows that the reshaping of elements of *A Clockwork Orange* frames de la Iglesia's thematic concerns on the violent treatment of homosexuality in authoritarian societies.

The pre-credits sequence opens with a television advertisement for the beverage 'Blue Drink', and the introduction of the main female character, Ana, who is watching TV. The news bulletin relates the deaths of young men at the hands of what the police describe as 'a mentally unstable murderer or a sick sadist with homosexual tendencies', seemingly establishing the link between crime, pathology, young men and homosexuality. Cut to the credits and a classical music score accompanies an aerial shot of the outskirts of a modern city, focusing on a building complex which the viewer soon realises is a hospital. We are

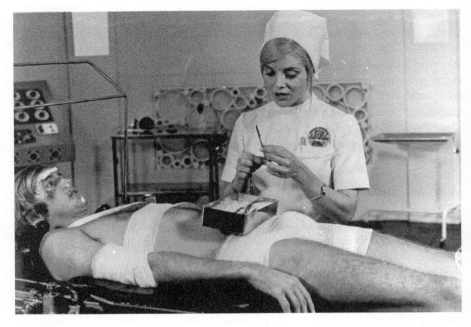

Figure 23   The male body on display in *Una gota de sangre para morir amando*.

reintroduced to Ana, this time in the context of an award ceremony held at the hospital's lecture theatre, where her remarkable work as a nurse is recognised by the board. Among the members of the board is Dr Víctor Senater (Jean Sorel), a psychiatrist and neurologist in charge of the mind-control experiments sponsored by the government in its attempts to eliminate crime. His romantic interest in Ana is evident in the next scene in the car park, when he invites her to dinner to celebrate her success. But the romantic moment is interrupted by the arrival of an ambulance which brings in a badly beaten-up young man, de la Iglesia himself, making his first cameo appearance inert on a stretcher that passes disruptively across the screen. Undoubtedly, this patient is destined to join other delinquent 'guinea pigs' in the medical experiments led by Dr Senater. The actual nature of the experiments and research being conducted at the hospital is introduced in the next two sequences: firstly, in a conversation between Víctor and Ana during their date in the restaurant through a conventional shot / reverse shot, and, secondly, mediated through the TV appearance of Víctor in a popular science lecture broadcast, where we adopt the point of view of Ana as she watches it. During his speech, Víctor advocates for the potential benefits of medical science in the treatment of the criminal condition, among them the rehabilitation of juvenile delinquents and their subsequent reinsertion in society as productive citizens (see Figure 23). The broadcast is interrupted by a short break for advertising slots. While the voiceover enthuses about the libido-enhancing properties of the product, 'Golden Slip Panther', the camera focuses on the muscular body of the male model and zooms in on his crotch. From here onwards, the coordination of shots intensifies the links to Kubrick and *A Clockwork Orange*. Cut to a gang of Droog look-alikes dressed in leather and futuristic orange helmets racing in a dune buggy through a tunnel. And cross-cut to the TV screen where a newsreader announces that '*A Clockwork Orange* (1971) from Warner Bros. and directed by Stanley Kubrick' is going to be shown after the lecture. The newsreader's description of the film as 'A symphony of violence' cues the eruption of on-screen violence in *Una gota de sangre para morir amando*, as the felonious gang invade and wreck a family home, beating and raping the couple inside.

Cinematography, *mise-en-scène* and editing probe the connections between medical discourse, violent totalitarian methods, criminality and homosexuality and bring together a visible dialogue of an otherwise invisible reality. The scene in which Dr Senater's team subject one of the patients to the electroshock treatment focuses on the punished and traumatised male body. In the tradition of the mad scientist, Dr Senater explains his method:

> our only aim is to cure your mind, release you from those instincts that have turned you into a criminal. We want you to become a proper, honest man, who is productive in society. Our aim is to reinsert you into society as a productive and law-abiding citizen.

This is followed by a cut to a TV studio where a male model is rehearsing an advertisement for pants under the hysterical direction of an effeminate director, an obvious clichéd stereotype of gay male sexuality in popular culture.

Like Kubrick's filmic production, controversy accompanied de la Iglesia's *Una gota de sangre para morir amando*. And like *A Clockwork Orange*, de la Iglesia's film quickly become a cult favourite among certain audiences. He was heavily criticised for his depiction of sex and violence, and censors and critics alike cut and curtailed the director's formal and aesthetic approach to genre filmmaking. Looking back at de la Iglesia's filmic production from the vantage point of the early twenty-first century makes it easier to perceive the formal and stylistic strategies used by the director to suggest and represent the homosexual motifs running through *Nadie oyó gritar*, *La semana del asesino* and *Una gota de sangre para morir amando*, developing the way a thematics and style anticipate his cinema of the Transition. In the highly politicised context of the Transition period, de la Iglesia would be able to produce an explicitly 'homophile cinema' (Mira 2004). But in the late Francoist period, his expression of this cinema could only be intimated and articulated through the horror / thriller genres. De la Iglesia's film cycle resists straight gender and generic definitions, escaping any classificatory system set on closing off either the complexities of desire or the (in fact) complex consumption behaviours of popular genres.

NOTES

1. 'Destape' describes a period of liberalisation in Spain in the mid-1970s after a partial relaxation of censorship whereby images of partial nudity made it into print material and films. 'Landismo' refers to a trend in a series of 1970s comedies starring Spanish actor Alfredo Landa (1933–), in which plots and film aesthetics reflected contemporary attitudes towards sex.
2. As part of his *Laws of Desire. Questions of Homosexuality in Spanish Writing and Film 1960–1990*.
3. Hopewell (1986), Smith (1992), Troppiano (1997) and, more recently, Mira (2004). Smith and Mira have acknowledged, for example, the 'homoerotic subtext' of *La semana del asesino* but merely in passing.
4. See 2003 and 2005.
5. Equivalent figures are 9,685,321 pesetas and 30 days for *Nadie oyó gritar*, and 11,642,000 and 48 days for *La semana del asesino*.
6. See, for example, promotional interviews in popular film magazines *Cine en 7 días* (1971 and 1972) and *Nuevo Fotogramas* (1971b).
7. Antonio Artero, José Luis Garci, Antonio Fos and Eloy de la Iglesia.
8. 'Tremendismo' can be translated as a literary style characterised by a coarse realism which dwells on the ugly and the shocking.
9. The film served as the vehicle for a change in direction in the career of the male lead, Vicente Parra, an established male sex-symbol who had played the figure of the 'galán' (i.e. matinee idol) in melodramas, musicals and plays throughout the 1950s and 1960s. As co-producer of the film, Parra saw it as an opportunity to move away from his previous roles and obtain the artistic kudos he was seeking. Some Spanish film posters sold the film on Parra as the established male sex-symbol.
10. The newspaper acknowledged receipt of the letter in its show business section in the 12 September edition (1973: 119) ('Se discute una película'). An interview with the director, 'Eloy de la Iglesia se defiende', was published ten days later, on 22 September 1973 (Flores 1973: 22–3).
11. Interestingly, his films would be defined as 'pamphlets' by the film theory journal *Contracampo* ('Countershot') in the late 1970s and early 1980s. See Llinás and Téllez (1981) and Vega (1981) for a discussion of how de la Iglesia's films are like political and controversial texts where the exposition of ideas is more important than attention to style.
12. See melonfarmers.co.uk/nasties/htm: 'The cover was a flimsy slip case that didn't last long so adding to the rarity of a mint condition cover. [The film] was re-released after 3 BBFC cuts in 1993 (Redemption). Current UK status: Passed 18 with 3 cuts.' Whilst most films came from the US and Italy, there were also four other Spanish films that made it into the list: *No profanar el sueño de los muertos*, a Spanish–Italian co-production; *La maldición de la bestia*; *El canibal / The Devil Hunter* (Jesús Franco, 1980), a Italian–Spanish–German co-production; and *Colegialas violadas*, a Spanish–German co-production.
13. The Movimiento, or Movimiento Nacional, was the only lawful political organisation during the dictatorship, and comprised members of the army, the Catholic Church and the Falange Española (Spanish Fascist Party).

14. 'Those who are found responsible of acts of homosexuality [. . .] shall be found guilty of social danger' (Domingo Lorén 1978: 46), in *Los homosexuales frente a la ley. Los juristas opinan*. The law also stipulated the prohibition against residing in a designated place or territory and against visiting certain areas or public spaces, and imposed obedience to the designated vigilance.

15. The popular press also enquired about the marital status of Eusebio Poncela once he established himself with the underground cinema of Zulueta and Almodóvar in the late 1970s and early 1980s.

5. DEVOTED TO HORROR: FROM *TERROR FANTASTIC* (1971–3) TO *2000MANIACOS* (1989–PRESENT)

Terror Fantastic and *2000maniacos* are landmark publications in the field of Spanish horror of the last four decades. The study of specialist film magazines and fanzines aids in an understanding of how different cultural producers not only think and write about the genre and adjacent subcultures but also act as cultural platforms for constructions of Spanish film history and its canon. These two publications provide a prime example of the cultural capital developing from and around horror cinema and the emergence of specific horror fan cultures in Spain. *Terror Fantastic* was the first specialist film magazine in horror and science fiction to be published in Spain in the early 1970s; *2000maniacos* is a fanzine edited by Manuel Valencia since 1989. Publications like *Terror Fantastic* and *2000maniacos* are not traditionally considered to be worthy objects of study because of their ephemeral character and their focus on specific subcultures. Whether considered as repositories of trivia or sites of marginalised subcultural ideologies, fanzines, for example, have been far removed from the centre of cultural debates and excluded from histories of Spanish horror cinema. But, as this chapter argues, they are the very lifeblood of horror culture.

Despite the sixteen-year gap that separates the last edition of *Terror Fantastic* in 1973 and the arrival of *2000maniacos* in 1989, and the fact that both publications have their own historical specificity, they share a number of points in common in the cultural lineage that I seek to draw. Firstly, they are cultural documents which provide us with actual examples of the discursive activities of 'genre-users'; secondly, they are sites of fandom which provide valuable insights into the (sub)cultures within which they circulate; thirdly, the writings of the editors of and contributors to these publications reveal a fruitful atlas of cultural and subcultural interventions in the field of Spanish horror culture; fourthly, their links to two genre festivals, the Sitges Festival – originally called the International Week of Fantasy and Horror Cinema – in the case of *Terror Fantastic* and the San Sebastián Horror and Fantasy Film Festival in the case of *2000maniacos*, highlight the role these institutions play in helping to shape and contextualise Spanish horror culture; and, finally, their emergence corresponds to peak periods in the cultural vitality of the genre across different media – that is, films, comics, specialist magazines or fanzines.

This chapter places *Terror Fantastic* and *2000maniacos* within their own historical specificity and in relation to contemporary mainstream and alternative publications. Thus while the lifespan of *Terror Fantastic* is informed by specific film experiences (for example, singular viewings, the double-bill programme or the cultural significance of the auteur) and institutions (censorship), the journey of *2000maniacos* goes hand in hand with the impact of VHS and the social and cultural significance of video stores throughout the 1980s and 1990s, the arrival of DVDs and the value of bonus features and paratexts in facilitating forms of criticism since the late 1990s, and the internet revolution (blogging, file-sharing, youtube.com, and so on) at the turn of the twenty-first century. Changes in viewing practices, consumption habits and the types of knowledge circulating around films are reflected in the pages of the fanzine, producing new forms of cinephilia, cinephagia and fandom around the genre, which, in turn, open up the cultural experience of horror and contribute to the revision of film histories, film canons and cultural histories. By and large, the contents of both publications are produced by avid movie fans. Whereas *Terror Fantastic* collaborators would describe themselves as *cinéphiles*, *2000maniacos* contributors would describe themselves as *cinéphages*, as Pedro Calleja, editor of fanzine *Serie B* in the early 1980s, argued in '¡Están vivos! Cultura basura, cine psicotrónico y espectadores mutantes' (2003b), focusing on theories and habits of film consumption in relation to psychotronic films. The suffixes '-phile' and '-phage' here indicate different ways of engaging with and, above all, consuming films.

The chapter is organised as follows. The section devoted to each individual publication is preceded by a general overview of how these two publishing ventures sat in relation to their contemporary publishing scenes. Whilst it is beyond the scope of this chapter to cover all horror-related publications and their contents, the personnel and their contributions, a general overview will give the reader an idea of the connections and overlaps which have been only partially explored in fanzines and e-publications. This is followed by a description of the contents and format of the magazine and the fanzine in order to give the reader a sense of their respective scopes, the range of contents, their diverse contributors, their international dimension and, above all, their specialist role in the dissemination of horror, fantasy and science fiction among Spanish general readers and genre aficionados.

Horror at the Kiosk

Comic books, graphic novels and magazines devoted to the horror genre and to science fiction proliferated in the late 1960s and early 1970s, attesting to their growing commercial importance, as well as to the significance of horror in the popular culture of the period. This is a fertile period in the history of genre publications in Spain. Yet their production, circulation and consumption belong to a specific historical and cultural juncture which goes beyond histories of Spanish horror culture, opening up its history to the international as well as the intermedial dimension of the contemporary cultural field of horror. The cultural historian could delve into the new business relationships and cultural blends between the American and European comic-book (and movie) businesses, and the role of American publishers and international art agencies in shaping aesthetics, trends and cycles which are, in turn, reflected in local practices (film and comic books). For example: the portfolio of Warren Publishing – *Eerie*, *Creepy*, *Famous Monsters of Filmland*, *Vampirella* – and Warren's operations in European countries made its way into Spanish publishing ventures; Spanish artists from the Barcelona studio agency Selecciones Ilustradas, led by Josep Toutain, became world-leading illustrators on the international comics scene,[1] their work being exported across the world and appearing in American Warren Publishing and later on in Skywald, and in the Spanish versions from the American publisher such as *Rufus*, *Vampus* and *Vampirella*; the imprint of Spanish illustrators who had worked in London's Fleet Street, producing the visual aesthetics of many adventure, war, western, thriller and romance comics and who at the time were putting their talent at the service of horror; or the recycling – repetition – and translation into Spanish of stories that had already been published in pulp publications and comic books in the US, France or Italy.

Historias para no dormir was a landmark in Spanish television and paved the way for the publication of horror across different media (pulp anthologies, graphic novels, comic books and specialist genre magazines) in the second half of the 1960s and first half of the 1970s. As I discussed in Chapter 3, the popularity of *Historias para no dormir* led to the publication of two titles with the same name, which capitalised on Ibáñez Serrador's horror brand. The first publication to reach the kiosks in 1966 was *Historias para no dormir* ('Novela gráfica para adultos'), which was published in Barcelona by Semic Española de Ediciones S. A.[2] Eight issues of horror graphic novels supplied by comic-book art agency Barton Art came out. The second collection, *Historias para no dormir* ('Revista Ilustrada'), published in Madrid by Julio García Peri, fared much better. Constructed around the figurehead 'Chicho', it generated more interest and performed much better commercially; a total of eight volumes and sixty-plus stories were published between 1967 and 1974. Classics of horror, suspense and science fiction, contemporary writings and scripts from the TV series were introduced by Narciso Ibáñez Serrador, his familiar face in the top corner of the front cover of the first issue, and the Master's ceremonial words on the back: 'the most scary horror stories of the past, the present and the future, horror that scares some, amuses others, entertains others, but that bores nobody'. Other horror and science fiction pulp anthologies, 'Narraciones Géminis de Terror' (Editorial Géminis, 1968–9), 'Terror Extra' (Editorial Romeu, 1968–9) and 'Relatos de terror y espanto' (Editorial Dronte, 1972–3) also piggybacked on the success of the TV series and its paper tie-ins.

The cultural effervescence of the horror genre peaked in 1971. Special horror issues were published in general culture magazine *Triunfo*, popular film weekly *Nuevo Fotogramas* and specialist genre magazine *Nueva Dimensión*; even satirical magazine *La Codorniz* dedicated an issue to the genre.[3] This is the year in which *Terror Fantastic* emerged. TVE could not escape the boom either. Cycles devoted to Frankenstein and Dracula in the programme *Cine-club*,[4] silent era classics in *Sombras recobradas* and a range of international suspense thrillers in *Intriga*[5] were broadcast on the small screen. At times, the programming of horror and fantasy films provoked controversy. *Ciclo cine-fantástico*, for instance, was cancelled by TVE after three films were aired (*King Kong* (Merian C. Cooper and Ernest B. Shoedsack 1933), *Cat People* (Jacques Tourneur 1942) and *Una invención destructiva* / *The Fabulous World of Jules Verne* (Vynález Zkázy 1958), the latter a last-minute replacement for the controversial *Invasion of the Body Snatchers* (Don Siegel 1956)) because of the pernicious effects of 'the fantastic film' upon audiences; trade journal *Teleprogramas* informed its readership that the television authorities had adduced that the genre was 'not of good taste', and was 'depressing' and 'scared viewers' (Yagüe in Cervera 1972a: 23).

Barcelona-based publisher Ibero Mundial de Ediciones launched *Dossier negro* and *Delta 99* in 1968, *Vampus* in 1971 and *Rufus* in 1973, all printed in black and white and featuring showy colour covers designed by well-known American and Spanish illustrators such as Sanjulián and Enrich. *Dossier negro* was a pioneer publication on the horror comic scene with its offer of 'Relatos gráficos de terror para adultos'. With a total of 217 issues between 1968 and 1988 under four different publishers, it remained a favourite among comics fans (see Figure 24). *Delta 99*, created by a young Carlos Giménez, offered an original blend of science fiction, mystery and romance scenarios. Both *Vampus* (1971–8) (see Figure 25) and *Rufus* (1973–8) were modelled on Warren Publishing products, the former on *Creepy* and the latter on *Eerie*,

Figure 24   Enrich's cover art for horror and suspense magazine *Dossier negro* (issue 33, 1972), originally published for American horror publication *Eerie* in January 1972.

although with the passing of time many issues included material from both, as well as other Warren publications like *Vampirella*, or from other American publishing houses: namely, Skywald, DC Comics and Archie Comics. When Ibero Mundial de Ediciones was acquired by Garbo Editorial, the publication of these graphic novels continued. Others such as the Spanish *Vampirella* (1974) were added to the group.[6] Many other publishing ventures, such as *Drácula – 'Revista de terror y fantasía para adultos'*, by Buru Lan S. A. de Ediciones – which published in instalments the works of Esteban Maroto and Enric Sió, only lasted a few issues through 1971; others like *Psico – 'Novelas gráficas de misterio para adultos'*, by Editorial Plan – had a shorter shelf-life, with only two issues. Two pioneering genre-based magazines emerged in this cultural milieu, *Nueva Dimensión* (Ediciones Dronte) and *Terror Fantastic* (Pedro Yoldi).

Figure 25   Sanjulián's cover art for horror and suspense magazine *Vampus* (issue 12, 1972), originally published in American horror publication *Creepy* in June 1972 (courtesy of tebeosfera.com).

TERROR FANTASTIC

Science-fiction aficionados had been enjoying the pages of *Nueva Dimensión* (Editorial Dronte) since 1968, the first specialist magazine dedicated to the genre.[7] *Nueva Dimensión* included short stories, articles and essays, book and film reviews, festival reports and general information, as well as visual material such as comic strips and comic art. Spanish horror film aficionados had to rely on French *Midi-Minuit Fantastique* (1962–70) and US publications such as *Famous Monsters of Filmland* or *Castle of Frankenstein* reaching specialist distributors and bookshops to read about and see images of their favourite genre. Although *Terror Fantastic* (TF) was not a horror companion to *Nueva Dimensión*, both publications shared a pool of contributors (Luis Vigil, Luis Gasca and Carlos Fabretti) and comic-art illustrators (José María Bea, Enric Sió). In the months leading up to *TF*'s launch, the pages of *Nueva Dimensión*, as well as those of *Nuevo Fotogramas*, carried promotional advertisements for *TF* which marketed the magazine in terms of its pioneering role ('The first magazine devoted to horror and fantasy in film and literature') and its daringly different approach, aimed as it was at an exclusive niche readership of fantasy-lovers ('Una revista nueva, diferente, audaz. Exclusivamente para amantes de lo imposible' [A new, different, bold magazine. Exclusively for lovers of the impossible']). When *TF* arrived in the Spanish kiosks in October 1971, prospective readers were able to acquire a large-format magazine (26 cm × 21 cm) with sixty-three pages of information, reviews and articles, as well as copious illustrations, on the horror, fantasy and science-fiction genres.

For the first issue, the publishers caught the eye of interested genre aficionados and general readers with a graphic and violent black-and-white image taken from Italian Mario Bava's *Reazione a Catena / Antefatto / La ecología del delito / Bay of Blood* (1971) (see Figure 26). For the price of 50 pesetas every month, or a subscription of 500 pesetas for 12 issues, the magazine promised fresh forays into the world of horror, science fiction and fantasy. The title *Terror Fantastic* was splashed in red across the top of the front cover, while the shocking murder scene from Bava's film, in which a man is speared through the abdomen, enticed prospective readers with an image from a contemporary horror film which had not been released in the Spanish market beyond the specialist context of the Sitges 'International Week of Fantasy and Horror Film' Festival. Also in red lettering in the bottom right-hand corner, two headlines, 'The Films of Boris Karloff' and 'Trieste's Film Festival', set up further expectations about the magazine's contents. The cover functioned as a letter of introduction to the commercial scope of the publication: its international dimension, its interest in the genre past and present, and its coverage of new developments in the specialised field of horror film and fantasy. The choice of cover worked on two further levels: firstly, it acted as a window display for the activities of the Sitges Festival, where Bava's film was being shown that year; and, secondly, it stood as a bold statement against censorship by offering a glimpse of a film which was not available to general Spanish audiences.

While the first cover showed a certain leaning towards the filmic rather than the literary, both the inside cover and the first page soon established other allegiances to related genres and forms of expression: namely, science fiction and comics. The promotion of *Nueva Dimensión* and *¡Bang! Revista de tebeos españoles* on the inside cover – two publications which offered a serious approach to writing about popular and mass culture – signalled a bond and a commonality with like-minded readers and the existence of a network of genre-based publications and subcultural communities. The right-hand margin of the first page details the names and roles of the creative team behind *TF*: Director José Cañas Aznar, Co-ordinator Francisco Montaner and a list of collaborators (Antonio Camín, Luis Gasca, Terenci Moix, Francisco Montaner, Carlos Nolla, Peñarroya, Enric Sió, Juan Tébar, Luis Vigil, Antonio Vilella and Pedro Yoldi), which would increase over the next two years with further additions (among them, Antonio Cervera, Carlos Fabretti, Carlos Garrido,

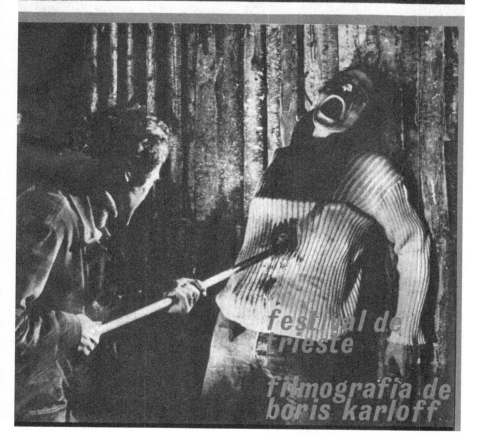

Figure 26 *Terror Fantastic*, front cover for the first issue published in October 1971.

Antonio Martín and Ornella Volta). From issue 2 onwards, Pedro Yoldi became the General Editor. The first table of contents served as the template for regular features and sections, which would remain virtually the same for another twenty-five issues and of which specific collaborators were in charge.

The sections which formed the backbone of the magazine were as follows: in 'Los hombres de la fantasía' Antonio Camín offered illustrated biographical profiles of fantasy film directors and actors,[8] whereas in 'Los mitos del terror' and 'Los mitos de la fantasía' Francisco Montaner focused on classic monsters and monstrous creatures in literature and film.[9] In 'El museo fantástico' Carlos Nolla documented and examined a repository of films, classic and modern, which were representative of horror, fantasy and science fiction,[10] while in 'La película olvidada' Luis Gasca unearthed long-forgotten films from Spain and abroad; many of the titles he reviews, such as the Spanish experimental fantasy *Al Hollywood madrileño* (Nemesio M. Sobrevilla 1927) and the Russian science-fiction film *Aelita* (Yakov Protazanov 1924) are linked to the Sitges Film Festival's special programming.[11] In 'La biblioteca del terror' Antonio Vilella and, later on, Carlos Garrido built up a library of classic Gothic, pulp mystery and science-fiction authors, also making space for less classifiable writers.[12] Through his section 'Los cómics fantásticos', Luis Gasca demonstrated an erudite knowledge of the national and international comic-book scene, making readers aware of the industrial and intertextual relationship between comics, pulp fiction and movies[13]; Gasca's connoisseurship was complemented by other *¡Bang!* collaborators like Antonio Martín, whose articles initiated a historiography of Spanish horror comics and introduced Spanish readers to, among other things, the worlds of American crime books and Marvel comics; Luis Vigil wrote on witchcraft, voodoo and the occult sciences; and the distinctive voices of Terenci Moix (Ramón Moix Messeguer (1942–2003)) and Pierrot (Antonio José Gracia (1943–2011)) opened up the magazine to other sensibilities and categories of intellectual taste, 'camp' readings of films in the case of Moix's essays, and theatre features linked to the 'Panic Movement' in the case of Pierrot's section 'Teatro-Terror'.

In addition to these various sections and regular contributors, the magazine also included letters to the editor ('¿Dígame?'), festival reports, reviews, cartoons, news and notes on upcoming Spanish productions ('Veremos' by Antonio Cervera from February 1972 onwards), snippets of information on current cultural events and publications on horror and science fiction in comics, television and the press ('TV y fantasía', 'Telex' and 'SF') and short fiction ('Usted lo cuenta'). Some articles appeared in instalments across a number of issues: personal travelogues by Juan Tébar on the *fantastique* scene in Paris ('La pantalla infernal: "a la recherche du fantastique"') and by Pierrot on Hamburg's red-light district; a journey through the world of Forrest J. Ackerman and his *Famous Monsters of Filmland* by Luis Vigil; or the tantalising visual documentation on international exploitation nudies collated by Sadko (pseudonym of Luis Gasca).[14]

One of the main values of the magazine as a cultural document clearly resides in the sheer eclecticism and approach to the material published. A sample of contributions will also be considered to discuss how different *TF* cultural producers thought and wrote about the genre. The distinctive voices of Moix, Pierrot, Gasca and Tébar will serve as examples. But let us look at the first editorial in detail, as well as some other of the magazine's editorials, in order to examine the ways in which *TF* positioned itself in relation to horror, to the existing market, to the institutional context of the Spanish film industry and to general and specific discourses around the field of horror. '¿Qué pretende ser "Terror-Fantastic"'? ('What is "Terror-Fantastic" trying to achieve?'), the title of the first editorial, is a letter of presentation to its potential readership (*Terror Fantastic* (1971)). The opening statement sets up 'the rules of the game' so that 'you, reader and friend, know when you are purchasing our publication what you are going to read and see.' Like a genre contract whereby producers and audiences agree on what to expect from a certain type of film, the contract between *TF* and its readership promises to honour expectations and a set of shared rules: *TF* 'aims to bring monthly "everything" related to the world of fantasy and the unusual' (1971: 5). Although 'its main subject matter will be cinema', the editors declared, 'other pages will be devoted to literature, painting, theatre, comic and any other cultural manifestation falling within this scope' (1971: 5). The ultimate goal of the *TF* creative team 'is to bring together in one publication a series of themes which are related to each other and can be of interest to a specific group of people' (1971: 5) – that is, a particular cultural community. This statement of intent implies an embracing approach to genre, media and cultural expression, a realisation that the topics and cultures to be featured in the magazine were interrelated, and an acknowledgement of the existence of communities that shared cultural sensibilities and tastes. Appropriately enough, the creative team saw themselves as 'modern Frankensteins', who had 'brought to life a new publication' and called upon readers to 'supply the necessary energy' (1971: 5) to keep their progeny alive. As far as the actual contents included in the first issue were concerned, the editorial sought to affirm the expectations of horror film enthusiasts with the choice of two iconic figures of the genre, Boris Karloff and Barbara Steele, as well as ample coverage of the genre in reviews and festival reports (Trieste and Sitges). Other fandom communities were interpellated with the inclusion of material on fantasy comics. The magazine also dedicated a space to short fiction in the field of horror and science fiction, which took the form of a regular fiction competition, the above-mentioned 'Usted lo cuenta' ('Your Story'). The specialist contributions of Luis Gasca, Terenci Moix and Juan Tébar were flagged up in a move to grant cultural and subcultural kudos to the new venture. While Tébar had established his reputation working with Ibáñez Serrador as a screenwriter for *Historias para no dormir* and *La residencia*, Gasca and Moix pioneered the study of comics as a mass media form, the former with *Los cómics en la pantalla* (1965) and *Tebeo y cultura de masas* (1966), the latter with *Los cómics, arte para el consumo y formas pop* (1968).

TF's editorials ranged from the magazine's broad opinions on the state of national and international horror film and fantasy film production and current developing trends[15] to general commentaries on the Spanish film industry and its institutions, in particular censorship, to related topical issues such as the droves of Spaniards travelling to the South of France to watch films that were censored in Spain,[16] and to general observations on a variety of events.[17] Editorials for issues 25 and 26 were attempts at reanimating the strained financial life of the magazine in order to keep it afloat. Added to its economic difficulties, legal action was taken against the magazine concerning the title copyright. The November 1973 editorial was replaced by two notes: one briefly informing readers of the legal appeal lodged against the magazine and a second one announcing that the magazine would be published bimonthly from January 1974 onwards under the new title of *Terror*, containing a hundred pages for the price of a hundred pesetas. *Terror* achieved only one issue.

By and large, *TF*'s discussion of the role of censorship focused on its effects on the distribution and exhibition of specific horror films in Spain, but it never reached the level of polemic articulated, for example, in weekly magazines *Nuevo Fotogramas* and *Triunfo* or film journals associated with the 'New Spanish Cinema'. Like any other publication, *TF* had to conform to the norms of the 'Ley de Prensa e Imprenta' ('Press Law') and was scrutinised by the censorship bureaucratic machinery. The impact of censorship practices on the circulation and exhibition of foreign horror films in Spain is addressed in 'Las que no veremos' ('The films we shall not see') (1972b: 7), where the limited access of Spanish mainstream audiences and horror aficionados to specific horror film cycles, or what puritan censors called 'dangerous and unpleasant films' (1972b: 7), is discussed. Spanish audiences did not see around half of the productions featuring the classic monsters Frankenstein (only 12 out of 22 were shown), Dracula (14 out of 23) and the werewolf (13 out of 26), and had hardly a peek at other monstrous creations such as Dr Jekyll (9 out of 25), the mummy (3 out 28) and zombies (3 out of 19). The January 1972 editorial had teasingly invited readers to become film tourists and to join the itinerant Spaniards searching out 'films that have not been censored' beyond the Pyrenees (1972b: 7). Discussion of these peculiarly Spanish film-going pilgrimages was the object of a two-page commentary, 'El cine, Perpignan y los españoles' (1973: 60–1), which was an en masse *TF* condemnation of an article entitled 'Los peregrinos del erotismo', penned in the Barcelona daily *El Noticiero Universal* by journalist Enrique Rubio. The commentary-cum-editorial included a full transcription of Rubio's piece and *TF*'s response to it. Rubio's piece makes interesting reading for, in the same article, he wittingly equates drugs, trips, eroticism and pornography, accusing these filmgoers, whom he describes as 'country bumpkins, simpletons, unsophisticated, and morbid', of offending and undermining the foundational Spanish institutions of 'family, marriage and manliness' (Rubio in *Terror Fantastic* 1973: 61). The *TF* editors dismantled Rubio's demonised version of the pilgrim filmgoer by exposing his ignorance and lack of discernment regarding the films and venues within the film tourist's reach, pointing out that it was films like *The Devils* and *A Clockwork Orange*, forbidden in Spain, which drew pilgrims – at least, these pilgrims – to places like Perpignan.

Together with censorship, the combination of horror, eroticism and sex in contemporary production trends was one of the recurrent discussion points of the editorials. The arguments in this respect were mainly related to production practices and to issues around quality and taste, rather than an analysis of changing social and sexual mores in contemporary Spain. In general terms, *TF* editorials rejected and condemned a particular brand of horror which they labelled as 'terror fácil' and invariably described as 'sexi-terror-show' (1972a: 7) or 'terro-horrorífico-eróticas' films (Montaner 1972b: 5). These products represented 'the gradual death of the horror film, which is increasingly giving way to what is only a purely erotic cinema with horror titles' (1972a: 7). In 'Erotismo en el terror', the editorial appealed for and justified 'the use of an enlightening / instructive eroticism, which justifies itself for clear artistic reasons; gratuitous eroticism is unacceptable' (1972a: 7). Another editorial, '¿Cine español de exportación?', rebuked double versions: 'one thing is the film exhibited on Spanish screens, a very different thing is what audiences see abroad, where the epidermis of our "stars" is exhibited in abundance in the most "artistic" poses and through the most unimaginable angles' (1973: 7). The editorial concluded that these films should be 'for export only' and should not be subsidised or released in Spain. Most reviews on the latest Spanish horror film releases put into practice these editorial views on the exploitative combination of sex and horror, with many a Jesús Franco film serving as the main target of criticism: 'the argument in *El proceso de las brujas* is merely a pretext to display countless gratuitous scenes' which are only destined to 'foreign cinemas specialized in sex and violence' (Vilella 1971a: 54), whereas in *La ciudad sin hombres* Franco exploited to the 'maximum cheap commercial elements' by 'sticking to the inexhaustible sadist-erotic-exotic gold-mine' (Vilella 1972b: 52). Other films were reviewed along similar lines, almost in a formulaic manner; thus, in *La llamada del vampiro / The Curse of the Vampyr* (José María Elorrieta 1972), the production of 'horror is neither the ultimate goal of the film nor its narrative basis. It is merely a pretext, an excuse to show us a display of young ladies more fitting in a variety show than in a horror film' (Nolla 1972: 48), while in *La noche del terror ciego* the camera focuses on 'an attractive female camper whose presence takes more than half of the reel in gratuitous exhibitionism, encounters with the monsters, escapes, sacrifices and various activities after she is dead' (Vilella 1972b: 60). Despite these views on the exploitative nature of 'sexi-terror-show' films, the magazine was generous with stills exhibiting scream queens, damsels in distress, femmes fatales and curvaceous Barbarellas and Vampirellas. It launched a new section, 'Veamos . . .' ('Let's see . . .'), exclusively devoted to sexy female starlets participating in Spanish horror films (to name but a few, Argentinean Cristiana Suriani (1973: 38–9), Spaniard Loretta Tovar (1973: 51–2) and Pole Dianik Zurakowska (1973: 54–5)), included extensive coverage of 'nudies' across five issues, and commercially exploited the combination of eroticism and horror with a special issue, 'Erotismo en el terror' (1972a), confirming the old cliché that sex – or the promise of it – sells. Apart from the undeniable commercial pull of these features, the contradiction also speaks to the publication's range of approaches.

The eclecticism and variety of TF's regular sections and diverse editorials can also be seen in the convergence of different approaches to the horror genre: from the mere compiling (or straight translation from foreign publications, in some instances) of information on directors, performers and films to traditional readings based on generic conventions, formulas and iconographies, and to the more countercultural and transgressive interpretations of texts, performers and modes of representation. Its pages included writings on household names and newcomers, classified filmmakers according to the familiar categories of auteurs, *metteurs-en-scène* and commercial opportunists, and covered mainstream, art-house and exploitation production. It became the channel through which unknown directors and films reached Spanish audiences. Gasca, for example, brought to the attention of horror aficionados the strange world of Brazilian Mójica Marins in 'Mójica Marins: donde el instinto supera a la razón' (1972a: 40–8), producing informative dossiers on the exceptional life of the director, his filmic output and the exploitation of his alter ego, Zé do Caixão, in TV, comics and merchandising, as well as the adventures of Mexican multimedia superhero and crime-fighter Santo, 'el enmascarado de plata' (1972b: 8–19). The interventions of Tébar, Pierrot and Moix are noteworthy in that they exemplify the plurality of discursive practices generated around the genre. In his 'Pantalla infernal' ('Infernal Screen'), Tébar sometimes examined the representation and adaptation for the screen of classic monsters (Dracula, Dr Jekyll and Mr Hyde, ghosts), while at other times he indulged his cinéphile fascination with Buñuel and Hitchcock, and regularly provided a first-hand description of horror film practices of exhibition, reception and consumption. For instance, his role as a horror correspondent in Paris, 'à la recherche du fantastique', lent the publication an air of cosmopolitanism which whetted the (filmic) appetite of readers. He recommends in his first instalment that 'the first thing that any Spanish cinéphile must do is to buy [the popular weekly magazine] *Pariscope*' for its comprehensive 'classification by genres' and 'the exactitude and precision of its film production lists' (1972a: 40). The places to go, he continued, are 'Pigalle, the Latin Quarter and Etoile', which offered the fantasy film lover more than sixty films at any given time. In his third instalment, Tébar explained how his fannish desire to watch those Corman films censored in Spain, which had always been mediated in his personal experience through the pages of *Midi-Minuit Fantastique*, was eventually realised 'in four consecutive days – "un film par jour", as the French would put it' (1972c: 17) in which he viewed the following Roger Corman films: *The Raven* (1963), *The Haunted Palace* (1963), *The Masque of the Red Death* (1964) and *The Tomb of Ligeia* (1964). Some of his other contributions provide a window on to localised cultural practices in Spain: his review of *La maldición de la Llorona / The Curse of the Crying Woman* (Rafael Baledón 1963), *Night of the Living Dead*, *Diabolik* (Mario Bava 1968) and *Un hacha para la luna de miel / Blood Brides* (Mario Bava 1970), which were shown at the Cinema Alexis in Barcelona, can also be read as an ambling description of the venue's programming of 'Terror a medianoche' ('Midnight Horror'), Barcelona's version of the Parisian (and New York's Times Square) midnight-movie phenomenon. Tébar described the success of the programme with local audiences – there were always 'long queues' and 'many people were left outside without a ticket' (1971: 45) – and their responses – for those who managed to go in screamed, laughed, stamped their feet and had a great time (1971: 45). There was a second contributor, Pierrot, whose personal travelogue brought the filmic (and sexual) attractions of Hamburg's red-light district, St Pauli, to the attention of *TF*'s readers.

Pierrot was in charge of the section 'Teatro-Terror'. Here he focused on the aesthetics and the affects of 'Grupo Pánico', an avant-garde performance arts movement created by Chilean Alejandro Jodorowsky in conjunction with Spanish playwright Fernando Arrabal and French artist and writer Roland Topor in 1962 in Paris, which called for the trangressive and affective potential of performance. Pierrot introduced himself to *TF* readers in issue 3, 'Auto-crítica – o así – de la obra por su "exquisito" autor' (1971: 50), giving an account of his influences (Sade, Artaud) and his drama activities as part of the Barcelona underground theatre scene. The 'Grupo Pierrot' had been staging absurdist and shocking 'efímeros' ('panic ephemeras' interventions, or happenings) following the Panic movement tactics of shocking audiences with horror, sadomasochistic eroticism, violence and humour. He had also been editing the fanzine *Teatro de Impacto*, which described itself as 'terror, sadism, madness, witchcraft, horror, crime'. From issue 4 onwards, his 'Teatro Terror' for *TF* introduced readers to a gallery of panic precursors (Marquis de Sade, Oscar Wilde, Ramón María del Valle Inclán) and contemporary practitioners (Alejandro Jodorowsky and Fernando Arrabal) in a series of very idiosyncratic – and demanding – writings arranged like dramatic works for the stage, with stage directions, absurd situations, bizarre dialogues and asides. Fragments of Jodorowsky's and Arrabal's avant-garde experimental works are unorthodoxly and ingeniously put together in 'Elucubraciones, desmayos y gritos sobre el Teatro-Pánico de Alejandro Jodorowsky' ('Lucubrations, Swoons and Screams about Alejandro Jodorowsky's Panic-Theatre') (1972: 58–9) and 'Teatro Terror presenta al loco, ventrudo y mamarracho Fernando Arrabal' ('Teatro-Terror presents the mad, potbellied and coarse Fernando Arrabal') (1972: 60–2), respectively. Pierrot went on to produce his own fanzine *Vudú* once *TF* disappeared, where he continued in a total of nine issues between January 1975 and June 1976 with his versatile and unconventional take on the horror genre, transgressing straight gender boundaries by publishing articles on gay and transsexual subcultures.[18] *Vudú* was a unique fanzine: its forty-eight pages in black and white brought together articles on international horror stars and film production, psychiatry, hypnosis and witchcraft, porn fiction and sadomasochistic comic books, the Rocky Horror Show, the Gay Liberation Front street theatre and Spanish variety-show artists.[19]

Moix too gave voice to gay sensibilities through his camp readings of international horror and fantasy cinema. He contributed four essays: three treatises on icons of camp style, Barbara Steele ('Barbara Steele. Diosa del Terror' (1971b: 60–3)), María Montez ('Antinea y Ayesha' (1971a: 51–3) and 'Cobra' (1972a: 4–6)), and one on the camp possibilities rendered by Gothic and exotic scenarios in horror and adventure films ('Goticismos del terror' (1971c: 4–5)). A fifth contribution, 'Entre Batman y Superman' (1972b: 40–1), which had already appeared as a chapter of his study *Los cómics. Arte para el consumo y formas pop*, compared the universes of these comic heroes in relation to their American context of production. The essay on Barbara Steele traced the rise and decline of the 'Queen of Gothic' in the films of Mario Bava, Roger Corman and Riccardo Fredda and her elevation through the construction of her iconic cult status in the pages of *Midi-minuit fantastique* to the pantheon of cinematic goddesses of the horror genre. Another queen, this time the 'Queen of Technicolor' María Montez, is the object of 'Cobra' and 'Antinea y Ayesha',[20] where Moix blends his love for exotic adventure epics, their fantastic and exaggerated scenarios and the sexual titillation of specific cinematic images; the iconic phallic snake-dance in *Cobra Woman* (Robert Siodmark 1944) is read through the lens of camp, and is therefore susceptible to a double interpretation: a gesture full of duplicity for the cognoscenti and another for outsiders. In these pieces Moix takes pleasure in his personal identification with the queer appeal of Steele and Montez, and the camp aesthetic qualities of the period and of costume adventures that they came to embody. Moix was certainly familiar with Susan Sontag's 'Notes on "Camp"' (1964), and most probably with American avant-garde artist Jack Smith's aesthetic manifesto 'The Perfect Film Appositeness of María Montez', published in *Film Culture* in 1962–3. Moix's time in Paris, London and Rome during the 1960s familiarised him with the recent theoretical debates on popular and mass culture examining spectatorial reception, as well as with textual and visual discourses circulating in international gay culture.

But what about the magazine's coverage and critical views of Spanish horror film (bearing in mind, of course, that a significant percentage of these films were co-productions)? While there was an article which charted the presence of the science-fiction film in Spanish cinema, 'La ciencia ficción en el cine de España' (Montaner 1973: 16–19), there was no attempt to map a history of the horror film in Spain or of the place of horror film in the history of Spanish cinema. Indigenous national film production was mainly represented in the form of direct access to information about the pre-production and production stages of a particular film in the section 'Veremos . . .' (We Shall See . . .'), reviews of the latest releases in the film review section, and interviews with some of the key players.[21] *TF* was markedly international, as my discussion of the choice of both the front covers and the contents has shown. Only two front covers were devoted to Spanish horror stars: Paul Naschy's werewolf alter ego in *Dr Jekyll y el hombre lobo* stared out at readers from the January 1972 cover (see Figure 27), while the sensual presence of Jesús Franco's muse Soledad Miranda in *Vampiros Lesbos* captivated readers in March 1972 (see Figure 28).[22]

The 'Veremos . . .' section acted as a showcase for upcoming releases, providing readers with the production details of the films being surveyed, orienting the prospective filmgoer on the generic categories which the films belonged to, and regaling fans with stills. Antonio Cervera reported on the productions of prolific filmmakers Franco, Klimovsky and Ossorio, the projects of other genre filmmakers entering the world of horror (for example, José Luis Merino, Francisco Lara Palop or José María Elorrieta), and the work of newcomers such as Carlos Aured, experimental directors like Pere Portabella with his *Vampir Cuadecuc*, or the multi-authored film *Pastel de sangre*. Most of the films featured in 'Veremos . . .' are well known among fans of Spanish horror film; more recently, they have been made available on VHS and DVD. But for the dedicated fan and collectionist 'Veremos . . .' is also an invaluable source of information that brings to light films which have not made it into general accounts of Spanish horror film or whose lack of availability through the decades has made them much sought-after commodities. Copies of *Ivanna / Altar of Blood* (José Luis Merino 1970, *La mansión de la niebla / Manic Mansion* (Francisco Lara Palop 1972) and *El espectro del terror* (José María Elorrieta 1973), for example, have eluded fans for years.

The film review section allows us to sample the reading protocols encountered in the magazine. In general terms, *TF* critics showed disdain towards local production mainly because of its often-gratuitous exploitation of sex and horror and its poor artistic quality. As Yoldi acknowledged in his review of *La mansión de la niebla*, 'we are in the habit of systematically scorning all that

Figure 27 *Terror Fantastic* acknowledged Paul Naschy's horror stardom.

comes with the "made in Spain" stamp on it, not without good reasons' (1972: 61–2). The views of specialist critics did not influence the kinds of films that were being made in Spain. Overall, the interpretive frameworks deployed in the reviews relied on generic conventions and connoisseurship, intertextual ref-

Figure 28 *Terror Fantastic* devoted its March 1972 cover to Soledad Miranda, Jesús Franco's muse in *Las vampiras*.

erences and extra-textual information. Paul Naschy's *La furia del hombre lobo* and *Dr Jekyll y el hombre lobo* were read in relation to and measured against the success of the first two instalments of his werewolf cycle – *La marca del hombre lobo* and *La noche de Walpurgis* – and linked variations introduced to the werewolf subgenre. *La furia del hombre lobo* left Yoldi with 'a bad taste in the mouth' because the werewolf here is 'in tatters and without bite' (1972: 47). The potentially interesting innovation of a female werewolf was worth exploring but her 'screen debut could not have been more unfortunate' (1972: 47). For Montaner, *Dr Jekyll y el hombre lobo* proposed 'an excellent idea with the confrontation between irrational evil (the lycanthrope) and conscious evil (Mr Hyde) in the same character', but once again characterisation and performance were a major cause of criticism: Paul Naschy 'seems to be a bit tired in his werewolf role' (1972a: 49). And Montaner complained about what he saw as a laboured enactment of specific conventions and formulas: firstly, 'there is no need to waste any film reel explaining for the umpteenth time that the lycanthrope metamorphoses on nights of a full moon, that he can only be killed with a silver bullet and blah, blah, blah' for a 'veiled allusion to the myth should suffice to situate the non-initiated' (1972a: 49), and, secondly, he was unhappy with 'the "happy endings" that go against generic conventions' (1972a: 49).

Terror Fantastic was the product of a shared historical moment, a confluence of people writing not only on horror and related genres but also on their manifestations in different media across popular and mass culture (film, comics, literature and theatre). Reading through the twenty-six issues reveals heterogeneous and versatile interests in and approaches to the horror genre. Among its regular contributors, one sees the formation of a first generation of critics and cultural analysts who produced insightful and rigorous articles on the field of mass media production, reception and consumption. Many contributors like Gasca, Moix or Tébar were particularly sensitive to the industrial aspects of popular culture and the links between the cultures of pulp, film, comics and television. For Spanish horror aficionados it was the first publication to provide fans with access to various forms of knowledge about films, directors, performers and international traditions. What is the legacy of *TF*? Its treatment of horror and science-fiction genre filmmaking as worthy of serious consideration provided a different approach to writing about these genres. To a certain extent, it legitimised writing about horror. It provided a training ground for young cultural producers. For many readers and fans, *TF* engendered a sense of fandom. From a contemporary point of view, *TF* is a foundation for historians of the genre.

HORROR'S WANING FORTUNES

The publishing house Garbo Editorial, which had been enjoying some success with the commercialisation for the Spanish market of *Creepy*, *Eerie* and *Vampirella*, enrolled a key *TF* player, Luis Vigil, to launch *Famosos monstruos del cine*, the Spanish spin-off of the American fan publication *Famous*

Monsters of Filmland, another Warren Publishing product which had been edited by Forrest J. Ackerman since 1958. Like previous Garbo Editorial comic-book magazines *Rufus* and *Vampus*, the twenty-four issues of *Famosos monstruos del cine* (April 1975 to April 1977) included translated material from the American original, brief articles and a generous supply of illustrations and graphic artwork.[23] In fact, *Famosos monstruos del cine* would be one of the last specialist magazines to be devoted to the genre in the 1970s. From the late 1970s to the early 1990s, the magazine and fanzine on offer to Spanish horror aficionados declined dramatically. Individual, isolated ventures took the form of fanzines produced by some of the names that had been associated with specific publications, as in the case of Salvador Sáinz with *Transilvania Express* (1980–1, 4 issues) and Sebastián D'Arbó with *Fantastik* (1985, 1 issue), both of whom had participated in *Vudú*, or newcomers who belonged to a second generation of fandom, among them Ángel Gómez Rivero with *Metrópolis* (1978, 2 issues), Alberto Santos with *Blagdaross* (1979), Carlos Águilar with *Morpho* (1980–1, 4 issues) or Pedro Calleja with *Serie-B* (early 1980s, 4 issues).

The decline in horror film production was part of a much larger series of changes within Spain and the Spanish film industry, as well as the international film industry. The end of the dictatorship was followed by a period of transition – *transición* – whereby Spain was transformed from an authoritarian Catholic regime to a secular democracy. The abolition of all media censorship on 11 November 1977 heralded a period of permissive experimentation in the press, television and film; the lifting of censorship enabled filmmakers, actors and producers to bring explicit sexuality to mainstream culture. Indeed, Spanish politicians, filmmakers, producers and performers presided over the development of a highly unusual experiment in adult cinema during the late 1970s and early 1980s, the S film. Part of a new rating system,[24] the S certificate put Spain ahead of other European countries regarding the screening of soft- and hard-core pornography and violent films which could be 'exhibited in any cinema in the country, their receipts [. . .] taxed like any other film and their publicity [. . .] unrestricted [. . .] Apart from the warning label, the S film was in every way a mainstream film product' (Kowalsky 2004: 191).[25] Some of the directors who had been producing horror films (Jesús Franco, Carlos Aured, Francisco Lara Palop, José María Zabalza, Miguel Iglesias) moved into the pornographic film industry and availed themselves of the new commercial opportunities that flourished in Spain between 1977 and 1982. The Socialist government of Felipe González abolished the S rating in February 1982, replacing it with the X-rated category and the creation from 1984 onwards of X-rated cinemas to conform to American and European standards and rating systems. As the state denies financial support for low-brow products, the so-called popular degenerate genres, subgeneric cinemas or *subproductos*, horror and soft-porn among them, vanished from Spanish screens. As Triana-Toribio has argued in *Spanish National Cinema,* 'a series of genres reminiscent of an undesirable past had to be killed off in order to "modernize"' (2003: 114) the country's filmic output. This modernisation of Spanish cinema was carried out via the Miró Law (Ley Miró (Real Decreto 3.304 / 1983 de 28 de diciembre sobre protección a la cinematografía española)), named after the Director General of Cinematography, Pilar Miró. The new film legislation introduced by the Socialist government changed not only the way in which films were to be subsidised by the state but also the type of films to gain state protection and subsequent promotion as cultural goods representing Spanish identity and cultural patrimony. Among other reforms, the Ley Miró was used to facilitate the production and distribution of 'quality' films – that is, auterist, middle-brow and high-brow products, which were based mainly on literary and historical sources. The serious art-film, the 'quality' cinema promoted by the Miró Law, was instituted as the new brand of official cultural cinema, bringing to an end a specific type of genre filmmaking.

Concurrent with the explosion of erotica and soft-core porn in the film industry, there was also a publishing boom in the porn magazine sector, as well as the adult comic industry. Josep Toutain, with his knowing commercial opportunism and the extensive portfolio of his agency 'Selecciones Ilustradas', again played a major role by invading the Spanish market with publications such as *Creepy, 1984, Zona 84, Comix Internacional, Totem* and *El víbora.* Much of the creative personnel whose artwork had appeared in American and Spanish horror and science-fiction comics throughout the 1970s (Esteban Maroto, Víctor de la Fuente) now illustrated these adult comic magazines. Likewise, the lifting of censorship on the one hand, and the development of youth subcultures associated with punk, the new wave and rock on the other, provoked an upsurge of alternative publications and fanzines. Kike Babas and Kike Turrón catalogue around five hundred fanzines produced between 1980 and 1995 in *De espaldas al Kiosko. Guía histórica de fanzines y otros papelujos de alcantarilla* (1995). These new fanzine scenes, emerging mainly in Madrid, Barcelona, Valencia and the Basque country, heralded a generational change and new forms of expression.

A new wave of fan magazines competed for the attention of genre enthusiasts throughout the first half of the 1990s. *Blade Runner Magazine* had a run of six issues (1990–1, Manhattan Transfer) and, as its name attests, privileged science fiction. Old hands from *Nueva Dimensión* and *Terror Fantastic,* such as Domingo Santos and Luis Vigil, as well as fanzine editors such as Carlos Díaz Maroto, once again displayed their fan connoisseurship. Vigil in particular re-emerged as director of science-fiction, horror and comic magazines *Star Ficción* (16 issues, 1990–3), *Fangoria* (35 issues, 1991–3), *Comics Scenes* (1991–2, 17 issues) and *SXF* (1996–7, 8 issues), all part of the Barcelona-based

Ediciones Zinco, which had specialised since the early 1980s in pulp novels and DC comics and would be associated with the diffusion and dissemination of *Dungeons and Dragons* and related fantasy role-playing games in the mid-1990s. These magazines replicated once more the *modus operandi* of Ibero Mundial Ediciones and Garbo Editorial two decades before: that is, they were the Spanish versions of recognised American and British publishing operations. Thus *Star Ficción* was primarily the translated edition of science-fiction magazine *Starlog* (1976–present, Starlog Group Inc.), *Fangoria* was a replica of the American original *Fangoria* (1979–present, Starlog Group Inc.), *Comics Scenes* ditto, and *SXF* was a spin-off of the British publication of the same name. There was an attempt to revive *Fangoria* and *Starlog* in the early 2000s, without too much success.

In the wake of the unprecedented commercial success of *Nightmare on Elm Street* (Sam Raimi 1984) and other 1980s horror franchises such as *Halloween* and *Friday the 13th*, which came to represent the escalation of on-screen gore, a group of fans who converged around the Festival Internacional de Cinema Fantástico de Sitges launched the *Freddy magazine*, a monograph devoted to their screen hero Freddy Krueger. For the second issue, *Freddy magazine* was retitled *Fantastic magazine* (Magazines Ediciones S. A.). Editors Erico Rodríguez, Ángel Sala, Marcos Ordoñez and Ramón García were behind the publication of eleven issues (July 1990 to August 1991), which comprehensively covered contemporary international horror and fantasy production and delighted genre aficionados with small doses of classic monster lore. Unfortunately, *Fantastic magazine* was discontinued after the tragic death of Erico Rodríguez. Comunicación y Publicidad S. A. acquired the magazine, newly subtitled 'Revista de cine fantástico, terror, aventura y ciencia ficción', and reanimated it for another three years (1992–4). Editorial directors such as Jorge de Cominges and Jordi Costa garnered an enthusiastic group of contributors drawn from the fanzine scene (among them Manuel Valencia, Jesús Palacios, Jaume Balagueró and Jordi Sánchez) and expanded the cultural – and subcultural – remit of *Fantastic magazine* beyond mainstream and independent fantasy and horror cinema. Changes in the publication moved it towards a more generalist approach associated with its mother magazine *Fotogramas*, which brought with it the progressive encroachment of mainstream Hollywood and Spanish cinema and the resultant loss of its hard-core readership. As one disaffected fan ranted in a letter to the editors of the new magazine *Invasión* a few years later, 'it is refreshing to find this [publication] in the kiosk after the much missed *Fantastic magazine* was turned into a bland *Super Pop* [in reference to a popular contemporary teen magazine]' (Julia Ladykiller in *Invasión*, 1996: 14). From the point of view of the promotion of horror cinema culture in Spain and of Spanish horror cinema in particular, the significance of the second phase of *Fantastic magazine* is threefold: firstly, it combined mainstream and marginal coverage of the genre; secondly, it brought together a generation of critics and fans united by the desire to present their own appreciation and criticism of genre films to a broader readership; and thirdly, it included first-hand coverage of the early filmic projects of emerging figures such as Álex de la Iglesia and Santiago Segura. Álex de la Iglesia's first feature film, *Acción mutante / Mutant Action* (1992), for example, is granted cult status in the pages of the magazine before it is even released. The decisive impact of the newly revamped *Fantastic magazine* is evident from a rereading of its first issues, which bear witness to the hatching of a nascent Spanish horror cinema culture where a new generation of film critics, future filmmakers and genre readers converged.

A few years later, the magazine *Invasión* (1996–7, Editorial Glénat) seemed to take up the baton, albeit on a much smaller scale. '*Invasión*', wrote its editor Manuel Romo in the first editorial,

> equals teenage films, B-movies, X-rated films and Z-movies, independent and alternative cinema, virtual reality, friends of *Kabuki* [Spanish manga-anime magazine], bustle and fun, underground culture, vulgar culture, chlorethyl, benzol and formol, fantasy cinema, horror cinema, monster movies, trash cinema, punk, Def con Dos [Spanish hip-hop and hard-core band], paranormal phenomena, radioactive matter, teen spirit, kids, disorderly nights, more culture, this time trash culture and a lot more. (1996: 4)

This multitude of paracinematic interests aligned the magazine with a thriving contemporary fanzine scene which had been developing during the first half of the decade. *Invasión* was well positioned in the cultural field of horror; its combined financial and creative resources ensured its positive contribution to an emerging Spanish horror film scene. Editorial Glénat was – and still is – a specialist publisher in comics and books on popular culture; Manuel Valencia, editor of *2000maniacos*, was enlisted as one of the designers and main contributors, and the editor-in-chief Manuel Romo had directed *Hijomoto vs zombies radioactivos / Hijomoto vs the Radioactive Zombies* (1993) and *Hijomoto 2: el ataque de las hordas sodomitas / Hijomoto vs the Sodomite Hordes* (1996) – two shorts which had had some success in specialist genre festivals.

Fanzines like *Sueño de Fevre* (1990) and *Vértigo. Fanzine de cine* (1992), both edited by Carlos Díaz Maroto, or *Tenebrae. El fanzine del fantástico* (1992), by Eduardo Escalante Ávila, were short-lived ventures. Jesús Palacios, whose voice would become familiar to genre aficionados, and his father Joaquín started fanzine *El Grito* in the late 1980s and maintained it throughout the 1990s, focusing mainly on horror literature. Different subcultural sensibilities are reflected in a variety of fan publications. *Zineshock. Revista de cine oscuro y brutal* (1991–4) by future director Jaume Balagueró specialised in the hard side of the horror film spectrum: that is, gore, mondo and snuff. *Annabel Lee* (1991–6, Rubén Lardín and Sandra Uve) was a very personal zine which combined personal musings – its motto was 'Estilo de ejercicio más que ejercicio de estilo' ['A style of practice rather than a practice of style'] – with a strong sense of acting as a network fanzine informing its readers about other fanzines, festivals and conventions. *ojalatemueras* (1999, Rubén Lardín and Hernán Migoya), which echoed Umberto Eco's seminal work on mass culture *Apocalittici e integrati* (1964) in its subtitle 'Apocalípticos Integrados', privileged horror, sexploitation and porn. In the early 2000s, *Mudhoney* tapped into the world of exploitation (juvenile delinquent films, women-in-prison films or the Troma factory[26]). *Quatermass* (1989–present, Javier G. Romero) has tended to concentrate on classic moments and national movements of the horror genre in its development from fanzine to monograph. And there are many others which contribute in one way or another to the cultural field of Spanish horror, such as *Suburbio* (Naxo Fiol, 1993–present), *Data* (Antonio Garrido, 1997–present), *Amazing Monsters* (Dani Moreno, 1997–present), *Monster World* (David García, 1998 and currently as mundomonstruo.blogspot.com), *Infernaliana* (Javier Ordás, 2004, and currently as a blog in infernalianablog.blogspot.com), *El buque maldito* (Diego López, 2005–present) or *Diabolik* (David Pizarro, 2006–7). The worldwide web also houses innumerable fan-created websites and blogs (pasadizo.com, revistafantastique.com, cinefantastico.com, aullidos.com), some of which provide highly specialised repositories of Spanish horror culture.

A look at any copy of *2000maniacos* from 1989 to the present day reveals a familiarity with 'paracinema' publications: for instance, Michael Weldon's completist guides to psychotronic cinema *The Psychotronic Encyclopedia of Film* (1983) and *The Psychotronic Videoguide to Film* (1996), cult movie fanzine *Psychotronic Video* (1989–2006), B-movie specialist magazines *Video Watchdog* and *Filmfax*, and, more recently, volumes such as Pete Tombs's *Mondo Macabro. Weird and Wonderful Cinema* (1997), whose translation into Spanish in 2003 contributed further to the dissemination of international exploitation traditions among Spanish exploitation fans. As Jeffrey Sconce (1995: 387) and Joan Hawkins (2000) have observed, 'paracinema culture is heavily indebted to video technology' (Hawkins 2000: 34), mail-order video and DVD catalogues. Both the home video market and international psychotronic film distributors (Video Watchdog, Sinister Cinema, Mondo Macabro) and, lately, internet file sharing and the online network YouTube have become common everyday ports of call among fans for personal consumption and for trading with other members of the community. Bootlegs, duped tapes and uncut copies become part of the quest for and consumption of these films. The reception of many traditions of exploitation cinema in general in Spain is therefore always mediated through fandom culture.[27] And *2000maniacos* is arguably the best example of such fan practices. Let us focus on this fanzine and the ways in which Manuel Valencia and his collaborators write about and read psychotronic cinemas.

2000MANIACOS

2000maniacos trades in horror, gore, porn and exploitation, covering the low end of the horror market and the high and low ends of the porn market. It provides its niche zine readership with a wealth of archival and collector information on international psychotronic culture. Taking its name from the classic exploitation gore picture, *2,000 Maniacs* (Herschell Gordon Lewis 1964), *2000maniacos* published its first issue in August 1989. One hundred copies were produced on a budget of 4,000 pesetas and the price tag was a hundred pesetas ($1). As is typical of fanzine publications, the release history of *2000maniacos* has not always been consistent (it has sometimes appeared quarterly, other times annually). However, it has now been in existence for over three decades, which makes it possibly the oldest fanzine in Europe. Like many other fanzines, copies of *2000maniacos* were initially sold at gigs, fanzine and comic conventions, genre film festivals, and independent record and comic shops. My own collection certainly started that way, with a first copy purchased from a local record store in my hometown of Zaragoza, after reading a reference to it in the pages of specialist music magazine *Ruta 66*. These days, the fanzine is distributed to major comic shops in Spanish cities by special effects company DDT and can be obtained by contacting its editor Manuel Valencia (pipoelpayasoborracho@yahoo.es).

The early visual aesthetics of *2000maniacos* attest to a do-it-yourself production ethic – itself an exploitation mode / code of practice – since most of the graphic material is poached from international catalogues and fanzines; likewise, the images of film promotional material are black-and-white or colour reproductions from video and DVD covers, and stills are home-made photographs taken directly from the television screen. There are two important turning points in the life of the publication. Its 'official' association with the San Sebastián Horror and Fantasy Film Festival since 1992, with a special issue celebrating the retrospective on Italian horror cinema 'Tutto Italia', has contributed to its much wider distribution (3,000 copies) and a production quality far removed from the do-it-yourself amateurism of the original bundle of black-and-white typewritten photocopies (the price these days is 7 euros ($10)); and its distribution went national with issue 13 (July 1993), devoted exclusively to porn queen Traci Lords. The use of desktop publishing, Xerox and computer scanning from issue 14 onwards (January 1994) have rendered better-quality reproduction of images and facilitated the move to colour covers.

The first issue's cover and content drew distinct cultural markers and alignments. Both the fanzine title, *2000maniacos*, and the cover image from *Freaks* (Tod Browning 1932) (see Figure 29) interpellate a community of self-confessed 'freaks' and invite the prospective reader to become 'one of us', to echo the famous line from Browning's film, forging links with a specific readership. Although no direct discussion of *Freaks* or *2,000 Maniacs* is featured in the forty pages of the first issue, the fanzine's founder and editor Manuel Valencia is visibly generating a sense of subcultural identity and taking a position within the fanzine scene. The graffiti-style '2000maniacos' masthead against the background of a hand-drawn brick wall, a paint tin and brush in the top right-hand corner, would identify the fanzine for the first seven issues, and denotes the punk do-it-yourself attitude of the editor. Six leads typewritten in capitals establish the fanzine's political affiliations with the alternative culture of pirate radios ('RADIOS LIBRES'), irreverent tastes ('MAL GUSTO', in reference to Peter Jackson's gory 1987 comedy *Bad Taste* and to the popular trading card collection 'PANDILLA BASURA' ('The Rubbish Bin Kids')) and generic preferences for horror auteur Sam Raimi and for *Nightmare on Elm Street* villain Freddy Krueger.

The next eight issues or so confirm the fanzine's trajectory in terms of content and anticipate its development of other enthusiasms. Issues 4 to 7, from June 1990 to June 1991, adopted the generic subtitle 'SF, Fantasy & Horror'. Individual issues give special focus to American horror auteurs Tobe Hooper, Joe Dante and Frank Henenlotter, and to actors Bruce Campbell (*Evil Dead*), Jeffrey Combs (*Re-animator*) and Robert Englund (Freddy Krueger), revealing a particular affection for gore and the combined generic excesses of comedy and horror. Other favourite topics of the fanzine are the brands of exploitation and sexploitation represented by the likes of directors Herschell Gordon Lewis and Russ Meyer, or producer Lloyd Kaufmann of Troma, whose works are exhaustively celebrated. But more conventional appraisals of classical myths and films also find a place in the fanzine. Reports on horror and fantasy film festivals such as Sitges or the now-defunct Imagfic show the presence and participation of *2000maniacos* fans in specialist events. Porn enters the publication mainly through the treatment of stars Ginger Lynn (issue 3), Traci Lords (issues 5, 8) and John Holmes (issue 2), and, with time, it becomes a major focus for Valencia, attracting some readers and alienating others. Indeed, Valencia and other pioneering contributors, such as Sergio Rubio, have been among the first critics seeking to vindicate the porn genre in Spain. Affinities with adjacent subcultures – adult comics, animation, cartoons – are reflected from the beginnings of the publication, while the always-limited coverage of music and literature would gradually disappear altogether. As the second editorial reiterated, 'our remit is horror and fantasy cinema, we want to touch upon erotic and porn cinema, and we are not going to turn our backs on comics. Rock music will be given a small space (but that is about it). Few

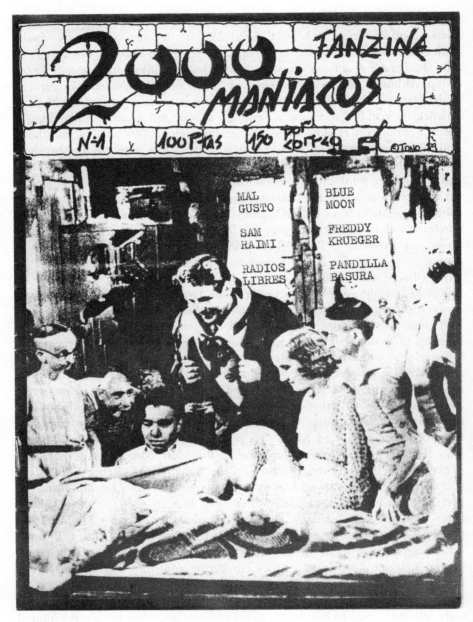

Figure 29 *2000maniacos*' front cover for the first issue is a declaration of principles.

(if none) have advocated for such a formula, but we accept the risks' (Valencia 1990: 3). By issue 25 (2002) and the editorial 'Esto es lo que hay' ('This is it'), the sense of the fanzine's identity is clear: 'Porn and Trash. If you read it quickly, it sounds like PORNOTRASH. Pure cacophony [. . .] In *2000maniacos* we only know how to talk about horror and sex' (2002c: 5).

While Valencia is the chief editor and writer, there have been a number of regular collaborators whose names are well known in the subcultural field of the Spanish fanzine scene of the mid-1980s to the early 2000s: Jesús Palacios, Alex Zinéfilo (real name Álex Mendíbil), Sandra Uve, Borja Crespo, Charly Álvarez and Casto Estópico, among others. The twentieth anniversary issue '20 años, 1989–2009' (2009), invited past and present contributors to reminisce about their first encounters with *2000maniacos*, to choose their most and least favourite issue and cover, and to assess whether the fanzine had 'aged well or terribly' (Valencia 2009: 28). The different replies confirm a sense of community and shared spaces, frequented sites and cultural artefacts. Here are some of the ways in which the fanzine's contributors first encountered the publication: at festivals ('the encounter between Manuel Valencia and Pedro Calleja (with Isabel Andrade) takes place at the Sitges Film Festival in 1991 or 1992' (Pedro Calleja in Valencia 2009: 29); or 'I got my first copy at the Donostia film festival' (Juanma Bajo Ulloa in Valencia 2009: 33)); at film genre seasons and retrospectives ('after a season of gore films organized in my university' (Txema Millán in Valencia 2009: 30; or 'the retrospective that the Spanish Film Institute devoted to Jess Franco in Madrid back in 1992' (Pedro Temboury in Valencia 2009: 29)); through like-minded individuals ('Daniel Monzón introduced me to the fanzine. It had been appearing for some years. I was then editor of *Fantastic magazine* and Monzón suggested to me that it would be a good idea to recruit Valencia, which it definitely was' (Jordi Costa in Valencia 2009: 29); or 'Pedro Calleja, Sara Torres and other degenerate types introduced me to it' (Jesús Palacios in Valencia 2009: 31)); and via comics shops and independent record outlets, as related by Charly Álvarez (in Valencia 2009: 35), Rubén Lardín (in Valencia 2009: 37) and Pablo Herránz (in Valencia 2009: 36). Perhaps Spanish singer Alaska – a key representative of the punk scene in Madrid in the 1980s –best captures the confluence of subcultural producers and consumers and their sense of a shared circuit of alternative publications: 'we also edited fanzines [*Kaka de Luxe*], had similar interests and had friends in common' (Alaska in Valencia 2009: 32). Valencia himself, reminiscing about how it all began, recalls his active participation in the alternative pirate radio scene of his home town Valencia, where he presented a programme devoted to comics, horror films, porn cinema and the world of fanzines on Radio Funny in the second half of the 1980s – and still airing. In true fanzine fashion, Valencia essentially created the fanzine he would have wanted to buy and read, a non-profit publication which reflected a desire to 'do-culture-yourself' and an 'an urge to disseminate culture' (1994: 3). Valencia cites two publications as major influences, Spaniard Pedro Calleja's *Serie-B* and American Michael Weldon's *Psychotronic*.

The forty-one issues published to date carry numerous items on the varied historical manifestations of psychotronia past and present, a vast quantity of interviews with directors, performers and producers of films and other media, and, above all, hundreds of film reviews. With the exception of letters to the editor, 'Pin-ups' (actually current news items), the comic strip 'El prisionero' and the review section 'Toxic Shrieks', which established themselves as regular features from very early on, the features of the fanzine tend to vary from issue to issue. Special issues started in 1992 with the Italian horror film special edition 'Tutto Italia' and have continued with monographs on porn (issues 13 (1993) and 18 (1997)) and horror traditions such as 'Chicas de miedo' (issue 15 (1994)), '100 años de terror' (issue 16 (1994)), 'México Loco Superespecial. Chilli Terror' (issue 22 (1999)), 'Eurovicio' (issue 24 (2001)), 'Bizarre Latino' (issue 26 (2002)), 'Euroheroes' (issue 29 (2004)) and 'Especial viejuno' (issue 38 (2008)). Anniversary editions – the tenth in 1999, fifteenth in 2005 and twentieth in 2009 – give the reader an idea of the diversity of the fanzine's output, as well as the types of fandom it accommodates. For example, *2000maniacos*' special issues function as significant repositories of connoisseurship of the international traditions of horror and respond to the fanzine's archivist tendencies. The aforementioned Mexican 'Chilli Terror' and 'Bizarre Latino' are representative of a long-standing collaboration between the 'Semana de Cine Fantástico y de Terror de San Sebastián' and the fanzine. The festival and *2000maniacos* have together provided different generations of horror fans with cultural spaces of fandom to indulge in horror pleasures, as well as with networks where 'fans from different walks of life gather together to share their fandom' (Hills 2002: 61) and invest their (sub)cultural capital as consumers and / or producers. For the Mexican 'Chilli Terror' issue, Valencia enlisted connoisseurs from different fields of cultural production. Academic Eduardo de la Vega Alfaro shed light on Fernando Méndez (Valencia 1999b: 32–7), archivist and curator Rogelio Agrasánchez Junior supplied inside knowledge about his father's productions (Valencia 1999b: 48–51) plus an exuberant selection of popular film posters from the Agrasánchez Film Archives collection for the delight of readers (Valencia 1999b: 76–7),[28] journalist and novelist Mauricio-José Schwarz analysed wrestling superheroes El Santo and Superbarrio from a sociological perspective (Valencia 1999b: 64–7), and Brian Moran, editor of American fanzine *Santo Street*, talked to Herránz about his fannish enthusiasm for women wrestlers, Aztec mummies and all things mexploitation (Valencia 1999b: 40–3). Added to these, contributions from Guillermo del Toro, a bibliography, a list of internet resources and even an index give the fanzine a scholarly air. Indeed, 'Chilli Terror' could be described as 'the fanzine-as-dissertation', 'a site where academic knowledge may also circulate outside the academy' (Hills 2002: 18) and therefore as a contribution to the historical and cultural valorisation of Latin American exploitation film history and, by extension, Spanish and Latin American cinematic encounters, histories and canons.[29]

Trying to determine a 'maniac philosophy' from *2000maniacos* would not do justice to the diversity of the fanzine's output, the wide range of material covered or the varied profiles of the contributors writing across its forty-one issues. Equally, when we talk about the fan community converging around the production and consumption of *2000maniacos*, we are not depicting a homogeneous group. We can nevertheless attempt a sketch of the fanzine's dominant subcultural sensibilities. I would like to focus on the tenth anniversary issue (1999) in order to map out a range of ways in which Valencia and other *2000maniacos* contributors approach and write about horror and psychotronic / trash (or *caspa*) cinema with particular attention to the following: firstly, I will consider the relationship the fanzine establishes with its subjects in articles and interviews, which is varied and ranges from the celebratory and cultish to traditional forms of auterism, as well as to the treatment of filmmakers as fellow fans. Jesús Franco, or 'Uncle Jess', as he is affectionately referred to in the pages of the fanzine, and Pedro Temboury, whose career runs parallel to the life of the fanzine and Franco's re-emergence from the mid-1990s onwards, will be my brief representative cases. And, secondly, I consider specific examples of the fanzine's treatment of Spanish horror film in order to indicate its key involvement in emerging trends within contemporary Spanish horror cinema: its coverage of gore shorts on the one hand, and the work of Álex de la Iglesia on the other. It can be seen that *2000maniacos* was a lead player in the revitalisation of the contemporary field of horror.

The tenth anniversary issue, entitled '1989–1999. Toda una década de caspa y puterío' ('1989–1999. A Decade of Trash and Porn'), includes, among the regular features and coverage of porn, the following material: interviews with Jess Franco (Susi Sexy in Valencia 1999a: 40–7), Mójica Marins (Álex Zinéfilo in Valencia 1999a: 48–51), Roger Corman (Guillot, Romo and Valencia in Valencia 1999a: 54–61) and Carlos Aured (in Valencia 1999a: 66–73), a guide on 'How to Make a Trash Film?' (Dr Relleno in Valencia 1999a: 13), an overview of world trash cinema via a delirious 'Trash Cinema "World Cup"' featuring key directors and stars (Valencia 1999a: 20–7), an article on American pulp fiction (Palacios in Valencia 1999a: 52–3) and an extensive film review section (Valencia 1999a: 30–9). The term 'caspa' (literally meaning 'dandruff' in Spanish) is often used in *2000maniacos* to define psychotronic or trash cinema. In relation to Spanish trash cinema, it is applied to the films of established filmmakers such as Jesús Franco and a new breed of contemporary directors such as Santiago Segura, Pedro Temboury, Manuel Romo and the late Antonio

Blanco, who emerged from the short film and festival circuit. In the interview with Franco as part of the tenth anniversary issue, the director himself describes *caspa* as 'a cinema that is not official, that is independently made, with cheap means of production but which can be much better than the so-called "official" cinema' (Valencia 1999a: 40), adding that 'for me it is not a pejorative term but rather a label to be put on the cover of the videotape or on the video store stalls' (Valencia 1999a: 40). The category of trash cinema is, for Franco, a commercial label that asserts both the market viability of this (his own) type of cinema and the existence of trash consumers. To these fans and readers he encourages a do-it-yourself approach to filmmaking: 'you must dare to do it, and move from being a cinéphile to becoming a director' (Valencia 1999a: 44). Franco places this type of *caspa* filmmaking outside mainstream official culture, a position with which the fanzine readership he is addressing identifies. His words cut across production, distribution and circulation practices, and speak to the modes in which films are classified and consumed in the marketplace.

Until very recently, the reception and consumption of Franco in Spain has always been mediated and constructed through fandom culture,[30] *2000maniacos* being a prime example. In fact, the resurgence of the fanzine as a cultural form in the early 1990s – alongside a boom in gore shorts – proved to be a determining factor in the celebration and revival of his work for new generations of fans in Spain and the ongoing construction, promotion and perpetuation of his cult reputation. Franco's media presence was significantly weakened by the disappearance of the 'S' category film and the decline of low-budget film production in the mid-1980s; still trading on his reputation from the 1960s and 1970s, the notoriously prolific director made relatively few features from the late 1980s to the early 1990s. But fresh impetus was given to Franco's career in 1991 when the Spanish Film Institute in Madrid organised a retrospective of his work. *2000maniacos* provided coverage of the retrospective and an interview with the director, whose name appears on the front cover of its 1991 issue. Retrospectives are key events in the galvanising of critical communities. The Spanish Film Institute event conferred auteur status on Franco within the traditional norms of auteurism; however, the retrospective also confirmed his status as cult auteur for an emerging fanzine audience. Franco's appeal to a young subcultural scene was confirmed in 1996 when he teamed up with indie rock band *Killer Barbys* in the direction of his gore-fest movie *Killer Barbys / Vampire Killer Barbys* (see Figure 30). Encouraged perhaps by the commercial successes of young directors de la Iglesia and Amenábar in the mid-1990s, the veteran director went on to produce a further five titles in the space of one year: *Tender Flesh* (1998), *Mari Cookie y la tarántula asesina / Mary Cookie and the Killer Tarantula in 8 Legs To Love You* (1998), *Lust for Frankenstein* (1998), *Vampire Blues* (1998) and *Dr Wong's Virtual Hell* (1998). Valencia and the retrospective put Franco back into circulation – from

Figure 30   Apart from the indie band Barby Killers, Jesús Franco also paired with
comics artist Miguel Ángel Martín to reach a new generation of fans in
Killer Barbys.

1992 onwards Franco's presence in niche publications is firmly established. Of
course, Franco's cinema had long been a staple of the international culture of
psychotronia; the retrospective gave institutional validation to a type of filmmaking whose contribution to an international trash film history was already
being celebrated in *2000maniacos*.

Two self-confessed Franco fan pieces accompany the 1999 interview, Álex
Zinéfilo's 'Jess perverso: descubre el tortuoso mundo sexual de Jesús Franco'
('Perverse Jess: Discover Jesús Franco's devious sexual world') (in Valencia
1999a: 45)[31] and Pedro Temboury's 'Yo trabajé en tres películas con el Tío
Jess y aún le quiero' ('I worked with Uncle Jess on three films and I still love
him') (in Valencia 1999a: 42–3). Zinéfilo catalogues for Franco neophytes

the director's loose adaptations of the Marquis de Sade's works and records 'the inimitable and inexpressible sexual aberrations' (in Valencia 1999a: 45) in, among others, *Marquis de Sade: Justine* (1969), *Women in Cell Block 9 / Tropical Inferno* (1978) and *Gemidos de placer / Cries of Pleasure* (1983). At the time of writing his note on Franco, Temboury had already worked with Franco as a production manager and second unit assistant director on three films, *Tender Flesh, Mary Cookie and the Killer Tarantula* and *Lust for Frankenstein. Vampire Blues* and *Dr Wong's Virtual Hell* would follow. Temboury describes how he fell in love with Franco's cinema at the Spanish Film Institute retrospective and explains how Franco's style made him realise that in order 'to make films you only need a bit of money, some friends and enthusiasm' (in Valencia 1999a: 42). Shortly thereafter, Temboury decided to pick up a super-8 camera and make shorts, one of which, *Psycho-lettes* (1996), a side-splitting, gory take on *She-Devils on Wheels* (Hershell Gordon Lewis 1968), was entered in film festivals and catapulted him to subcultural fame, bringing him to the attention of Franco.[32] Temboury acknowledges that he learnt his trade by watching Franco films and later on by working for the director. As a follower of Franco, Temboury ends his note with a cry for action: 'Freaks of the world, unite and make *caspa* films right fucking now' (in Valencia 1999a: 43). Subsequent coverage of Temboury's feature films, *Kárate a muerte en Torremolinos* (Karate to the Death in Torremolinos (2003)) and *Ellos robaron la picha de Hitler* (They Stole Hitler's Cock (2006)) in *2000maniacos* frames this relationship in terms of a subcultural lineage – 'Jesús Franco, true Zinematographic (yes, with capital Z as in grade-Z movie) father of Temboury' (Valencia 2002b: 16).[33]

2000maniacos has featured numerous articles on and interviews with Franco and provided the (cult) fan with stories and anecdotes that have helped to cement his iconic status.[34] The work of other directors from the 1970s and 1980s, such as León Klimovsky, Carlos Aured, Eugenio Martín and Juan Piquer Simón, has also been the subject of interviews and film reviews. But the main contribution of the fanzine to the resurgence of Spanish horror cinema lies in its championing of a new generation of filmmakers whose shorts and first feature films responded not only to the tastes and generic preferences of *2000maniacos* (gore-comedy), but also to the do-it-yourself attitude of the fanzine. The fanzine provided the platform for the dissemination of these shorts and films to a broader fan community.

Recalling the period from the early 1990s to the early 2000s, regular fanzine collaborator Charly Álvarez writes:

> the first shorts of directors such as Manuel Romo, Borja Crespo, Koldo Serra or Pedro Temboury, even the first crazy shorts [*primeras locuras*] made by people who are now consecrated such as Santiago Segura,

Álex de la Iglesia or Paco Plaza served to bring together these young rogues under the dubious label of *generación CASP* (*Casposos Aunque Sobradamente Preparados*) [generation Trash (Trashy Although Fully Qualified)]. *Caspa* is to cinema what punk was to music. (Valencia 2009: 20)

One of the main architects behind the coinage of the term *caspa* was Manuel Romo, whose shorts *Hijomoto vs zombies radioactivos* and the sequel *Hijomoto vs las hordas sodomitas* exemplify this mode of filmmaking. Responding to the rallying call of Jesús Franco and others to take up arms in the *caspa* cause, Romo, one of the fanzine contributors, duly took up his camera. The resulting short gave rise to the character of Hijomoto, a cross between a manga Kamen rider and a Tromaesque leather-clad biker-superhero whose crusading mission is announced in the form of a cross on his helmet, a 'Christ Loves You' on the back of his jacket and a religious print on the front. In the first instalment, Hijomoto wipes out a legion of radioactive zombies, while in the second and final part he returns from retirement to save the town from a very contemporary plague of young urban professionals and the values they embody. From the pages of the magazine *Invasión*, which Romo edited (and to which Valencia himself contributed), he plugged his own work and endorsed the *caspa* generation: 'promoters and lovers of Z-series, [producers of] alternative, underground and fanzine culture, in other words, cultural terrorists, they represent a generational change associated with the cinema of Franco. They are the *generación CASP*' (1996: 19).

Another collaborator to *2000maniacos* from 1992 onwards, and to *Invasión*, was Borja Crespo.[35] Crespo's short, *Snuff 2000* (2002), exhibits far better production values than Romo's, but its approach to its subject matter, deployment of humour and circulation in the same contexts of reception and consumption (festivals and fanzines) make it part of the same 'gore movement'. *Snuff 2000* is a fusion of the comic of the same title by comic artist Miguel Ángel Martín (*Snuff 2000* (1998, La Factoría de Ideas)), porn imagery, myths around snuff movies, and black humour. Crespo's *Snuff 2000* illustrates once again the close intersection of different subcultural scenes (gore shorts, festivals, comics and fanzines) with shared tastes and sensibilities (see Figure 31). In an interview published in *2000maniacos*, Crespo described it as a 'morbid absurdity [majadería enfermiza]', 'a Monty Python sketch filmed by David Cronenberg', and '*Funny Games* in a Dunkin' Donuts coffee shop' (Crespo in Suzy Sexi 2002: 13). The opening credits of *Snuff 2000* introduce the viewer to a video camera, tapes, a computer, and surgical instruments meticulously arranged in an aseptic space akin to an operation theatre, which doubles up as a film studio. A close-up of the video camera held by one of the torturers mediates between the viewer and the gagged, almost naked victim – a

Figure 31   Comics artist Miguel Ángel Martín contributed with his distinctive
aesthetics to Borja Crespo's short *SNUFF 2000*.

pregnant young woman, the snuff girl. From then onwards, the viewer's attention is drawn to the two male characters, Rubberface and Rubberman: to the
fuchsia rubber suit of Rubberman and the immaculate white shirt and fuchsia
tie of Rubberface, their gas masks, their mundane dialogue and their measured, mechanical actions. Torture, mutilation, rape and murder take place off
screen. A 'Game Over' intertitle gives way to the second segment of the short,
in which we are presented with two young male characters (man in white and
man in yellow) commenting on the content and quality of the snuff videos they
are watching, as if it were the most natural thing in the world (the titles of the
videos they are watching, 'Pregnant' and '2000 snuff', being a self-reference to
the previous segment). A third segment, entitled 'How to be a successful serial
killer', reintroduces Rubberface talking straight to the camera and advising the
viewer on the key rules that must be observed in order to avoid capture.

But perhaps the gore landmark *par excellence* of this period is Antonio
Blanco's and Ricardo Llovo's film *La matanza de los garrulos lisérgicos /
Cannibal Massacre* (1993). As directors Blanco and Llovo admit in an interview with Valencia, their film 'is a pillaging of Tobe Hooper's classic [*The
Texas Chainsaw Massacre*] and Herschell Gordon Lewis's *2,000 Maniacs*.
We are not creators or geniuses. We are like sponges that absorb everything
within our reach' (Valencia 1994: 28): in other words, cinéphages. As for
their film practice, 'we vindicate the use of the video format to make rabid
films, following what punk did with rock'n'roll' (Valencia 1994: 28). Indeed,
the film packs in 'Mutilations, Cannibalism, Rape, Incest, Murders, Drugs,
Necrophilia, Sadism, Wild Beasts in Captivity'. As the video cover tagline
blithely announces, 'More atrocities for less money!'. For the price of 1,999

pesetas, *2000maniacos* readers could obtain what was immediately heralded as a cult movie among Spanish horror fans. Unfortunately, the early offerings of Blanco and Llovo were cut short by the untimely death of Blanco. However, the cultural afterlife of Blanco and *La matanza de los garrulos lisérgicos* continues, due in no small part to the fanzine's initial profiling.

A different type of landmark was provided by the early works of Álex de la Iglesia, his short *Mirindas asesinas / Killer Mirindas* (1991) and his first feature film, *Acción mutante*. *Mirindas asesinas* is the only short to have been granted a *2000maniacos* front cover – issue 10 in 1992 (see Figure 32). *Acción mutante* also took centre-stage in the following edition (11 November 1992), as did his second film, *El día de la bestia*, three years later in issue 17 (1995). From the pages of the fanzine, as well as those of *Fantastic magazine*, de la Iglesia was hailed as the spearhead of a new Spanish horror and fantasy cinema, *fantastique* or *caspa*, and both *Mirindas asesinas* and *Acción mutante* were predicted to become cult movies. In fact, *2000maniacos* and *Fantastic magazine* chose the same *Acción mutante* still for their front covers (see Figure 33). In issues 10, 11 and 17 Valencia gives extensive coverage on the director's career as a fanzine editor of *No!, el fanzine maldito*, as author of comics, as artistic director and artistic designer in shorts and feature films by other Basque filmmakers, such as Pablo Berger (*Mama* (1988)) and Enrique Urbizu (*Todo por la pasta / Everything for the Money* (1991)), and as set designer for a number of television shows on Basque regional television. The macabre storyline, the twisted sense of humour and the visual aesthetics of *Mirindas asesinas* were just right for the profile of the fanzine. A seemingly normal guy (played by Álex Angulo) goes into a bar and orders a *mirinda* (a Spanish fizzy drink); when asked by the bartender to pay for his drink, he loses his temper and turns into a 'tubular psycho-killer', shooting the bartender and another costumer. De la Iglesia's filming of *Acción mutante* offered Valencia and other genre fans the opportunity to witness *in situ* the return of horror and fantasy film production in Spain. Valencia succeeded in providing insider knowledge of the film: production history details, storyboard images, anecdotes about the shoot, and serious discussion of the film's science-fiction and gore aesthetics with particular attention to the craftsmanship of SFX designer Hipólito Cantero and set designer Emilio Ruiz. While Valencia situates de la Iglesia's production as part of the fanzine's enthusiasm for gore and psychotronic / trash cinema and links it to contemporary production trends such as Troma, the director tactfully qualifies his association with these traditions by expressing his dislike for 'trash cinema à la Troma' and his concern that *Acción mutante* might be seen through that lens. Although de la Iglesia accepts the presence of gore-comedy in his film, the director's affiliations lay elsewhere: on the one hand, with the Spanish dark comedy tradition of Marco Ferreri's *El cochecito* (1960) and Luis García Berlanga's *El verdugo / The Executioner* (1963), and, on the other,

Figure 32   De la Iglesia's short *Mirindas Asesinas* had full coverage in *2000maniacos*.

Figure 33   *Fantastic magazine* and *2000maniacos* illustrated their covers with an image from Álex de la Iglesia's *Acción mutante.*

with auteurs like Hitchcock and Polanski. *2000maniacos* and *Fantastic magazine* welcomed de la Iglesia as the vanguard of a long-awaited Spanish *freak* cinema movement, which suited the director's conscious targeting of different audiences and tastes in the film's promotion, although de la Iglesia and his producers were keen for his work to be co-opted by the mainstream media. Even at the level of production, de la Iglesias's *Acción mutante* is far removed from the gore films of Romo or Blanco as it was sustained by the financial backing and marketing machinery of El Deseo, Agustín and Pedro Almodóvar's production company (see Figure 34).

CONCLUSION

The fanzine title *2000maniacos* indicates a pointedly self-conscious frame of reference that produces a sense of subcultural identity. The invitation to become a *maniaco* paid dividends, turning readers into potential collaborators and fans into filmmakers. Regular *2000maniacos* collaborators, such as Jesús Palacios (*Goremanía* (1995) and *Planeta zombi* (1996)) and Rubén Lardín (*Las diez caras del miedo* (1996)), represent a significant section of the players who have actively contributed to the thriving Spanish fanzine scene and the world of specialist genre publications appearing throughout the 1990s. Other

Figure 34   Producer Pedro Almodóvar and director Álex de la Iglesia pose with the freaky *Acción Mutante* commando.

contributors have found a home in the new portal of fanzine culture, the internet blog: Pedro Calleja (pedrocalleja.blogia.com), Borja Crespo (infraser. com), Sandra Uve (sandrauve.wordpress.com), Alex Zinéfilo (franconomi-con.wordpress.com and expandedexploitation.blogspot.com) or El Abuelito (eldesvandelabuelito.blogspot.com). The line-up of zinesters has remained reasonably constant, for which Manuel Valencia deserves praise. For Valencia himself, the fanzine has acted as a platform which has enabled him to collaborate in mainstream commercial publications (*Fantastic magazine*, *Primera línea*) and adult comics publications (*El víbora*, *Kiss comics*), and to write guides and specialist books on gore and porn cinema (*Videoguía X* (1994), *Breve historia del cine X* (co-authored with Sergio Rubio, 1995), *Sangre, sudor y vísceras: Historia del cine gore* (co-authored with Eduardo Guillot, 1996) and *Pornomanía* (1999)). More recently, he has directed his first film *Manolín* (2007), an idiosyncratic 'biopic' with no dialogue, shot entirely with a digital camera; it works as a video diary of Valencia's favourite beloved places, family moments and situations.

The journey of *2000maniacos* from its micro-media cut-and-paste origins in 1989 to its current position as a niche media publication with the financial and institutional support of the San Sebastián Horror and Film Festival from the mid-1990s onwards continues into its third decade. *2000maniacos* has remained true to its original non-profit fanzine remit and its aim to inform and entertain its readers. For more than three decades the fanzine has inde-fatigably propagated information on psychotronia, grade B and Z movies, and porn, catering to a wide variety of subcultural fan communities, mainly oriented towards exploitation and cult interests. Just as *Terror Fantastic* did in the early 1970s with international horror traditions and subcultural forms of expression such as comics, Valencia's *2000maniacos* has helped to import into Spain a psychotronic movie canon which had been largely constructed in the US by publications such as *The Psychotronic Encyclopedia of Film* and *Video Watchdog*. As Jordi Costa recommended to Valencia back in issue 27, 'you should be our Michael Weldon and think of *2000maniacos* as a mission, a necessity, a drug served in regular doses' (Costa in Zinéfilo 2003: 65).

NOTES

1. See Sennit (1999).
2. Semic stands for SEries and coMIC. From 1963 Semic had been publishing serials based on TV series such as *Eddie Constantine*, *El Santo* or *Super Agente 86*. Comic artists for these anthologies were drawn from the Agency Bardon Art.
3. *Triunfo*'s understanding of the term terror cuts across politics, sociology, psychol-ogy, history and culture; the term is used to discuss it as an emotional state, and as a weapon used by totalitarian and democratic states to intimidate and punish people, as well as the literary and filmic genre of horror. The issue compiled the expert opinions of writer Ana María Moix ('El terror en la infancia'), playwright Alfonso Sastre ('Ensayo sobre Drácula'), pathologist Professor Fernández-Cruz ('Bases psicobiológicas del terror y del miedo'), historian Jordi Borja ('El manual de los inquisidores'), cultural and political commentators Eduardo Haro-Tecglen ('Miedo y sociedad. El "Gran Terror" y el "Pequeño Terror"') and Manuel Vázquez Montalbán ('Hacia un terror sin humanismo'), and film critics Diego Galán ('El terror en el cine') and Fernando Lara ('Y los fantasmas vinieron a nuestro encuen-tro'). *Triunfo*'s archives can be accessed via triunfodigital.com. *Fotogramas*'s focus on the topic, on the other hand, was merely filmic, featuring articles by Román Gubern, José Luis Guarner and Luis Gasca, and interviews with Narciso Ibáñez Serrador and Suzy Kendall.
4. Shown between June and July 1972: *Drácula* (Tod Browning 1931), *La hija de Drácula* (Lambert Hillyer 1936), *El hijo de Drácula* (Robert Siodmark 1943), *La mansión de Drácula* (Erle C. Kenton 1945) and *La sangre de Drácula* (Herbert L. Strock 1958).
5. *El sabor del miedo*, *La escalera de caracol*, *Cartas envenenadas*, *El mon-tacargas*, *Al morir la noche*, *La muchacha del trapecio rojo* and *La mujer del cuadro*.
6. See tebeosfera.com for detailed information (format, price, periodicity, table of contents and so on) on *Dossier negro*, *Rufus*, *Vampus* and *Vampirella*.
7. The editors were Sebastián Martínez, Domingo Santos and Luis Vigil. The publica-tion was discontinued in 1982 after 148 issues.
8. Boris Karloff (issue 1), James Whale (issue 2), Terence Fisher (issue 3), Roger Corman (issue 4), Lon Chaney (issue 5), Inoshiro Honda (issue 6), Jack Arnold (issue 7), Ricardo Freda (issue 8), Ingmar Bergman (issue 12), F. W. Murnau (issue 13), Bela Lugosi (issue 14), Christopher Lee (issue 15), Mario Bava (issue 16), William Castle (issue 17), Fritz Lang (issue 19), Barbara Steele (issue 20),

Vincent Price (issue 21), Lon Chaney Junior (issue 22), Paul Naschy (issue 23), Tod Browning (issue 24) and Alfred Hitchcock (issue 25).

9. Frankenstein (issue 2), Dracula (issue 3), the werewolf (issue 4), the mummy (issue 5), zombies (issue 6), Dr Jekyll and Mr Hyde (issue 7), minor vampires (issues 11, 13 and 15), James Bond (issue 8), Tarzan (issue 9), giant insects (issue 17), apes (issue 18), the invisible man (issue 22), Fu Manchu (issue 23) and Sherlock Holmes (issue 24).

10. The films covered ranged from the silent era to contemporary productions: *Freaks, La semilla del diablo, Psycho, The Most Dangerous Game, 2001. A Space Odyssey, Night of the Living Dead, Häxam, M, Planet of the Apes, Dr Caligari, Dies Irae, The Birds, Marat / Sade, The Day the Earth Stood Still, I Married a Monster From Outer Space, Island of Lost Souls, Repulsion, Vampyr, Metropolis* and *Yellow Submarine.*

11. *Just Imagine, The Mask of Fu Manchu, Al Hollywood madrileño, Dante's Inferno, Forbidden Planet, Mysterious Dr Satan, El manuscrito encontrado en Zaragoza, The Phantom Empire, Aelita, Attack of the Fifty Foot Woman, The Colossus of New York, Artistas y modelos.*

12. Percy Bysshe Shelley, Bram Stoker, Edgar Allan Poe, H. P. Lovecraft, Robert Louis Stevenson, Ian Flemming, Edgar Rice Burroughs, Jules Verne, H. G. Wells, Agatha Christie, Henry James, Aldous Huxley, Théophile Gautier, Gustav Meyrink, Ray Bradbury, Franz Kafka, Dante Alghieri, Gustavo Adolfo Bécquer.

13. Captain Marvel, El hombre enmascarado, Flash Gordon, Batman, Mandrake, the Magician, Buck Rogers, Superman, Ace Diamond, Barbarella, Modesty Blaise.

14. In issues 20, 21, 22, 23 and 25.

15. Issue 11, 'A vueltas con el terror', on the popularity of the genre; issue 13, 'Triste realidad', on the sorry state of the genre in Spain due to the commercial opportunism of producers and directors.

16. Issue 5, 'Cine y Turismo'.

17. Issue 6, 'En busca del turismo'. on recent anthropological studies on vampirism; issue 14, 'Brujería ¿Última moda?', on witchcraft and parapsychology; issue 16, 'Ciencia Ficción', on science fiction; or the untitled issue 17, on Disney film animation.

18. From 1976 onwards, Pierrot devoted his life to gay and transsexual culture, contributing to gay magazines such as *Party, Privadísimo* and *Revista Pierrot* and working in the cabaret and variety show scene in Barcelona.

19. Among its contributors were Paul Naschy, Salvador Sáinz, Sebastián D'Arbó and Manuel Domínguez.

20. The titles make reference to exotic adventure films *Cobra Woman, The Siren of Atlantis* and *She.*

21. Paul Naschy in issue 2, Narciso Ibáñez Serrador in issue 11 and Javier Aguirre in issue 25. Paul Naschy featured regularly, as well as those products associated with his name. Although Jesús Franco's films were duly reported, too, promises of interviews and a comprehensive profile of the filmmaker never materialised.

22. The front cover for issue 12 featured an image from *El espanto surge de la tumba / Horror Rises from the Tomb.*

23. Manuel Domínguez, who at the time was also contributing to *Vudú*, was the translator of the material.

24. All audiences, over 14 years of age, over 18 and the S rating.

25. See Bassa and Freixas (1996) and Kowalsky (2004). For a visual record of S film posters, visit 'Clasificada "S": El negocio de la Transición' at miscartelesdecine. blogspot.com.

26. Troma is an independent American film production and distribution company specialising in exploitation movies.
27. As part of the global consumption of psychotronia, a parallel could be drawn with the reception and consumption of mexploitation cinema in the US: in the words of Syder and Tierney, 'mexploitation has acquired a growing reputation in America among fans of cult and psychotronic cinema who in turn have their own sites of exhibition and sets of reading protocols' (Syder and Tierney 2005: 50).
28. The contribution of Rogelio Agrasánchez Junior coincided with the publication of his *Mexican Horror Cinema. Posters from Mexican Fantasy Films* (1999).
29. See Lázaro-Reboll (2009).
30. With the exception of the journalistic and cinéphile interventions – and their enthu-siasm as fans – of Carlos Águilar, Joan Bassa and Ramón Freixas in the early 1990s, and the official recognition attached to the recently awarded Goya de Honor, 2009, for Franco's lifetime achievement in Spanish cinema. Águilar organised a retrospec-tive at the Filmoteca Española in 1991; Bassa and Freixas interviewed Franco for *Archivos de la Filmoteca* (1991a); and Águilar, Bassa and Freixas are the main contributors to the *Dezine* special issue entitled *Jesús Franco: francotirador del cine español* (*Dezine* 1991).
31. Álex Mendíbil, Zinéfilo's real name, has devoted a blog (written in Spanish) to Franco's work: franconomicon.wordpress.com.
32. Temboury's three shorts – *Psycho-lettes*, *Generador adolescente* and *Muerte de un coleccionista de discos* – were commercialised by Subterfuge Video.
33. See Valencia (2002b: 14–16 and 2005: 42–50). See also Calleja (2003a).
34. Issue 7 (1991) featured the first article on Franco, with a particular focus on the director's engagement with various genres.
35. Borja Crespo's previous video shorts, *El Trivial Exterminador* (1995) and *El Trivial Exterminador 2* (1995), had been exhibited on the festival circuit and distributed by Subterfuge in a gore-pack together with two Koldo Serra shorts, *Photomatón* and *Photomaton II: The Avenger*, in 1998. Concurrent with his con-tributions to *2000maniacos*, Crespo collaborated with other alternative publica-tions such as *Burp! La comictiva* and *Quatermass*. During the 1990s he was chief editor at fanzine *Subterfuge* and Subterfuge Comix, publishing arm of indie record label Subterfuge Records. He is also author of comic books such as *Tales from the Splatter Family* (1995, Subterfuge Comix) and *Comic Horror Freak Show* (2001, Hilargi). Currently, he is in charge of Arsénico Producciones P. C., together with Koldo Serra, Nacho Vigalondo, Borja Cobeaga and Nahikari Ipiña.

6. POST-1975 HORROR PRODUCTION

The production of horror in the late 1970s and during the 1980s decreases dramatically, for reasons that have been addressed in the previous chapter: firstly, the boom in historical and political films during the period of the Transición and the early years of democracy; secondly, the film legislation established by the Socialist government in 1983, the so-called Ley Miró, which privileged the production of high-quality films, based mainly on literary or historical sources; and, thirdly, changing habits in the production, circulation and consumption of audiovisual material. It is not until the mid- to late 1990s and the early 2000s that Spanish horror cinema reaches another production peak, although this does not begin to approach the high-volume output of the period 1969–75, covered in Chapter 1. Looking at the fantasy and horror film section of the filmography collated by Águilar in his *Cine fantástico y de terror español: 1984–2004* (2005), one can see the production lows and highs of the genre: a dearth of films in the 1980s (7 films in 1984, 5 in 1986 and 5 in 1988), a lowermost point in the early 1990s (4 in 1991, 3 in 1992 and 2 in 1994), an ascending line in the second half of the 1990s (7 in 1995, 8 in 1996 and 11 in 1997) and a resurgence in the early 2000s (18 in 2001, 19 in 2002 and 13 in 2004). It is beyond the scope of this chapter to cover the entire horror production of the last three decades. Moreover, my aim here is not to provide a catalogue of contemporary Spanish horror films but rather to map out the commercial return of horror to the marketplace. In order to do so, the chapter examines positions taken in the field of contemporary Spanish horror film from the 1980s to the late 2000s by considering the ways in which specific horror

figures and films, cycles and production trends have been positioned in relation to Spanish and international horror cinema by producers, directors and
critics. By mobilising specific commercial discourses and generic formations,
these industrial and cultural agents have sought to reach beyond core horror
audiences nationally and internationally. I therefore propose to examine how
contemporary Spanish horror films have been 'situated – how they "behave",
so to speak – when they arrive in the market place' (Hantke 2004: x).

The chapter focuses on a number of industrial and cultural examples of the
marketing and creation of horror: Paul Naschy as a representative of the old
guard holding sway in the late 1970s and early1980s; the B-movie products
of Sebastiá D'Arbó and Juan Piquer Simón in the 1980s; the commercial successes of young directors Álex de la Iglesia (*El día de la bestia*) and Alejandro
Amenábar (*Tesis*), whose work made possible a renaissance of horror films at
the turn of the twenty-first century; examples of the so-called 'terror juvenil a
la española' (Spanish teen-horror) of the late 1990s and early 2000s; the products of the Barcelona-based genre specialist production company the Fantastic
Factory; and, finally, the 'phenomenon' of *El orfanato*, whereby Mexican
director Guillermo del Toro acted as the patron of debutant filmmaker Juan
Antonio Bayona. Each of these horror productions is representative of a
certain type of horror movie made in Spain, showing the variety and versatility
of Spanish horror production. As the chapter will demonstrate, these horror
manifestations occupy different spaces within the field of horror, draw upon
diverse horror tropes and traditions, and represent distinctive bids for different
audiences and cultural credentials.

In fact, during the last decade, the Spanish horror film genre has dominated
the Spanish box office, in 2001, 2007 and 2009. *Los otros / The Others* was
the box-office hit of 2001, confirming the domestic and international bankability of Amenábar, and making his film the top-grossing film product in the
history of Spanish cinema (27 million euros and over 6 million spectators);
Amenábar's film is followed by the 2007 hit, *El orfanato / The Orphanage*,
which launched the career of Bayona, outperformed Hollywood products such
as *Shrek the Third* and *Pirates of the Caribbean: At World's End* on Spanish
screens by grossing 25 million euros, and 'salvaged Spanish cinema's pride' that
year, according to the annual report published by trade journal *Cineinforme*[1];
the second to top-grossing Spanish film in 2007 was *[•REC]* by genre practitioners Jaume Balagueró and Paco Plaza, which earned over 8 million euros,
its sequel *[•REC2]* performing reasonably well in 2009 by making 5 million
euros. The most recent horror success has been *Los ojos de Julia / Julia's Eyes*
(Guillem Morales 2010), which grossed over 7 million euros.

OLD DOG, NEW TRICKS: PAUL NASCHY

One casualty of the changed industrial circumstances of the 1980s was Spain's most notorious screen werewolf, Paul Naschy (also known as Jacinto Molina). (A fuller treatment of Naschy's key role in the Spanish horror boom can be found in Chapter 2.) The Naschy brand created by Molina was embodied in the figure of Waldemar Daninsky, a tormented aristocrat at the mercy of his lycanthropic condition. Daninsky's first screen outing resulted in the unprecedented success of *La noche de Walpurgis* and was followed by a werewolf cycle which was commercially exploited until the mid-1970s. Parallel to the werewolf cycle, Naschy expanded his monster repertoire through his participation in other horror and horror-related movies, in particular through his collaboration with genre production company Profilmes. During the second half of the 1970s Molina started to direct his own films, which connected thematically and aesthetically with the Naschy products made earlier in the decade.[2] Thus, in the witch-hunt movie *Inquisición / Inquisition* (1976), Naschy plays a dual role as a medieval inquisitor and the Devil incarnate, modelling his performance on another of his fictional creations, Alaric de Marnac (based on the historic figure of Gilles de Rais), whom he had portrayed in *El espanto surge de la tumba* and *El mariscal del infierno / Devil's Possessed* (León Klimovsky 1974); in *Látidos de pánico / Panic Beats* (1983), Naschy presents a variation on this same character; in the rural psycho-thriller *El huerto del francés / The Frenchman's Garden* (1977), he plays a serial killer who commits brutal murders that remind the viewer of the *giallo* elements of *Los ojos azules de la muñeca rota*; while in the Spanish–Japanese co-production *El carnaval de las bestias / The Carnival of Beasts* (1980) Molina repeats the scenarios and situations of *Los ojos azules de la muñeca rota*.

Naschy continued to market his lupine creation Daninsky well into the 1980s with a number of variations on the werewolf theme, *El retorno del hombre lobo* (1980) and *El aullido del diablo* (1988). But for mainstream critics the Naschy brand was fast losing its commercial mileage or 'bite' and, for all but the most diehard of Naschy fans, the 1980 film was an 'anachronistic film for the period' (Sala 2010: 168). Apart from the fact that low-brow genre production in Spain could no longer benefit from state subsidies, these films could not compete commercially or aesthetically with new trends in contemporary American horror (slasher, gore, science fiction and adventure pictures, all taking advantage of the latest SFX), or with emerging horror stars in the making. In terms of its reflexive engagement with Naschy's own production and the history of horror film in general, Naschy's second film is a much more interesting proposition. It works as an autobiographical meta-commentary on Naschy's roles and position in the international hall of monsters, as well as a tribute to the conventions, myths and *leitmotifs* of classic and contemporary traditions of the horror genre. The personal nature of the project is reflected in the fact that Jacinto Molina signs the film as his alter ego Paul Naschy and dedicates the film to Boris Karloff, Bela Lugosi, Lon Chaney and (Universal make-up artist) Jack Pierce, self-consciously placing himself among these celebrated international horror stars. The plotline of *El aullido del diablo*, however, is illustrative of the weakened narrative charge and diminished scare value of the Naschy label and the brand of horror it represented. The film tells the story of Héctor Doriani (Paul Naschy), a failed and forgotten actor, who lives in an isolated mansion with his orphan nephew Adrián (played by Jacinto Molina's son Sergio Molina) and his loyal butler Eric (played by Franco regular and Eurohorror star Howard Vernon). Eric kidnaps young women hitch-hiking in the surrounding area for the sadistic pleasures of his master. Once these women are brought back to the mansion, their bodies are disposed of in a variety of vicious ways by a host of monsters, all of which 'are trotted out for the edification of our (and Paul Naschy's) fandom' (Robert Monell 2002). The multi-monster narrative is a throwback, then, to Naschy's much-admired Universal movies of the early 1940s. Apart from being a self-reflexive commentary on a long-gone tradition of filmmaking represented by Naschy himself, having a cast of Eurohorror actors (Howard Vernon, Caroline Munro and Fernando Hilbeck) and following genre formulas, the project clearly reflects the difficulties of this type of film in gaining audience and critical attention.

In the 1990s and 2000s, several retrospectives in specialist genre festivals, the publication of his autobiography *Paul Naschy. Memorias de un hombre lobo*, coverage in Spanish and foreign fanzines, and the reissue of unavailable videos (Suevia Films and Tripictures),[3] as well as his participation in films such as *School Killer* (Carlos Gil 2001), *Mucha sangre / Gangsters vs Aliens* (Pepe de las Heras 2002) and *Rojo sangre* (Christian Molina 2004), repackaged Naschy for contemporary audiences and revitalised his career until his death in 2009. In this, his fate can be likened to that of Jesús Franco, whose revival and recycling among younger audiences came via fanzines such as *2000maniacos*, magazines such as *Invasión*, and his collaboration with the rock band Killer Barbys.

THE PARANORMAL ACTIVITIES OF SEBASTIÀ D'ARBÓ

Among the few productions related to horror and adjacent genres to buck the trend of the early 1980s, the films of Sebastià D'Arbó (Sebastià Arbonés Subirats) deserve a brief mention since they represent a cycle of films touching upon the virtually uncharted territory of paranormal phenomena in Spanish popular cinema. D'Arbó's film trilogy, *Viaje al más allá* (1980), *El ser / Psicophobia* (1982) and *Más allá de la muerte* (1986), constitutes a genuine attempt to market for a 1980s audience the interest in paranormal activities that had permeated different media throughout the 1970s and that had been part of the specialist magazine and fanzine scene. His own pioneering role in the dissemination of the occult sciences in Spain across the mass media (press, radio, television and cinema) and his active participation in the specialist publications emerging in the early 1970s linked him to the lively field of horror, fantasy and science-fiction cultures of the period: D'Arbó was co-founder of the pioneering specialist magazine *Karma-7* devoted to parapsychology, of which he was editor between 1973 and 1977, advisor to *Terror Fantastic* on the occult during 1973, and contributor to Pierrot's fanzine *Vudú* for the period 1975–6. His move into film directing in the early 1980s[4] was an attempt to disseminate these interests to a wider audience and to provide a credible big-screen treatment of paranormal discourses within a horror narrative template. Although it was made in the context of B-movie production and narrative strategies, D'Arbó fully believed in the didactic purpose of his trilogy.

D'Arbó's first feature, *Viaje al más allá*, is a portmanteau film based on a number of factual cases and follows the format of some British Amicus horror productions. Promoted as 'the first Spanish parapsychology film based on real facts and directed by a professional parapsychologist: D'ARBÓ' and qualified as 'This is not a horror film!', the film's subtitle promised an exploration of 'the frontiers of the unknown'. The publicity material posed a question and gave a disquieting yet categorical answer: 'Is it possible to travel beyond life and . . . return? Scientifically: Proven.' The narrative is preceded by a prologue in which Professor D'Arbó explains to viewers the authenticity of the events they are about to see and the educational pretensions of his project. Then the narrative introduces us to Doctor Meinen, specialist in parapsychological phenomena and alter ego of D'Arbó, and the five people he has invited to a suitably sinister mansion in the Pyrenees to narrate their experiences of psychic phenomena. such as demonic possessions, poltergeists and reincarnations. (Doctor Meinen is played by Narciso Ibáñez Menta, who appears in each of the three films, and whose regular presence in *Historias para no dormir* and Spanish horror production would have provided audiences with an explicit reference to a not-so-distant televisual and cinematic tradition.) Paranormal themes had certainly been used in Spanish horror productions: for example, in the voodoo-inspired products of Paul Naschy such *El espanto surge de la tumba*. Whereas Naschy presented such themes within a traditional multi-monster narrative, D'Arbó employed scientific framing devices, such as his scholarly prologue and experiments, to establish the authenticity of the film. For many critics the film was a 'bad hybrid: neither documentary nor horror; neither science nor fiction' (Interino 1981: 65), for the supposedly true stories are dramatised 'using old methods, obsolete conventions. The spooky house, the fog, the storm, lightning and vampires [. . .] they are all worn out, stale effects [which make the spectator] lose interest in the paranormal aspect of the film' (1981: 65). Nevertheless, in true horror exploitation fashion, his work set off a further cycle of films on psychic phenomena, among them *Sexo sangriento* (Manuel Esteba 1980), *Regreso del más allá* (Juan José Porto 1982) and *Secta siniestra / Bloody Sect* (Ignacio F. Iquino 1982).

As opposed to the episodic nature of *Viaje al más allá*, *El ser* and *Más allá de la muerte* each present a single plot. Based on a supposedly true case D'Arbó documented in a house in Barcelona, *El ser* shifts the action to an unidentified country in central Europe to tell the story of a widow whose domestic life following the death of her husband is disturbed by strange cacophonies and apparitions. This time it is parapsychology expert Doctor Oliver (Ibáñez Menta) who investigates the entity manifesting itself in the house. The concluding film, *Más allá de la muerte*, originally entitled 'The Man Who Returned From Death' and 'Life After Death', appeared to offer a more credible underpinning story. According to D'Arbó, the feature is based on historically documented experiments performed by Nazi doctor Joseph Mengele in Auschwitz, whereby Jewish prisoners were subjected to torture almost to the point of death and brought back from its brink to explain their near-death experiences. In the film a psychiatrist-cum-detective searches for a doctor who collaborated with the Nazis and ends up joining in his experiments on clinically dead patients.

Although D'Arbó did not see himself as a horror director, his films represent a unique moment in Spanish horror production. The films' tepid contemporary reception must be attributed to the less than auspicious industrial circumstances in which D'Arbó was working; indeed, it is these very conditions that make his project so exceptional. But there were other factors too: D'Arbó's paranormal enthusiasms were not well served by the somewhat clunky narrative machinery employed in the films, which in any case had limited audience reach beyond a hardcore (paranormal) fan following.

JUAN PIQUER SIMÓN'S B-MOVIES

Juan Piquer Simón was one of the few directors of the period to find an international market for his films by responding quickly to horror (and fantasy) production trends in the US. Neither part of the horror boom of the 1970s nor part of the contemporary revival of the genre, Piquer Simón can best be described as a sharpshooter within the declining fortunes of genre filmmaking in the 1980s. He specialised in popular adventures based on literary fantasy classics (*Viaje al centro de la tierra / Journey to the Center of the Earth* (1977), *Misterio de la isla de los monstruos / Mystery Monster Island* (1981), *Los diablos del mar / Sea Devils* (1982)) and spin-offs from Hollywood science-fiction blockbusters (for example, his psychotronic *Supersonic Man* (1979) followed on from *Superman* (Richard Donner 1978) and *La grieta / The Rift* (1989) belongs to the cycle of films exploiting the success of *The Abyss* (James Cameron 1989)).[5] However, his gore B-movie horror productions *Mil gritos tiene la noche / Pieces* (1982)[6] and *Slugs, muerte viscosa / Slugs: The Movie* (1988), which were co-productions between Spain and the US, brought Piquer Simón to the attention of international horror aficionados because of the films' strong relationship with American genre products. The feature *Pieces* was entirely conceived with the international horror circuit in mind. Shot in English, *Pieces* had a wide release in the US (it was exhibited in 97 screens in New York alone) and the impressive box-office returns were such that it even earned a mention in *Variety*.[7]

Originally entitled 'Jigsaw', *Pieces* had the financial backing of Steve Minician,[8] producer of *Friday the 13th* (Sean S. Cunningham 1980), and adhered to the commercial, narrative and aesthetic strategies of successful contemporary 'slasher' films in the style of *Halloween* and *Friday the 13th*, as well as the body count of many a *giallo*. The pre-credit sequence places the action in Boston in 1942. A teenage boy kills his repressive mother with an axe after she has found her son completing a jigsaw with the image of a naked woman. The credit sequence intercuts the credit titles, the arrival of a female family friend and the boy cutting his mother's body into pieces. An intertitle moves the action forward forty years to an American college campus, where young female students are being murdered and mutilated. A police investigator (Lieutenant Bracken, played by Christopher George), an undercover policewoman (Mary Riggs, played by Linda Day George) and the boyfriend (Kendall James, played by Ian Sera) of one of the gruesomely mutilated girls join forces to uncover the criminal. Whilst Piquer Simón deployed the formulaic nature of the American slasher film, the graphic, shocking nature of the murder scenes, as well as the gratuitous sex, is characteristic of Spanish horror products of the 1970s. *Pieces* was an 'invitation to horror' with a warning 'Don't come alone . . . just in case,' as one of the taglines from the Spanish campaign read. (The American taglines were 'Pieces . . . It's exactly what you think it is!' and 'You Don't Have to Go to Texas for a Chainsaw Massacre.') Promotional material for the film featured two posters; in the first, the illustrated figure of the killer fused elements of the pulp character 'The Shadow', splatter movies – the chainsaw as a weapon of choice – and the *giallo*-killer costume, while the second foregrounded the helpless, terrified expression of a female victim who is about to be slaughtered. Contemporary Spanish critics described the film as 'execrable' and 'tasteless' (Santos Fontenla 1982: 48), slating every single narrative and stylistic aspect of the film. Yet this and other B-movie products by Piquer Simón proved to be a hit with local audiences and were 'an indispensable presence in the double-bills of neighbourhood cinemas and in the video stores during the eighties' (Valencia 2010: 66). His films were regularly and extensively profiled in subcultural publications like *2000maniacos*, whose emergence is closely associated with the arrival of VHS and DVD releases, which have facilitated their cult status.

Many other B-movies of the 1980s, whose distribution and exhibition went unnoticed, ended up in the direct-to-video market. A few examples of the products which are now being reclaimed and reviewed by inveterate cinéphages in fanzines, internet forums and blogs are *Trauma* (León Klimovsky 1977), *Aquella casa en las afueras / That House in the Outskirts* (Eugenio Martín 1979), *Morir de miedo* (Juan José Porto 1980), *Más allá del terror / Further than Fear* (Tomás Aznar 1980), *Morbus (o bon profit) / Morbus* (Ignasi P. Ferré 1982), *La capilla ardiente* (Carlos Puerto 1983), *El enigma del yate / The Enigma of the Yacht* (Carlos Aured 1983) and *El invernadero* (Santiago Lapeira 1983).

BIDS FOR PRESTIGE

Both De la Iglesia and Amenábar emerged as the bright hopes of contemporary Spanish cinema in the mid-1990s with films which did not shy away from the commercial realities of the horror film and which drew upon horror traditions, themes and conventions in a savvy and self-reflexive manner. In placing their products in the changing Spanish media landscape of the mid-1990s, both directors combined the commercial appeal of popular genres and the exploitation strategies associated with alternative cultures with the discourses of art-cinema and auterism. With above-average budgets at the disposal of these young directors (2 million euros for *El día de la bestia* and around 800,000 euros for *Tesis*), the films benefitted from the reputation and *savoir-faire* of their respective producers; Vicente Andrés Gómez, who had a successful track record with his company Lolafilms, produced de la Iglesia's second film, while José Luis Cuerda, up until this point dedicated to directing, ventured into production with the founding of Producciones del Escorpión S. L. These producers were also able to provide access to media platforms nationwide. *El día de la bestia* and *Tesis* were promoted and reviewed extensively in the mainstream Spanish press and fully exploited their exposure on the pages of cultural trendsetters such as the cultural supplements of national dailies *El país* and *El mundo*. De la Iglesia and Amenábar placed the aesthetic languages of television, video and new technologies at the centre of their narratives, operating as filmic mediations of the directors' personal concerns; in *El día de la bestia* the format of the TV reality show is parodied through Professor Caván's parapsychology programme *La zona oscura*, whereas in *Tesis* digital video plays a key role aesthetically and narratively.

As far as their relation to the horror genre is concerned, De la Iglesia and Amenábar painstakingly qualified their films' association with the genre in a patent endeavour to affirm the cultural prestige of their respective films. Product differentiation in the case of *El día de la bestia* and *Tesis* is markedly activated by the filmmakers themselves, who distanced their films from lowbrow Spanish horror traditions, past and present, and enforced the distinction by making a number of aesthetic and moral claims designed to cultivate their artistic pretensions. Chapter 5 touched upon how De la Iglesia took up a cultural position in relation to his first feature film, *Acción mutante*, in the context of my discussion of fanzine *2000maniacos* and genre specialist magazine *Fantastic magazine*; while he used these publications to acknowledge the presence of elements of gore-comedy in his film, he also underlined his affiliations with the Spanish cinematic tradition of early 1960s *esperpento*, or dark comedy, and with auteurs *par excellence* such as Hitchcock and Polanski. With *El día de la bestia*, De la Iglesia once again sought to differentiate his work from contemporary representations of gore without alienating those fans who had connected with his subcultural sensibilities. Similarly, Amenábar aligned his *Tesis* with psychological horror thrillers rather than gore, or, as he referred to it in many an interview in the mainstream media, visceral horror. Unlike De la Iglesia, who had emerged out of the fanzine scene and whose films had been profiled by *2000maniacos*, among others, Amenábar did not court the fanzine circuit and the alternative press showed hardly any interest in *Tesis*.

The two directors' bids for prestige were successful. Their works were officially endorsed by the Spanish Film Academy, which awarded six Goyas to *El día de la bestia* in 1996 and seven to *Tesis* in 1997; were popular at the box office – 'the national cinematic phenomenon of the year' (Cerdán 1995: 328) in the case of De la Iglesia's film (800 million pesetas and more than 1 million spectators), and a profitable sleeper in the case of *Tesis* (around 400 million pesetas and 900,000 spectators); and gained international distribution (*El día de la bestia* had been distributed in the UK, France and Japan by the end of 1996; *Tesis* was sold to thirty countries). The official Spanish institutions had found the new representatives of contemporary Spanish cinema and embraced the viability – industrial and commercial – and quality – artistic and auterist – of *El día de la bestia* and *Tesis*.

Despite the relative commercial and critical success of *Acción mutante* in Spain and abroad, it took de la Iglesia and co-screenwriter Jorge Guerricaechevarría two years – January 1993 to late 1994 – to find a producer willing to chance his or her arm with a plotline involving a priest and the arrival of the Anti-Christ in present-day Madrid and a product whose generic hybridity (part-black comedy, part-supernatural horror, part-thriller) made its placement in the Spanish marketplace a challenging prospect. Throughout this time, the script underwent a number of revisions, as de la Iglesia himself revealed to journalist and critic Marcos Ordóñez in *La bestia anda suelta. ¡Álex de la Iglesia lo cuenta todo!* (1997: 130–2). Inspired by H. P. Lovecraft's Cthulhu Mythos, the original draft was set in 1920s Toledo, where an old priest and professor of theology begins to prophesy the imminent arrival of the 'Great Old Ones' and the tragic implications for humanity. In a second version, a younger priest is introduced into the story and the setting moves to Madrid, where he warns about the arrival of the Anti-Christ. It is not until the third revision that de la Iglesia and Guerricaechevarría decided to introduce a sidekick for the priest, a character who would act as the priest's interlocutor in the same way that Sancho Panza served Don Quijote. After it had been rejected by a number of production companies – among them Almodóvar's El deseo, which had financed *Acción mutante* and was concerned about the satanic theme – and twice by the Spanish Ministry of Culture, producer Andrés Vicente Gómez picked up the project, as part of a deal with film production company Sogetel and multimedia conglomerate PRISA to produce thirty films between 1994 and 1996. Assisted by the publicity machinery of these influential media corporations, *El día de la bestia* achieved maximum exposure across different mainstream media. Interest in the movie was generated largely by the cultural pages of 'El País de las Tentaciones', the Friday arts review supplement of *El país*, as well as 'Cinelandia', the film magazine put out by national daily *El mundo*, from which the arrival of *El día de la bestia* was unreservedly welcomed. Circulation in specialist genre festivals positioned the film on the European fantastic film festival circuit, commencing in Sitges in September 1995 and continuing throughout the following year in Gérardmer, London and Brussels, where it obtained the prestigious Méliès d'Or for the Best European Fantastic Film.

Coverage in 'El País de las Tentaciones', which carried an image of the film's protagonist, Padre Berriartúa, on its front cover, gun in hand, next to the defiant title 'Satán, te voy a enviar al infierno' ('Satan, I am going to send you to Hell') (de la Iglesia 1995: 1–6), functioned as a letter of presentation to fans and to a wider audience, as well as a guide to the film. It included De la Iglesia's chronicles of the ordeals and (cannily manufactured) urban legends surrounding the film, his explanations of the cultural and generic references shaping his project in the piece 'De Sancho Panza a Blade Runner', and his review of the film's audiovisual aesthetics, ranging from 'death metal subculture which uses satanic imagery' to 'the *kitsch* patina of Tele 5' (1995: 7). De la Iglesia presented different segments of the audience with a range of references and tastes which positioned his film in relation to national and transnational artistic traditions and to debates in the contemporary media landscape. For mainstream and cinéphile audiences, the director drew an analogy with Hitchcock's *Vertigo* by describing *El día de la bestia* as the story of an unfortunate man who finds himself in an incredible story. For his hardcore fans, the tagline 'A comedy of satanic action' carried over the gore-comedy elements present in *Mirindas Asesinas* and *Acción mutante* and signalled the fact that horror was embedded in a climate of comedy and satire. For horror aficionados, de la Iglesia drew prospective viewers with overt gestures to national and international horror traditions: the design of the film's poster, created by Oscar Mariné, evoked Ibáñez Serrador's *Historias para no dormir* logo for many Spanish spectators, whereas de la Iglesia's relation of spooky anecdotes surrounding the conception and shooting of the film followed the 'black legend' histories generated around previous landmark devil movies such as *Rosemary's Baby* (Roman Polanski 1968), *The Exorcist* and *The Omen* (Richard Donner 1976). In a bid for authenticity, the director also recounted his meeting at a horror genre festival with William Peter Blatty, author of the novel *The Exorcist* and leading expert in the occult sciences, who supplied him with a list of names, 'the pick of the international occult sciences scene', some of whom worked as advisors throughout the film (de la Iglesia 1995: 3); he also described his own and Guerricaechevarría's research on genuine early modern European witchcraft texts, such as the *Malleus Maleficarum* (1487), and historical evidence of devil invocations such as that linked to seventeenth-century French Catholic priest Urbain Grandier. For the consumers and connoisseurs of bad taste TV reality and celebrity shows, he related how a news item on the well-known Spanish medium and astrologist Rappel uncannily resembled one of the key scenes in the film while it was still in the pre-production stage (Rappel had been tied up, gagged and threatened with a shotgun in his flat in the same way that Professor Caván is tied up and gagged in his flat by Padre Berriartúa). For those with a taste for sensationalism, he disclosed the fact that he received countless anonymous letters from satanists, that voodoo dolls were regularly found on the set, and that some 'orthodox religious associations tried to prevent the filming of the sequence in which Satan is invoked' (de la Iglesia 1995: 3). The director laid out the narrative and aesthetic universe of *El día de la bestia* in 'De Sancho Panza a Blade Runner': it is a story of apocalyptic horror inspired by the writings of H. P. Lovecraft; a story not dissimilar to *Don Quijote*, in which 'the priest is a madman in search of adventures, looking for ghosts, and being helped by a chubby and good-natured squire' (de la Iglesia 1995: 11); and a story set in a Madrid indebted to the apocalyptic urban landscapes of Los Angeles in *Blade Runner* and Gotham City in *Batman*.

But *El día de la bestia* was not only a popular genre product destined for entertainment; it was also a cultural artifact with a message and a meaning related to contemporary topical concerns around sensationalist TV programming and the representation of violence in the media. According to de la Iglesia, the film contained 'a fierce criticism of television and the model represented by Berlusconi's Tele 5' (de la Iglesia in García 1995: 40), participating therefore in a wider cultural debate about the changes taking place in Spanish television. *El día de la bestia* took issue with the sensationalist contents and aesthetics of 'reality' TV shows that were being programmed by new private channels Telecinco and Antena 3. In the words of de la Iglesia, the misery of TV game-shows and "reality" TV debates is where the devil truly lies. People live and think through these programmes [. . .] That's why I believe that programmes which exploit people's emotions are much more dangerous and violent than fiction movies. (de la Iglesia in García 1995: 40)

Furthermore, these programmes provided 'an intellectual alibi for the intro- duction of despicable, ultraconservative and reactionary content' (de la Iglesia in Cervera 1995: 136). By linking his film to contemporary topicality and arguing for its immediate cultural relevance, the director is enabling a type of critical attention for *El día de la bestia* whose function is dual: on the one hand, to guide the reception of the film by critics, who, in turn, picked up these arguments, and, on the other, to bestow cultural and moral value on the film, a strategy typical of auterist discourses.

Auterism was certainly one of the main frames of reference for the critics in the interpretation of de la Iglesia's work. Overall, most film critics welcomed the arrival of de la Iglesia on the contemporary film scene, noting the director's novel and original world view. *El mundo*'s Alberto Bermejo greeted 'the stimu- lating reappearance of a figure like Álex de la Iglesia', whose *El día de la bestia* 'expands the limited scene of contemporary Spanish cinema' (1995: 90); *La vanguardia*'s Bonet Mójica saluted 'the boldness and talent of a director who fortunately goes beyond the conventions [of Spanish cinema]' (1995: 39); and influential film critic Torreiro of *El país* observed that *El día de la bestia* was 'an original contribution to the history of Spanish cinema' (1995: 44). Other reviewers belittled the film's aesthetics, its (lack of) cultural credentials and its narrative construction. Thus in *ABC* Rodríguez Marchante dismissed *El día de la bestia* as the director's 'second *filmcomic*' and sneered at its cultural value: 'there can be no doubt that if somebody chooses not to watch this film, his cultural level will remain unaffected. [If he chooses to watch it, on the other hand,] other levels will surge: levels of adrenalin, of bafflement, of a need to pee' (Rodríguez Marchante 1995: 82); Rey in *Ya* concurred with Rodríguez Marchante – 'too close to [the aesthetics] of comics' – and measured the film against realist aesthetics – 'not plausible enough' (Rey 1995: 48); and in film magazine *Dirigido por . . .*, Losilla disapproved of the film's accumulation of 'gags and scenes of violence [which] seem to be autonomous [and] conceived and executed for their own sake, as if their function within the overall struc- ture of the film was not important' (Losilla 1995: 12).

By approaching de la Iglesia's production via the prism of auterism, however, critics like Torreiro distinguished his film from previous low-brow genre tra- ditions, since 'the director wipes out with one stroke the distinction between genre cinema and auteur product', showing 'marks of authorship' within the conventions of horror cinema (Torreiro 1995: 44). Moreover, Torreiro made a clear distinction between de la Iglesia's films and Spanish horror traditions, whether these were the exploitative products of the late 1960s and early 1970s or the Tromaesque gore-comedy of contemporary products championed in alternative publications. The film's treatment of Satanism, noted Torreiro, is far removed from 'those tasteless Spanish subgeneric products made 20, 25 years ago' (1995: 44). But, above all, the textual references mentioned by Torreiro and others connected the film to a Spanish literary and cinematic canon and imaginary far removed from the world of Spanish horror film. Two obvious examples are the references to Miguel de Cervantes's early seventeenth-century literary classic *Don Quixote*, which elevated the film from the base low-brow pleasures of gore-comedy to the realm of artistic sophistication, and to the indigenous cinematic traditions of dark comedy of the early 1960s, which offered an acerbic critique of Francoist institutions and society. Thus Bermejo described *El día de la bestia* as 'a fantastic adventure with evident Cervantine inspiration' (1995: 90), Bonet Mójica called it 'a picturesque cross between *The Exorcist, Rosemary's Baby,* and *The Omen*, recycled by an advanced pupil of screenwriter Rafael Azcona' (1995: 39), and Pérez Gómez in *Reseña* referred to it as 'a "dark" film [*película negra*], in the literal sense of the word, disguised as a horror and intrigue film, peppered with buckets of physical and visual violence, and with high doses of *esperpento*' (1996).

The commercial and cultural pretensions of Amenábar with his *Tesis* were well defined and struck a chord with large sectors of the industry, the critical intelligentsia and official film institutions. The débutant director stated that, 'from an entrepreneurial point of view, what I wanted to do with *Tesis* was to win the trust of my producers so that I could make a second film' (Amenábar in Mendoza 1997: 70), thus employing the proven formula of first-time directors who use genre filmmaking as a stepping-stone into the industry. As Amenábar explains in 'The Making of *Tesis*' DVD extras, the thriller was an obvious genre choice: 'it's an easy genre' and 'it's very mathematical.' The generic adoption of the thriller, as well as the conventions and themes of horror, proved to be a successful formula. The relationship of *Tesis* vis-à-vis horror was manifested commercially, narratively and aesthetically. From an artistic standpoint, although Amenábar sought to differentiate his work from contemporary gore representations of violence in Spanish cinema, the film exploited the very same themes, tropes and tools of low-brow exploitation filmmaking. In this respect, *Tesis* represented a calculated cultural straddling of exploitation and art. The director mobilised, on the one hand, the commercial, formal and stylistic strategies of exploitation cinema and, on the other hand, the institutional discourses of art-cinema and auterism. Amenábar and his producers Producciones del Escorpión S. L. utilised the discourses of art-cinema in the pressbook and in promotional interviews: namely, in their claims about the intellectual and moral value of the film. Critical reception at film festivals and in the mainstream press weighed in to validate the film's cultural discourse and its (moral) message.

Tesis introduces us to Ángela (Ana Torrent), an Audiovisual Communication and Media PhD student, who is working on a thesis on the representation of violence in audiovisual media. Her supervisor, Professor Figueroa (Miguel Picazo), informs Ángela that the university video library holds copies of some extremely violent films which he could make available for her project. The following day, however, Ángela finds Figueroa dead – a heart attack – in one of the projection rooms. She takes the tape left in the video machine. At home, Ángela cannot bring herself to watch the tape and decides to play only the audio, revealing to her and the audience the distressing screams of a woman. When she shows the videotape to her classmate Chema (Fele Martínez), a gore and porn fan with an extensive film collection, he confirms that the tape is an actual 'snuff movie': the recording in real time of a woman's torture, mutilation and death. While Ana is distressed by the actual nature of the images, Chema focuses on their quality and texture, remarking that the camera used for the recording is the same model used in their faculty, a Sony XT-500. Together they begin to investigate who is behind the filming of the snuff movie. Some days later, Ángela meets another fellow student, Bosco (Eduardo Noriega), who carries a very similar camera. Ángela's investigations reveal that the victim on the videotape was one of Bosco's closest friends. In the mean time, Professor Castro (Javier Elorriaga) is appointed as Ángela's new supervisor. During their first meeting Castro demands that Ángela returns the videotape – her possession of it has been recorded on CCTV. The closer Ángela gets to Bosco, the more attracted she is to him. Feeling hounded, Bosco kidnaps Ángela and ties her to a chair, ready to record the torture and murder of his latest victim. But Ángela manages to escape and to shoot Bosco dead, while the camera films her act of murder.

The pressbook provided just a brief synopsis of the film, instead offering an explanatory statement about *Tesis*'s plotline. 'What is *Tesis*?' probed the pressbook:

> Thesis is a story about TV violence, pornography and the 'snuff movie', as the ultimate manifestation of terror in cinema.
>
> The progressive demystification of old social taboos, for example, sex, pain, and death, and their transmission by the mass media, makes very difficult their visual treatment in film. To call the public's attention to these matters is not easy in a media culture where everything has already been shown. For this reason we chose the opposite course, to show nothing. The public will see the protagonists looking at images in an almost pathological mood but the images will never be seen on-screen.
>
> The public, for whom these images are the main source of interest, is

thereby 'punished', but this punishment is compensated by a script full of tricks, and designed for its entertainment.

However, at several points the film script also invites subtle reflection on the future of the audio visual market: on the pressure of the American Movie Industry, the main example of movies dominated by economic interests; the growing diffusion of 'snuff movies' (in which human beings are murdered in front of the camera) on video circuits; the legitimization of violence in TV news; the dominance of images over words; the individualization of the public by means of TV and video; and their insensibilization and loss of contact with reality. We think that THESIS is an interesting and necessary movie, due to the fact that it is one of the first films about 'snuff movies', and, also, because its style, dramatic and frenetic simultaneously, is very rare in the Spanish movie industry.[9]

Themes typical of horror – and the academic study of horror – are invoked in this statement, among them: spectatorship and voyeurism, the broadcasting and representation of shocking media images and the notorious pathology of horror audiences. The academic subject matter and tone of this blurb positioned *Tesis* in the domain of a sophisticated self-reflexivity normally associated with art-cinema. *Tesis* was therefore a filmic and academic exercise – that is, a film about horror – which transcended the horror genre. And, indeed, academic theory was repeatedly cited by Amenábar in promotional interviews as the principal source of inspiration, in particular a book he had read as an undergraduate student which included a section on snuff movies, *La imagen pornográfica y otras perversiones ópticas* (1989, reissued 2005), written by Román Gubern, a distinguished Professor of Audiovisual Communication in Spain. In the chapter devoted to 'the pornography of cruelty' (2005: 284), which mainly focuses on the horror genre and its subgenres, Gubern had written the following about snuff movies: '*snuff movies*, with real murders of unsuspecting prostitutes or aspiring actresses in front of the camera, constitute the ultimate point of convergence between horror film and hardcore pornography, and, ultimately, their last possible frontier' (2005: 322); further, that they represent the 'most extreme case of sadist scoptophilia' (2005: 323). The 'Introduction' and 'Post-Scriptum' to the 2005 re-edition of *La imagen pornográfica y otras perversiones ópticas* are framed with admiring (and self-validating) references to *Tesis*:

> The main satisfaction that this piece of work gave me was to read some years later that a very young filmmaker unknown to me then, called Alejandro Amenábar, stated in several press interviews that the idea for his film *Tesis* was inspired by his reading of my book, more specifically the last chapter, in which I introduced for the first time in Spanish film

and media studies the topic of snuff movies [. . .] In truth, with this unique outcome, which initiated the successful filmography of Amenábar, the publication of this book was more than justified for me. (Gubern 2005: 7)

Amenábar's cultivated auteurist and scholarly pretensions had come full circle.

In addition to the academic standing of his *Tesis*, Amenábar also summoned the urban-legend status of snuff movies through references to media coverage of 'organized rings' producing and trafficking in snuff movies (Amenábar in Leyra 1996: 72) and to the unlikely availability of the 'real thing': 'I have never seen a *snuff* movie, not even the ones I describe as *soft*, that is, images that are part of documentaries. Some [*snuff* movies] were offered to me, but I did not want to watch them' (Amenábar in Leyra 1996: 72). Amenábar constantly emphasised that he never wanted 'to give publicity to *snuff* movies' (Amenábar in Mendoza 1997: 68) and expressed his concern that 'some spectators may think that my film is a eulogy to *snuff* movies, when my intention is quite the opposite' (Amenábar in Gil 1996: 58). One of the specific questions that Amenábar's film posed is whether 'television would be capable of broadcasting *snuff* images' (Amenábar in Mendoza 1997: 68), and, more generally, a critical meditation on the nature of TV reality shows. These days, Amenábar's official website describes his work thus: 'My movies are not movies of answers but of questions.'

In interviews, the first-time director fused the rhetoric of commerce and of film-art: 'Quality and commercialism are compatible' (Amenábar in Leyra 1996: 72); 'the commercial and the personal [i.e. auterism] can be perfectly united. In this respect, I think that *Tesis* is a cross between American cinema [Hollywood] and European cinema [auteur cinema]' (Amenábar in Gil 1996: 58). The mechanics of auterism are noticeably at work in the self-reflexive nature of the film: it is academically inspired; it is topical in its intervention in contemporary debates around the production and circulation of violent media representations; it portrays the two main characters as representatives of specific cultural practices and knowledges – namely academic and horror fandom – Ángela as a PhD researcher and Chema as a horror fan; it calls attention to the technology of horror filmmaking by foregrounding the role of digital cameras, on-screen and off-screen violence and other genre conventions; it self-consciously stages 'what it imagines the aesthetics of snuff to be' (Tierney 2002: 49); and it interrogates the very act of viewing. A strong sense of moral duty also came across in interviews. *Contra* the often-quoted words of one of the film's main characters, Professor Castro, to his audiovisual media students ('The American industry is out there poised to trample on you, and there is only one way to compete with it: give the public what it wants. Don't forget that!'), Amenábar did not believe that 'a director has to do everything that audiences want – yes, audiences are very important, but it is not a case of anything goes' (Amenábar in Leyra 1996: 72); he strongly believes that 'the public can be educated' (Amenábar in Leyra 1996: 72), despite claims made in the pressbook concerning the avoidance of a didactic message.

Amenábar's discourse was replicated by producer José Luis Cuerda, who accentuated the 'honesty and seriousness with which the film tackles a subject matter so morally sensitive as [the representation of] violence as spectacle', an approach which 'makes of this film a filmic and sociological challenge of the first order' (Cuerda in Floresta 1996: 4). And critics confirmed the claims made by the director and the producer. For *Diario 16* reviewer Bejarano, the film provoked

> an interesting and much needed moral reflection: [. . .] to beware of those who proclaim for all to hear that the public should be given what it wants; it also poses the question of the limits of censorship in a sibylline manner and whether the premise of 'anything goes' could be applied to the media business. (1996: 15)

Bejarano concluded that 'the majority of the audience would be able to form their moral opinion on the sickening practice' of *snuff* movies (1996: 15) after watching *Tesis*. Bonet Mójica in *La vanguardia* stated that Amenábar 'does not traffic in morbid pleasure, but rather uses the underworld of *snuff* movies to articulate an argument whose progressive turning points allow him to strike forceful blows against television *reality shows*' (1996: 48). *ABC* reviewer Rodríguez Marchante praised the film's storyline because it 'tackles the latest theories and narrative niches that dazzle generations "x", "y" and "z"' (1996: 86); its approach to the 'foul' and 'indecent' subject of *snuff* movies and their links to the 'socially accepted vulgarity of *reality shows*' was treated 'with lots of tact', making of *Tesis* a quality suspense film (1996: 86).

The projection of *Tesis* at international film festivals was also carefully orchestrated to guarantee coverage in the Spanish national press. Such was the case with the Berlinale, the Berlin Film Festival. The controversial subject matter of the film fitted the profile of Berlin's 'Panorama' section, in which *Tesis* was entered in February 1996. As a showcase for début films and exciting new discoveries, Amenábar and his *Tesis* were positioned as part of contemporary trends in art-house world cinema. According to Heredero, the film had an 'excellent reception' which 'left nobody indifferent' in spite of 'some evident naiveties' typical of débutant directors (1996: 32). Heredero's review gave prominence to an anecdote that generated further interest and polemic, as it continued to feature in subsequent reviews: Amenábar had failed Production as part of his degree programme, a course taught by Antonio Castro – Professor at the University Complutense of Madrid and also a film critic – on whom the character of Professor Jorge Castro appears to be modelled. 'The *tribe* of film correspondents in the Spanish media', observed Heredero, 'exchanged juicy and facetious commentaries' on the matter (1996: 32). Writing for *El país*, M. Torreiro described the controversy as 'a settling of scores' (1996: 43) and used his review to defend his colleague Castro and to put 'The student Amenábar', as he entitles the review, in his place: '*Tesis* is a clever but not successful *thriller*, it is more *efectista* [sensationalist] than *efectivo* [effective]. It has a serious problem: its script is deplorable' (1996: 43). Other critics were also unimpressed by Amenábar's film. For Casas, it was 'a shallow exercise in suspense which is resolved satisfactorily but it is less thrilling that we were led to expect' (1996: 62); Bou and Pérez acknowledged that the generic adoption of the psycho-thriller was a 'formula for success' which was, none the less, simply a 'shamelessly imitative, final-year dissertation' (1996: 8).

Not all film critics therefore joined in with the critical championing of *Tesis* nor the elevation of Amenábar as the new wunderkind of Spanish cinema. Perhaps the strongest dissent comes in the form of a comic strip from film critic and cultural commentator Jordi Costa. 'Mis problemas con Amenábar' ('My problems with Amenábar'), published periodically in the pages of fanzine *Mondo Brutto* between 2005 and 2010 and collected in 2009 in a comic book with the same title,[10] developed from a personal feud that harks back to Costa's negative experience on a press junket during the filming of *Tesis* and was exacerbated by his negative review of the film in *Fotogramas*, where he argued that it was a badly assimilated version of Gubern's book and a patchwork of genre conventions. Costa's fictionalised hatred of Amenábar is first and foremost, however, a scathingly perceptive representation of how critical prestige can be discursively constructed by the film industry and the critical intelligentsia. Costa's comic book draws attention to what he calls 'the machinery of prestige' (see Figure 35), the polished workings of a marketing operation that would enhance the success of Amenábar's subsequent cinematic products, *Abre los ojos* / *Open Your Eyes* (1997), *Los otros* /*The Others* (2001), *Mar adentro* / *The Sea Inside* (2004) and *Agora* (2009).

Spanish Teen Horror

The globally popular slasher pic *Scream* (Wes Craven 1996) and its offshoots loom large in the production, marketing and reception of *El arte de morir* / *The Art of Dying* (2000), as well as other titles from the early and mid-2000s such as *Tuno negro* / *Black Serenade* (Pedro L. Barbero and Vicente J. Martín 2001), *School Killer* (Carlos Gil 2001), *Más de mil cámaras velan por tu seguridad* / *More Than a Thousand Cameras are Working for Your Safety* (David Alonso 2003), *Ouija* (Pedro Ortega 2004) or *La monja* / *The Nun* (Luis de la Madrid 2005). Producer Francisco Ramos, screenwriters Juan Vicente Pozuelo and Francisco Javier Royo, and director Álvaro Fernández Armero deliberately

Figure 35   *Mis problemas con Amenábar.*

modelled *El arte de morir* on the teen horror films of the late 1990s and early 2000s, a hugely successful and popular Hollywood production trend.[11] *El arte de morir* was very much a calculated commercial project designed to yield maximum financial returns. Its spectacular weekend opening (31 March 2000) made it an instant local hit and brought a much-needed injection of capital into the ailing coffers of national production; as *Screen International* dramatically described it, 'Spanish Film Stays Alive with *Art of Dying*' (Green 2000c). The producers certainly showed commercial *savoir-faire* since the film grossed $1.3 million in the two weeks following its nationwide release on 179 screens and attained a domestic box-office total of $3,328,702.[12] As for its life beyond Spain, *Variety*'s reviewer gives a realistic prediction of the possibilities for the film in the highly competitive horror market: 'pic is down-the-line mainstream [. . .] Offshore buyers and auds may feel material is too standard issue to perk much interest' (Holland 2000) – a fair assessment, given the fact that *El arte de morir* grossed a meagre $36,207 and only lasted a few weeks in US theatres (11 September to 30 November 2001).[13]

In what ways, then, is *El arte de morir* a film 'like *Scream*'? It was developed as an in-house project by Aurum Producciones, the Spanish distributor for New Line Cinema (which, in turn, is associated with several slasher hits), and producer Ramos commissioned the script from Pozuelo and Royo, offering the project to Fernández Armero, who took it on as a genre assignment. The filmmaker had established his name as a comedy director with *Todo es mentira* (1994), *Brujas* (1996) and *Nada en la nevera* (1998), a series of films focusing on the lives of urban, middle-class adolescents and young people, which had given him the credentials among this demographic to depict their lives realistically. His first and only foray into the horror genre had a considerable budget for a Spanish genre production, 300 million pesetas (approximately $2.5 million), plus the collaboration of Spanish TVE and the participation of Canal Plus.[14] The production and marketing strategy capitalised on the *Scream* series in a number of ways, including script and production decisions, publicity and media commentary, and generic markers. Scriptwriters Pozuelo and Royo explained the premise behind the project in the pressbook: namely, to produce a Spanish version of contemporary American teen horror films: 'throughout the long process of its gestation we found that some elements of the latest American horror cinema were translatable into Spanish tastes.' In what would become a common rhetorical operation throughout the promotional campaign, the acknowledgement of the source of inspiration is immediately followed by a disclaimer: 'but we also realized that Spanish audiences demanded something more, some narrative complexity which American teen horror films lacked'. Their distancing from the 'unsophisticated', 'juvenile' American horror genre is replicated by the director in interviews: 'I am aware that my audience and that of *Scream 3* are the same' but 'we have added another turn of the screw

Figure 36   *Scream*-like poster for the Spanish teen horror film *El arte de morir*.

to the narrative to give the story a European touch,'; or 'my film belongs to another genre [. . .] psychological horror. And I believe it is much more intelligent' (Belinchón 2000: 5). These promotional tactics reveal a two-pronged manœuvre aimed at targeting particular audience segments, while, at the same time, presenting *El arte de morir*, through its thematic and stylistic association with 'European' art-film, as a sophisticated alternative to the popular genres produced by Hollywood. The producers and creators were at pains to differentiate *El arte de morir* from the likes of *Scream*, then, asserting its qualitative difference and positioning it in a cinematic tradition that would elevate it to the higher end of the market and please middle-brow tastes. Let us examine the elements that shaped these tactics.

The poster for *El arte de morir* bears an uncanny resemblance to those advertising *Scream 2* and *Scream 3* (see Figure 36). A group portrait presents the defiant faces of the six young characters – Iván (Fele Martínez), Clara (María Esteve), Carlos (Adriá Collado), Patricia (Lucía Jiménez), Candela (Elsa Pataky) and Ramón (Sergio Peris-Mencheta) – and, in the background, the menacing presence of Nacho (Gustavo Salmerón) looms above them. The *Scream*-like scenario is counterpoised to the arty font used for the film title, which has marked artistic and intellectual pretensions far removed from the bodily and emotional reactions elicited by low body genres. 'El arte de morir is the literal translation of *ars moriendi*,' a Western medieval literary tradition, which provided guidance to the dying, write Pozuelo and Royo in the press-book notes, in an attempt to lend the film an air of seriousness and respectabil-ity and to clothe the story in a philosophical and metaphysical subtext. Nacho, an up-and-coming avant-garde artist who is obsessed with representations of death, is the character through whom this theme is articulated in the narrative. In spite of these studious framing devices, the *ars moriendi* motif was largely ignored by the media, though the philosophical and metaphysical subtext was picked up by some reviewers, who argue that the real protagonist in the film is conscience (Villar 2000) and the storyline involves spectators in a confronta-tion with their own ghosts (Piña 2000).

Undoubtedly, death is the structuring element in *El arte de morir*, as it is in any other slasher film where the protagonists are picked off one by one by the killer(s). Films like *Scream* present a whodunnit structure populated predominantly by young characters who have to probe into 'the past – either their own past or the past of the community – in order to make sense of the present and then be able to act decisively on the basis of the knowledge thus acquired' (Hutchings 2004: 215). What this probing into the past achieves is putting the group's interpersonal relationships to the test and asking the indi-vidual characters to face up to their past actions. *El arte de morir* is formulaic in this respect. The tagline for *El arte de morir* clearly establishes the ominous presence of the past: 'if you have to dig up your past, don't dig too deep.' Only Iván, ridden with guilt, is prepared to dig deep. A practical joke gone wrong ends with Nacho drowning in the swimming pool of an abandoned country house, where he is hastily buried. Four years later, when the case is reopened, the group deny that Nacho had been with them on the weekend in question and refuse to admit any involvement with his disappearance. Panic and friction set in when the group decide to recover the body and remove any incriminating evidence. Their plan goes wrong when a fire breaks out at the house and they are forced to flee. After this incident, one by one, the characters begin to die.

As with its American counterparts, part of the cast of *El arte de morir* came from the world of television. Sergio Peris-Mencheta, Lucía Jiménez and Elsa Pataky had appeared in the popular Telecinco series *Al salir de clase* (1997–2002), which attracted audiences of 3 million in the afternoon slot (an audience share of 22%). This TV series appealed to both male and female audiences in the 13–24 age group, a segment of viewers which would make up the main target audience for the film's producers. By exploiting the popularity of certain members of the cast due to their appearance in the TV series, the producers succeeded in attracting a mixed-gender teen and youth mainstream audience. Casting decisions were also made to promote the film as a showcase for a new generation of actors, whose looks, attitude and 'coolness' were highly marketable in the media; mainstream film magazines *Cinemanía* and *Fotogramas* featured glossy reports on the cast and their roles in the film. But *El arte de morir* did not just entice TV audiences dying to see their TV crush and the genre's core teen audience hungry for the Spanish *Scream*; Spanish horror fans were also attracted, as the casting of Fele Martínez in the lead role of Iván allowed this specific segment of the audience to make cross-cinematic connections with his appearances in Amenábar's *Tesis* and *Abre los ojos*, and added credibility to Fernández Armero's take on the genre. And credibility was a quality (desperately) sought after by the director, who expressed his love for and commitment to the genre in promotional interviews ('I'm a big horror fan and I've always wanted to make a horror film' (Fernández Armero in Belinchón 2000: 5), and by the scriptwriters, who described their work as 'a pure exercise in genre filmmaking'. Yet their claims to authenticity and their declared engagement with generic conventions, whether those of the American teen horror film or the psychological thrillers of Amenábar, constituted a risky tactic that would be put to the test by reviewers.

Scream acts as a critical yardstick to measure the film's performance in almost every review. 'Gritos a la española', reads the review title in *El Levante* (Guillot 2000). 'Terror juvenil a la española', advertises the guide *Metrópoli* (Calleja 2000: 12). The plot 'smells like *Scream* or *I Know What You Did Last Summer*', writes Belinchón (2000) in *El país*, but he qualifies his statement, remarking that *El arte de morir* 'steers clear of the usual commonplaces typical of the genre' (2000). Similarly, the feeling of *déjà vu* experienced by the critic of *El correo español* when confronted with the plot is soon dispelled by an involving storyline ('the way in which the narrative is presented to the audience') and the importance of the 'psychological process at work' (Belinchón 2000). These reviewers, like those in *Cinemanía*, *Fotogramas* and *Imágenes*, reproduce the call for distinction mobilised by producers and screenwriters in the pressbook and in the media: the call, that is to say, to differentiate *El arte de morir* from the formulaic slasher films coming from Hollywood, and, at the same time, to differentiate Spanish audiences – discerning, sophisticated – from the average (American) teen consumer. In fact, the (lack of) genre-knowingness displayed by *El arte de morir* is its major critical downfall. Genre commentators at home and abroad lambasted the horror competencies of Fernández Armero and Pozuelo and Royo. For British horror specialist magazine *Shivers*, the film is guilty of 'drawing heavily from several sources and doing justice to none of them' (Botting 2000a: 47). In *Cine para leer*, journalist Cobeaga Eguillor makes a clear distinction between the commercial aesthetics of the film and its attempt to engage generically with *Scream*. On the one hand,

Cobeaga Eguillor applauds Aurum Producciones' ambitions to produce commercial cinema 'designed for immediate consumption' and 'to reach audiences' (2000: 50) by combining a charismatic cast, an efficient promotion machinery and an entertaining and thrilling ride that is profitable at the box office (2000: 49–50); on the other hand, *El arte de morir*'s pretensions to be 'like *Scream*' are cancelled out by the creators, who show a

> total ignorance of the horror genre (it looks as if neither the scriptwriters nor the director have ever seen a horror film in their lives) and their lack of humour (the main feature in the series created by Wes Craven and Kevin Williamson). (2000: 51)

Thus, as a purely commercial exercise, *El arte de morir* cunningly exploited the formula of a scary brand name and horror cycle, and delivered an 'energetic piece of entertainment' (Holland 2000) for Spanish audiences. However, thematically, it offered no meditation on 'the art of dying' nor on the *Scream* blueprint, failing to produce a local rebranding of contemporary American horror conventions. The commercial life of *El arte de morir* slowly died through the summer of 2000.[15] R.I.P.

A number of subsequent autochthonous takes on the teen-horror movie attempted to piggy-back on the production strategies and commercial achievements of *El arte de morir* with varying degrees of success at the box office, although they were generally slated by critics as yet another Spanish *Scream* rip-off. Such was the case with *Tuno Negro*, *School Killer*, *Más de mil cámaras velan por tu seguridad*, *Ouija* and *La monja*. Heavy-handed dialogue, such as that used in the *La monja* trailer, did nothing to persuade audiences and critics: 'Are you trying to tell me that all this is some sort of "I know what you did eighteen summers ago"? Bullshit.' Directors and scriptwriters tended to qualify the position of their respective films in relation to *Scream*, and, by extension, the American teen-horror movie, in the pressbooks and in interviews. For instance, *Tuno Negro* aimed, as the directors explained,

> to take the concept [of *Scream*] and adapt it to the realities of Spanish university life, which is much richer than in the States. So we have a film which is fundamentally very Spanish – Salamanca, *La Tuna*[16] and the character of the people – but the framing, the pacing and the inclusion of plenty of action, chases, and suspense make the film very American in presentation. (Barbero and Martín in Hodges 2003: 57)

In the Spanish university town of Salamanca, a psycho-killer has infiltrated the *Tuna*. Selecting his victims through the internet, he applies very simple reasoning to his actions: the worst students in each class must die. *School Killer* and *La monja* proposed similar scenarios and narrative structures. *School Killer* introduces the viewer to a group of students, who in 1973 hold a party in an abandoned school that ends in massacre. Only one of the six students survives, and the murderer, believed to be the school caretaker (played by Paul Naschy), is never found. Twenty-seven years later, a group of six teen-agers decide that the same abandoned building is the perfect place to throw a weekend party. Ramón, the son of the only survivor of the 1973 crimes, is part of the group. It is within this scenario that the caretaker and the ghosts of the murdered teenagers reappear to the young protagonists, who soon believe, as the film's tagline declares, 'Nos van a matar a todos' (They're going to kill us all). 'Reza para que no aparezca' (Pray you don't see her) was the public-ity tagline for *La monja*, which tells the story of six girls who are haunted by the vengeful spectre of the Mother Superior they murdered while they were at Catholic boarding school. The action then situates us seventeen years later, when two women from the group are brutally murdered. Knowing that the murders are linked and that the nun must be seeking revenge, the remaining survivors decide to return to the place where it all began years ago. Critical reception of these Spanish teen-horror products followed a familiar pattern: references were made to the *Scream* franchise and / or to *El arte de morir*, there was often pointed commentary on the inability of the directors to repli-cate *Scream*'s smart knowingness about genre conventions, and the films were generally disparaged. The reviews of *School Killer* and *La monja* serve as an example here: *School Killer* 'aims to emulate the recent success of *El arte de morir*', is nothing more than 'an unoriginal teen-horror-formula' and 'lacks the double-entendre of *Scream*' (Barredo 2002: 280–1), while *La monja* incurred the wrath of the reviewer – this film 'is a filmic spit' at the audience, 'a terrible copy of already derivative copies', and an insult, 'since *School Killer* I have never felt so embarrassed during a premiere' (Barredo 2006 235).

Most of these teen-horror movies were either genre assignments or the work of first-time directors with hardly any links to the cultural field of horror. The only exception to this was *La monja*'s Luis de la Madrid, who had worked as editor on *El espinazo del diablo* and *Los sin nombre* and whose name was linked throughout the early 2000s to the Fantastic Factory, a Barcelona-based genre-production label focusing on fantasy and horror set up in 1999 as part of the Filmax group.

'SPANISH HOUSE OF HORROR': FANTASTIC FACTORY[17]

The association of Julio Fernández, President of Filmax, and American horror filmmaker Brian Yuzna – whose horror genre credentials include such gore clas-sics as *Society* (1989), *Bride of Re-Animator 2* (1990), *Necronomicon* (1993) and *The Dentist* (1996) – was forged at a specialist genre festival, Sitges, in

1998. The initial objective of the Fantastic Factory was 'to produce up to six $4m–$6m English-language horror and sci-fi films [annually], marrying Spanish creative talent with English-speaking actors in search of international audiences' (Green 2002a: 12) and to 'make Barcelona the centre of genre filmmaking in the world' (Yuzna in Mendik 2004: 183); in order to maintain a steady stream of production, the output target would change to a more moderate two or three movies a year, plus one bigger-budgeted effort. As Yuzna related to *Screen International*, the philosophy behind the creation of the label was to 'foster identification among buyers and loyalty among audiences' (Green 2002a: 34). Vital to the success of the label was the role of the international sales department in controlling the destiny of the product: namely, to reach the international marketplace in a Hollywood genre style and to ensure video, DVD and television sales.

The first three works to come out of the Fantastic Factory were shot in English and directed by Americans: *Faust. La venganza está en la sangre / Faust: Love of the Damned* (Brian Yuzna 2000), *Arachnid* (Jack Sholder 2001) and *Dagon. La secta del mar / H. P. Lovecraft's Dagon* (Stuart Gordon 2001). These products, as Willis has noted, 'clearly aimed to sit alongside other low- to mid-budget American horror films without drawing attention to their production roots, attracting cinemagoers, and more likely DVD renters, through their generic elements rather than their national origins' (2008: 32). This production trend continued with other works by Yuzna: *Beyond Re-Animator* (2003), which was a reawakening of Gordon's 1985 gory *Re-Animator* and Yuzna's own 1990 *Re-Animator 2*; *Bajo aguas tranquilas / Beneath Still Waters* (2005); and *Rottweiler* (2005). *Beneath Still Waters* was the last film released under the banner of the Fantastic Factory, which ceased production as a label after the departure of Yuzna in 2005. Although, on many levels, these first Fantastic Factory products were Spanish enterprises (shot on location in and around Barcelona, members of the artistic crew), the label's initial mode of production was, for some Spanish critics, 'un-Spanish'. *Faust*, for example, was based on an American comic book of the same name by artist Tim Vigil and writer David Quinn, proposed a violent superhero played by Jeffrey 'Re-Animator' Combs and blended horror, thriller and action-movie conventions. Such labelling was rejected by Yuzna, who described these critics as 'reactionaries [. . .] wary of changing traditional ways of conceptualizing, financing and making films in Spain' (Green 2002a: 34). In fact, one of the directions taken by Yuzna and Fernández was to spot and support Spanish talent through 'Fantastic Discovery' by producing the works of up-and-coming new directors, among them Jaume Balagueró and Paco Plaza, who later teamed up for the successful [●REC] series.

While still keeping the international market in mind, the production strategies of films such as *Beyond Re-Animator, Dagon, Romasanta. La caza de*

SPANISH HORROR FILM

la bestia / Romasanta: The Werewolf Hunt (Paco Plaza 2004) and *La monja* introduced some 'Spanish' elements, or, as Willis puts it, 'a shift to a more identifiable Spanish horror' (2008: 36). Thus *Beyond Re-Animator*, a sequel to the entertaining obsessions of mad scientist Herbert West, included 'effective use of Spanish locations' and 'the self-reflexive casting of local pop culture icons such as Santiago Segura [. . .] and pin-up [actress] Elsa Pataky' (Mendik 2004: 189). *Dagon* and *Romasanta* were set in Galicia and incorporated characters based on local folklore, *La monja* in a Spanish Catholic boarding school. This shift allowed specialist reviewers such as Antonio José Navarro from the pages of *Dirigido por* . . . to identify a fundamental rift between the base commercialism of the 'American defectors', the 'mercenaries of the Factory' (that is, Yuzna, Gordon and Sholder) and 'the cinema of Jaume Balagueró and Paco Plaza', who conceived their films as 'art and commerce' (2005b: 14).

As one of the few Spanish interventions in the werewolf subgenre not associated with Spanish werewolf *par excellence* Paul Naschy (the 1970 *El bosque del lobo* comes to mind), *Romasanta. La caza de la bestia* is a historically based approach to the werewolf myth, which was not seen as a typical product coming out of the Fantastic Factory. The film is an adaptation of the novel *Memorias inciertas del hombre-lobo* (Alfredo Conde), which is based on the true-life murder case against Manuel Blanco Romasanta, a travelling salesman, who confessed to the murder of thirteen people in Allariz, Galicia, in the mid-nineteenth century, blaming his actions on his lycanthropic condition. The film focuses on Manuel (Julian Sands) and his affair with villager Maria (Maru Valdivieso), who lives with her daughter Teresa (Luna McGill) and sister Barbara (Elsa Pataky), who is also in love with Manuel. When mutilated corpses begin to appear in the village, among them the bodies of Maria and Teresa, the local authorities begin to investigate and attention turns to Manuel. Manuel's former partner in crime, huntsman Antonio (John Sheridan), warns Barbara about Romasanta. Barbara plans to avenge the death of her relatives. The film blends drama, romance and horror, and belongs to the tradition of Gothic horror tales in which superstitious beliefs – in this instance the local inhabitants' beliefs regarding the 'Werewolf of Allariz' – are pitted against the rationality of science, embodied in the figures of lawman Luciano de la Bastida (Gary Piquer) and the British Professor Philips (David Gant). While the representatives of scientific knowledge attempt to explain the actions of Romasanta through reference to medical discourses, the horrific and fantastic elements are introduced from the point of view of Romasanta and the versions of the story given the villagers.

Apart from *Romasanta. La caza de la bestia* and *La monja*, other Spanish films appeared in the Fantastic Factory catalogue in the early 2000s: *Darkness* (Jaume Balagueró 2002), *El segundo nombre / Second Name* (Paco Plaza 2002), *Trece campanadas / Thirteen Chimes* (Xavier Villaverde 2002), *Palabras enca-*

denadas / *Killing Words* (Laura Maña 2003) and *Frágiles* / *Fragile* (Jaume Balagueró 2005). Since Yuzna's departure, Filmax has continued producing horror and horror-related films: the suspense-thriller *Bosque de sombras* / *The Backwoods* (Koldo Serra 2006), *Los abandonados* / *The Abandoned* (Nacho Cerdà 2006), *KM31*. *Kilómetro 31* / *KM31: Kilometre 31* (Rigoberto Castañeda 2007), *[•REC]* (Jaume Balagueró and Paco Plaza 2007) and its sequels *[•REC2]* (Jaume Balagueró and Paco Plaza 2009), *[•REC3] Genesis* (Paco Plaza 2012) and the fourth and final instalment, *[•REC4] Apocalypse* (Jaume Balagueró) – the last one in production at the time this book was being completed – and *Mientras duermes* / *Sleep Tight* (Jaume Balagueró 2011). Filmax also attempted to spread its genre production to the television medium with the ambitious *6 Películas para no dormir* / *Six Films to Keep You Awake*, TV movies which brought together household name Narciso Ibáñez Serrador, his landmark *Historias para no dormir* and contemporary genre practitioners Álex de la Iglesia, Jaume Balagueró, Paco Plaza, Mateo Gil and Enrique Urbizu. Filmax Televisión joined forces with Telecinco's Estudios Picasso to produce quality Spanish TV horror and to export it abroad. However, only the first two episodes were aired by Telecinco: de la Iglesia's 'La habitación del niño' / 'The Baby's Room' and Balagueró's 'Para entrar a vivir' / 'To Let'. The four remaining episodes – Ibáñez-Serrador's 'La culpa' / 'Blame', Gil's 'Regreso a Moira' / 'Spectre', Urbizu's 'Adivina quién soy' / 'A Real Friend' and Plaza's 'Cuento de Navidad' / 'The Christmas Tale' – went directly to video and DVD rental.

PATRONAGE AND *El orfanato*

Juan Antonio Bayona's *El orfanato* 'is a compelling exercise in *mainstream* horror' (2007a: 40), which demonstrates a 'deep knowledge of [the genre's] classic forms', wrote film critic Jordi Costa in *El país*. Costa also highlighted the 'referential voracity' of a film which echoes, among others, the Deborah Kerr of *The Innocents* – or perhaps her 'digest through the sieve of *Los otros*' (2007a: 40) – through the remarkable performance of the female protagonist Laura (Belén Rueda), or the memorable medium scene in *Poltergeist* (Tobe Hooper 1982). 'If one was to read Bayona's debut film with malicious eyes,' Costa conjectured, 'the *high concept* to sell the film to a Hollywood executive could be "the atmosphere / mood of *Los otros* with the actress of *Mar adentro*"' (2007a: 40). And the critic concluded: '*El orfanato*, therefore, is not the work of an auteur, but rather the work of a strategist' (2007a: 40), who 'keeps in one hand a virtual *Manual To Please Guillermo del Toro in Ten Easy Steps*, and, on the other, an essay on the art of seducing (the masses)' (2007a: 40). Comparisons with Amenábar also run through Tonio L. Alarcón's comments on the film for *Dirigido por* . . . :

Juan Antonio Bayona learnt very well Amenábar's magisterial lessons [in *Los otros*]. There is no doubt that the key to his overwhelming success lies here [. . .]: in order to enjoy the misfortunes of [main lead] Belén Rueda, there is no need to know M. R. James, Jack Clayton or Robert Wise (not even Shyamalan) [for *El orfanato*] is more a bid for those foreign to the genre than for horror aficionados. (2009: 37)

We turn now to the commercial and artistic strategies that made *El orfanato* the most successful film at the Spanish box office in 2007, grossing 19.1 million euros and drawing over 3.5 million spectators, as well as a hit at international festivals, with trade journals such as *Variety* and *Screen International*, and with the Hollywood industry (New Line Cinema bought the rights for an American remake as soon as the film entered the festival circuit).

The films of Amenábar, in particular *Los otros*, and the patronage of del Toro paved the way for the debut of Bayona. With the backing of the Mexican director, *El orfanato* maximised the bankability and reputation of del Toro and adopted the profitable marketing and distribution strategies of *El laberinto del fauno*, which had reaped nominations and awards the world over and broken industry records in the American, Spanish and Mexican markets throughout 2006. The tagline 'Produced by Guillermo del Toro' acted as a guarantee of access to international markets and ensured that Spanish horror cinema would be put on the global filmic map; Warner Bros. Pictures International Spain acquired the multi-territory distribution rights for the film in Spain and Latin America, Wild Bunch bought the rights to international sales and Picturehouse picked up all North American rights. In Spain, Producciones Cinematográficas Telecinco, as co-producer with production company Rodar y Rodar, ensured the productive synergy between cinema and television, in particular the key role of private TV channel Telecinco[18] in the successful placing of *El orfanato* in the marketplace; an aggressive advertising and promotional campaign was mounted that covered the whole media spectrum (from traditional to new media outlets) in order to reach the widest possible audience (and to replicate the phenomenal box-office takings of *El laberinto del fauno* and *Alatriste* (Agustín Díaz Yanes 2006)). The spot advertising campaign on television was vigorous, with spots and trailers shown repeatedly on Telecinco to promote specific sellable elements of the film: 'Guillermo del Toro Presents', the presence of lead actress Belén Rueda, and tantalising glimpses of the strange costumes and masks worn by the ghostly children. Likewise, fragments from the film and its 'Making of . . .' footage, as well as clues about the plot, were regularly posted on myspacetv.com to drum up general interest and to feed prospective fans.

The international success of the film at art-house and genre film festivals replicated the course traced by *El laberinto del fauno* a year earlier: world premiere at Cannes, North American screenings in New York and Toronto, and official presentation to genre specialists at Sitges' forthieth anniversary. The Sitges connection between del Toro and Bayona came into the stories that both directors relayed to the press. As a teenager, Bayona had interviewed del Toro in Sitges in 1993 for a local TV station when del Toro's first film, *Cronos*, played the festival; since then he had cultivated their friendship and kept del Toro abreast of his projects. Like *El laberinto del fauno*, *El orfanato* premiered at the Sitges Festival, which acted as the launch pad for the film in the Spanish media. Press attention escalated in the cultural sections and weekend supplements of the two main newspapers, *El país* and *El mundo*, as well as in popular and specialist film publications, especially after *El orfanato* was selected as the Spanish entry at the 80th Academy Awards.[19] The film was released on 11 October 2007. The following day saw its release nationwide on 350 screens, and it took 6 million euros in its first weekend, which represented the second-highest-grossing film in the history of Spanish cinema.

Del Toro's patronage and legitimation of Bayona's début feature film not only were impressed upon critics and audiences in interviews and through his gregarious physical presence at premieres but also were officially inscribed in *El orfanato*'s pressbook, where the Mexican director wrote about the film's genre credentials, its generic affiliations and its distinctive contribution to the field of contemporary horror. Del Toro begins by expressing his admiration for Bayona's shorts, *Mis vacaciones / My Holidays* (1999) and *El hombre esponja / The Sponge Man* (2002) – two imaginative tales about children growing up, told through the aesthetic lens of *Xanadú* (Robert Greenwald 1980) and films and comics about superheroes, respectively – and his work for the music video industry, the quality of which 'vociferously demanded the opportunity to direct a film'. His expectations of the script penned by Sergio G. Sánchez[20] were surpassed, for 'it was not just a crowd-pleasing rehash of the emblematic elements of the genre: haunted houses, ghosts, parallel universes . . . It had a depth which is unusual and powerful.' *El orfanato*, del Toro stated, 'worked not only as a horror film' which 'rereads in a personal manner the genre's commonplaces', but also expertly brought into play other generic markers – 'mystery', 'suspense' and 'melodrama' – through the emotional depths of pain and loss which link the characters. Correspondingly, the film was marketed as transcendent of genre; Spanish posters, for example, promoted the melodramatic and horrific modes with the tagline 'Un cuento de amor. Una historia de terror' ('A love tale. A horror story').

El orfanato displayed production values usually associated with Hollywood products; Sandra Hermida, *El orfanato*'s Director of Production, affirmed that 'we have made a film with an "American" production quality but using the Spanish production system' (*Cineinforme* 2007: 38). In the 'Production Notes' included in the pressbook, Bayona stated that his film relates to a type of *cine fantástico* that is not produced any more. It is a type of horror which starts out from quotidian elements, it is then gradually tainted until it moves into the realms of dread and absolute madness [. . .] In this story fear originates in an idyllic setting, at the heart of a perfect family. And it grows in unexpected ways threatening to destroy this family completely.

The aesthetics of modern classic horror films *The Innocents* and *The Haunting* 'surged through my head', Bayona asserted, 'so the film had to be shot classically, that is, using a studio setting' – eight percent of the film was shot in a Barcelona studio. The film unabashedly makes use of a classic haunted house production design to convey the grief, distress and madness germinating in the female protagonist's psyche. Storyboards and animatics, *mise-en-scène*, cinematography and post-production were aimed at reproducing the look and feel of the haunted house genre and at conveying a tale of haunting which ambiguously straddles the line between reality and fantasy, the sane and the mad, the haunter and the haunted.

Laura (Belén Rueda) returns with her family, husband Carlos (Fernando Cayo) and seven year-old Simón (Roger Príncep), to the long-abandoned orphanage where she grew up thirty years ago to reopen it as a haven for disabled children. Soon after arriving at the new home, Simón, who does not know that he is both adopted and HIV-positive, claims that he has some invisible friends. When Simón goes missing, Laura believes that something terrible, related to the orphanage's past, is lurking at the heart of the house and trying to hurt her family. The unsuccessful investigation carried out by the police and a police psychologist and Laura's growing despair lead her to enlist a team of paranormal experts, among them a medium (Aurora, played by Geraldine Chaplin) to confront the ghosts in the house. While in a trance, Aurora reveals that Simón's disappearance is linked to the fortunes of Laura's fellow orphans three decades ago. Laura's grief and obsession escalate, and she embarks on a search in which the real and imaginary ghosts of her past and present blur together (see Figure 37).

The ominous skyline with which the pre-credit sequence opens sets the mood of the film. Our first view of the orphanage's façade is framed in a long take that slowly moves to Laura and her orphan friends, who are playing a 'freeze' game in the garden, and the sing-song refrain, 'One, two, three, knock on the wall', that we hear in these first moments will be eerily replayed at the end of the film. The portentous sky and façade will provide a recurring *leitmotif* that links the orphanage of past and present with Laura's progressive mental deterioration. The sequence neatly establishes Laura's childhood at the orphanage and the fact of her later adoption. The black screen following the stylised credits *à la* Saul Bass – wallpaper being ripped off to reveal the names

Figure 37   Waiting for the ghost to manifest in *El orfanato*.

of the producers and the director– is punctured by a little boy's voice calling 'Mummy!' and the introduction of the now-adult Laura in a medium close-up, looking dazed and confused after being abruptly woken up by her son's call. Laura's comforting of Simón promptly sets up the mother–son bond, as well as key themes in the film – game-playing and make-believe, through Laura's pretend restoration of the abandoned lighthouse nearby through the moon's reflection in a clock face, and through Simón's initial references to his imaginary friends Watson and Pepe, who will soon be replaced by a new set of invisible others. The straddling of reality and fantasy is central to the carefully constructed ambiguity upon which the film's dual reading relies; whether the narrative events are the product of Laura's psyche or supernatural in origin is to be determined by the viewer. Ambiguity is formally and stylistically con-structed through Laura's point of view and the technologies of horror and suspense, which convey the experiences of a haunted mind reckoning with its ghosts and reproduce the staple atmosphere of the haunted house genre. The sequence where the medium Aurora attempts to summon the orphanage's ghosts captures the two possible readings: horror, if we, like Laura, accept the presence of ghosts, or hoax, if we believe that the roles and methods of the parapsychologists are mere trickery. The sequence also encapsulates Bayona's self-reflexive use of the technology of horror and his cinematic lineage.

Accompanied by Laura, Carlos and Pilar the psychologist (Mabel Rivera), parapsychologists Balabán (Edgar Vivar) and Enrique (Andrés Gertrudix) set up their operations room, which resembles a video editing suite, to monitor and record Aurora's attempts to contact the spirits of the house. A night vision camera tracks Aurora's movements around different rooms in the residence and recording equipment captures what the medium sees and hears. While Carlos and Pilar express their mistrust of the powers of the medium and her assistants ('This is a farce, a sideshow trick,' declares Pilar), an enthralled Laura follows Aurora's every movement in search of signs or sightings of

Simón. As the sequence develops, the viewer increasingly shares Laura's point of view and is therefore placed in an empathetic relationship with her and develops a willingness to believe in the existence of ghosts in the house. In fact, the episode represents a turning point in the narrative, as Carlos decides to leave the house and Laura poignantly intensifies her search for Simón within the walls of the orphanage.

When Carlos questions Aurora, he says 'Are you telling us that there are ghosts in this house?' The beginning of the reply comes through Balabán, whose question 'What is a ghost, Carlos?' is continued by Aurora, who addresses Laura directly:

> When something terrible happens, sometimes it leaves a trace, a word that acts as a knot between two time lines, it's like an echo, repeated over and over, waiting to be heard. Like a scar [. . .] that begs for a caress to relieve it.

The traces, timelines and echoes alluded to by Aurora function narratively and allegorically as a way of saying that the ghostly resides in the living. But Balabán's question in the voice of Mexican actor Edgar Vivar and Aurora's words in the voice of Geraldine Chaplin also carry intertextual echoes that speak to a recent cinematic past. On the one hand, it repeats the central idea of Guillermo del Toro's ghost story *El espinazo del diablo*, and, on the other, it links *El orfanato* with *Cría cuervos* (Carlos Saura 1975), a canonical film in the history of Spanish cinema, through the casting of Geraldine Chaplin. In *Cría cuervos*, Chaplin's dual role as María, a terminally ill mother, and Ana, María's grieving daughter, two decades later provides a complex exploration of emotional thresholds and traumas and of the knotted lines of past, present and future.

Through a calculated – some might say aggressive – marketing strategy, *El orfanato* attracted more mainstream audiences. The deliberately crafted ambiguity of the plot and its elegant 'synthesis of *The Innocents*, *The Others* and every other cinematic chiller about a woman's psychic fixation with some not-so-innocent children' (Chang 2007) blended melodrama and ghost story and found a broad audience beyond the horror genre crowd. As Bayona acknowledged to horror magazine *par excellence Fangoria*, 'I love the genre, but I want to transcend it too, and that's my personal triumph with *The Orphanage*' (Bayona in Jones 2008: 35). Undeniably, del Toro's successful supernatural horrors *El espinazo del diablo* and, more particularly, *El laberinto del fauno* paved the way for Bayona's début chiller. His artistic and industrial patronage enabled a first-time director like Bayona to realise his own vision. More recently, del Toro co-produced another feature debut with Barcelona-based Rodar y Rodar, *Los ojos de Julia* by Guillem Morales, replicating the marketing template and quality-horror production values that had proved so effective in *El orfanato*. Bayona looks set to follow in his patron's benevolent footsteps: 'The only condition that Guillermo imposed is that I should sponsor a debutant in the future, as he has done with me' (Bayona in Belinchón 2007: 14).

From the industrial lows of the late 1970s and the 1980s to the arrival of a new generation of filmmakers in the mid-1990s and the dizzying box-office heights of the 2000s, contemporary Spanish horror film has moved from the margins to the mainstream. What is clear is that *El día de la bestia*, *Tesis*, *El arte de morir* and *El orfanato* owe their commercial success to the role played by their respective production and distribution companies, whose marketing and publicity tactics drew audiences to the cinemas and mediated the reception of the films. Mainstream critical response (and academic writing) in Spain is coming to terms with what is mostly perceived as a purely commercial film culture. However, genre critics and fans consume and write about these films in a different way by engaging with generic conventions, diverse national and international horror traditions, and the cross-fertilisation between films and comics, cinema and television – in other words, by participating in the construction of a Spanish horror film culture. As a thriving culture and industry, Spanish horror continues to forge its place in the global horror market.

Notes

1. See *Cineinforme* (2008: 16–25).
2. Parallel to his role as director, he acted in numerous films, among them *Secuestro* (León Klimovsky 1976), *Pecado mortal* (Miguel Ángel Díez 1977), *El transexual* (José Lara 1977), *El francotirador* (Carlos Puerto 1978) and *Comando Txikia, muerte de un presidente* (José Luis Madrid 1978).
3. The former *Látidos de pánico* and *Licántropo*; the latter *El retorno del hombre lobo*, *El espanto surge de la tumba*, *El jorobado de la morgue*, *El mariscal del infierno*, *La maldición de la bestia*, *El carnaval de las bestias*, *Exorcismo*, *Una libélula para cada muerto*, *Los ojos azules de la muñeca rota* and *La rebelión de las muertas*.
4. D'Arbó's entry into filmmaking came via his apprenticeships in the popular genre film industry, in particular IFI productions, which specialised in low-budget thrillers and *film noir*, and Balcázar studios, which specialised in spaghetti westerns in the late 1960s and early 1970s.
5. Piquer Simón also produced *Escalofrío* (Carlos Puerto 1978) and *Más allá del terror / Further than Fear* (Tomás Aznar 1980).
6. The film is available on DVD: a Spanish edition marketed by Filmax Home Video as part of their 'DVD Bizarro: Cine de Terror Español' collection (2007), and an American edition with extra features sold though Grindhouse Releasing DVD (2008).
7. Distributed by Film Ventures International, *Pieces* made $604,510 in its opening weekend, ranking in 14th position, and made a total $2,032,311.
8. As well as that of Dick Randall and Tonino Mori.
9. This text is also available in Spanish and in English at clubcultura.com/club-cine/clubcineastas/amenabar/tesis.htm, which houses Amenábar's official website

(accessed 30 June 2010). For purposes of clarity, I have made a number of stylistic changes to this statement as it appears in the pressbook and on Amenabar's official website.

10. Jordi Costa and Darío Adanti (2009), *Mis problemas con Amenábar* (Barcelona: Glénat).

11. Among the films in this cycle of American teen horror of the late 1990s and early 2000s, the following titles can be mentioned: the two sequels of the *Scream* franchise (*Scream 2* (1997) and *Scream 3* (2000)), *I Know What You Did Last Summer* (Jim Gillespie 1997), *I Still Know What You Did Last Summer* (Danny Cannon 2000), *Urban Legend* (Jamie Blanks 1998) and *Final Destination* (James Wong 2000).

12. That same year it was only outperformed at the box office by *Año Mariano* (Karra Elejalde and Fernando Guillén Cuervo), *La comunidad* (Álex de la Iglesia) and *You're the One* (José Luis Garcí).

13. Box-office and rental grosses have been obtained from variety.com and mec.es.

14. Television channels were complying with current film legislation whereby TV operators had to invest 5 per cent of their annual revenues in local cinema.

15. The film's afterlife is limited to its distribution abroad for the US Hispanic video and DVD market via Venevision International, and to screenings on Spanish TVE-2 (11 October 2002 on TVE-2's *Versión española*, featuring a discussion with director Fernández Armero, scriptwriter Royo and actress María Esteve; and 25 August 2006 in *Cine con Ñ* as part of a late-night horror double-bill with *Mucha sangre*).

16. *Tunas* are groups of university students dressed in seventeenth-century costumes, who play guitars, lutes and tambourines and go serenading through the streets singing traditional Spanish songs, often of a bawdy nature.

17. I borrow this intertitle from an article published in *Screen International* (Stephanie Green 2002: 12). The activities of Filmax Entertainment cut across production and post-production, distribution and exhibition of audiovisual material. As its website publicises, the company's catalogue includes 'more than 2,000 works – feature films, TV series and documentaries, and TV movies – which cater to the cultural sensibilities and different tastes of national and international audiences'. Thus Filmax Televisión and Filmax Animation produce TV movies and animation feature films, respectively. See filmax.com, accessed 29 June 2010.

18. See cine.telecinco.es/ELORFANATO.htm.

19. The film did not make the final shortlist for the Best Foreign Film Oscar.

20. The script underwent different versions: Sánchez wrote it originally in 1996 as 'Sé que estás ahí' / 'I Know You Are There', reworked it during his stay at the Sundance Institute, made it into a short entitled *7337*, and then passed Bayona the libretto after they met at a festival of shorts in Mallorca. During the early 2000s Sánchez and Bayona rewrote the script that would become *El orfanato*. The work of a decade was rewarded in 2008 when the film was awarded Best Original Screenplay at the Goyas.

7. TRANSNATIONAL HORROR AUTEURS: NACHO CERDÀ, JAUME BALAGUERÓ AND GUILLERMO DEL TORO

Horror magazine *Fangoria* hailed Jaume Balagueró, Nacho Cerdà and Guillermo del Toro as 'The Future of Fear' in its 200th issue. The report profiled '13 rising horror talents who promise to keep us terrified for the next 200 issues and beyond' (2001: 80), including directors, writers and a make-up artist.[1] *Fangoria* greeted the 'somber, chilling power' of Balagueró's first feature film, *Los sin nombre / The Nameless* (1999), as a movie that 'is as quietly chilling as any movie from any country in the past several years' (Gingold 2001: 80);[2] invited its readers to 'witness the creation of a major force in horror as Nacho Cerdà moves up to features' (Totaro 2001: 82) following his short film trilogy – *The Awakening* (1990), *Aftermath* (1994) and *Genesis* (1998) – which was packed with 'the sort of cinematic know-how and formal control to whet one's appetite for a future film showcase' (Totaro 2001: 82); and recognised approvingly that del Toro was 'doing his part for the genre' with the successes of *Cronos* (1993) and *Mimic* (1997), and was in fact already in 'preproduction on the Wesley Snipes vampire sequel *Blade 2: Blood Hunt* while still in postproduction on his Spanish Civil War ghost story *The Devil's Backbone*' (Bernstein 2001: 83). Brief interviews with the three directors also provided the *Fangoria* readership with their views on horror film in general, their latest projects and the mandatory affirmation of their horror fandom. Thus del Toro raved about 'films that have heralded things to come', such as *Blair Witch Project* (Daniel Myrick and Eduardo Sánchez 1999), *Videodrome* (David Cronenberg 1983) and *Lost Highway* (David Lynch 1997), and expressed his disappointment with those directors who use the genre as merely a 'stepping stone', a 'transitional genre', concluding that 'as long as I live [. . .] I will do horror' (del Toro in Bernstein 2001: 83); Balagueró defined his approach to the genre as 'investigating new ways to scare people' (Balagueró in Gingold 2001: 82); and Cerdà located his work in relation to trends in contemporary Spanish horror production thus:

> until a few years ago, there seemed to be an obsession with young Spanish filmmakers to do horror films with a humorous tone, and that is something I never really liked, especially as the only approach. Those films should co-exist with other types of horror films that are serious and harsher, like *The Nameless* by Jaume Balagueró and the new movie *The Others* by Alejandro Amenábar – films that work as true classic horror stories. (Cerdà in Totaro 2001: 82)

A decade later, Balagueró and del Toro have consolidated their respective filmographies, while Cerdà's involvement in a number of projects throughout the 2000s has led to the production of just one feature film, *Los abandonados / The Abandoned* (2006), and a couple of documentaries, *Ataúdes de luz* (2000) / *Coffin of Light* (2009) and *Pieces of Juan (Piquer Simón)* (2008).[3] Balagueró, whose name has been closely associated with Filmax and the Fantastic Factory, has been producing competitive products for the international commercial horror film market – *Darkness*, *Frágiles* and *Mientras duermes* – and, together with Paco Plaza and still under the umbrella of Julio Fernández's Filmax, has co-directed the reality TV horror *[•REC]* and *[•REC2]*, the third instalment *[•REC3] Genesis* (2011) directed by Plaza, and the forthcoming *[•REC4] Apocalypse* to be helmed by Balagueró. With seven films under his belt to date – *Cronos*, *Mimic*, *El espinazo del diablo*, *Blade 2*, *Hellboy*, *El laberinto del fauno* and *Hellboy 2: The Golden Army*, del Toro has become a bankable transnational figure whose name is highly regarded in the global film industry. Del Toro's standing also means that smaller film industries like that of Spain benefit when he is fronting co-productions and acts as the producer of commercial ventures, such as *El orfanato* and *Los ojos de Julia*, as his name is a guarantee of access to international markets and of putting Spanish cinema on the global film map.[4] As Evan Calder Williams has pointed out in relation to del Toro's latest assignment as producer, the remake of 1973's *Don't Be Afraid of the Dark* (2011) by Canadian Troy Nixey, the name of the Mexican director has become 'a discernible franchise and banner, complete with discernible – and requisite – tendencies' (2011).

The accuracy of *Fangoria*'s horror forecast has been borne out in the significant contributions of Balagueró, Cerdà and del Toro to the field of contemporary Spanish horror. This final chapter focuses on the productive cross-fertilisation of diverse horror traditions in their works; the transnational reach of their filmmaking, intended to engage horror audiences across the world; and their status as horror auteurs across the globe. Producers and distributors have sold and promoted their films not only through the traditional pledges and frights of horror promotion but also through the cultivation of an auteurist sensibility. A survey of the profiles of Balagueró, Cerdà and del Toro in feature articles, their interventions in promotional interviews and the critical receptions of their respective films shed light on their status as horror auteurs.

My choice of these horror genre directors also enables me to draw together some of the various threads woven through the course of this book. Cerdà and Balagueró represent shifts in production that have characterised Spanish horror film over the last four decades; from their initial local productions, shorts and début features, they moved on to international co-productions under the auspices of Filmax and their latest projects belong to a wider transnational mode of filmmaking, which is readily associated with del Toro. The move towards filmmaking for each of these directors was strongly grounded in and driven by horror fan culture, a shared starting point that marked their familiarity with many of the Spanish as well as international horror traditions discussed in previous chapters. Drawing on low-brow, art-house and / or mainstream strategies in a bid to engage different horror fandoms, they consciously position themselves within the wider cultural field of horror.

NACHO CERDÀ

Cerdà's horror auteur (and cult) reputation has been built upon three shorts made in the 1990s, especially the second one entitled *Aftermath*, which has been a favourite of international horror culture and horror film magazines since it won the Audience Award for the best short film at Fant-Asia, Montreal, in 1997. Its screening, which followed *Cannibal Ferox* (Umberto Lenzi 1981), provoked such strong reactions in critics and audience that commentaries on the film quickly filled the pages of publications on both sides of the Atlantic, among them North American *Rue Morgue*, *Ultra Violent Magazine*, *Carpe Noctem* and *Shock Cinema*, British *Shivers*, *Flesh and Blood* and *Is it Uncut?*, and French *Mad Movies* and *Assault*, which certainly contributed to disseminating its 'worldwide fandom infamy'.[5] *Aftermath* went on to accrue a substantial fan base through its circulation as a bootlegged tape among horror fans all over the world in the late 1990s and early 2000s. More recently, its DVD commercialisation as part of the 'La Trilogía de la Muerte' / 'Trilogy of Death' package (Versus Entertainment, 2008) for the Spanish market, as well as through North American-based DVD outlets Xploited Cinema and Unearthed Films, which released limited special editions, have furthered renewed interest in Cerdà's productions. While Cerdà himself intended these shorts to work as a trilogy and the recent DVD packages have cemented such a reading among critics, fans and distributors retrospectively, it has been *Aftermath* that has generated substantial popular and critical controversy in genre magazines, something quite unique for a horror short.

Produced in the space of eight years, 1990 to 1998, the trilogy is composed of *The Awakening*, *Aftermath* and *Genesis*. As the pressbook for *Aftermath* explains, *Aftermath* 'is not a one-off movie; on the contrary, it is closely tied to *The Awakening*'. According to Cerdà, 'my intention [in *The Awakening*] was to film the death of the soul from a sterile, distant standpoint. In a way, *Aftermath* is the second part of a diptych: death from the point of view of the body, of the flesh,' that is, what the body is subjected to in a mortuary during an autopsy, 'the solitude, the violence, the inhumanity of the act'. The pressbook for *Genesis* considers the thematic and stylistic similarities and differences within the trilogy.

> Death is at the core of *Genesis*. This theme dominated both of director Nacho Cerdà's previous short films: *The Awakening* (1990) and *Aftermath* (1994) [. . .] Whereas the first film, shot in 16 mm, approached the subject matter from a spiritual angle, and the second from a physical, visceral standpoint, *Genesis*, shot in anamorphic 1.235, deals with the subject [of death] from the point of view of someone who has survived the death of a loved one. Seen from this perspective, Nacho Cerdà's latest short completes a kind of trilogy that progressively widens its scope to encompass on the wide screen the end of all living things.

Cerdà's thematic preoccupation with death is conveyed in a filmic language which juxtaposes the genre-film vocabulary of spectacle and doses of gore with the art-film vocabulary of psychological depth and self-reflexive narration.

The Awakening was a film project which Cerdà, in collaboration with classmates Ethan Jakobson and Francisco Stohr, shot as a student at the University of Southern California Summer Film School in 1990. Drawing on horror and science-fiction conventions and indebted to *The Twilight Zone*, it centres on a high-school student who finds himself drifting off to sleep in class. When he wakes up, time has stopped. The student, named as 'the soul' in the closing credits, realises that he cannot leave the room. Fleeting moments of his life (as a baby with his mother, a birthday cake) and the last things he has seen (the Great Seal on a dollar bill, the crucifix in the classroom) flash before him, as he slowly becomes aware of what is happening. He is witnessing his own death, signalled by the CPR procedure being performed on his prostrated body and the vision of a woman, 'The Angel', beckoning him from the threshold of the door. While the short adheres to the typical production strategies of shorts – that is, shot in 16 mm and black and white, and lacking dialogue, the treatment of the subject matter and the visual language deployed by Cerdà made it a distinctive product when regarded in relation to the contemporary Spanish short scene of the early 1990s.

Although *Aftermath* coincided with the mid-1990s boom in gore shorts (see Chapter 5) and critics and audiences tended to link it to the gore subgenre, it was also a different filmic proposition in terms of both its taboo content – death and necrophilia – and the seriousness of Cerdà's approach, with the short offering an extremely graphic and realistic depiction of the world of autopsies with no space for gory humour. Cerdà's art-house pretensions can be set within the context of Joan Hawkins's thesis in *Cutting Edge* (2000) on the ways in which lowbrow body genres and high art traffic in the same tropes, taboo subjects and shock tactics, amongst others. The production values of *Aftermath* departed noticeably from contemporary short productions entered in film festivals, as well as from many Spanish feature films of that period. For example, Cerdà had a budget of 35,000 euros, of which 8,000 were destined to SFX; the 35 mm short contained no dialogue, was thirty minutes long, and was produced in colour; and the storyboard included 500 drawings over 125 pages. In sum, *Aftermath* was a defiant and uncompromising work by Cerdà, who scripted, directed and produced it.

Aftermath's initial reception at the 1994 Sitges Festival, where it was entered in the short competition, provoked a divisive reaction among audience and critics.[6] As current Director of the festival and then genre journalist Ángel Sala recalls in his audio-commentary for *Aftermath*, it was 'one of the most disturbing experiences I had at Sitges [. . .] Even the hardened horror festival audiences found it tough to sit through.' As Sala puts it, for some it was an 'obscene' piece of work; for others it 'became a cult phenomenon' straight away. The short met with a similarly polarised reception across the Atlantic some three years later at the 1997 Fant-Asia Festival, upping Cerdà's reputation among underground and gore audiences all over the world. Most notoriously, Chas. Balum of gore title *Deep Red Magazine* (and author of *Gore Score. Ultraviolent Horror in the 80s* (1987)) launched a verbal attack on Cerdà's short, describing it as 'pornographic', or 'gorenography', for its use of graphic violence, continuing his attack in the pages of the magazine ('Aftermath: Is the Spanish Shocker the next Guinea Pig?' (1997)).[7] Associations with the controversial and censored Japanese 'Guinea Pig' series of the mid- to late 1980s and Jorg Buttgereit's *Nekromantic* (1987) would follow Cerdà. At the other end of the spectrum, Donato Totaro of online film journal *Offscreen*, a regular contributor to *Fangoria*, became an advocate of the 'necrophilic art' and of Cerdà's ability to create 'poetic beauty for the ugly and the grotesque' (1997a). Horror fans were advised on the virtues and depravities of *Aftermath* from the pages of international genre magazines. Gingold informed *Fangoria* readers that the short 'sharply divides the crowd: it is extremely well-made, but extremely disgusting' (1998: 17), whereas *Rue Morgue*'s Rod Gudino described it as a

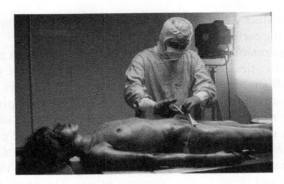

Figure 38   The post-mortem examination is about to start in *Aftermath*.

'visual assault' (1999: 8), 'a revolting little piece of cinema, clinically executed and clinically removed from any narrative judgment (moral or otherwise) in its study of what happens [. . .] during a post-mortem' (1999: 27). Jason J. Slater warned *Dark Side* readers of the potential affects and effects of viewing *Aftermath*:

> For the seasoned gore fan, *Aftermath* is sheer nirvana. For the casual viewer, intrigued by curiosity, this Spanish short will make them reach for the nearest sickbag. For the intelligentsia amongst us, they will find that this film asks more questions than it answers. Certainly a horrific picture, it is not suitable to label *Aftermath* as a splatter film. Amongst the body parts and buckets of goo, lies a film with social and personal comment. (1998: n.p.)

Aftermath is relentless in its crude representation of what happens in an autopsy room when bodies are under the knife during post-mortem examinations (see Figure 38). Cerdà's approach to the filming of the autopsy room and the coroner's actions is distant and clinical, attaining a documentary quality that makes the coroner's shocking rape of a female corpse all the more disturbing. The documentary-like quality, as Cerdà explained in interviews, was supported by conscientious research at the mortuary of a Barcelona hospital, where he witnessed three real autopsies and the SFX work of company DDT, whose craftsmanship contributed to the short's graphic aesthetics.[8] The choice of this very same mortuary as the location for the shoot and the use of knives, pliers, scalpels, electric drills and coroner's uniforms from the autopsy room as props for the *mise-en-scène* further added to the authenticity and realism of the story (see Figure 39).

The magazine *Shivers* described *Aftermath* as '[P]erhaps the most gut-wrenchingly violating and relentlessly subversive piece of cinema for many,

Figure 39   All in order in the autopsy room.

many years' (Mitch 1997: 38). Mitch vividly described the beginning of *Aftermath*:

> Translucent red tissue pulsates in close-up on the screen as a throbbing heartbeat tears the soundtrack to pieces. Soon this sound is replaced with a new one – that of screeching tyres followed by a terrified shriek and a pulverizing crash as the tissue onscreen obliterates before your eyes to surrealistically reveal a mutilated dog. (1997: 38)

The soundscape of tragic horror and the gruesome image of the blood-spattered entrails of the dog are followed by the cold, clinical introduction of the film's main location, an autopsy room. Close-ups of the head of a female corpse toe-tagged as Marta Arnau, on which a shroud is being placed, are alternated with static shots of medical instruments neatly arrayed in stainless steel trays. The name of the director in red lettering gives way to a young mortuary attendant pulling a trolley along the morgue's basement corridors and sliding the cadaver into a refrigeration compartment. A crosscut takes the viewer to a waiting room, where an unidentified doctor is handing a necklace and crucifix to a grieving couple. The next sequence presents in painstaking detail the perfor-mance of autopsies by two coroners at their dissection tables, drilling skulls and removing brains, ruthlessly cutting open sternums, crudely eviscerating the bodies of their internal organs, and eventually sewing up the corpses.[9] The visceral messiness of the dissection is counterpoised to the aseptic composition of the shots as the camera focuses on the surrounding medical paraphernalia.

A fade to white one-third of the way into the short introduces a shift in the formal and stylistic tone of *Aftermath*. From this moment onwards, the viewer is made privy to the assault on Marta Arnau's corpse by one of the coroners. The disturbing necrophile desires of the coroner are unflinchingly conveyed through the physical intimacy he establishes with the cadaver and the shocking abuse he inflicts on it, undressing it, masturbating while touching it, savagely and repeatedly knifing its vagina and brutally raping it.[10] In what looks like a well-established ritual, the coroner duly records the defiled and mutilated body with a photographic camera. A fade to black marks the end of the coroner's pathological exploits and a return to the methodical and meticulous sanitisation of the utensils and the post-mortem table, another ritual in itself. In a final act of desecration, the coroner takes away the cadaver's heart in his briefcase. The closing sequence shows the coroner puréeing the heart in a food processor and emptying it into a dog bowl, which ironically sits on top of a sheet of newspaper containing Marta Arnau's obituary: 'died 25 December; her parents, relatives and friends pray that her soul may rest in peace.'

Despite (or even because of) its disturbing portrayal of necrophilia and the documentary-like visual aesthetics deployed by Cerdà, *Aftermath* is a landmark in Spanish and international horror film production. Whereas detractors of the film have focused on the gore and necrophiliac credentials of the film, its defenders have stressed that necrophilia is derived from the character's pathology, that the actions are shot in a distanced, clinical manner and that Cerdà's serious treatment of the subject of death is 'a cinematic thesis' and 'not about getting noticed' (Sala in DVD audio-commentary). Cerdà stated that his interest lay in 'the post-mortem manipulation and humiliation one suffers after one's death' (Cerdà in Cristóbal Borra 1999: 29) and not in necrophilia. But the recurrent and unavoidable question thrown at Cerdà was 'Is *Aftermath* a gore movie?' His response has been consistent throughout the years: '*Aftermath* has got a lot of blood and guts. But the film is not about blood. The difference is that the gore genre takes things in a festive way' (Cerdà in Gudino 1999: 9); 'My approach only uses gore to show what really happens there [in autopsy rooms]. It isn't gratuitous' (Cerdà in DVD audio-commentary). Certainly, *Aftermath* did not suit the cinematic tastes of alternative publications like *Ruta 66*; in 'Spanish Gore: Sangre y Caspa', for example, Sabino Méndez acknowledged that the short was 'unusually interesting' but that it

> was a pity that it takes itself so seriously. Not even the slightest sense of humour or a sarcastic note. And, to tell you the truth, if there is a future for Spanish horror and fantasy cinema in a third-world industry like ours, it should go down the line of excess, self-parody and original wit. So, be careful, my friend, if you go on doing films like this, you will end up being the Alain Tanner of Spanish fantasy cinema. (1995: 39)

Even so, the gore tag proved difficult to shake, as the short was frequently measured against the contemporary boom of such films (*Evilio* (Santiago Segura 1992), *Perturbado* (Santiago Segura 1993), *Mirindas Asesinas* (Álex de la Iglesia 1991)), and showcased in film events like 'Bad Taste II', as part of the 1995 Gijón Film Festival. And yet Cerdà, as well as Balagueró in the wake of his shorts *Alicia* (1994) and *Días sin luz* (1995), continued to distance himself from gore: 'Jaume Balaguero + Nacho Cerdà: Esto no es gore', declared cultural magazine *A Barna* (del Pozo 1994: 15); '*Aftermath* is not another gore flick' (M. M. 1995: 7), asserted subcultural publication *Brut Art*. When events like 'Bad Taste II' catalogued *Aftermath*, Cerdà felt the need to clarify his short's relationship to gore and the *raison d'être* behind what proved to be a very personal story, although this account would not form part of subsequent interviews. In a letter published in the festival gazette (28 November 1995), he wrote:

> I would not like to leave Gijón without clarifying a misunderstanding [concerning my short]: *Aftermath* is not a gore film as it has been said on a number of occasions, it is a documentary. Marta existed, I know that's the truth because I had her in my arms, talked to her, loved her. After that terrible car accident I always wanted to know where my girlfriend's corpse was taken.

And the director goes on to poignantly describe the aftermath of the event, the arrival of the ambulance and the removal of the corpse to a mortuary. 'Where was my Marta taken? At last, I had the answer which I waited for so anxiously. AFTERMATH is what I witnessed and that's why I tell you about it.'

Like *Aftermath*, the production values used in the making of *Genesis* were those of a feature-length film. Again, it was shot in 35 mm widescreen and fully storyboarded. It became a landmark in the Spanish short scene since it included 'the most elaborate sets ever constructed for a short film in Spain' (Perks 1998: 8). This time, the Gothic love story seemed to be to the taste of genre festivals and official institutions alike; *Genesis* claimed the Best Short prize at the two most important horror festivals on Spanish territory, Sitges and San Sebastián in 1994, and earned a nomination for Best Short at the Spanish Academy Awards, the Goyas. Similarly, international genre publications *Shivers* and *Flesh and Blood* gave the film detailed coverage. *Rue Morgue* confirmed the director as 'Spain's New Face of Death' (Gudino 1999: 8–10) and *Shock Cinema* described him as 'one of the most unsettling new filmmakers of this era' (1999: 9). As the final chapter of the trilogy, *Genesis* also brought with it a re-viewing of *Aftermath* and *The Awakening*, and the consolidation of the three shorts as a triptych, which prompted critics to trace thematic and stylistic continuities between the three. Fastasporto and Brussels screened the three shorts together, instigating an exhibition practice that saw them as a coherent whole.

Genesis focuses on the character of an artist (Pep Tosar), who has lost his wife (Trae Houlihan) in a car crash. The opening is imbued with a sense of nostalgia, conveyed through Super 8–style footage that evokes memories of a loving relationship and introduces the artist's obsession with his dead wife. Unable to handle her death, he desperately recreates her full body image in clay. But one day, while working on the sculpture, he notices that a small area of the clay figure is bleeding and human tissue is visible underneath it; his wife is returning to life through his art. The gradual animation of the sculpture coincides with the artist's own petrification and results in a beautiful final transformation, when husband and wife become conscious of each other for a fleeting moment.

Genre publications qualified the love story as Gothic, thus aligning the short with the Gothic mode: the death of a beautiful woman, the desperation and solitariness of human experience, death-like states, and intense, universal emotions such as guilt and the haunting of the psyche by the loss of a beloved. The short also draws upon mythological, artistic and psychoanalytic figurations characteristic of the art-film: the Pygmalion-like artist, the stage-like performance space of the sculptor's atelier, the *mort vivant* motif personified in the artist, whose inner death manifests itself in his compulsive pursuit of the lost object and repetition of the traumatic event in nightmarish flashes and in his turning into stone. Cerdà therefore reworks the classical theme of life and death through the modern trope of bodily transformation and such modernist narrative strategies as the disruption of linear temporality or the insertion of dream sequences. The sculptor's attempts to recover his irrevocable loss are reflected not only through sculpture but also through the medium of film, running throughout the short as a self-reflexive motif, first in the opening Super-8 footage and then through the projection of this very same Super-8 movie on to the finished clay statue.

Thematic and stylistic comparisons with *Aftermath* are inescapable. The car crash as the cause of a woman's death, the centrality of a dead female body to the narrative and the male protagonists' relationship with the female corpse (whether through medical implements, carving tools or explicit physical contact) represent the death drive at the core of Cerdà's work. *Genesis* is as consciously constructed and technically competent as *Aftermath*, signalling a distinctive aesthetic preference for a slow editing pace and repeated cinematographic palette to convey mood and atmosphere, for extreme close-ups lingering obsessively and unnervingly on inanimate objects and for classical music scores.

Aftermath and *Genesis* did not conform to the emerging – and soon to be dominant – trends of Spanish horror cinema in the 1990s. Cerdà carved out a distinct and recognisable style, although for many critics this did not fully transfer to his first feature film. For many horror publications such as *Fangoria*, however, the question was whether Cerdà would survive 'the curse of Too Much Potential' (O'Brien 2007: 65).[11] After ten years in development, two working titles ('The Bleeding Compass' and 'Bloodline') and the final involvement of three scriptwriters (Cerdà himself, and Canadian horror film directors Karim Hussaim and Richard Stanley), Julio Fernández's Filmax produced *Los abandonados*. Like many other Filmax products, *Los abandonados* was destined for the international marketplace; it was shot in English with an international cast, set in the Eastern European backwoods (Bulgaria standing in for Russia) and presented a narrative that crossed national borders and temporalities. Its mainstream generic and narrative values were highlighted in a run-of-the-mill and deficient marketing campaign on both sides of the Atlantic. The tagline for the American market – 'Death never runs out of time' – as well as the Spanish – '40 years for the truth to be revealed. 24 hours to survive it' – seemed to drive the story towards the territory of thrillers. The director's desire 'to assault the viewing public with terror for 90 minutes', as expressed in the pressbook, was not transferred to the publicity material. Despite being the first début feature film to be released outside Spain first (the US on 23 February 2007 and Spain on 20 April 2007) and the second Spanish film to have more copies in the US market (1,250) (only surpassed by *The Others*), *Los abandonados* was 'rather unceremoniously dumped into U.S. theatres sans previews by Lionsgate' (Harvey 2007). On release for two weeks, it made $782,000 in its opening weekend, ranking nineteenth in the box-office charts and totalling $1,331,137 overall. The film also gained effective exposure among genre fans as part of the 2007 *Fangoria* / After Dark Films' *Horrorfest (8 Films to Die For)* package. In Spain the film was a commercial failure, taking only $515,659 in the space of two months and ranking in 201st position in 2007, a year which had been tremendously successful for other Spanish horror productions, *El orfanato* and *[•REC]* topping box-office ratings.

The storyline of *Los abandonados* follows American movie producer Marie Jones (Anastasia Hille) to the Russian backwoods, where she has inherited a family homestead. Abandoned and uninhabited for more than forty years, the farm stands in total disrepair and neglect. Soon after arriving, Marie unexpectedly meets a man who claims to be her twin brother, Nikolai (Karel Roden), who is also there to claim his inheritance. Together they come face to face with their doppelgangers, dead versions of themselves, and discover that the farm holds secrets to their past, their mother's murder and their abandonment as babies. The pre-credit sequence links present and past and family lineage. The 'Somewhere in Russia, 1966' intertitle and a female voiceover, which corresponds to Marie's daughter Emily, establish the narrative temporalities as well as the main themes – the return of the past, family history and individual identity:

> My mother never told me about her parents. She regretted having to hide such a pretty Russian name like Milla with the name her foster family gave her. She told me: 'the past was another country, now best forgotten' [. . .] Just because you are through with your past, doesn't always mean that your past is ever really through with you.

Spatially, a montage of still frames introduces the viewer to scenic woodland, soon to be disturbed by ominous skies and further disrupted by a cut to a close-up of a truck hurtling down the forest track until it comes to an abrupt stop outside a farm. When the camera focuses on the truck's cabin, it reveals the dead body of a young woman at the wheel and two babies, whose piercing cries close the sequence. A fade to light blue and the intertitle '40 years later' move the narrative forward to a plane landing in a non-specified location in Russia and the arrival of the main female character, Marie. The rest of the credits and the opening sequence establish Marie's character and the motive behind her journey. Marie is alone in a foreign country, unable to connect emotionally with her daughter during a brief phone conversation and, as her pill-taking seems to suggest, under considerable mental strain. Her meeting with notary Mr Misharin (Valentin Ganev) brings to light a past unknown to her: her true identity and a link to her Russian roots through the inheritance of a property. Marie's journey to the backwoods and the framing of the farm follow horror conventions to the letter: a mysterious and frightening driver who disappears as soon as they arrive at their destination, a remote, uninhabited location cut off from the mainland, and, awaiting her arrival, a haunted house. As soon as Marie sets foot in the abandoned farmhouse, the uncanny manifests itself through the motif of the double, in mirrored reflections. The twins are haunted by their past, by their doppelgangers; as Nikolai puts it to Marie, 'we are haunting ourselves,' 'They are our deaths, Marie, our futures.' Apparitions and dream sequences work as horror set pieces that recurrently and progressively reveal a terrible personal and family tragedy in the past: Marie's and Nikolai's father attempted to drown them when they were born, and they were only saved when their mother shot him. Forty years later, the father's spirit seeks to reclaim the life of the children who survived. The closing sequence, with its images of the landscape, returns us to Emily's voiceover and her expressed desire to lay family secrets to rest:

> When she left for Russia, I knew I'd never see her again. It's been a long time since she left but I'll never go after her. Never try to find out what became of her parents. It's better that way. Better not to know, but still to forget, best of all to be abandoned.

Although, formally and stylistically, *Los abandonados* continued the thematic and aesthetic preoccupations established by Cerdà in 'The Trilogy of

Death', notably the vivid repetition of traumatic events conveyed through dream sequences, nightmarish flashes and haunting images, the long-awaited first feature film did not succeed in reaching mainstream horror audiences. Despite punching 'well above the genre norm', as the *Variety* review puts it, this 'brand of arty, surreal Euro-horror is more beloved by cultists than teenage mallrats' (Harvey 2007). Cerdà's reputation among cult, underground and gore fans still rests chiefly on his shorts. Perhaps his new project, an adaptation of the French vampire comic *I Am Legion*, which pits vampires against Nazis in the Second World War, might enable Cerdà to move beyond a niche horror market that had nevertheless granted him auteur status before he made a transition to the big screen.

<h2 style="text-align:center">JAUME BALAGUERÓ</h2>

Balagueró's trajectory over the last two decades can leave us in no doubt about his horror credentials and is concurrent with major developments and trends in the field of contemporary Spanish horror: in the early 1990s his fanzine *Zineshock. Revista de cine oscuro y brutal*, devoted to gore and trash cinema, was part of the emerging fanzine culture of the time; his shorts, *Alicia* (1994) and *Días sin luz* (1995), trod avant-garde and exploitation territory and performed exceptionally well on the official and alternative festival circuits; his first feature film, *Los sin nombre* (1999), gained him critical and international acclaim, paving the way for his professional association with the Fantastic Factory and Filmax in the 2000s on *Darkness* (2002) and *Frágiles* (2005), his participation in the TV series *Películas para no dormir*, and his most recent film *Mientras duermes* (2011), released when this book had already been completed. And, together with another Fantastic Factory director, Paco Plaza, he has been responsible for the *[•REC]* franchise, which will be addressed in the conclusion of this volume. Balagueró's career, therefore, has been devoted to the horror genre and its revival. For all these reasons Balagueró is seen as a horror auteur.

When listing his cinematic influences, Balagueró aligns himself with horror auteurs such as David Cronenberg and Dario Argento, among others, associations which serve to place his work primarily in the field of horror and within a particular horror lineage. The reputation of Balagueró as a cult and horror connoisseur was cemented in his fanzine *Zineshock* (see Figure 40). The do-it-yourself look of the first issue, published in the summer of 1991, was an overt statement of artistic alliances and interests, with the cover lines forewarning dark celluloid: gore underground, snuff cinema, Troma Inc. and Mondo films. The editorial, typewritten by Balagueró and preceded by a Pablo Picasso quotation which announced the fanzine's relation to questions of taste ('The main enemy of creativity is good taste'), confirmed its stance:

Figure 40   Jaume Balagueró edited fanzine *Zineshock* during the early 1990s. Cover art for issue 1994 above.

Decidedly, pretty birds, almond trees in bloom and happy endings are not for us. We support obscure and wicked cinema. From the ridiculous to the obscene, from the candid to the outrageous, we are interested in cinema which is peripheral to bourgeois good taste, that is, illegitimate and bizarre cinema. Thus ZINESHOCK embarks upon a crazy journey towards that weird and marginal filmic universe in search of the most outlandish B-movie products, radical gore movies, disturbing shockers, all things underground, irreverent, extraordinary and brutal. Dare to descend with us into the cinematic hells of excess. The 'other' cinema awaits; we are set to leave for its most inhospitable places. (1991: 2)

Its manual for self-styled 'shockomanos' (shock-o-maniacs) (1991: 19–22) offered various pointers for the acquisition of horror booty: frequenting video stores ('if you're lucky, you may be able to find marvels such as the classic *Emmanuel y los últimos caníbales* [*Emanuelle and the Last Cannibals* (1977)] by Joe D'Amato or the ultra-gore *Zombi Holocaust* [1980] by Frank Marti, Franco Martinelli, that is' (1991: 19)), neighbourhood cinemas ('militant

B-movies are shown for the first time in these types of venue' (1991: 20) and kiosks ('do not underestimate alternative points of sale for videotapes' (1991: 20)); acquiring pioneering volumes such as *Les Visages de l'horreur* or *The Pyschotronic Encyclopedia of Film*, as well as specialist genre magazines and fanzines ('Publications such as *Video Watchdog* or *Psychotronic Video* are excellent from start to finish' (1991: 21)); and, above all, committing oneself to the search for the next obscure film. A total of five *Zineshock* issues were published between 1991 and 1993.

By the mid-1990s, then, Balagueró was an established name on the fanzine scene and his horror pedigree was indisputable. 'He is one of us' (1999: 60), wrote Rubén Lardín in the fanzine *ojalatemueras* when he covered the director's film début, reassuring his readers that Balagueró was a *real* fan. But Balagueró's commitment to alternative culture and 'obscure and brutal' traditions of horror did not mean he rejected film as a commercial venture. 'I think my shorts are commercial. Yes, they are weird, but I believe they are commercial because they are very *guarros* (dirty)' (Balagueró in Lardín 1999: 64). In *Alicia* and *Días sin luz*, Balagueró showed a predilection 'for pus, for degradation, for the decay of flesh (and perhaps that of the soul). He definitely is a horror *freak*' (Llopart 1999: 55). The silent, black-and-white *Alice* depicts a tale of puberty whose surreal nightmarish visual world is reminiscent of filmmakers Lynch and Cronenberg and photographer Joel Peter Witkin. It presents the abduction of a teenage girl by insect-like 'Rubbermen' in sadomasochistic gear and their subsequent preparation of their sacrificial victim as an offering to a supreme female 'Ogre'. The 1995 San Sebastián Horror and Fantasy Film Festival catalogue described the garlanded *Días sin luz*, co-produced by Nacho Cerdà, as 'a purulent nightmare' which presented the viewer with 'a genetic cross between the world of David Cronenberg and the paintings of Lucien Freud' and an unrelenting 'descent into the sepia-toned hell of family life' (1995: 79). The short follows the misfortunes of a boy via a narrative voiceover that informs us of his life as an orphan, abandoned by his mother, his adoptive parents and their 'strange games' (an S&M relationship), and his inability to understand why 'mums abandon their children'.

References to Balagueró as a fan and (commercial) horror auteur that had been circulating in fanzine publications eventually seeped through to mainstream journalism with the arrival of fanzine writers into mainstream media (see Chapter 5). Thus Calleja, regular contributor to *2000maniacos* and by then writing for the cultural supplement of major national daily *El mundo*, described him as a 'true freak' who 'has an exquisite bad taste', crowning him as 'el Príncipe de las Tinieblas' ('The Prince of Darkness') (Calleja 2002). For many mainstream critics, therefore, Balagueró's work was already strongly defined within the contours of auterism. Such is the treatment reserved for him in the high-brow film magazine *Dirigido por...* , which included him among the key directors of contemporary horror film production on the international scene ('Dossier nuevo cine de terror. Diez directores fundamentales del género' (Navarro 2006)). Genre critic Tonio Alarcón mapped out some of the director's recurrent concerns, his visual signature and his relation to international horror traditions in 'Jaume Balagueró ¿Quién puede torturar a un niño?' (2006: 56–8). Among his obsessions, Alarcón credits Balagueró with physical and psychological torture, in particular that of children, an investigation into pure evil and the horrors of the past, and 'a dark vision of human existence', all conveyed through recurrent visual imagery (old photographs, medical paraphernalia, the presence of bodily fluids and water), cinematography and editing style (2006: 57). In this respect, the Balagueró look is also the work of regular collaborators, whose names are credited across different films, among them cinematographer Xavi Giménez in the shorts and *Los sin nombre*, *Darkness* and *Frágiles*, and editor Luis de la Madrid in all but *Frágiles*.

Reviews and interviews in *Dirigido por . . .* have consistently framed the reception of his production in auteurist terms. An example of the construction of Balagueró as an auteur is provided by Navarro's review of *Frágiles*: 'an œuvre à la Balagueró is beginning to take shape' through the 'consolidation of a personal visual style of telling stories' (2005a: 26). However, whilst there seems to be a critical consensus on Balagueró's visual signature, many critics have also identified certain weaknesses in his construction of narrative action. *Los sin nombre* presented, in the words of a *Reseña* reviewer, an 'unbalanced script' where 'the second half of the narrative accumulates characters in an arbitrary and unexplained manner leading to a hurried finale' (Bejarano 2000: 509). Balagueró's second film, *Darkness*, according to *Dirigido por . . .*, confirmed 'his remarkable talent for constructing disturbing visual textures, while, at the same time, it evinces substantial lacks in narrating the story in a coherent manner' (Navarro 2002b: 30). Equally, the international industry press drew attention to the technical qualities present in Balagueró. *Darkness*, wrote Holland in *Screen International*, 'is ultimately just an efficient exercise in style' and 'a series of powerful sequences that fail to cohere [narratively]' (Holland 2004). What these reviews seem to suggest is that Balagueró's name performs a classificatory function in the fields of international horror production and reception but that Balagueró, as a true 'horror auteur', is still 'in the making'.

Los sin nombre, Balagueró's debut film, was loosely based on an adaptation of British horror author Ramsey Campbell's *The Nameless* (1981).[12] According to Balagueró,

> what really captivated me in Ramsey Campbell's novel, apart from the very terrifying and very original storyline, was the treatment given to evil and perversion. The way perversity attracts some of the characters in the novel, the fascination that evil wields over them. (see Filmax DVD sleeve)

But, thematically and visually, Balagueró's psychological horror draws from the work of American director David Fincher: namely, the inexplicable cruelty of human nature, the bleak atmosphere and claustrophobic cinematography of films such as *Alien 3* (1992) and *Seven* (1995). The cinematography of Xavi Giménez in the credit sequence draws upon Fincher's dark urban settings and derelict industrial landscapes. In a forbidding, abandoned factory the police have found the body of a six-year-old girl. The police contact the Gilfords, whose daughter Ángela is missing, because the victim's body presents the same physical feature – one leg is shorter than the other. The cross-cutting between the crime scene, the Gilfords' bedroom and the post-mortem examination connects the present and the past, deepening the sense of parental agony and communicating to the viewer detective Bruno Massera's (Karra Elejalde) reopening of an unsolved case. The 'Five years later' intertitle reintroduces us to Claudia Gilford (Emma Vilasarau), who seems to have moved on personally by separating from her husband, and professionally, by furthering her career in the publishing industry. However, Claudia is still grieving, time and again replaying home videotapes of her daughter. Her despair and pain are unexpectedly deepened by a harrowing phone call, her daughter Ángela's voice muttering, 'Mummy, it's me.' A second call – 'Come get me at the sanatorium on the beach. You know where it is' – sets in motion a desperate search for her lost daughter and Claudia's progressive mental disintegration. Recognising the sanatorium from one of the videotapes, she goes there to find a building in ruins; among the rubble, Claudia comes across old photos and records of hospital patients, medical leaflets and texts, and a box with an orthopedic boot. Unable to make any sense of what is happening to her, she contacts detective Massera. Massera himself is mourning the loss of his wife and readjusting to civilian life after leaving the police force. Together, their investigations lead them to an orphanage, to similar cases of missing girls, and to the activities of a sect called 'The Nameless'. Finally, they track down Santini, the imprisoned leader of the para-religious sect; this man's personal history is linked to the Nazi Holocaust when he was prisoner in a concentration camp; the occult craze in 1960s London as an author of articles on occultism and esotericism; and to a trail of child kidnappings and disappearances in Spain in the early 1980s, for which he has been jailed. The character of Santini, who preaches 'annihilation, torture, the practice of terror as a way of purification' (*Los sin nombre*'s publicity tagline), embodies evil as a living entity, and foreshadows narrative developments by directing Claudia to look for Ángela 'where it all began' and by announcing Massera's death ('You're dead'). When Quiroga (Tristán Ulloa), a journalist specialising in occultism and contemporary sects through his work on a magazine devoted to parapsychology, receives a videotape with Claudia's telephone number on its label, containing scenes from snuff movies and a recording of Claudia's search in the sanatorium, he contacts Claudia and Massera. They all embark upon a desperate search to uncover the dark truth. The last third of the narrative focuses on the detective's and the journalist's parallel investigations: while Massera delves into Santini's past and tracks him to the psychiatric prison where he is held, Quiroga follows up leads from an article on 'The Nameless' published by a retired colleague – specifically, the involvement of a German doctor in Nazi medical experiments in Dachau. Massera, Claudia and Quiroga will converge on an abandoned motel, where it all began for Claudia with the conception of her daughter and where it will all end for Massera and Quiroga. In the motel Claudia is met by members of the sect and is reunited with her former husband, who reveals that he claimed their daughter for the sect, 'a pure child to be perverted from the beginning'. The family reunion leads to a bleak ending: Ángela shoots her father and seeks forgiveness from her mother. But in a final, chilling twist, she kills herself in front of her mother with the words 'This way you'll suffer more [. . .] I'll call you.' Claudia's entrapment in a world haunted by the returned Ángela is signified by a fade to black and the insertion of a static-blurred image.

Specific narrative and aesthetic features contribute to the film's focus on an agonised mother unable to discern the living from the dead and its construction of a plot about the relationship between haunter and haunted. Like some of its contemporary Japanese horror film counterparts such as *Ringu* (Hideo Nakata 1998), the telephone and the videotape as generators of terror drive the mechanics of the horror and thriller plot forward, enabling the past and present to co-exist in the narrative. The non-diegetic intercuts accompanied by non-diegetic sound are privileged as an editing device to activate the uncanny, to convey the mother's psychological breakdown, and, ultimately, to suggest the interminable replay of Claudia's traumatic loss. Among the intercuts, we view old photographs, a 'not dead' sign written in blood, fragments of a snuff movie, and images of Ángela dressed in white, prefiguring the narrative resolution. Interspersed throughout the narrative, some of these inserts will rematerialise in the final sequence as a replay of Claudia's living nightmare.

Darkness, Balagueró's second feature film, became Filmax International's flagship production of 2002. Building on the horror themes and aesthetics established in *Los sin nombre*, the teaser trailer promised 'a new brand of evil', a filmic experience 'beyond the limits of terror'. The film's official homepage whetted fans' appetites by daring potential browsers to enter a house of horrors ('A House. A Past. A Secret. Will You Dare Enter?'), emphasising the film's horrific elements and economically inserting the film into the haunted house subgenre. The publicity campaign in Spain and abroad conveyed the traditional promises and frights of horror promotion ('You will fear it again . . .') and fostered the cultivation of an auteurist sensibility ('A Film by Jaume Balagueró'). *Darkness* was conceived for the international market as part of the

Fantastic Factory's goal to produce competitive English-language horror films, and therefore adapted to transnational business models in operation in the contemporary industry. The English-language product attracted investors and pre-sales with a teaser trailer and the promise of an international cast (Anna Paquin, Lena Olin and Iain Glen). The integration of transnational elements in the plot – namely, an American family relocating to Spain – also contributed to its global appeal. Filmax acted as partners with Miramax through its genre arm, Dimension Films, and sold them the distribution rights in the US and other English-speaking territories for $4 million. This commercial operation, plus other major pre-sales to European, Latin American and East Asian territories, helped boost the budget to $11 million. In its world premiere in Sitges at the 35th International Film Festival of Catalonia, the film was showcased for potential distributors and die-hard genre fans and built enough momentum to be released for the general public on almost 300 screens in Spain (taking $1.14 million), mainly in multiplexes. Filmax's marketing director Carlos Rojano explained to *Screen International* that the concept of *Darkness* was 'fear rather than horror. Our audience is young, the kind of audience that goes to see films like *The Sixth Sense* or *The Others*' (Green 2002b: 12). *Darkness* did not descend on American theatres until Christmas Day 2004, when it was part of holiday counterprogramming (1,700 screens), yielding a total of $22,163,442 in the space of three months. As these figures show, Balagueró's film was extremely lucrative for Filmax and a valuable investment for Dimension Films. To these profits, one needs to add the value of *Darkness* in the local and global TV, home video and DVD markets, for which it was mainly conceived. In the Hispanic world, video and DVD were commercialised by Filmax Home Video, which marketed the film individually and as part of a DVD pack entitled 'El cine de terror de Jaume Balagueró', exploiting the horror fans' and collectors' market. In the US, Buena Vista simultaneously released the unedited and unrated version in what was, for many DVD reviewers, just 'a marketing gimmick' catering for the sensibilities of genre fans.

Like *Los sin nombre*, *Darkness* presents an act of inconceivable evil. In both films 'the antagonist isn't really a physical person or a concrete entity, but something much more abstract' (Balagueró in Hodges 2004: 24); the house is home to an all-pervasive darkness and the site of an abominable secret from the past. Again, occult rituals lie at the centre of the narrative. Forty years prior to the current action, seven children went missing and only one of them, Marco, was found; the other six were cruelly murdered in a satanic ritual. The secrets of the house are unearthed when an American family moves from the US to Spain to live in the father's childhood home; the various members of the family are soon affected by the change. While the teenage daughter, Regina (Paquin), resents the family's relocation, despite starting a new relationship with boyfriend Carlos (Fele Martínez), and her younger brother Paul (Stephan

251

Enquist) senses the ghosts of the six young children, the parents grow apart physically and emotionally; the mother Maria (Olin) becomes more distant from her daughter and estranged from her husband Marco (Glen), whose physical and mental deterioration from Huntington's disease is rapid. Not unlike Claudia in *Los sin nombre*, the family has been drawn to the house by evil spirits in order to re-enact the failed or incomplete ritual. The bleak ending is reminiscent of *Los sin nombre*: when Regina, Carlos and Paul drive away from the house, the final image is of them driving into a dark tunnel.

Despite its commercial success in the US, reviews ranged from the scathing to the downbeat. According to *The Hollywood Reporter*, '*Darkness* should never have seen the light' (Scheck 2004). The *Village Voice* derided the film along the same lines – '[R]arely has a film's tagline been more fitting: "Some secrets should never come to light"' (Blaylock 2004). *Entertainment Weekly* disparaged the film's technical qualities: '*Darkness* was clearly tossed together like salad in the editing room, since it's little more than the sum of its unshocking shock cuts' (Gleiberman 2004). And some websites, such as metacritic. com, ranked it among 'The Worst Horror Films Since 2000' (Thompson 2010). While *The Austin Chronicle* slammed it as 'Eurotrash for the new millennium' (Savlov 2004), it shed light on the film's distribution history, which perhaps accounted for some negative responses to *Darkness*, in particular concerning its editing:

> by all reports, it's been sitting on Miramax's shelf for the better part of two years, and the version the Weinstein brothers have so graciously chosen to release has been editorially hung, drawn, and quartered to the point that the story makes no sense whatsoever. To make matters worse, the recutting (necessary to bring the film down to a PG-13 level from its previous hard R) seems to have been performed by a blind marionette-operator on crack. (Savlov 2004)

'Both psychology and plot are bargain-basement. Strictly for horror fans,' warned *Variety* (Holland 2004), whose high hopes after the 'genuinely disturbing' *The Nameless* were dampened by its successor's emergence from the 'noisy, high-budget, color drenched school of hard shocks'.

Spanish critics were more benign and responded to the director's positioning of the film in relation to a larger international horror tradition (Navarro 2002a, 2006; Calleja 2002). They invariably rooted *Darkness* in the haunted house subgeneric tradition (Fernández 2002; Navarro 2002a; Zambrana 2002) – in particular, classic contemporary films such as *The Amityville Horror* (Stuart Rosenberg 1979) and *The Shining* (Stanley Kubrick 1980) – as, in both of these films, the house is linked to the father's process of derangement. Other reviewers looked for literary influences – namely, Lovecraftian lore: 'The darkness of

Balagueró's film could well be called Yog-Sothoth' and its conception could be out of *The Lurker at the Threshold* (August Derleth and H. P. Lovecraft),' wrote Fernández in *Fotogramas* (2002: 20).

Following the same production strategies of *Darkness*, *Frágiles* is another example from Filmax Entertainment of the transnational nature of contemporary Spanish horror production and how it taps into global horror film trends. A Spanish / British co-production, shot in English with an international cast led by Calista Flockhart, *Frágiles* is a ghost story set in an isolated Victorian hospital on the British Isle of Wight; its plot integrates a fertile cross-breeding of horror influences in its treatment of ghostly beings, drawing in particular on classical ghost stories and the horror aesthetics characteristic of the contemporary *J-Horâ* boom. In his third film, Balagueró moves from a haunted house setting to the Mercy Falls Hospital, a building with a past, at which the main character, American nurse Amy Nicholls (Flockhart), arrives to replace another nurse prior to the hospital's closure. Amy too is haunted, by traumatic memories of her professional past: the death of a patient due to her medical negligence. Self-medicating as a response to the guilt, Amy soon befriends orphan Maggie (Yasmin Murphy), a child who is terminally ill, and begins to find a sense of purpose by looking after her. When Maggie claims that she can hear and sense a spirit living on the abandoned second floor of the hospital – Charlotte, the 'mechanical girl', as Maggie calls her, Amy starts to experience signs of the spirit's presence (flickering lights, strange sounds, a malfunctioning lift). Amy's questions are ignored by hospital director Mrs Folder (Gemma Jones) and nightshift doctor Robert Kerry (Richard Roxburgh), who represent the voice of rational social authority, and also by dayshift nurse Helen (Elena Anaya), whose refusal to acknowledge what is happening hardens into a silent dread. But Amy's persistence leads her, first, to two mediums, who inform her that 'there is something in that hospital from the other world, something that doesn't accept or hasn't understood that it has died,' warning her that ghosts can only be seen by those who are about to die, and subsequently to a search of the hospital records for any information relating to a patient named Charlotte. With Maggie's help, Amy ventures to the disused second floor to look for further clues. There she is confronted with the first apparition of the mechanical ghost, a shadowy figure at the end of a derelict corridor, and comes across dated medical equipment, ragged toys, a black-and-white photo of a nurse and a girl seated in a wheelchair with the text 'Charlotte and Mandy, 1959' written on the back, and a 16 mm film. The found footage, which Amy shares with Dr Kerry, reveals a medical recording of a little girl being treated for brittle bone disease. It is as if the playing of the found film releases the hospital's ghosts, and from this point onwards havoc ensues.

The unearthing of the hospital's dark secret is presented through parallel editing. Thus, while Amy is learning the truth from Mrs Folder during a journey back to the hospital to evacuate the children, Dr Kerry replays the tape and identifies the people in the film and the photograph: nurse Charlotte Rivers and child-patient Mandy Phillips, together in 1959. According to Mrs Folder, the nurse became obsessed with Mandy, provoking the child's bone fractures and ultimately suffocating her because she could not bear the idea of her leaving the hospital; Charlotte was found in the lift shaft wearing the girls' orthopedic limbs. Forty years later, and coinciding with the immanent closure of Mercy Falls Hospital, Maggie goes missing and Charlotte's ghost seems bent on keeping the children within the hospital's confines. In her final endeavour to save Maggie, Amy is confronted by a hideous, imp-faced, straggly-haired old woman, who is claiming the lives of those remaining in the hospital. In scenes reminiscent of a disaster movie and far removed from the restrained build-up and atmospherics of the rest of the narrative, a critically wounded Amy rescues Maggie from the falling rubble, to no avail. As Amy is being artificially resuscitated, she has a vision of Maggie kissing her. A fade to black introduces the viewer to the closing sequences. The image of Amy in a hospital room with Dr Kerry and the two mediums is followed by a final shot of Amy resting, Maggie – or is it her ghost? – sitting with her on the bed.

Frágiles was described by many Spanish reviewers as 'a classic, good "ghost story" [. . .] deeply rooted in Gothic fiction' (Navarro 2005c: 30–1) – namely, Victorian ghost stories[13] – and appreciative of the role of the supernatural in the genre. And most mainstream film magazines, such as *Cinemanía*, agreed that the film enjoyed 'an impressive quality and the look of a big production' (Ángulo 2005: 109) akin to contemporary international horror productions.[14] But *Frágiles* failed to impress international trade journals such as *Variety* and *Screen International*, which remained unconvinced of Balagueró's horror competencies. For *Variety* the film was a 'badly written, poorly acted, and drearily predictable shocker' (Felperin 2005), Balagueró and co-scriptwriter Jordi Galcerán demonstrating 'a lack of imagination about how to generate fear', although perhaps 'it delivers just enough off-the-shelf scares to satisfy horror fans' (Felperin 2005). The *Screen International* reviewer was equally despondent: *Frágiles* 'is a stale spooky-hospital yarn' which 'suffers from poor suspense management and the gelid obnoxiousness of the central nurse character, played by US loan Calista Flockhart', which, above all, felt dated 'when compared to recent Japanese horror imports' (Marshall 2005).

With his latest film, *Mientras duermes*, Balagueró is still searching for new ways of scaring audiences. In his words, he 'wanted to go back to investigate the more sophisticated mechanics of the thriller and suspense genre', following *[•REC]* and *[•REC2]*, 'both radical and brutal films in their form and narrative' (Director Notes). In promotional interviews, the director has insisted that '*Mientras duermes* is not a horror film, although it is arguably one of the most terrifying I have ever made' (Balagueró in De Fez 2011: 100). The film is based on a script by Filmax regular Alberto Marini,[15] who turned it into a novel of the same title as the film was being shot. *Mientras duermes* takes the viewer into the twisted mind of its central protagonist César (Luis Tosar), a porter in a block of flats in Barcelona, who knows everything about the residents in the block, in particular happy-go-lucky Clara (Marta Etura), with whom he becomes obsessed. Unhappy and unable to understand the happiness of others, he delights in their pain and anguish and is set on destroying Clara's life. Balagueró's deployment of the mechanics of the thriller and suspense genres has been favourably received by Spanish critics, whose textual and cinematic references hint at a coming-of-age auteurism in Balagueró. For Boyero in *El país*, 'Balagueró tells this disturbing story with visual prowess, without *coups de théâtre*, and with a tone and atmosphere that remind me of Polanski at his best' (2011).

GUILLERMO DEL TORO

El laberinto del fauno's official homepage summarises del Toro's professional journey thus: he 'has shuttled between independent projects and mainstream Hollywood filmmaking, bringing to each his own distinctive Gothic sensibility'.[16] This sensibility comes through with his creative depiction of monstrous creatures and settings, the powerful and persistent presence of irrational forces and of restless spirits in his fictional worlds, the allegorical bent of his narratives, the merging of religious and secular iconography, and, above all, his commitment to the fantastic, fairy tales and mass-mediated horror traditions. Moving between his native Mexico, Hollywood and Spain, del Toro has become synonymous with horror auteurism and the transnationality of horror. Many cultural commentators describe del Toro as fan, connoisseur, craftsman, cinéphile and auteur, since he is equally comfortable talking about films in Cannes as he is discussing them in front of fans at comic conventions. For example, Mark Kermode of *Sight and Sound* has stressed the director's ability to charm 'both hard-core horror fans' and 'the upmarket critical cognoscenti' (2006: 20), and, more recently, Kim Newman in *Nightmare Movies* has described him as a contemporary horror auteur who is 'infectiously enthusiastic about film fantasy' (2011: 509). As A. O. Scott put it, in his review of *El laberinto del fauno* for *The New York Times*: del Toro 'swears allegiance to a pop-fantasy tradition that encompasses comic books, science fiction and horror movies, but fan-boy pastiche is the last thing on his mind. He is also a thoroughgoing cinéphile, steeped in classic technique and film history' (2006).

In Spain, del Toro's original take on the vampire movie tradition, *Cronos*, made an instant impact on the specialist genre festival circuit (Sitges 1993 edition), in genre publications such as the Spanish version of *Fangoria* and in fanzines like *2000maniacos*.[17] His début in the American film industry with *Mimic* was duly covered in mainstream film publications, as were his comic-book adaptations of superheroes *Blade* and *Hellboy*. But it was in the 2000s that he truly came to the fore of the Spanish horror film culture scene. Fanzine *2000maniacos* repeatedly and reverentially acknowledged his standing with his fans, hailing del Toro as 'one of us' (Valencia 1999b: 5). Del Toro even collaborated with the fanzine for the special issue 'México loco superespecial. Chilli Terror' ('Superspecial Mad Mexico. Chilli Terror'), published in 1999 after the San Sebastián Horror and Fantasy Film Festival's retrospective on 'Cine psicotrónico mexicano'. In his article, del Toro laid bare 'his hard-core fan heart' and shared 'his very personal inventory of Mexican psychotronia' (Valencia 1999b: 5). But it is with *El espinazo del diablo* and *El laberinto del fauno* that del Toro has succeeded in speaking directly to the contemporary Spanish psyche, tapping in particular into current topicality with debates around the legacy of the Civil War and *memoria histórica*. These debates intensified following the excavation of mass graves and the exhumation of the victims of Fascist repression demanded by the Asociación para la Recuperación de la Memoria Histórica (Association for the Recovery of Historical Memory), founded in 2000, and other grassroots organisations such as the Foro por la Memoria (Forum for Memory),[18] as well as the controversial Ley de la Memoria Histórica (Historical Memory Law), which acknowledges the memory of victims of the Spanish Civil War, passed by the Socialist government of José Luis Zapatero in 2007. While these two films are patent examples of the transnationality of contemporary Spanish horror, del Toro's so-called 'Spanish films', unlike Balagueró's and Cerdà's productions, engage with the established local cinematic tradition of films on the Spanish Civil War.

When it comes to transnational credentials, *El espinazo del diablo* and *El laberinto del fauno* certainly fit the bill. The former was a co-production between the Spanish El Deseo and the Mexican Tequila Gang and Anhelo Producciones, in association with Sogepaq, Canal Plus (Spain). The film targeted not only the expanding Spanish and Latin American markets but also a wider international audience, being distributed through a truly global film cartel and pre-sold heavily to many major territories. It was then picked up by the Sony Pictures Classic studio for US distribution. On the back of heavy marketing and nationwide screening in Spain, the film had a very successful first weekend at the box office. First released in Spain on 19 April 2001, *El espinazo del diablo* had to compete with a product of global proportions, *Los otros* (Alejandro Amenábar), and one local blockbuster, *Torrente 2. Misión en Marbella* (Santiago Segura). Caught between the global and the local, this Mexican–Spanish co-production was the sixth most successful film of the year, taking 2,981,037 euros and bringing 705,531 spectators to the cinema. November saw the release of the film in the US market, where it was exhibited in multiplex cinemas such as the Cineplex Odeon chain and art-house venues alike, grossing $755,249. *El laberinto del fauno* brought together five producers working with a budget of $19 million: Bertha Navarro (from Mexican Tequila Gang), Alfonso Cuarón, Guillermo del Toro, Frida Torreblanco (Spanish OMM) and Álvaro Augustín (Spanish Estudios Picasso, the production arm of Spanish TV channel Telecinco). Warner Bros. Pictures International acquired the multi-territory distribution rights for the film in Spain and Latin America, while Wild Bunch bought the rights for international sales and Picturehouse picked up all North American rights. To date, its box-office takings have been phenomenal and have broken some industry and personal records in the US, Spanish and Mexican markets. With a worldwide gross of $82,048,724, del Toro's film appealed, and continues to appeal, to broad and diverse audiences across the globe.

During the promotional interviews for *El laberinto del fauno*, del Toro referred to the fact that the original script for the film preceded that of *El espinazo del diablo*.[19] As he explains in the Production Notes, *El laberinto del fauno* was set in the Victorian period and told

> the story of young pregnant woman who arrives with her husband at a secluded countryside house they intend to restore. During their stay, she discovers a labyrinth in the garden where she meets a faun. After they have a sexual relationship, the faun proposes that she sacrifice her newly born baby so that she can live eternally in the labyrinth. It has nothing to do with the film I ended up making but some elements are still there. (del Toro in Costa 2006: 14)

El espinazo del diablo was an old project of del Toro's ('I actually wrote it as my thesis for my class in screenwriting' (del Toro in Chun 2002: 29)), originally conceived as a ghost story set in a religious school in the historical context of the Mexican revolution. In del Toro's words, the story was 'a homage to "Luvina", a story by [Mexican writer] Juan Rulfo', with a twist – 'like a putrid Western seen through the eyes of Mario Bava' (del Toro in Khan 2001: 63). During the 1998 Sitges International Film Festival, del Toro, who was acting as a juror on the back of his success at previous festivals with *Cronos* and *Mimic*, received a script entitled 'La bomba' from Antonio Trashorras and David Muñoz, scriptwriters, comic artists and film critics. Soon after, del Toro contacted Trashorras and Muñoz and offered to buy their script, rewrite it and turn it into a film. Director and scriptwriters conflated del Toro's old project 'El espinazo del diablo' and 'La bomba', which was situated in an orphanage. As the script developed, the origins of the project were recontextualised from the Mexican revolution to the Spanish Civil War.

Related thematically and aesthetically, *El espinazo del diablo* and *El laberinto del fauno* share settings, child protagonists, the use of horror conventions and a pop-fantasy sensibility that cuts across genres: namely, horror, fantasy, war movies and melodrama. Cinematographer Guillermo Navarro, production designer Eugenio Caballero, special effects house DDT FX, composer Javier Navarrete, comic artist Carlos Giménez – as set designer of the Pale Man's dwelling – and the cameo appearance of Federico Luppi allowed for visual and aural continuities in the films. Both films are set during the Spanish Civil War and its immediate aftermath; each film unfolds through the eyes of the children while at the same time presenting an adult horror allegory on Fascism; both present strong visual concepts related to the aesthetics of comics in the case of *El espinazo del diablo* and of classic fairy-tale illustrations in *El laberinto del fauno*; and both evoke a Spanish cinematic tradition in which the protagonist is a child dealing with traumatic experiences, as seen before in Erice's *El espíritu de la colmena* (1973) and Saura's *Cría cuervos* (1975). In fact, comparisons with Erice's film were common currency in reviews of *El laberinto del fauno* in Spain and abroad: for Costa in *El país*, *El laberinto del fauno*

> could be seen as a *freak* version of *El espíritu de la colmena*, but it is more than that. As in Erice's work, the child's gaze transforms real horror and imaginary horror (or not so imaginary) into communicating vessels, but the Mexican director's film establishes a dialogue with the discourse he himself has articulated in works like *Cronos* and *El espinazo del diablo*. (Costa 2006: 43)

As Smith has observed, the young girl Ofelia's replacement of the missing eye of a mysterious stone figure with which she comes face to face in the woods at the beginning of *El laberinto del fauno* is a very 'precise reference' (2007: 5) to the little girl Ana (Ana Torrent) in *El espíritu de la colmena*, in her schoolroom, replacing the missing eye of a human manikin. Other points of comparison with *El espíritu de la colmena* are the temporalities framing the narratives – the combination of the once-upon-a-time device and specific historical dates, the foregrounding of the narratives' self-reflexive mode of telling, the manifestations of the spirit to Ana and the appearances of the Faun to Ofelia, and, from the point of view of critical reception, the interpretation of both films as political allegories.

Set against the backdrop of the Spanish Civil War, *El espinazo del diablo* follows the life of ten-year-old Carlos (Fernando Tielve), who arrives in Santa Lucía, a crumbling Republican orphanage for boys run by Carmen (Marisa Paredes), widow of a left-wing poet, with the assistance of Dr Casares (Federico Luppi), a liberal Argentinian immigrant, and Jacinto (Eduardo Noriega), the young caretaker and Carmen's lover. Carlos and the other orphans are haunted by the spectre of Santi (Iñigo Garcés), who mysteriously disappeared the same night that a Fascist bomb was dropped on the courtyard during an air raid. Summoned by the ghostly presence of Santi and drawn to the unexploded (but defused) bomb, Carlos learns about the orphanage's inhabitants, their dark secrets and hidden treasures, and, finally, about the identity of Santi's murderer. Set in 1944 in post-Civil War Spain, *El laberinto del fauno* follows Ofelia (Ivana Baquero) and her heavily pregnant mother, Carmen (Ariadna Gil), as they move to a rural military outpost in Fascist-ruled Spain to live with her new stepfather, Francoist Captain Vidal (Sergi López), whose mission is to eliminate any remaining anti-Fascist guerrillas hidden in the mountains of the area. Uprooted and terrified of her sadistic stepfather and the unfathomable cruelty around her, Ofelia seeks refuge in fairy tales and in her imaginative life; she finds an ally in Mercedes (Maribel Verdú), the rebellious housekeeper, who is secretly helping the Resistance. Ofelia discovers the ruins of a labyrinth, where she meets a faun (Doug Jones) who reveals to the girl her true identity: Ofelia is a princess, Princess Moanna, and in order to return to her underground kingdom she must accomplish three tasks before the moon is full.

Although both films are rooted in local history, their respective plot, story and characterisation contribute to a transnational comprehension of the historical background for audiences, and lend themselves to allegorical textual interpretations. Thus, in the case of *El espinazo del diablo*, the walled confines of the isolated orphanage act as a microcosm for the conflict taking place outside. Likewise, the unexploded bomb at the centre of the courtyard is a constant reminder of the war. Carmen and Casares can be interpreted as symbols of a collapsing world and a lost cause through their physical lacks (an amputated leg and sexual impotence, respectively), while Jacinto's spiralling violence conveys the conduct of a newly emerging Fascist Spain. Roger Ebert noted that the use of 'buried symbolism will slip past American audiences not familiar with the Spanish Civil War', but 'del Toro's symbols work first as themselves, then as what they may stand for, so it does not matter if the audience has never heard of Franco as long as it has heard of ghosts' (2001). In *Variety* the symbolism was further reduced to a narrative of 'good and bad guys' which neutralised ideological differences:

> elegant, cultured Casares (Federico Luppi from *Cronos*) and one-legged Carmen (Marisa Paredes) are a late-middle-aged couple who run an orphanage in the desert. They also use it as a hiding place for Republican (i.e. good guy) funds, in the form of gold ingots. An unexploded bomb, dropped by a Fascist (i.e. bad guy) airplane sits in the middle of the court-yard. (Holland 2001: 28)

The allegorical intentions of the film were neatly translated into American generic forms, therefore providing a familiar template and a narrative resolution which resituated the film in American film-going culture; the film evoked 'a proud movie lineage of strike dramas and populist westerns, in which the people, united, can never be defeated' (Scott 2001). Thus the emphasis was shifted away from the historically specific and translated back into familiar generic conventions. The review of *El espinazo del diablo* in *Empire*, though brief, was very positive: this 'ghost story contains more substance and is executed with more style than half a dozen Hollywood monster movies' (Kennedy 2001: 130). *Empire*, as well as *Entertainment Weekly* and *The New York Times*, linked the film with Amenábar's *The Others* and other contemporary US productions such as *The Sixth Sense* (M. Night Shyamalan 1999) or *What Lies Beneath* (Robert Zemeckis 2000), offering audiences familiar references. *The Hollywood Reporter* recommended this 'classical ghost story', which mixed the supernatural and the allegorical, as a 'crowd-pleaser': it 'is loaded with visual style and startling images to dazzle the art house crowd while delivering enough goose bumps and horror for genre movie lovers' (Honeycutt 2001). The film could also 'entice a mainstream audience', according to this same critic. Del Toro's film deploys commercial expertise and knowledge of popular tastes by bridging the gap between art house, mainstream and horror, producing a film with international currency.

As seen in the reviews of Ebert, Holland and Scott, the horrific and melodramatic elements of the film are pushed to the foreground, while the culturally and historically specific aspects are downplayed. But, as a foreign horror film, *El espinazo del diablo* went a step further than other foreign movies, for it was also dubbed into English and released in dubbed version for other windows of consumption (the horror market) and exhibition (DVDs). Such neutralisation of the film's language places the film outside the art-house circuit and transforms it into a global popular product, rendered more legible for a broader American public and a mainstream horror audience. In this context, horror-film publications such as *Fangoria* described the film as a classical ghost story with nuanced qualifications: 'a period ghost story' (Salisbury 2001: 30), 'a neoclassical ghost story' (Jones 2001: 40). As well as positioning the film in relation to classic horror traditions, and more specifically to the renewed interest in the ghost story in contemporary US products like *The Sixth Sense* and *What Lies Beneath*, the *Fangoria* horror fan community inserted del Toro's work into the international world of horror cinema.

The universal appeal of *El laberinto del fauno* was explicitly asserted in Del Toro's authorial declarations ahead of the film's release, when he emphasised both the film's condemnation of Fascism and his use of an allegorical mode to articulate its message. In 'Allegory: the international language', an article featured in *Screen International*, del Toro's *El laberinto del fauno* was selected to address one of the key questions facing the film industry:

the international market is obsessed with the question of how to unite a global audience divided linguistically and culturally while retaining a sense of purpose and integrity. Guillermo del Toro, whose *Pan's Labyrinth* opens worldwide later this year, believes one answer lies in allegory [which, according to the director], politically, is the most powerful form of discussion. (*Screen International* 2006: 7)

For del Toro, universal themes, archetypes and imagery

can be turned to a political purpose [. . .], in this case a passionate anti-fascism: 'the best opposition to choice and imagination is fascism. If imagination is the multiplicity of choice, then fascism is imagination by a group. It is evil without responsibility' (2006: 7)

Anglophone mainstream film criticism certainly read the film through these grids: that is, as a film with an allegorical message and as a denunciation of Fascism. For *Total Film*, del Toro's picture 'dissect[ed] the horror of fascism under the guise of a fantasy film' (2006); for *Variety*, *El laberinto del fauno* presented 'the plight of children living under fascist rule' (Chang 2006); for *The Austin Chronicle*, the child protagonist has no other choice than to 'retreat into the imagination' in order to cope with the horrors of war (Baumgarten 2007). Horror genre websites, such as *Film Threat*, also stressed the film's 'strong anti-fascist message that needs to be heard more often in our modern day world' (2006). As for del Toro's use of figurative language, *El laberinto del fauno* has been variously interpreted as 'a political fable in the guise of a fairy tale. Or maybe it's the other way round' (Scott 2006), a 'morality tale' (Atkinson 2007: 52), 'a parable [. . .] part war film, part fairy tale fable' (Kermode 2006: 23), and, above all, as an allegory which can be interpreted locally and universally; as Philip French put it in *The Observer*, del Toro's film can be read as '[an allegory] about the soul and the national identity of Spain, and, in a wider sense about the struggle between good and evil, between the humane and the inhumane, the civilized and the barbaric' (2006: 14). José Arroyo observed, in his *Sight and Sound* review, that 'in a Spain currently obsessed with issues of historical memory arising from the Civil War, [*El laberinto del fauno*] is bound to cause comment' (2006: 66).

Although del Toro was generally praised for his innovative and alternative intervention in contemporary representations of the Civil War dominated by a realist aesthetics (Costa (2006), Torreiro (2006: 44), Bermejo (2006)), some reviewers were suspicious of the Mexican director's intentions – the director's 'fixation with the Spanish Civil War is not a political act but an aesthetic intuition' (Molina Foix 2007) – and contemptuously reproving of his approach to the topic – 'this Mexican director hasn't got a clue about what happened here [in Spain] in the forties. [He has] converted the dark reality of that Spain into a *tebeo* [children's comic]' (Reguera 2006). The allegorical potential of the two films has also generated a number of academic articles in the field of Spanish film and cultural studies, which have examined the relationship between history and its representation within the films, and the films' ability to tap into contemporary anxieties about historical memory.[20] My own readings of *El espinazo del diablo* and *El laberinto del fauno* form part of this critical debate by examining how del Toro's films address and engage history – the legacy of the Spanish Civil War and its aftermath – through the possibilities of the horror genre for political allegory.

In *Shocking Representation: Historical Trauma, National Cinema and the Modern Horror Film* (2005), Adam Lowenstein frames his exploration of the relationship between allegory, history, trauma and the horror film with two questions: 'what does cinematic horror have to tell us about the horrors of history?' (2005: 1) and how does a film access 'discourses of horror to confront the representation of historical trauma tied to the film's national and cultural context?' (2005: 9). The main theoretical underpinnings for his argument on the ways in which the horror genre registers national traumas is provided by Walter Benjamin's thoughts on the literal and transformative value of allegory and, more particularly, his notion of *Jetztzeit*, whereby the past and present collide through a powerful image 'capable of blasting open the continuum of history' (2005: 15). Drawing upon the Benjaminian images of the 'death's head' and the 'corpse', ruins and fragments, Lowenstein focuses on how specific horror films, which he describes as 'shocking representations' (2005: 6), have dealt with national traumas in France (*Eyes Without a Face* (Georges Franju 1960)), Britain (*Peeping Tom* (Michael Powell 1960)), Japan (*Onibaba* (Shindo Kaneto 1964)), the US (*The Last House on the Left* (Wes Craven 1972)) and Canada (*Shivers* (David Cronenberg 1975)). According to Lowenstein,

> Benjamin's images exist in the allegorical moment *between* being and appearance, *between* subject and object, *between* life and death. This allegorical (and dialectical) between-ness of the image is indicated by the 'meaningful' corpse and crystallized by the death's head – what Benjamin refers to as 'the heart of the allegorical way of seeing'. The realm of the image, with its connotations of ruins, fragmentation, and death, is thus also, for Benjamin, the realm of history's representation. (2005: 13)

In the opening moments of *El espinazo del diablo* and *El laberinto del fauno*, del Toro offers up such images, forcing the viewer to put death and history in direct relation and to acknowledge historical representation as allegory. Both openings conjure images of the death's head and the corpse: the fatally

Figure 41   The haunting motif inscribed in the tagline and the visual imagery of *El espinazo del diablo*.

wounded body of Santi in the basement of the orphanage and the subsequent disposal of the corpse in the cistern in *El espinazo del diablo*; and a close-up of Ofelia's wounded face as she lies dying within the ruins of the labyrinth in *El laberinto del fauno*. These opening moments also mobilise the trope of haunting, basements and ruins being among the favourite haunts of ghosts (see Figure 41). In the case of *El espinazo del diablo*, the motif of haunting is reinforced by the musings of the narrative voiceover: 'What is a ghost? A tragedy condemned to repeat itself time and again', which accompanies the image of a bomb being dropped from the hatch of a bomber. The voiceover continues to muse: 'an instant of pain, perhaps; something dead which still seems to be alive', as a fatally injured Santi is revealed to us, sinking to his watery grave in the cistern. Again the voiceover: 'an emotion suspended in time. Like a blurred photograph. Like an insect trapped in amber', while the image of the sinking body dissolves into a foetus with a malformed backbone. The opening sequence locates the action in a desolate, barren landscape marked by the ravages of war. The still frame is disrupted by a car cutting across the landscape and a cut to the interior of the car, introducing Carlos, the child protagonist, as he arrives at the isolated orphanage of Santa Lucía. The viewer is invited to share Carlos's point of view as he explores his new surroundings, discovers the unexploded bomb in the middle of the orphanage courtyard and becomes aware of a ghostly presence. During his first night in the dormitory, Carlos is allocated bed number twelve, whose previous occupant, Santi, has scratched his name on the wall above the bed; as soon as Carlos reads out the name, Santi's ghost manifests itself as a lurking shadow, sighing terribly, with echoing footsteps and even footprints. From this moment onwards, Carlos deals with the traces of a past haunting the lives of the orphans. The beginning of *El laberinto del fauno* presents evident similarities. The initial close-up of Ofelia in her final moments is accompanied by the humming of a haunting lullaby and an intertitle locating the narrative in 'Spain, 1944', where 'hidden in the mountains, armed men are still fighting the new Fascist regime'. The voiceover and the searching camera seamlessly transport us to a fantastic subterranean environment and the world of fairy tales:

> A long time ago, in the Underground Realm, where there are no lies or pain, there lived a Princess who dreamt of the human world [. . .] one day, eluding her keepers, the Princess escaped. Once outside, the bright sun blinded her and erased her memory.

A blinding light marks the transition to a rural landscape above ground, to a landscape ravaged by war and decay,[21] and to the ruins of a labyrinth. The voiceover continues relating the events that took place prior to the commencement of the story, suggesting a continuation of the story rather than a new beginning:

> The Princess forgot who she was and where she came from. Her body suffered cold, sickness and pain. And eventually she died. However, her father, the King, always knew that the Princess's soul would return, perhaps in another body, in another place, at another time. He would wait for her, until he drew his last breath, until the world stopped turning.

Concurrent with the last words of the voiceover, a procession of cars bearing Fascist symbols irrupts across the still frame. Ofelia and her mother Carmen are travelling in one of the cars, talking about the value of the fairy-tale books Ofelia holds close. When the car stops by the road so that Carmen can vomit, Ofelia explores the woods, becomes captivated by an insect and comes across a mysterious Celtic-looking stele. Ofelia replaces the missing eye of the figure. Her inquisitive nature is further established when they arrive at the mill and she discovers the labyrinth. With these opening scenes, del Toro guides our point of view in the film, creating a sense of continuity between the real world and the fantasy world, and declaring his own cinematic lineage. Like the begin-

Figure 42   Comics artist and author of *Paracuellos* Carlos Giménez contributed to *El espinazo del diablo*'s storyboard.

ning of *El espíritu de la colmena*, the once-upon-a-time device in *El laberinto del fauno* frames the narration atemporally, placing us in the fantasy dimension that corresponds to fairy tales, while the intertitles and the arrival of Carmen and Ofelia at Captain Vidal's headquarters anchor the narrative in a very specific historical context. With openings that echo each other, the viewer of *El espinazo del diablo* and *El laberinto del fauno* is forced to confront the reality of a specific moment in the history of Spain and the fiction emerging from the screen.

While Ofelia's visits to the fantasy world and her encounters with the Faun and the Pale Man are mediated through the lens of fairy tales, Carlos's search for and confrontation with the ghost in *El espinazo del diablo* are mediated through a sketchbook kept by another of the orphans, the bully Jaime, whose drawings act as a summary of the main events in the story and anticipate Carlos's encounter with Santi's ghost. The eventual meeting with the ghost is dramatised through Carlos Giménez's storyboard (see Figure 42). Giménez's influential comic-book series *Paracuellos*, in which he made an autobiographical record of everyday life in a Francoist orphanage in post-war Spain, is allegorically inscribed in del Toro's film.[22] In his search for the ghost, Carlos feels compelled to go outside in the middle of a stormy night; a high angle frames his dwarfed figure as he approaches the bomb in the orphanage courtyard and stands before it, magnifying the strips of coloured ribbon attached to the bomb's tail assembly. 'Bomb, are you alive? Tell me where Santi is,' asks a frightened Carlos. A red ribbon becomes detached from the tail and is blown away in the direction of the kitchen. The fluttering red ribbon, captured by the fluid camerawork of the whole sequence, leads Carlos to Santi. The next shot directs our attention to Carlos's face in the foreground and, through depth of focus, to the kitchen doorway, where the ghost first materialised upon his arrival in Santa Lucía. A tracking shot follows Carlos's eyes as they follow the red ribbon. A cut introduces a shift in point of view by placing the viewer on the other side of the open kitchen door, the camera now turned on Carlos, who is framed by the doorway. Standing there, Carlos is about to enter the ghost's space by crossing the boundary between his present and the orphanage's not-so-distant past, between the living and the dead. Through Carlos's eyes we see a medium long shot of Santi's back and, soon afterwards, a ribbon of blood floating away from a gash in Santi's head. Although defused, the bomb clearly loses none of its dramatic charge; the graphic match between the red ribbon and the slow unfurling of Santi's blood provides an early visual clue to Santi's fate and whereabouts, and, while his death is not a direct consequence of the war, it is ineluctably tied to its destructive force. 'Many of you will die,' the ghost laments. As the ghost attempts to reach out to Carlos, he escapes into the courtyard, running for shelter into the main building. But there is no escape for him, as the ghost is always a step ahead, always already there. Carlos will finally confront the ghost and act on its demands for justice: 'Jacinto. Bring him.' Jacinto's death at the hands of the children might be read as an act of revenge, 'an act of reparation' (Labanyi 2007: 101), yet the man's greed, bitterness and vindictiveness, when he returns to steal the gold ingots hidden away by Carmen for the Republican army, extend to his disavowal of the children's lives and memories ('They've no parents. They've no one. Who'll miss them? We're at war'). Consigned to oblivion, they are potentially denied memory. But the phantom returns. At the end of *El espinazo del diablo*, Santi's ghost has vanished but the dead reappear in the guise of Casares, who had died in an explosion following the fire caused by Jacinto. In a final narrative twist, the narrator, whose voiceover opens the film, is revealed in the film's final shot to be the ghost of Casares repeating the film's opening words and framing the whole narrative 'as his retrospective account from beyond the grave' (Labanyi 2007: 102): 'What is a ghost? A tragedy condemned to repeat itself time and again? An instant of pain, perhaps? Something dead which still seems to be dead? A sentiment suspended in time. Like a blurred photograph. Like an insect trapped in amber?', but with an added final answer: 'A ghost. That's what I am.' The final scene shows Casares's ghost from behind, looking across the plain as he stands in Santa Lucía's gateway.[23]

The fairy-tale narrative and stylistic framework functions as yet another allegorical layer contributing to the dialectical form of representation mobilised in *El laberinto del fauno*. The seamless merging of the fantasy world and the real world is articulated through parallel plotting and montage. Fairy-tale conventions and tropes structure Ofelia's narrative development and transform her from Ofelia into Princess Moanna. The three trials set by the Faun become the quest through which Ofelia's true nature will be tested. Firstly, she must obtain a magic key from the belly of a monstrous toad; the key will then enable her to access the netherworld dwelling of the Pale Man, from where she will recover a dagger; and, finally, the Faun will request from her that she sacrifice the innocent blood of her newly born brother in order to enter the realm of Princess Moanna's palace. As del Toro explained in the Production Notes,

Figure 43   Guillermo del Toro on the set of *El laberinto del fauno*.

El laberinto del fauno is a 'dark fairy tale about choice'. Ofelia's actions and choices follow a 'common thread between the "real world" and the "imaginary world", which I found in one of the seminal bloodlines within fairy tales: the bloodline choice' (del Toro in Kermode 2006: 22). Her choices function as counterpoints to 'the institutional lack of choice, which is fascism' (del Toro in Kermode 2006: 22). In the real world, her choice is to withhold her brother from Vidal, an act of defiance for which she pays with her life; in the parallel fantasy world, she refuses the Faun's request to sacrifice her brother, but this act of defiance is, in fact, a fulfilment of the third and final test and ensures her access to the netherworld. At the end of the film, Ofelia gives birth to herself by entering the netherworld and reuniting with her 'real father', the King. Vidal is killed by the *maquis*, who refuse to grant his final wish that his son be told his name and the time at which he dies. It is here that the narrative returns to the film's opening image of Ofelia's corpse lying within the ruins of the labyrinth, and the narrative voiceover re-emerges:

> It is said that the Princess returned to her father's kingdom. That she reigned there with justice and a kind heart for many centuries. That she was loved by her people. And that she left behind small traces of her time on earth, visible only to those who know where to look.

The circular structure of both narratives, therefore, returns the viewer to haunting motifs (ghosts and traces) and to the realm of allegory. Through *El espinazo del diablo* and *El laberinto del fauno*, del Toro confronts recent Spanish history and exhumes memories buried by *el pacto del olvido* (see Figure 43). The haunting trope and the allegorical moment function as 'a strategy for ensuring the ghostly returns in the future of history's victims: that is, ensuring that those who were not allowed to leave a trace on the historical stage do leave their trace in the cultural arena' (Labanyi 2002: 6). In this respect, del Toro's intervention in a Spanish cinematic tradition dealing with the Spanish Civil War reconfigures cinematic codes and 'truths', and refuses to be contained in generic frameworks which have legislated dominant representations of the conflict and its legacy.[24]

The commitments of these self-made horror auteurs to the genre can be traced to their relation with the cultural experience of horror and the institutional contexts associated with the genre. Like-minded producers and consumers, their (sub)cultural capital and sensibilities, as well as their filmic talent, have developed in and around fanzines, genre publications, video stores and specialist film festivals. Horror auterism is an established critical practice, which they have performed in fanzine writing, in the case of Balagueró and del Toro; likewise, Balagueró's and Cerdà's short filmography is driven by auteurist pretensions. In fact, my search for advertising and promotional material, press coverage and magazine profiles on Cerdà's film shorts, specifically, was always rewarded with an extraordinary amount of material the director himself had collated. As part of an extremely competitive commercialising horror film culture, the horror auteurism of Cerdà, Balagueró and del Toro is a major commercial marketing strategy that the industry – and the directors themselves – mobilise in the production and promotion of their films. Film and DVD releases market Cerdà, Balagueró and del Toro as auteurs to invoke a distinctive horror brand name and an original confection of horror traditions, and to exploit the horror fans' and collectors' market. Horror film publications *Fangoria* and *Shivers* recurrently read and evaluate their films in terms of their status as horror auteurs.

Fangoria marked its 300th issue by compiling 'the mother of all horror-movie lists' (Alexander 2011: 3). The inclusion of *Cronos, Blade II, El espinazo del diablo* and *El laberinto del fauno* positioned del Toro as a major contemporary force in the field of international horror production. The presence of *Los sin nombre* acknowledged Balagueró's 'talent for inexorably building a sense of doom that really gets under your skin' (Gingold 2011: 64), as well as the 'international sensation' of *[•REC]* (Gingold 2011: 72). And Cerdà? Some might argue that, if *Aftermath* had been a feature film, it would undeniably have made the list. Other contemporary Spanish horror products that made the cut (*El día de la bestia, Los otros* and *El orfanato*) reflect the vigour of the genre, whereas the presence of 1970s cult classics such as *Horror Express, Horror Rises From the Tomb, Let Sleeping Corpses Lie, Who Can Kill a Child?* and *Tombs of the Blind Dead* attest to the status of Spanish horror film in a transnational horror culture.

NOTES

1. The other ten talents were directors Jamie Blanks, Shusuke Kaneko, William Malone, Mike Mendez, Hideo Nakata, Mark Pavia and Rob Zombie; author

Gerard Daniel Houarner; screenwriter Neal Marshall Stevens; and make-up FX artist Adrien Morot.

2. *Los sin nombre* had already been featured a few months earlier in issue 194, 'The Nameless Scares You Senseless' (Hodges 2000: 22–5).

3. *Ataúdes de luz* (Coffin of Light) is a documentary about 1970s Spanish director Sergio del Monte, who was murdered while making his début feature film in 1974. The archival film footage focused on sects and the dictatorship's manipulation of the masses through propaganda. Cerdà's footage consists of interviews with key players of the Spanish horror scene of the period: namely, Jesús Franco, Paul Naschy, Narciso Ibáñez Serrador, Amando de Ossorio and Fernando Jiménez del Oso. The *Pieces* documentary features an interview with director Juan Piquer Simón, included in the DVD release for the US market in 2008.

4. *El laberinto del fauno* has reaped nominations and awards all over the world: from the industry (3 Oscars in Hollywood; three BAFTAs in the UK; six Goyas in Spain; nine Ariels in Mexico), the critical establishment (Film of the Year for the National Society of Film Critics in the US, the UK Regional Critics Film Awards, Fantasia Empire Awards, and included in hundreds of critics' lists of the ten best films of 2006) and the horror festival circuit (Zone Horror Fright Fest, Fantasporto).

5. This is the advertising line used in the Fant-Asia compilation as part of the 'Small Gauge Trauma' DVD, featuring thirteen award-winning shorts.

6. The film was also entered in the Bilbao Short Film Festival (1994), the Valencia International Film Festival (1995) and the Sevilla Week of Fantasy Cinema (1996). Other festivals, such as the one held in Huesca, did not accept it due to its subject matter.

7. Balum taking Cerdà to task is recorded in the festival documentary *The Belly of the Beast* (1997), which covered the 1997 Fant-Asia event.

8. When asked in interviews whether Mondo films or death-documentaries were part of his research, he replied, 'I've seen *Faces of Death* and *Killing of America* but nothing else. No *Mondo Cane*, *Death Scenes* or *Traces of Death*. I've heard a lot about this genre so I bought the book *Killing for Culture* to learn more' (Cerdà in Slater 1998).

9. Barcelona-based company DDT were in charge of the SFX. The authenticity of the material used (polyurethane SkinFlex3) and their craftsmanship were celebrated in *Fangoria*.

10. The original script featured a sodomy scene for the rape. However, as the director explained, the SFX were only constructed face-up and he could not film from that particular angle.

11. Eight years of cinematographic silence in which Cerdà's projects failed to come to fruition. 'Cerdà hopes *Genesis* will help him raise finances to make a full-length haunted house movie' (Perks 1998: 10). 'I'm working on a script about a world-wide plague [. . .] it's called "Dante" and it's a story about a plague that affects you on a mental, not biological, level' (Cerdà in Gudino 1999: 10).

12. Published as *La secta sin nombre* in Barcelona in 1988 by Ediciones Vidorama.

13. *The Oxford English Book of Victorian Ghost Stories* (eds Michael Cox and R. A. Gilbert, Oxford: Clarendon, 1989).

14. Other critics, such as *Reseña*'s Fernando Bejarano, used *Frágiles* as an excuse to berate Balagueró's standing in Filmax, and to vent their customary disapproval against the horror production company: 'Jaume Balagueró does not seem to have risen to the challenge of becoming the great white hope of autochthonous horror, as planned by his habitual producer Julio Fernández', whose company is characterised by 'producing mainly Spanish horror cinema of low quality and distributing vile American cinema' (2006: 165).

15. Marini has participated in projects such as *[•REC]*, *Frágiles* and *Romasanta*.
16. Accessed 24 August 2007.
17. See 'Cronos, tiempo y sangre' (Vié 1994: 48–51).
18. See memoriahistorica.org, foroporlamemoria.info and www.foroporlamemoria.es.
19. In the DVD audio-commentary, del Toro dates the first ideas on *El laberinto del fauno* back to 1993.
20. On *El espinazo del diablo*, see, for example, Smith (2001), Hardcastle (2005), Labanyi (2007: 101–2) and Lázaro-Reboll (2007). On *El laberinto del fauno*, see Smith (2007) and Gómez López-Quiñones (2009). And, for a comparative analysis, see Enjuto Rangel (2009).
21. The location for this scene is the Aragonese village of Belchite, devastated by the Republican troops during the Civil War. The village remains ruinous even today, as a mark of the fratricidal conflict.
22. Although the influence of *Paracuellos* was duly acknowledged by Spanish film critics (Santamarina 2001, Costa 2001, Khan 2001, Garrido 2001), the aesthetic and political significance of Carlos Giménez's work in the film was overlooked. As I have argued elsewhere (Lázaro-Reboll 2007), the aesthetic and political significance of *Paracuellos* in *El espinazo del diablo* lies in the comic series' account of a slice of public history and popular culture rendered invisible in official histories. Carlos Giménez's collaboration with del Toro extended from the casting of the children to the narrative, through the recreation of specific dialogues, episodes and themes reminiscent of *Paracuellos* (privation and suffering, fear and bullying, survival and solidarity) and to the *mise-en-scène*, which contribute to the recreation of the world of the orphanages depicted in the comic.
23. 'Played by the Argentinian Federico Luppi, one might wonder whether Casares's accent inscribes a final tour de force in the film, conjuring up other *desaparecidos*' (Lázaro-Reboll 2007: 49).
24. Del Toro had planned a third film on the theme of the Spanish Civil War, '3993', based on a script by Sergio S. Sánchez, which has not come to fruition.

CONCLUSION

The field of contemporary Spanish horror film is broad. Horror event movies, such as *El orfanato* and *Los ojos de Julia*, reflect changes in industrial practices and reach mainstream audiences. The do-it-yourself attitude of niche horror production company Chaparra Entertainment, 'making Spanish Monster Movies since 1997' (chaparraentertainment.com), is channelled and circulated via the internet, with the character of 'Amazing Mask, El Asombroso Luchador Enmascarado' as the main superhero in the episodes 'Amazing Unmasked vs. El Doctor Calavera Maligna' and 'Amazing Mask vs. La sobrenatural Mujer Voodoo', celebrating the world of the Mexican horror / wrestling movie and in particular the extensive body of films which featured Santo, 'el enmascarado de plata'.[1] Even Almodóvar, whose only claim to horror is the opening of *Matador* (1986), where the protagonist masturbates while watching Jesús Franco's *Colegialas violadas* / *Bloody Moon* (1981), has made a foray into horror territory with *La piel que habito* / *The Skin I Live In* (2011), drawing upon the mad-plastic surgeon tradition exploited by Franco in his Dr Orloff cycle in the wake of Franju's successful *Eyes Without a Face*. The *[•REC]* saga has become the first horror franchise to come out of Spain. The genre has also been popular in the world of television; patterned upon teenage horror production practices (shot in HD and starring a young cast) and narrative conventions, the series *El internado* / *The Boarding School* (Antena 3) ran for seven seasons (2007–10), with an average of 3.5 million viewers and a 19.4 audience share; a strong internet following and the profitable sale of ancillary products – books and a videogame – demonstrate that the genre struck a chord with a certain demographic. Horror film reception and consumption therefore operate in traditional and innovative media contexts, as well as in different markets.

The internet, as other media technologies – VHS, DVD – have done in the last three decades, has contributed to the circulation of horror and related genre films. In the introductory pages of *Horror Zone. The Cultural Experience of Contemporary Horror Cinema*, Conrich addresses the significance of the internet in providing 'a 'supporting culture of discussion groups, fan appreciation, bloggers, independent reviewers, and online trailers, that have expanded the connections of a horror community that was before more dependent on a print culture of fanzines and specialist magazines' (2010: 2). A survey of the current Spanish fanzine, e-zine and blog writing scene devoted to the unearthing of obscure films of the horror genre, for example, would require a separate chapter; Exhumed Movies, Psychotronic Kult Video, La abadía de Berzano and Cine de Medianoche are amongst the most notable researchers of cult classics, long sought-after and obscure films, raiding video store and mail order catalogues and trafficking peer-to-peer file-sharing archives.[2] These and other fans, bloggers and collectors (re)discover and (re)mediate Spanish horror films past and present – as well as other traditions of the international world of exploitation / psychotronic cinema – for generations of fans. Horror fan communities, or as Matt Hills describes them, 'flesh-and-blood genre communities' (2010: 87), gather in horror genre-focused film festivals.

As two of the most important specialised genre festivals in Europe, the Sitges International Film Festival of Catalonia, founded in 1968, and the San Sebastián Horror and Fantasy Film Festival, operating since 1990, have established themselves as meccas for industry, specialist press and fans alike. A discussion of their significance in the development of the (sub)cultural field of horror in Spain in the last four decades has been explored in Chapter 5 and elsewhere in this volume. Apart from their role in the dissemination of local and international horror traditions and in showcasing the latest world horror production, both festivals have championed underground strands of horror and programmed retrospectives of horror auteurs and cycles. The San Sebastián Festival's publishing ventures, supported by Donostia Kultura, range from monographs and edited collections on individual filmmakers and international horror traditions to the periodical *Dezine*, which acted as an unofficial publication for the festival for six volumes, as well as to regular collaborations with fanzine *2000maniacos* from the mid-1990s onwards.[3] The festival has therefore provided different generations of horror fans with venues at which to indulge their horror pleasures, as well as with networks where 'fans from different walks of life gather together to share their fandom (Hills 2002: 61) and invest their (sub)cultural capital as consumers and / or producers. In this respect, the festivals have become a training ground for genre film critics,

Figure 44   Enter the world of [•REC].

whose writings can be traced from fanzines and specialist film publications to the mainstream press, and for emerging Spanish horror filmmakers such as Jaume Balagueró or Paco Plaza, whose fandom and professional career – shorts, first features and subsequent productions – developed alongside the festivals. Indeed, the launching platform for Balagueró's and Plaza's collaborative work [•REC] was Sitges.

Since the release of [•REC] in 2007 (see Figure 44), the franchise has spawned two sequels, [•REC2] and [•REC3] Genesis, with a final instalment, [•REC4] Apocalypse currently in pre-production and announced for 2013. A brief discussion of [•REC] is perhaps a fitting way to bring this volume to a close. Its commercial and critical success is representative of the local and global impact of 'quality horror titles' (Evans 2010: 32) produced in Spain by 'savvy' and 'internationally-minded genre specialists' (2010), as reported in leading trade journals Screen International[4] and The Hollywood Reporter,[5] respectively. In 2007, just three titles caught the eye of the Hollywood remake machinery: [•REC], Nacho Vigalondo's Los cronocrímenes / Time Crimes and Juan Antonio Bayona's El orfanato. For the time being, the only one to be finalised is the American remake of [•REC], Quarantine (John Erick Dowdle 2008), which virtually replicates the Spanish original shot by shot, notwithstanding the relocation of the action to a downtown Los Angeles apartment. Like the films of other Spanish horror directors discussed in the volume, Balagueró's and Plaza's [•REC] is a creative and resourceful refashioning of international horror traditions and individual commercial successes. It is yet another offspring of the zombie / infected subgenre, as well as a variation on the contemporary 'reality horror' subgenre, in particular visual progenies such as *Last Broadcast* (Stefan Avalos and Lance Weiler 1998) and *Blair Witch Project* (Daniel Myrick and Eduardo Sánchez 1999). But the plague-zombie narrative, the predictable body count and the faux documentary angle of *[•REC]* are further updated by the narrative techniques of television: a horror story told live and in real time through the perspective of a single video camera. The premise behind *[•REC]*, according to Balagueró and Plaza, who scripted it with Luis Berdejo, was to experiment with televisual language – 'reality TV' – and contemporary media culture in the horror genre. Modelled on contemporary Spanish 'reality TV' programmes such as *España Directo* (TVE) or *Espejo Público* (Antena 3), the film introduces the viewer to young female reporter Ángela (Manuela Velasco) and the crew of the TV programme 'While you're asleep', who are filming a documentary on local firemen on their night shift in Barcelona. When they receive a routine call to attend an old lady trapped in her flat, they find themselves caught in the building, quarantined by health officials in an attempt to contain the outbreak of an unknown virus. Ángela and her cameraman Pablo (played by director of photography Pablo Rosso) grab the opportunity to record the unfolding events live on camera. Their motto '¡Grábalo todo!' (Tape everything!) and *modus operandi*, '¡No dejes de grabar!' (Keep rolling!), drive the narrative forward and maintain suspense as the source of the infection is never, in fact, revealed.

What also made the first *[•REC]* stand out in the context of contemporary Spanish horror cinema was the way the film was marketed and promoted through new media's social networking sites. Apart from the internet viral campaign and the franchise's presence on social networks Facebook and Twitter, Castelao Productions teamed up with global telecommunications company Nokia to exploit novel ways of promoting and marketing the film. As Balagueró explained to *Fangoria* readers, Plaza had the idea of filming

> the Sitges premiere audience with a night-vision camera, and make a trailer from the footage. Several films have done this before, but the media really reacted to this Internet viral campaign, and it became a major news item on Spanish TV. 'It's a frightening film, and look at the reaction' was the thrust of the stories, and it made *[•REC]* a word-of-mouth sensation. (Balagueró in Jones 2007: 33)

The trailer rapidly spread via YouTube – over a million hits in a matter of days – and gathered further momentum when it was broadcast as part of an intensive TV spot campaign. Internet dissemination expedited the film's global dissemination, soon transforming *[•REC]* into a transnational film franchise.

And keeping up with the expanding commercial operations of the franchise, [•REC3], the videogame, was scheduled for 2012. The survival horror game is said to 'faithfully reproduce the content of much of the story, divided into four worlds, one for each part of the franchise'.

The [•REC] saga, like horror film in general, promises more of the same but different. The final twist in the first instalment comes in the form of the 'Medeiros girl' in the attic of the building (is she or is she not the source of the infection?), leaving the door open for a sequel that picks up the girl's suggested demonic possession. 'Do you dare to return?', was the question posed to prospective Spanish viewers in the official poster. The tagline for the American market, 'Fear Revisited', augured a repetition of the affective experience delivered in the first instalment. Indeed, [•REC2] opened where the first film ended, exactly fifteen minutes later in narrative time, when the authorities have lost contact with the TV crew and have decided to send a SWAT team into the building. This time, the sense of immediacy is achieved through the built-in cameras on the SWAT team helmets (cinematographer Pablo Rosso plays one of the SWAT cops in charge of filming the rescue operation). Once inside the block, they find camcorder footage filmed by the now-missing cameraman. Although the narrative strand exploring the virus outbreak is developed through the actions of the medical and police teams, led by medical officer Dr Owen (Jonathan Mellor), the sequel has a more pronounced occult bent. Again, the possibility of another sequel was built into the ending; as the *Variety* reviewer bluntly put it, 'the final twist can be seen coming from miles away, leaving the door more than ajar for [•REC]3' (Van Hoeij 2009). And some classic strategies of horror marketing are currently at work with the [•REC3] promotional campaign: 'It's new, it's different, it's the reinvention of the saga! [. . .] Paco Plaza is pumping new blood into the [•REC] franchise.' The trailer, the teaser poster and the first images released by Filmax promote an unconventional scenario for a horror film – a wedding – and a change in tone, with the infection spreading beyond the building and filming taking place in broad daylight (see Figure 45). The franchise will no doubt be revisited in light of the forthcoming [•REC4], and will set in motion further fan writing and a revision of the saga.

Critics and scholars may well censure the absence in this volume of a detailed discussion of Erice's *El espíritu de la colmena*; some will reprimand the lack of references to Iván Zulueta's metafictional reflection on the vampiric nature of filmmaking in *Arrebato / Rapture* (1980) or Bigas Luna's self-reflexive postmodern exercise on voyeurism and sadism in *Angustia / Anguish* (1987). Art-house horror aficionados might have expected an examination of Agustí Villaronga's *Tras el cristal / In a Glass Cage* (1986) – and Villaronga is one of those directors who has not received, as yet, the critical attention he deserves. All these films are steeped in the traditions of horror cinema but, as Newman

Figure 45   The blissfully unaware happy couple in *[•REC3]*.

neatly puts it in the postscript to his updated edition of *Nightmare Movies*, 'the story of horror in the cinema is larger than the story of the horror film' (2011: 582). Fans of obscure horror production will perhaps insist on the inclusion of *Las flores del miedo* (José María Oliveira 1973) or *Cada ver es* (Ángel García del Val 1981), to name just two. These (and other) omissions are partly due to the necessary publishing constraints of a critical history on Spanish horror film. Then again, genres 'depend directly and heavily on the identity and purpose of those using and evaluating them' (Altman 1999: 98): that is, on the discursive activities of 'genre users' or 'user-groups' whose experiences of watching and consuming horror movies are continually mediated and remediated by institutions and technologies. Critical commentary and fan writing, as well as the industry and audiences, all participate in the social process of genre classification. In this respect, my own intervention in the cultural fields of Spanish horror and international horror traditions aims to contribute to a richer picture of the cultural history of Spanish horror film and to refigure related film histories.

NOTES

1. Chaparra Entertainment also publishes the genre magazine *Amazing Monster*.
2. Exhumed Movies (exhumedmovies.com) was started by a group of four horror fans on their annual pilgrimage to the San Sebastián Horror and Fantasy Film Festival in 2005; Psychotronic Kult Video (psychotronickultvideo.blogspot.com) has reviewed, among other movies, over 150 Spanish horror films since it was founded in 2006; La abadía de Berzano (cerebrin.wordpress.com) has catered for 'los cinéfagos más desprejuiciados' (the most unprejudiced cinéphages') since 2007; and Cine de Medianoche (cinemedianoche.blogspot.com), created in 2008 by current *2000maniacos* contributor Gerard Fernández Ordel, plunges into exploitation paraphernalia.
3. Since 1997, the festival has published several volumes on international horror film

traditions: for example, *Cine fantástico y de terror italiano. Del giallo al gore* (Loris Curci, Jesús Palacios, Ángel Sala, Juan Antonio Molina Foix 1997), *El cine fantástico y de terror de la Universal* (AA. VV., 2000), *Cine fantástico y de terror japonés. 1899–2001* (Carlos Águilar, Daniel Águilar, Toshiyuki Shigeta, 2001), *Cine fantástico y de terror alemán, 1913–1927* (AA. VV., 2002), *David Cronenberg: los misterios del organismo* (Quim Casas (ed.), 2006) and *American Gothic: Cine de terror USA, 1968–1980* (Antonio José Navarro, 2007), all with Donostia Kultura. It has also sponsored special issues of fanzines *ojalatemueras* for its 1999 and 2000 issues and *2000maniacos* throughout the 2000s (see, for example, issues 24, 'Eurovicio' (2001); 26, 'Bizarre Latino' (2002); 29, 'Euro Heroes' (2004); 35, 'America apesta' (2005); and 39, 'Terror majareta' (2008)).

4. See Evans (2010).
5. See *The Hollywood Reporter* (2011).

SELECT FILMOGRAPHY

99 mujeres / *99 Women* (Jesús Franco, 1969)
Abandonados, Los / *The Abandoned* (Nacho Cerdà, 2006)
Acción mutante / *Mutant Action* (Álex de la Iglesia, 1992)
Al otro lado del espejo / *The Obscene Mirror* (Jesús Franco, 1973)
Angustia / *Anguish* (Bigas Luna, 1987)
Aquella casa en las afueras / *That House in the Outskirts* (Eugenio Martín, 1979)
Arachnid (Jack Sholder, 2001)
Arrebato / *Rapture* (Iván Zulueta, 1980)
Asesino de muñecas, El / *Killing of the Dolls* (Miguel Madrid, 1975)
Ataque de los muertos sin ojos, El / *Attack of the Blind Dead* (Amando de Ossorio, 1973)
Aullido del diablo, El / *Howl of the Devil* (Jacinto Molina, 1988)
Bajo aguas tranquilas / *Beneath Still Waters* (Brian Yuzna, 2005)
Bésame monstruo / *Kiss Me Monster* (Jesús Franco, 1969)
Bestia y la espada mágica, La / *The Beast and the Magic Sword* (Paul Naschy, 1983)
Beyond Re-Animator (Brian Yuzna, 2003)
Bosque del lobo, El / *The Ancine Woods* (Pedro Olea, 1970)
Bosque de sombras / *The Backwoods* (Koldo Serra, 2006)
Buque maldito, El / *The Ghost Galleon* (Amando de Ossorio, 1974)
Cada ver es (Ángel García del Val, 1981)
Campana del infierno, La / *Bell of Hell* (Claudio Guerín Hill, 1973)
Canibal, El / *The Devil Hunter* (Jesús Franco, 1980)
Capilla ardiente, La (Carlos Puerto, 1983)
Cartas boca arriba / *Cartes sur table* (Jesús Franco, 1966)
Castillo de Fu Manchu, El / *Sax Rohmer's The Castle of Fu Manchu* (Jesús Franco, 1969)
Ceremonia sangrienta / *Bloody Ceremony* (Jorge Grau, 1973)
Colegialas violadas / *Bloody Moon* (Jesús Franco, 1981)

Colegio de la muerte, El / *School of Death* (Pedro Luis Ramírez, 1975)
Conde Drácula, El / *Count Dracula* (Jesús Franco, 1969)
Corrupción de Chris Miller, La / *The Corruption of Chris Miller* (Juan Antonio Bardem, 1973)
Cronocrímenes, Los / *Time Crimes* (Nacho Vigalondo, 2007)
Dagon. La secta del mar / *H. P. Lovecraft's Dagon* (Stuart Gordon, 2001)
Darkness (Jaume Balagueró, 2002)
Démons, Les / *She-Demons* (Jesús Franco, 1973)
Día de la bestia, El / *Day of the Beast* (Álex de la Iglesia, 1995)
Diablos del mar, Los / *Sea Devils* (Juan Piquer Simón, 1982)
Drácula contra Frankenstein / *The Screaming Dead* (Jesús Franco, 1971)
Dr Jekyll y el hombre lobo / *Dr Jekyll and the Werewolf* (León Klimovsky, 1972)
Dr Wong's Virtual Hell (Jesús Franco, 1998)
Ellos robaron la picha de Hitler / *They Stole Hitler's Cock* (Pedro Temboury, 2006)
Endemoniada, La / *The Possessed* (Amando de Ossorio, 1975)
Enigma del ataúd, El / *Les Orgies du Dr Orloff* (Santos Alcocer, 1967)
Enigma del yate, El / *The Enigma of the Yacht* (Carlos Aured, 1983)
Espanto surge de la tumba, El / *Horror Rises from the Tomb* (Carlos Aured, 1973)
Espectro del terror, El (José María Elorrieta, 1973)
Espinazo del diablo, El / *The Devil's Backbone* (Guillermo del Toro, 2001)
Espiritista, El (Augusto Fernando, 1974)
Espíritu de la colmena, El / *The Spirit of the Beehive* (Víctor Erice, 1973)
Eugenie / *Eugénie . . . The Story of Her Journey into Perversion* (Jesús Franco, 1969)
Exorcismo / *Exorcism* (Juan Bosch, 1975)
Faceless / *Les Prédateurs de la nuit* (Jesús Franco, 1988)
Faust. La venganza está en la sangre / *Faust: Love of the Damned* (Brian Yuzna, 2000)
Flores del miedo, Las (José María Oliveira, 1973)
Frágiles / *Fragile* (Jaume Balagueró, 2005)
Fu Manchu y el beso de la muerte / *The Blood of Fu Manchu* (Jesús Franco, 1968)
Furia del hombre lobo, La / *The Wolfman Never Sleeps* (José María Zabalza, 1972)
Garras de Lorelei, Las / *The Lorelei's Grasp* (Amando de Ossorio, 1974)
Gota de sangre para morir amando, Una / *Murder in a Blue World* (Eloy de la Iglesia, 1973)
Gran amor del Conde Drácula, El / *Count Dracula's Great Love* (Javier Aguirre, 1972)
Grieta, La / *The Rift* (Juan Piquer Simón, 1989)
Gritos en la noche / *The Awful Dr Orloff* (Jesús Franco, 1962)
Hija de Drácula, La / *Daughter of Dracula* (Jesús Franco, 1972)
Huerto del francés, El / *The Frenchman's Garden* (Paul Naschy, 1977)
Inquisición / *Inquisition* (Paul Naschy, 1976)
Invernadero, El (Santiago Lapeira, 1983)
Ivanna / *Altar of Blood* (José Luis Merino, 1970)
Jack el destripador de Londres / *Seven Murders for Scotland Yard* (José Luis Madrid, 1973)
Jorobado de la morgue, El / *Hunchback of the Morgue* (Javier Aguirre, 1973)
Juego del diablo, El / *Devil's Exorcist* (Jorge Darnell, 1975)
Kárate a muerte en Torremolinos / *Karate to the Death in Torremolinos* (Pedro Temboury, 2003)
Killer Barbys / *Vampire Killer Barbys* (Jesús Franco, 1996)
KM31. Kilómetro 31 / *KM31: Kilometre 31* (Rigoberto Castañeda, 2007)
Laberinto del fauno, El / *Pan's Labyrinth* (Guillermo del Toro, 2001)
Látidos de pánico / *Panic Beats* (Paul Naschy, 1983)
Libélula para cada muerto, Una / *A Dragonfly for Each Corpse* (León Klimovsky, 1973)

Licántropo. El asesino de la luna llena / Lycanthropus. The Moonlight Murders (Rafael Rodríguez Gordillo, 1996)
Llamada del vampiro, La / The Curse of the Vampyr (José María Elorrieta, 1972)
Lust for Frankenstein (Jesús Franco, 1998)
Maldición de Frankenstein, La / The Erotic Rites of Frankenstein (Jesús Franco, 1972)
Maldición de la bestia, La / The Werewolf and the Yeti (Miguel Iglesias Bonns, 1975)
Malenka, la sobrina del vampiro / Fangs of the Living Dead (Amando de Ossorio, 1969)
Mansión de la niebla, La / Manic Mansion (Francisco Lara Polop / Pedro Lazaga, 1972)
Marca del hombre lobo, La / Frankenstein's Bloody Terror (Enrique López Eguíluz, 1968)
Mari Cookie y la tarántula asesina / Mary Cookie and the Killer Tarantula in 8 Legs to Love You (Jesús Franco, 1998)
Mariscal del infierno, El / Devil's Possessed (León Klimovsky, 1974)
Más allá de la muerte (Sebastià D'Arbó, 1986)
Más allá del terror / Further than Fear (Tomás Aznar, 1980)
Más de mil cámaras velan por tu seguridad / More Than a Thousand Cameras are Working for Your Safety (David Alonso, 2003)
Mientras duermes / Sleep Tight (Jaume Balagueró, 2011)
Mil gritos tiene la noche / Pieces (Juan Piquer Simón, 1982)
Miss Muerte / The Diabolical Dr Z (Jesús Franco, 1966)
Misterio de la isla de los monstruos / Mystery Monster Island (Juan Piquer Simón, 1981)
Monja, La / The Nun (Luis de la Madrid, 2005)
Monstruos del terror, Los / Assignment Terror (Hugo Fregonese and Tulio Demicheli, 1969)
Morbus (o bon profit) / Morbus (Ignasi P. Ferré, 1982)
Morir de miedo (Juan José Porto, 1980)
Mucha sangre / Gangsters vs Aliens (Pepe de las Heras, 2002)
Nadie oyó gritar / No One Heard the Scream (Eloy de la Iglesia, 1972)
Noche de las gaviotas, La / Night of the Seagulls (Amando de Ossorio, 1975)
Noche de los brujos, La / Night of the Sorcerers (Amando de Ossorio, 1973)
Noche del terror ciego, La / Tombs of the Blind Dead (Amando de Ossorio, 1972)
Noche de Walpurgis, La / The Shadow of the Werewolf (León Klimovsky, 1970)
Noches del hombre lobo, Las / Nights of the Werewolf (René Govar, 1968)
No profanar el sueño de los muertos / The Living Dead at Manchester Morgue (Jorge Grau, 1974)
Novia ensangrentada, La / The Blood-Spattered Bride (Vicente Aranda, 1972)
Odio mi cuerpo / I Hate My Body (León Klimovsky, 1974)
Ojos azules de la muñeca rota, Los / Blue Eyes of the Broken Doll (Carlos Aured, 1973)
Ojos de Julia, Los / Julia's Eyes (Guillem Morales, 2010)
Ojos siniestros del Dr Orloff, Los / The Sinister Eyes of Dr Orlof (Jesús Franco, 1973)
Orfanato, El / The Orphanage (Juan Antonio Bayona, 2007)
Orgía de los muertos, La / Terror of the Living Dead (José Luis Merino, 1973)
Orgía nocturna de los vampiros, La / The Vampires' Night Orgy (León Klimovsky, 1972)
Orloff y el hombre invisible / Orloff Against the Invisible Man (Jesús Franco, 1970)
Otros, Los / The Others (Alejandro Amenábar, 2001)
Ouija (Pedro Ortega, 2004)
Palabras encadenadas / Killing Words (Laura Maña, 2003)
Pánico en el Transiberiano / Horror Express (Eugenio Martín, 1973)
Pastel de sangre (Frances Bellmunt, Jaime Chávarri, Emilio Martínez Lázaro, José María Vallés, 1971)
Piel que habito, La / The Skin I Live In (Pedro Almodóvar, 2011)

Proceso de las brujas, El / *Night of the Blood Monster* (Jesús Franco, 1970)
¿Quién puede matar a un niño? / *Who Can Kill a Child?* (Narciso Ibáñez Serrador, 1976)
[•REC] (Jaume Balagueró and Paco Plaza, 2007)
[•REC2] (Jaume Balagueró and Paco Plaza, 2009)
[•REC3] Genesis (Paco Plaza, 2012)
[•REC4] Apocalypse (Jaume Balagueró, forthcoming)
Rebelión de las muertas, La / *Vengeance of the Zombies* (León Klimovsky, 1972)
Refugio del miedo, El / *Refuge of Fear* (José Ulloa, 1974)
Regreso del más allá (Juan José Porto, 1982)
Residencia, La / *The Finishing School* (Narciso Ibáñez Serrador, 1969)
Retorno del hombre lobo, El / *Night of the Werewolf* (Paul Naschy, 1980)
Retorno de Walpurgis, El / *Curse of the Devil* (Carlos Aured, 1974)
Rojo Sangre (Christian Molina, 2004)
Romasanta. La caza de la bestia / *Romasanta: The Werewolf Hunt* (Paco Plaza, 2004)
Rottweiler (Brian Yuzna, 2005)
School Killer (Carlos Gil, 2001)
Secreto del Dr Orloff, El / *Dr Jekyll's Mistresses* (Jesús Franco, 1964)
Secta siniestra / *Bloody Sect* (Ignacio F. Iquino, 1982)
Segundo nombre, El / *Second Name* (Paco Plaza, 2002)
Semana del asesino, La / *Cannibal Man* (Eloy de la Iglesia, 1972)
Ser, El / *Psicophobia* (Sebastià D'Arbó, 1982)
Serpiente de mar / *Sea Serpent* (Amando de Ossorio, 1984).
Sexo sangriento (Manuel Esteba, 1980)
Siniestro Dr Orloff, El / *The Sinister Dr Orloff* (Jesús Franco, 1982)
Sin nombre, Los / *The Nameless* (Jaume Balagueró, 1999)
Slugs, muerte viscosa / *Slugs: The Movie* (Juan Piquer Simón, 1988)
Sobrenatural / *Supernatural* (Eugenio Martín, 1983)
Supersonic Man (Juan Piquer Simón, 1979)
Techo de cristal, El / *The Glass Ceiling* (Eloy de la Iglesia, 1971)
Tender Flesh (Jesús Franco, 1998)
Tesis / *Thesis* (Alejandro Amenábar, 1996)
Tras el cristal / *In a Glass Cage* (Agustí Villaronga, 1986)
Trauma (León Klimovsky, 1977)
Trece campanadas / *Thirteen Chimes* (Xavier Villaverde, 2002)
Tuno negro / *Black Serenade* (Pedro L. Barbero and Vicente J. Martín, 2001)
Vampiras, Las / *Vampiros Lesbos* (Jesús Franco, 1971)
Vampir Cuadecuc (Pere Portabella, 1970)
Vampire Blues (Jesús Franco, 1998)
Venganza de la momia, La / *Vengeance of the Mummy* (Carlos Aured, 1973)
Venganza del Dr Mabuse, La (Jesús Franco, 1972)
Venus in Furs / *Paroxismus* (Jesús Franco, 1969)
Viaje al centro de la tierra / *Journey to the Center of the Earth* (Juan Piquer Simón, 1977)
Viaje al más allá (Sebastià D'Arbó, 1980)

SHORTS

Aftermath (Nacho Cerdà, 1994)
Alicia (Jaume Balagueró, 1994)
Amazing Mask vs. La sobrenatural Mujer Voodoo (Dani Moreno, 2004)
Awakenings, The (Nacho Cerdà, 1990)

Días sin luz (Jaume Balagueró, 1995)
Evilio (Santiago Segura, 1992)
Evilio vuelve (El Purificador) (Santiago Segura, 1994)
Generador adolescente (Pedro Temboury, 1998)
Genesis (Nacho Cerdà, 1998)
Hijomoto vs zombies radioactivos / Hijomoto vs the Radioactive Zombies (Manuel Romo, 1993)
Hijomoto 2: el ataque de las hordas sodomitas / Hijomoto vs the Sodomite Hordes (Manuel Romo, 1996)
Matanza de los garrulos lisérgicos, La / Cannibal Massacre (Antonio Blanco and Ricardo Llovos, 1993)
Mirindas asesinas / Killer Mirindas (Álex de la Iglesia, 1991)
Perturbado (Santiago Segura, 1993)
Psycho-lettes (Pedro Temboury, 1996)
Snuff 2000 (Borja Crespo, 2002)
Trivial Exterminador, El (Borja Crespo, 1995)
Trivial Exterminador 2, El (Borja Crespo, 1995)
Unmasked vs. El Doctor Calavera Maligna (Dani Moreno, 2009)

TV SERIES

6 Películas para no dormir / Six Films to Keep You Awake (Estudios Picasso, Filmax Telecinco, 2006): Episodes 'La habitación del niño' / 'The Baby's Room' (Álex de la Iglesia), 'Para entrar a vivir' / 'To Let' (Jaume Balagueró); 'La culpa' / 'Blame' (Narciso Ibáñez Serrador), 'Regreso a Moira' / 'Spectre' (Mateo Gil), 'Adivina quién soy' / 'A Real Friend' (Enrique Urbizu) and 'Cuento de Navidad' / 'The Christmas Tale' (Paco Plaza)
Historias para no dormir / Stories to Keep You Awake (TVE, Narciso Ibáñez Serrador, 1966–8)
Internado, El / The Boarding School (Antena 3, Rafael de la Cueva, 2007–10)
Mis Terrores Favoritos (TVE, Narciso Ibáñez Serrador, 1981–2)

BIBLIOGRAPHY

ABC (1973), 'Se discute una película', 12 September: 119.

Acevedo-Muñoz, Ernesto R. (2008), 'Horror of Allegory: *The Others* and its Contexts', in Jay Beck and Vicente Rodríguez-Ortega (eds), *Contemporary Spanish Cinema and Genre*, Manchester: Manchester University Press, pp. 202–18.

Agrasánchez Junior, Rogelio (1999), *Mexican Horror Cinema. Posters from Mexican Fantasy Films*, Mexico: Agrasánchez Film Archive.

Águilar, Carlos (1991), 'Jesús Franco: de la cinefilia a la autofagia', *Dezine*, 4: 4–11.

— (ed.) (1999a), *Cine fantástico y de terror español: 1900–1983*, San Sebastián: Donostia Kultura.

— (1999b), *Jess Franco. El sexo del horror*, Firenze: Glittering Images.

— (ed.) (2005), *Cine fantástico y de terror español: 1984–2004*, San Sebastián: Donostia Kultura.

Águilar, Carlos, Dolores Devesa, Carlos Losilla, Francisco Llinás, José Luis Marqués, Alicia Potes and Casimiros Torreiro (1996), *Conocer a Eloy de la Iglesia*, San Sebastián: Filmoteca Vasca.

Alarcón, Tonio L. (2006), 'Jaume Balagueró. ¿Quién puede torturar a un niño?', *Dirigido por . . .*, July / August, 358: 56–8.

— (2009), 'Apocalípticos y desintegrados: una panorámica sobre el cine fantástico español reciente', *Dirigido por . . .*, October, 393: 36–42.

Alexander, Chris (2011), 'Horror Rises from the Tomb', *Fangoria* 300: 43.

Altman, Rick (1999), *Film / Genre*, London: BFI.

A. M. O. (1971), '*La noche de Walpurgis*', *Arriba*, 27 May: n.p.

Andrews, Stuart (2007), 'Ghosts of the Past', *Rue Morgue*, May, 67: 24–5, 28.

Ángulo, Javier (2005), '*Frágiles*', *Cinemanía*, October, 121: 109.

Anon. (1969), 'Dickens, Hitchcock y . . . Juan Tébar', *Nuevo Fotogramas*, 2 May, 1072: 12.

Anon. (1970a), '*La residencia*: ¿un nuevo cine español?', *Cineinforme*, October, 112–13: 31–2.

Anon. (1970b), 'Panorámica', *Reseña*, March, 33: 171–2.

Anon. (1971a), 'Confirmación de una gran actriz', *Pueblo*, 11 May.

Anon. (1971b), '*El techo de cristal*', *Arriba*, 7 May.
Anon. (1971c), '*El techo de cristal*', *Nuevo Diario*, 9 May: n.p.
Anon. (1971d), '*La noche de Walpurgis*', *Pueblo*, 20 May: n.p.
Anon. (1972a), 'Eloy de la Iglesia: "Bebo en las fuentes del pueblo"', *Nuevo Fotogramas*, 10 March, 1221: 12–13.
Anon. (1972b), '*La noche del terror ciego*', *Arriba*, 16 April: n.p.
Anon. (1972c), '*La noche del terror ciego*', *Pueblo*, 2 May: n.p.
Anon. (1972d), '*La semana del asesino*', *Nuevo Fotogramas*, 16 June, 1235: 70.
Anon. (1972e), 'Sangre, terror y sexo: *La noche del terror ciego*', *Pueblo*, 2 May: n.p.
Anon. (1973a), '*El espanto surge de la tumba*', *Arriba*, 3 May: n.p.
Anon. (1973b), 'Horror ingenuo: *La rebelión de las muertas*', *Pueblo*, 9 July: n.p.
Anon. (1975a), '*Exorcismo*', *La vanguardia*, 6 March: n.p.
Anon. (1975b), '*La orgía de los muertos*', *Cineinforme*, October: n.p.
Anon. (1976a), '¿Estamos educando a los niños para la violencia?', *ABC*, 29 May: 41–2.
Anon. (1976b), '*¿Quién puede matar a un niño?*', *Actualidad*, 17–24 May: n.p.
Anon. (1976c), '*¿Quién puede matar a un niño?*', *Nuevo Diario*, 8 May: n.p.
Anon. (1976d), '*¿Quién puede matar a un niño?* Una película para pensar', *Pueblo*, 28 April: n.p.
Anon. (1982), '*Mil gritos tiene la noche*, de J. P. Simón', *ABC*, 31 August: 48.
Aranda, Joaquín (1970), '*La residencia*', *Heraldo de Aragón*, 20 January: n.p.
Arroita-Jaúregui, Marcelo (1974), 'Símbolo de una frustración: *Odio mi cuerpo*', *Arriba*, 11 June: n.p.
— (1976), '*¿Quién puede matar a un niño?*', *Arriba*, 22 April: 42.
Arroyo, José (2006), '*Pan's Labyrinth*', *Sight & Sound*, December, 16(12): 66.
Atkinson, Michael (2007), 'Moral Horrors in Guillermo del Toro's *Pan's Labyrinth*: the Supernatural Realm Mirrors Man's Inhumanity to Man', *Film Comment*, 43: 1, 50–3.
Babas, Kike and Kike Turrón (1995), *De espaldas al Kiosko. Guía histórica de fanzines y otros papelujos de alcantarilla*, Madrid: El Europeo and La Tripulación.
Baget Herms, Josep María (1993), *Historia de la televisión española, 1956–1975*, Barcelona: Freed-Back.
Balagueró, Jaume (1991), 'Editorial', *Zineshock*, 1: 2.
Balbo, Lucas (ed.) (1993), *Obsession: The Films of Jess Franco*, Berlin: Graf Haufen and Frank Trebbin.
Balum, Chas. (1987), *Gore Score. Ultraviolent Horror in the 80s*, New York: Fantaco.
— (1997), 'Aftermath: Is the Spanish Shocker the Next Guinea Pig?', *Deep Red Magazine*, Fall, 8: n.p.
Barredo, Iván (2002), '*School Killer*', *Cine para leer 2001*, Bilbao: Mensajero, pp. 280–1.
— (2006), '*La monja*', *Cine para leer 2005*, Bilbao: Mensajero, pp. 235–6.
Bassa, Joan and Ramón Freixas (1991a), 'El increíble hombre mutante (entrevista con el heterónimo Jesús Franco)', *Archivos de la Filmoteca*, 8: 39–51.
— (1991b), 'Jesús Franco. Prolífico, desconocido y vilipendiado', *Dezine*, 4: 12–23.
— (1996), *Expediente 'S': softcore, sexploitation, cine S*, Barcelona: Futura, D. L.
Baumgarten, Marjorie (2007), '*Pan's Labyrinth*', austinchronicle.com, 12 January, accessed 5 April 2007.
Beck, Jay and Vicente Rodríguez-Ortega (2008), *Contemporary Spanish Cinema and Genre*, Manchester: Manchester University Press.
Bejarano, Fernando (1996), '*Tesis*', *Guía del Diario 16*, 19 April: 15.
— (2000), 'Los sin nombre', *Cine para leer 1999*, Bilbao: Mensajero, p. 509.
— (2006), '*Frágiles*', *Cine para leer 2005*, Bilbao: Mensajero, p. 165.
Belinchón, Gregorio (2000), 'El terror también da dinero al cine español', *El país*, 23 April: 5.
— (2007), 'La nueva casa del miedo', *El país EP3*, 5 December: 12–15.
Bermejo, Alberto (1995), 'Apocalipsis en la Castellana', *El mundo*: 20 October: 90.

— (2006), 'Cuento de terror y posguerra', elmundo.es, 18 October, accessed 5 March 2007.

Bernstein, Charles (2001), 'The Future of Fear: Guillermo del Toro', *Fangoria*, March: 83.

Blaylock, David (2004), 'Darkness', villagevoice.com, 21 December, accessed 5 May 2007.

Bonet Mójica, Lluís (1995), 'De la Iglesia y el Anti-Cristo', *La vanguardia*, 1 November: 39.

— (1996), '"Snuff movies" facultativas', *La vanguardia*, 25 April: 48.

Boquerini (2000), *'El arte de morir'*, *Imágenes*, April, 191: 102.

Borau, José Luis (ed.) (1998), *Diccionario del cine español*, Madrid: Fundación Autor y Alianza.

Botting, Jo (2000a), *'El arte de morir'*, *Shivers*, 79: 47.

— (2000b), 'The Slain in Spain . . .', *Shivers*, July, 77: 32–7.

— (2003), 'Genre and Authorship in the Spanish Horror "Boom", 1968–1975: The Films of Paul Naschy and Jorge Grau', MA Research Thesis.

Bou, Núria and Xavier Pérez (1996), 'La formula de l'èxit', *Avui*, 21 April: 8–11.

Boyero, Carlos (2006), 'La imaginativa e inquietante "El laberinto del fauno" despide con brilliantez la grisácea sección oficial', elmundo.es, 28 May, accessed 27 October 2006.

— (2011), 'El que acecha en el umbral', elpais.com, 14 October, accessed 12 December 2011.

Briz (1973), *'Una gota de sangre para morir amando*: Cine de imitación', *Cinestudio*, 126: 51.

Bronce (1976), *'¿Quién puede matar a un niño?'*, *La codorniz*, 9 May: n.p.

Burrell, Nigel J. (2005), *Knights of Terror. The Blind Dead Films of Amando de Ossorio*, Huntingdon: Midnight Media.

Busquets, Antonio (ed.) *Flash-Back*, Autumn: 4.

Calhoun, John (2007), 'Fear and Fantasy', *American Cinematographer*, January, 88(1): 34–45.

Calleja, Pedro (2000), 'Terror juvenil a la española', *Metrópoli*, 31 March.

— (2002), 'El Príncipe de las Tinieblas', elmundo.es/laluna, 4 October, accessed 3 August 2007.

— (2003a), '¿Te atreverás a ver esta película?', elmundo.es/laluna, 14 March, accessed 20 May 2009.

— (2003b), '¡Están vivos! Cultura basura, cine psicotrónico y espectadores mutantes', *Cultura porquería. Una espeolología del gust*, Barcelona: Centro de Cultura Contemporània de Barcelona, pp. 155–60.

Camilo Díaz, Adolfo (1993), *El cine fantaterrorífico español. Una aproximación al género fantástico español a través del cine de Paul Naschy*, Gijón: Santa Bárbara.

Camín, Antonio (1973), 'Los hombres de la fantasía: Paul Naschy', *Terror Fantastic*, August, 23: 31–40.

Caparrós Lera, José María (1983), *El cine español bajo el régimen de Franco, 1936–1975*, Barcelona: Universidad de Barcelona.

Casas, Quim (1996), 'Pánico en la Universidad', *El periódico*, 21 April: 62.

Cascajosa, Concepción (2011), 'Narciso Ibáñez Serrador, an early pioneer of transnational television', *Studies in Hispanic Cinemas*, 7(2): 133–45.

Castilla, Paquita (1976), '"Chicho" Ibáñez Serrador, otra vez en la cima de la popularidad', Ama, *Catálogo VI Semana de Cine Fantástico y de Terror* (1995), 'Días sin luz': 79.

Catálogo de la VI Semana de Cine Fantástico y de Terror de San Sebastián (1995), San Sebastián: Kultur Udar Patronatua.

Cebollada, Pascual (1971), *'El techo de cristal'*, Ya, 4 May: n.p.

— (1973), *'Una gota de sangre para morir amando'*, Ya, 25 August: n.p.

Cerdán, Josetxo (2004), 'España fin de milenio. Sobre *El día de la bestia* (1995)', in

Rafael Ruzafa Ortega (ed.), *La historia a través del cine: transición y consolidación democrática en España*, Bilbao: UPV/EHU, pp. 235–55.
Cerdán, Josetxo, Mar Binimelis and Miguel Fernández Labayen (forthcoming), 'From Puppets to Puppeteers. Or How Franco's Regime Became Modern through an Austrian Vaudeville Show, an Uruguayan's Horror Series and a Rumanian's Avant-Garde Parodies', in Peter Goddard (ed.), *Uncertain Entertainment: Popular Television in Totalitarian Europe*, Manchester: Manchester University Press.
Cervera, Antonio (1972a), 'Hemos visto . . .', *Terror Fantastic*, April, 7: 23.
— (1972b), 'Un cómic con Waldemar Daninsky', *Terror Fantastic*, May, 8: 55.
— (1973), 'Dos películas de Amando de Ossorio', *Terror Fantastic*, April, 19: 50–3.
Cervera, Rafa (1995), 'Álex de la Iglesia se atreve con Lucifer', *Man*, November: 136–9.
Chang, Justin (2006), '*Pan's Labyrinth*', variety.com, 27 May, accessed 12 December 2006.
— (2007), '*The Orphanage*', variety.com, 21 May, accessed 18 September 2007.
Chun, Kimberly (2002), 'What is a Ghost? An Interview with Guillermo del Toro', *Cineaste*, Spring: 28–31.
Cine-Asesor (1971), 'Hoja de información: *El techo de cristal*', March: 102.
— (1974), 'Hoja de información: *La semana del asesino*', March: 82.
Cine en 7 días (1971), 'La nueva Carmen Sevilla', 8 May, 526: 23.
— (1972), 'Parra: La Nueva Imagen', 25 March, 572: 6–11.
Cineinforme (2007), 'Hemos hecho una película de factura "americana", utilizando el sistema de producción español', *Cineinforme*, September: 38–40.
— (2008), '"El orfanato" salva el orgullo del cine español', *Cineinforme*, January: 16–25.
Cine para leer (1974), 'Editorial', in Equipo Reseña (eds), *Cine para leer*, Bilbao: Mensajero, pp. 21–5.
Clover, Carol J. (1992), *Men, Women and Chain Saws: Gender in the Modern Horror Film*, London: BFI.
Cobeaga Eguillor, Borja (2000), 'El arte de morir', *Cine para leer*, January / June: 49–52.
Colón, Antonio (1976), '¿Quién puede matar a un niño?', *ABC*, 21 April: 35.
Company, Juan Manuel (1974), 'El rito y la sangre (aproximaciones al subterror hispano)', in Equipo 'Cartelera Turia', *Cine español, cine de subgéneros*, Valencia: Fernando Torres, pp. 17–76.
Conrich, Ian (ed.) (2010), *Horror Zone: The Cultural Experience of Contemporary Horror Cinema*, London: I. B. Tauris.
Corrigan, Timothy (1991), 'The Commerce of Auteurism: Coppola, Kluge, Ruiz', in *A Cinema Without Walls: Movies and Culture after Vietnam*, New Brunswick, NJ: Rutgers University Press, pp. 101–36.
Costa, Jordi (1999), 'Entrevista. Jesús Franco', in Carlos Aguilar (ed.), *Cine fantástico y de terror español: 1900–1983*, San Sebastián: Donostia Kultura, pp. 145–96.
— (2001), '*El espinazo del diablo*', *Fotogramas*, April: 14.
— (2006), 'Un laberinto para perder el sentido', elpais.es, 7 October, accessed 20 October 2006.
— (2007a), 'Encerrados en el limbo', *El país*, 12 October: 40.
— (2007b), 'Los 10 caminos imposibles de Guillermo del Toro', *Fotogramas*, 1956: 98–101.
Costa, Jordi and Darío Adanti (2009), *Mis problemas con Amenábar*, Barcelona: Glénat.
Crespo, Pedro (1973a), '*El Conde Drácula*', *Arriba*, 18 March: n.p.
— (1973b), '*Una gota de sangre para morir amando*', *Arriba*, 28 August: n.p.
Cristóbal Borra, Carlos (1999), 'Nacho Cerdà, esteta del horror', *Opus Cero*, July / September, 6: 28–31.
De Cuenca, Luis Alberto (1999), 'Paul Naschy: el hombre de las mil caras', in Carlos Águilar (ed.), *Cine fantástico y de terror español: 1900–1983*, San Sebastián: Donostia Kultura, pp. 259–70.

— (2000), *Las tres caras del terror. Un siglo de cine fantaterrorífico español*, Madrid: Alberto Santos.

De Fez, Desirée (2011), 'Balagueró y su psicópata', *Fotogramas*, 2016: 98–100.

De la Iglesia, Álex (1995), 'Satán, te voy a enviar al infierno', *El País de las Tentaciones*, 13 October: 1–7.

De Obregón, Antonio (1971), '*El techo de cristal*', *ABC*, 7 May: n.p.

— (1973), '*El Conde Drácula*', *ABC*, 19 March: n.p.

Del Corral, Enrique (1966a), 'Cine y TV. "La broma"', *ABC*, 19 June: 119.

— (1966b), '"El asfalto", obra maestra', *ABC*, 3 June: 111.

— (1966c), 'El pacto', *ABC*, 27 March: 117.

— (1966d), 'La bodega', *ABC*, 6 March: 91.

— (1966e), 'Repugnancia innecesaria. "La sonrisa"', *ABC*, 5 June: 119.

— (1967), 'N.I.S. "La pesadilla"', *ABC*, 22 October: 105.

Del Pozo, Óscar (1994), 'Jaume Balagueró + Nacho Cerdà: Esto no es gore', *A Barna*: 15.

Dezine (1991), *Jesús Franco. Francotirador del cine español*, 4, San Sebastián: Ayuntamiento de San Sebastián.

Díez Borque, José María (1972), *Literatura y cultura de masas*, Madrid: Al-Borak.

Domingo Lorén, Victoriano (1978), *Los homosexuales frente a la ley. Los juristas opinan*, Esplugas de Llobregat, Barcelona: Plaza & Janés.

Donald (1973), '*Una gota de sangre para morir amando*, mimetismo vulgar', *ABC*, 8 September: 72.

Dopazo Jover, Antonio (1972), '*La semana del asesino*', *Pantallas y escenarios*, 117: n.p.

Ebert, Roger (2001), 'The Devil's Backbone', suntimes.com, 21 December, accessed 4 August 2005.

El País de las Tentaciones (1995), 'De Sancho Panza a "Blade Runner"', 13 October: 12–13.

Enjuto Rangel, Cecilia (2009), 'La Guerra Civil española: entre fantasmas, faunos y hadas', *Vanderbilt e-journal of Luso-Hispanic Studies*, 5, accessed 21 February 2011.

Equipo 'Cartelera Turia' (1974), *Cine español, cine de subgéneros*, Valencia: Fernando Torres.

Escamilla, Bárbara (2000), 'Terror español taquillero', *Cinemanía*, May, 56: 108.

Evans, Chris (2010), 'The Insiders', *Screen International*, 5 February, 1719: 31–42.

Falquina, Ángel and Juan José Porto (1974), *Cine de terror y Paul Naschy*, Madrid: Editorial Madrid.

Fangoria (2001), 'The Future of Fear', March, 200: 80–4.

— (2004), 'Darkness (Finally) Rises', *Fangoria*, 233: 22–6.

Felperin, Leslie (2005), 'Fragile', variety.com, 8 September, accessed 12 December 2005.

Fernández, Fausto (2002), '*Darkness*', *Fotogramas*, October, 1908: 20.

Fernández Blanco, Víctor (1998), *El cine y su público en España. Un análisis económico*, Madrid: Fundación Autor.

Fernández Labayen, Miguel and Elena Galán (2006), 'Historias para no dormir', in Manuel Palacio (ed.), *Las cosas que hemos visto. 50 años y más de TVE*, Madrid: IORTVE, pp. 32–3.

Film Threat (2006), 'Pan's Labyrinth', filmthreat.com, 30 December, accessed 5 March 2007.

Flesh and Blood (1998), 'Cerdà on Love, Death & Life', *Flesh and Blood*, 10: 60–3.

Flores, Miguel Ángel (1973), 'Eloy de la Iglesia se defiende', *ABC*, 19 September: 22–3.

Floresta, Mayte (1996), 'Morbo, violencia y cintas de video', *Guía del Diario 16*, 12 April: 4–5.

Fordham, Joe (2007), 'Into the Labyrinth', *Cinefex*, 109: 32–45.

Franco, Jesús (2004), *Memorias del tío Jess*, Madrid: Aguilar.

French, Philip (2006), '*Pan's Labyrinth*', *The Observer*, 26 November: 14.

Galán, Diego (1976), 'Eloy de la Iglesia, cine marginal', *Triunfo*, 15 May, 694: 65–6.

— (1983), 'La salvaje infancia *¿Quién puede matar a un niño?*', *El país*, 19 July: n.p.

Garci, José Luis (1968), 'El escalofrío antes de dormir', *Cinestudio*, 66: 22–3.

García, Pedro (1973a), 'Para un cine de terror nacional', *Cine en 7 días*, 21 July, 641: 16.

— (1973b), 'Para un cine de terror nacional', *Cine en 7 días*, 29 September, 651: 10.

García, Rocío (1995), '"Creo en Dios, pero creo más en el Diablo", afirma Álex de la Iglesia', *El país*, 18 October: 39–40.

García Escudero, José Manuel (1962), *El cine español*, Madrid: Rialp.

García Fernández, Emilio (1992), *El cine español contemporáneo*, Barcelona: CILEH.

García Santamaría, José Vicente (1981), 'Entrevista con PAUL (Jacinto) NASCHY (Molina)', *Contracampo*, October, 24: 51–6.

García Serrano, Federico (1996), 'La ficción televisiva en España: del retrato teatral a la domesticación del lenguaje cinematográfico', *Archivos de la Filmóteca*, June–October, 23/34: 71–89.

Garcival (1973), '*Una gota de sangre para morir amando*', *ABC*, 28 August: n.p.

Garrido, Inma (2001), '*El espinazo del diablo*: un fantasma en la guerra civil española', *Cinemanía*, May: 71.

Gasca, Luis (1965), *Los cómics en la pantalla*, San Sebastián: Festival Internacional de Cine de San Sebastián.

— (1966), *Tebeo y cultura de masas*, Madrid: Prensa Española.

— (1972a), 'Mójica Marins: donde el instinto supera a la razón', *Terror Fantastic*, February, 5: 40–7.

— (1972b), 'Santo, el enmascarado de plata', *Terror Fantastic*, September, 12: 8–19.

Gil, Cristina (1996), 'Mi generación está marcada por la violencia en el cine y la televisión', *Ya*, 10 April: 58.

Giménez, Carlos (2000), *Paracuellos*, Barcelona: Glénat.

Gingold, Michael (1998), 'Fear and Laughing in Montreal', *Fangoria*, March, 170: 17–19.

— (2001), 'The Future of Fear', *Fangoria*, 200: 80.

— (2011), '*The Nameless*', *Fangoria*, 300: 64.

Gleiberman, Owen (2004), '*Darkness*' (*Entertainment Weekly*), metacritic.com, accessed 5 May 2007.

Gómez López-Quiñones, Antonio (2009), 'Hadas, maquis y niños sin escuela: la infancia romántica y la Guerra Civil en *El laberinto del fauno*', *Vanderbilt e-journal of Luso-Hispanic Studies*, 5, accessed 21 February 2011.

González Egido, Luciano (1976), '*¿Quién puede matar a un niño?*', *Pueblo*, 10 May: n.p.

Un gorila que no es Morgan disfrazado (1973), 'Una gota de sangre para morir amando', *Nuevo Fotogramas*, 2 November, 1307: 13.

Grant, Catherine (2000), 'www.auteur.com?', *Screen*, 41: 1, 101–8.

Green, Jennifer (2000a), 'Filmax Develops English-Language Trio', www.screendaily.com, accessed 24 July 2007.

— (2000b), 'Filmax Partners with Miramax on *Darkness*', screendaily.com, accessed 24 July 2007.

— (2000c), 'Spanish Film Stays Alive with *Art of Dying*', screendaily.com, accessed 24 July 2007.

— (2001), 'Filmax Closes More Cannes Slate Deals', screendaily.com, accessed 24 July 2007.

— (2002a), 'Close Up: Brian Yuzna', *Screen International*, 25 October: 34.

— (2002b), 'Sitges to open with Darkness', *Screen International*, 18 July: 12.

Green, Stephanie (2002), 'Spanish House of Horror', *Screen International*, 27 September: 12.

Guarner, José Luis (1971), 'Spanish Speaking Terror, o los monstruos también pueden llamarse González', *Nuevo Fotogramas*, 9 April, 1173: 12–13.

Gubern, Román (1974), 'Prólogo', in Equipo 'Cartelera Turia', *Cine español, cine de subgéneros*, Valencia: Fernando Torres, pp. 9–16.

— (1981), 'La nueva edad del terror', *Contracampo*, October, 24: 35–46.

— (1989), *La imagen pornográfica y otras perversiones ópticas*, Madrid: Akal.

— (2001), 'El cine español mete miedo', *El mundo*, 27 June, elcultural.es/version_papel/ CINE/751/El_cine_espanol_mete_miedo, accessed 27 May 2005.

Gubern, Román and Domènec Font (1975), *Un cine para el cadalso. 40 años de censura cinematográfica en España*, Barcelona: Euros.

Gudino, Rod (1999), 'The Faces of Death of . . . Nacho Cerda', *Rue Morgue*, January / February: 8–10.

Guillot, Eduardo (2000), 'Gritos a la española', *El Levante*, 31 March: n.p.

Hantke, Steffen (ed.) (2004), *Horror Film. Creating and Marketing Fear*, Jackson: University Press of Mississippi.

Hardcastle, Anne E. (2005), 'Ghosts of the Past and Present: Hauntology and the Spanish Civil War in Guillermo del Toro's *The Devil's Backbone*', *Journal of the Fantastic in the Arts*, 15: 119–31.

Harvey, Dennis (2007), '*The Abandoned*', variety.com, 23 February, accessed 5 September 2007.

Hawkins, Joan (2000), *Cutting Edge, Art-Horror and the Horrific Avant-garde*, Minneapolis: University of Minnesota Press.

Heredero, Carlos (1996), 'La "Tesis" de Alejandro Amenábar', *Diario 16*, 17 February: 32.

Heredero, Carlos and José Enrique Monterde (eds) (2003), *Los 'Nuevos Cines' en España. Ilusiones y desencantos de los años sesenta*, Valencia: Generalitat Valenciana.

Hills, Matt (2002), *Fan Cultures*, London: Routledge.

— (2005), *The Pleasures of Horror*, London: Continuum.

— (2010), 'Attending Horror Film Festivals and Conventions: Liveness, Subcultural Capital and "Flesh-and-Blood Genre Communities"', in Ian Conrich (ed.), *Horror Zone: The Cultural Experience of Contemporary Horror Cinema*, London: I. B. Tauris, pp. 87–102.

Hodges, M. (2000), 'The Nameless Scares You Senseless', *Fangoria*, July, 194: 22–5.

— (2003), 'Black Serenade: Spanish Stalker', *Fangoria*, January / February, 219: 55–7.

— (2004), 'Darkness (finally) rises', *Fangoria*, June, 233: 22–6.

Holland, Jonathan (2000), '*The Art of Dying*', variety.com, 29 May, accessed 14 August 2007.

— (2001), '*The Devil's Backbone*', *Variety*, 30 April–6 May: 28.

— (2004), '*Darkness*', variety.com, 26 December, accessed 5 August 2007.

Honeycutt, Kirk (2001), '*The Devil's Backbone*', hollywoodreporter.com, 13 September, accessed 4 August 2005.

Hopewell, John (1986), *Out of the Past: Spanish Cinema after Franco*, London: BFI.

Hutchings, Peter (1993), *Hammer and Beyond: The British Horror Film*, Manchester: Manchester University Press.

— (2004), *The Horror Film*, London: Pearson Longman.

— (2008), 'Monster Legacies: Memory, Technology and Horror History', in Lincoln Geraghty and Mark Jancovich (eds), *The Shifting Definitions of Genre*, Jefferson: McFarland Press, pp. 216–28.

Interino (1981), '*Viaje al más allá*', *ABC*, 21 May: 65.

Jancovich, Mark (2000), '"A Real Shocker": Authenticity, Genre and the Struggle for Distinction', *Continuum: Journal of Media and Cultural Studies*, 14(2): 23–35.

— (2002), 'Cult Fictions: Cult Movies, Subcultural Capital and the Production of Cultural Distinctions', *Cultural Studies*, 16(2): 306–22.

Jancovich, Mark, Joanne Hollows and Peter Hutchings (eds) (2002), *The Horror Film Reader*, London: Routledge.

Jones, Alan (2001), 'Breaking the Devil's Backbone', *Shivers*, 93: 40–3.

— (2006), 'Pan's People', *Shivers*, 130: 14–18.

— (2007), '[•REC]', *Fangoria*, October, 267: 233–5.

— (2008), 'Success is an orphanage', *Fangoria*, January / February, 269: 35.

Jordan, Barry (2008), 'Audiences, genre and snuff: Revisiting Amenábar's *Tesis*', in Joan Ramón Resina (ed.), *Burning Darkness. Half a Century of Spanish Cinema*, New Haven: Yale University Press, pp. 173–93.
Kapsis, Robert E. (1992), *Hitchcock: The Making of a Reputation*, Chicago: University of Chicago Press.
Kay, Jeremy (2006), 'Faun-language market', *Screen International*, 15 December: 36.
Kendrick, James (2004), 'A Nasty Situation. Social Panics, Transnationalism and the Video Nasty', in Steffen Hantke (ed.), *Horror Film. Creating and Marketing Fear*, Jackson: University Press of Mississippi, pp. 153–72.
Kennedy, Colin (2001), 'The Devil's Backbone', *Empire*, December: 130.
Kermode, Mark (2006), 'Girl Interrupted', *Sight & Sound*, December: 20–4.
Khan, Omar (2001), 'El fantasma más hermoso', *Cinemanía*, May: 62–5.
Kowalsky, Daniel (2004), 'Rated S: softcore pornography and the Spanish transition to democracy, 1977–1982', in Antonio Lázaro-Reboll and Andrew Willis (eds), *Spanish Popular Cinema*, Manchester: Manchester University Press, pp. 188–208.
Labanyi, Jo (2000), 'History and Hauntology, or, What Does One Do with the Ghosts of the Past?: Reflections on Spanish Film and Fiction of the Post-Franco Period', in Joan Ramón Resina (ed.), *Disremembering the Dictatorship: the Politics of Memory in the Spanish Transition to Democracy*, Amsterdam: Rodopi, pp. 65–82.
— (2002), 'Introduction: Engaging with Ghosts, or, Theorizing Culture in Modern Spain', in Jo Labanyi (ed.), *Constructing Identity in Contemporary Spain: Theoretical Debates and Cultural Practice*, Oxford: Oxford University Press, pp. 1–14.
— (2007), 'Memory and Modernity in Democratic Spain: the Difficulties of Coming to Terms with the Spanish Civil War', *Poetics Today*, 28(1): 89–116.
La Codorniz (1971), 'Extra Suspense', 1532, 28 March.
Lahosa, J. E. (1973), '*Una gota de sangre para morir amando*', *Nuevo Fotogramas*, 19 October, 1305: 41.
Landis, Bill and Michelle Clifford (2002), 'The Liberty and the Cinerama: Showcases for Eurosleaze', *Sleazoid Express*, New York: Fireside, pp. 177–213.
La pantera rosa (1973), 'Una gota de sangre para morir . . . riendo (por no llorar)', *Nuevo Fotogramas*, 5 October, 1303: 8.
Lara, Fernando (1976), 'Niños donde había pájaros', *Triunfo*, 1 May, 692: 62.
Lara, Fernando, Diego Galán and Ramón Rodríguez (1973), 'Eloy de la Iglesia y la violencia', *Triunfo*, 22 September, 573: 61–3.
Lardín, Rubén (1996), *Las diez caras del miedo*, Valencia: Midons.
— (1999), 'Jaume Balagueró', *ojalatemueras*, 1: 60–5.
Latorre, José María (1970), '*La residencia*', *Film Ideal*, 217/218/219: 482–5.
Lázaro-Reboll Antonio (2004), 'Screening "Chicho": The Horror Ventures of Narciso Ibáñez Serrador', in Antonio Lázaro-Reboll and Andrew Willis (eds), *Spanish Popular Cinema*, Manchester: Manchester University Press, pp. 152–68.
— (2005), '*La noche de Walpurgis / Shadow of the Werewolf*', in Alberto Mira (ed.), *The Cinema of Spain and Portugal*, London: Wallflower, pp. 219–27.
— (2007), 'The Transnational Reception of *El espinazo del diablo* (Guillermo del Toro, 2001)', *Hispanic Research Journal*, 8(1): 39–51.
— (2008), '"Now Playing Everywhere": Spanish Horror Film in the Marketplace', in Jay Beck and Vicente Rodríguez-Ortega (eds), *Contemporary Spanish Cinema and Genre*, Manchester: Manchester University Press, pp. 65–83.
— (2009), '"Perversa América Latina": the Reception of Latin American Exploitation Cinemas in Spanish Subcultures', in Victoria Ruétalo and Dolores Tierney (eds), *Latsploitation, Latin America, and Exploitation Cinema*, London: Routledge, pp. 37–54.
— (2012), 'Horror', in Jo Labanyi and Tatjana Pavlovic (eds), *Film Noir, the Thriller, and Horror: A Companion to Spanish Cinema*, Oxford: Wiley-Blackwell.

Lázaro-Reboll, Antonio and Andrew Willis (eds) (2004), *Spanish Popular Cinema*, Manchester: Manchester University Press.

Lerman, Gabriel (1997), 'Entrevista a Guillermo del Toro', *Dirigido por . . .*, October: 34–7.

Leyra, Paloma (1996), 'Alejandro Amenábar', *El semanal*, 18 February: 72.

Llinás, Francesc and José Luis Téllez (1981), 'El primer plano y el aceite de colza. Entrevista con Eloy de la Iglesia', *Contracampo*, 25/26 November: 27–36.

Llopart, Salvador (1999), 'Jaume Balagueró: "además de entretener el cine debe producir emociones fuertes"', *La vanguardia*, 9 October: 55.

López Sancho, Lorenzo (1973), *ABC*, 4 October: n.p.

— (1976), 'Vigoroso relato entre el horror y la ciencia-ficción: ¿Quién puede matar a un niño?', *ABC*, 24 April: 58.

Losilla, Carlos (1995), 'El día de la bestia', *Dirigido por . . .*, November, 240: 12.

Lowenstein, Adam (2005), *Shocking Representation: Historical Trauma, National Cinema and the Modern Horror Film*, New York: Columbia University Press.

Lucas, Tim (1990), 'How To Read a Franco Film', *Video Watchdog*, 1: 18–34.

— (ed.) (2000), *Video Watchdog* 'Tales from the Attic: Special Paul Naschy Edition', December: 66.

— (2010), 'Jess Franco: Tim Lucas on the Early Films', *Video Watchdog*, 157: 16–49.

Marías, Miguel (1970), 'La residencia', *Nuestro Cine*, March, 95: 72–3.

Marsh, Steven (2006), *Popular Spanish Film under Franco: Comedy and the Weakening of the State*, Basingstoke: Palgrave.

Marshall, Lee (2005), 'Fragile', screeninternational.com, 15 September 2005, accessed 5 May 2007.

Martialay, Félix (1971), 'La marca del hombre lobo', *El Alcázar*, 24 August: n.p.

— (1972), 'La noche del terror ciego', *El Alcázar*, 14 April: n.p.

Martínez, A. (1976), '¿Quién puede matar a un niño?', *La vanguardia española*, 28 April: n.p.

Masó, Ángeles (1976), 'Narciso Ibáñez Serrador', *La vanguardia española*, 24 April: 51.

Matellano, Víctor (2009), *Spanish Horror*, Madrid: T & B Editores.

Méndez, Sabino (1995), 'Spanish Gore: Sangre y Caspa', *Ruta 66*, February, 103: 36–9.

Mendik, Xabier (2004), 'Trans-European Excess: An Interview with Brian Yuzna', in Ernest Mathijs and Xabier Mendik (eds), *Alternative Europe: Eurotrash and Exploitation Cinema Since 1945*, London: Wallflower, pp. 181–90.

Mendoza, Javier (1997), 'Alejandro Amenábar', *Man*, 1 April: 68–70.

Miles, Robert J. (2011), 'Reclaiming Revelation: Another Look at *Pan's Labyrinth* and *The Spirit of the Beehive*', *Quarterly Review of Film and Video*, 28(3): 195–203.

Mira (2004), *De Sodoma a Chueca: historia cultural de la homosexualidad en España 1914–1990*, Madrid: Egales.

Mitch (1997), 'Sitges Festival', *Shivers*, December, 48: 38.

M. M. (1995), '*Aftermath* is not another gore flick', *Brut Art*: 7.

Moix, Terenci (1968), *Los cómics, arte para el consumo y formas pop*, Barcelona: Llibres de Sinera.

— (1971a), 'Antinea y Ayesha', *Terror Fantastic*, December, 3: 51–3.

— (1971b), 'Barbara Steele. Diosa del Terror', *Terror Fantastic*, October, 1: 60–3.

— (1971c), 'Goticismos del terror', *Terror Fantastic*, November, 2: 4–5.

— (1972a), 'Cobra', *Terror Fantastic*, March, 6: 4–6.

— (1972b), 'Entre Batman y Superman', *Terror Fantastic*, October, 13: 40–1.

Molina, Jacinto (1976), 'El hombre lobo por el hombre lobo: Paul Naschy', *Vudu*, March, 8: 23–9.

— (1998), 'El hombre lobo español', tentaciones.elpais.es, 29 May, accessed 3 June 1998.

— (2001), 'El cine español mete miedo', *El mundo*, 27 June 2001, elcultural.es/version_papel/CINE/751/El_cine_espanol_mete_miedo, accessed 27 May 2005.

Molina Foix, Juan Antonio (1999), 'Entrevista. Paul Naschy', in Carlos Águilar (ed.),

Cine fantástico y de terror español, 1900–1983, San Sebastián: Donostia Kultura, pp. 287–305.
Molina Foix, Vicente (2007), 'Mexican Gothic', letraslibres.com, December 2006, accessed 5 March 2007.
Monell, Robert (2003), 'El aullido del diablo', naschy.com, accessed 16 April 2008.
Montaner, Francisco (1972a), '*Dr Jekyll y el hombre lobo*', *Terror Fantastic*, October, 13: 49.
— (1972b), 'Los mitos del terror: el hombre lobo', January, 4: 8–15.
— (1972c), '*La residencia*', *Terror Fantastic*, August, 11: 19.
— (1972d), '*La semana del asesino*', *Terror Fantastic*, August, 11: 75.
— (1973), 'La ciencia ficción en el cine de España', *Terror Fantastic*, January, 16: 16–19.
Monterde, José Enrique (1993), *Veinte años de cine español (1973–1992): un cine bajo la paradoja*, Barcelona: Paidós.
Naschy, Paul (1997), *Paul Naschy. Memorias de un hombre lobo*, Madrid: Alberto Santos.
Navarro, Antonio José (2002a), 'En el corazón de las tinieblas', *Dirigido por . . .*, October, 316: 30–1.
— (2002b), 'Jaume Balagueró', *Dirigido por . . .*, October, 316: 32–3.
— (2005a), 'Jaume Balagueró', *Dirigido por . . .*, September, 348: 26–8.
— (2005b), '*La monja*', *Dirigido por . . .*, November, 350: 14.
— (2005c), 'Una historia macabra', *Dirigido por . . .*, September, 348: 30–1.
— (2006), 'Dossier nuevo cine de terror. Diez directores fundamentales del género', *Dirigido por . . .*, July / August, 358: 36–55.
Nazzaro, Joe (2006), 'Creature Features Great and Small', *Fangoria*, 253: 60–5.
— (2007), 'Monsters in the Labyrinth', *Shivers*, 132: 15–17.
Newman, Kim (1988), *Nightmare Movies*, New York: Harmony.
— (2011), *Nightmare Movies*, London: Bloomsbury.
Nolla, Carlos (1972), '*La llamada del vampiro*', *Terror Fantastic*, October, 13: 48.
Nueva dimensión (1971), 'Número dedicado al terror en nuestro tiempo', July, 24.
Nuevo Fotogramas (1971a), 'Especial Terror', 9 April, 1173.
— (1971b), 'Vuelve violento Vicente Parra', 1 October, 1198: 26–7.
O'Brien, Joseph (2007), '*The Abandoned*', *Fangoria*, 65.
Olano, Antonio D. (1972), 'Racial Eloy de la Iglesia', *Cine en 7 días*, 5 April, 575: 5–8.
— (1973), 'Entrevista a Jesús Franco', *Cine en 7 días*, 17 February, 619: 9–12.
Ordóñez, Marcos (1978), 'Entrevista Eloy de la Iglesia. Del esperpento a la dialéctica', *Nuevo Fotogramas*, 30 June: 20–2, 43.
— (1997), *La bestia anda suelta. ¡Álex de la Iglesia lo cuenta todo!*, Barcelona: Glénat.
Palacio, Manuel (2001), *Historia de la televisión en España*. Barcelona: Gedisa.
Palacios, Jesús (1995), *Goremanía*, Madrid: Alberto Santos.
Pavlović, Tatjana (2003), *Despotic Bodies and Transgressive Bodies. Spanish Culture from Francisco Franco to Jesús Franco*, Albany: SUNY.
Peláez, Jesús (1973a), '*La furia del hombre lobo*', *El Alcázar*, 29 May: n.p.
— (1973b), '*Una gota de sangre para morir amando*', *El Alcázar*, 3 September: n.p.
— (1974a), '*La semana del asesino*', *El Alcázar*, 2 May: n.p.
— (1974b), '*Las vampiras*', *El Alcázar*, 1 June: n.p.
— (1976), '*La noche de las gaviotas*', *El Alcázar*, 4 August: n.p.
Pelayo, Antonio (1970), '*La residencia*', *Cinestudio*, February, 82: 39–40.
Pérez Gómez, Ángel A. (1970), '*La residencia*', *Reseña*, March, 33: 172–5.
— (1996), 'El día de la bestia, de Álex de la Iglesia', in Equipo Reseña (ed.), *Cine para leer*, Bilbao: Mensajero.
Perks, Marcella (1998), '*Genesis*: Visit to the set', *Shivers*, 53: 8–11.
Picas, Jaume (1971a), '*El proceso de las brujas*', *Nuevo Fotogramas*, 2 June, 1181: 39.
— (1971b), '*El techo de cristal*', *Nuevo Fotogramas*, 24 September, 1197: 41.
— (1971c), '*La noche de Walpurgis*', *Nuevo Fotogramas*, 30 July, 1189: 41.

Pierrot (1971), 'Auto-crítica – o así – de la obra por su "exquisito" autor', *Terror Fantastic*, December, 3: 50.

— (1972a), 'Elucubraciones, desmayos y gritos sobre el Teatro-Pánico de Alejandro Jodorowsky', *Terror Fantastic*, January, 4: 58–60.

— (1972b), 'Teatro Terror presenta al loco, ventrudo y mamarracho Fernando Arrabal', *Terror Fantastic*, April, 7: 60–2.

Piña, Begoña (2000), 'Fernández Armero explora el género del terror en su nuevo filme *El arte de morir*', *La Vanguardia*, 30 March.

Pirie, David (1973), *A Heritage of Horror: The English Gothic Cinema 1946–1972*, London: Gordon Fraser.

Regal, Lake (1984), 'Spain's "Mr. Monster"', *Classic Images*, 114: 10–11.

Reguera, Iván (2006), 'El laberinto del fauno y los fachas de fijador, brillantina y correaje', blogs.periodistadigital.com, 23 October, accessed 5 March 2007.

Rey, José Ramón (1995), 'Satanismo de tebeo', *Ya*, 30 October: 48.

Riambau, Esteve and Casimiro Torreiro (1999), *La Escuela de Barcelona: El cine de la 'gauche divine'*, Barcelona: Anagrama.

Rodríguez Marchante, E. (1995), '"El día de la bestia": de Madrid al infierno', *ABC*, 21 October: 82.

— (1996), '"Tesis": hay películas que matan', *ABC*, 13 April: 86.

Rodríguez-Ortega, Vicente (2005), 'Snuffing Hollywood: Transmedia Horror in *Tesis*', *Senses of Cinema*, July–September, 36, sensesofcinema.com.

Romero, Javier G. (2002), *Quatermass*, Autumn: 4–5.

Romo, Manuel (1996), 'Editorial', *Invasión* 1: 4.

Rubio, Miguel (1972a), '*Jack el destripador de Londres*', *Nuevo Diario*, 17 November: n.p.

— (1972b), '*La noche del terror ciego*', *Nuevo Diario*, 2 May: n.p.

— (1973), 'El cine, Perpignan y los españoles', *Terror Fantastic*, June, 9: 60–1.

— (1974), '*La semana del asesino*', *Nuevo Diario*, 27 April: n.p.

Sáinz, Salvador (1975), 'Paul Naschy', in *Vudú*, February, 2: n.p.

— (1981), *Transylvania Express* 'Especial Paul Naschy, el lobo mesetario', March: 2.

— (1989), *Historia del cine fantástico español (de Segundo de Chomón a Bigas Luna)*, Ibiza: Festival de Cine.

Sala, Ángel (1999), 'Las "pulp-legends" de Amando de Ossorio', in Carlos Águilar (ed.), *Cine fantástico y de terror español: 1900–1983*, San Sebastián: Donostia Kultura, pp. 309–29.

— (2010), *Profanando el sueño de los muertos*, Pontevedra: Scifiworld.

Salisbury, Mark (2001), 'Real Backbone', *Fangoria*, 201: 30–4.

Salvador, Lola (1969), '"Monstruo sagrado" de TVE rueda "La Residencia"', *Nuevo Fotogramas*, 2 May, 1072: 12–14.

Santamarina, Antonio (2001), 'Un sugerente melodrama gótico', *Dirigido por . . .*, April: 22–4.

Santos Fontenla, César (1974), 'Muñeca muerta', *Informaciones*, 13 August: n.p.

— (1982), '*Mil gritos tiene la noche*', *ABC*, 31 August: 48.

Savater, Fernando (1998), 'Hermano lobo', *Nosferatu. Revista de cine*, March, 27: n.p.

— (1999), 'Bendita familia', in Carlos Aguilar (ed.), *Cine fantástico y de terror español: 1900–1983*, San Sebastián: Donostia Kultura, pp. 193–6.

Savlov, Marc (2004), 'Darkness', austinchronicle.com, 31 December, accessed 5 May 2007.

Schaefer, Eric (1999), *'Bold! Daring! Shocking! True!' A History of Exploitation Films, 1919–1959*, Durham, NC, and London: Duke University Press.

— (2007), 'Pandering to the "Goon Trade": Framing the Sexploitation Audience through Advertising', in Jeffrey Sconce (ed.), *Sleaze Artists. Cinema at the Margins of Taste, Style and Politics*, Durham, NC, and London: Duke University Press, pp. 19–46.

Scheck, Frank (2004), 'Darkness' (*The Hollywood Reporter*), metacritic.com, accessed 5 May 2007.

Schneider, Steven Jay (2003), *Fear Without Frontiers: Horror Cinema Across the Globe*, Surrey: FAB.

Schneider, Steven Jay and Tony Williams (2005), *Horror International*, Detroit: Wayne State University Press.

Sconce, Jeffrey (1995), '"Trashing" the Academy: Taste, Excess and an Emerging Politics of Cinematic Style', *Screen*, 36(4): 371–93.

Scott, A. O. (2001), 'Dodging Bombs and Ghosts in Civil War Spain', 21 November, nytimes.com, accessed 4 August 2005.

— (2006), 'Pan's Labyrinth', *New York Times*, 29 December, nytimes.com, accessed 5 May 2007.

Screen International (2006), 'Allegory: the International Language', 25 August: 7.

Sennit, Stephen (1999), *Ghastly Terror. The Horrible History of the Horror Comics*, Manchester: Headpress.

Serrano Cueto, José Manuel (2007), *Horrormanía. Enciclopedia del cine de terror*, Madrid: Alberto Santos.

Serrats Ollé, Jaime (1971), *Nuestros Contemporáneos: Narciso Ibáñez Serrador*, Barcelona: Dopesa.

Shapiro, Steven (1993), *The Cinematic Body*, Minneapolis: University of Minnesota Press.

Shivers (1998), 'Genesis Set in Stone', *Shivers*, May, 53: 8–11.

Shock Cinema (1997), '*Aftermath*', *Shock Cinema*, Spring, 10: 9.

— (1999), 'Nacho Cerdà's *Genesis*', *Shock Cinema*, Fall / Winter, 15: 9.

Skal, David (1993), *The Monster Show: A Cultural History of Horror*, London: Plexus.

Slater, Jason (1998), '*Aftermath*: Interview with Nacho Cerda', *Dark Side*, April / May, 72: n.p.

Smith, Paul Julian (1992), *Laws of Desire. Questions of Homosexuality in Spanish Writing and Film 1960–1990*, Oxford: Clarendon.

— (2001), 'Ghost of the Civil Dead', *Sight and Sound*, December: 38–9.

— (2007), 'Pan's Labyrinth', *Film Quarterly*, Summer, 60: 4–8.

Smith, R. H. (2000), '*Cannibal Man*', *Video Watchdog*, 66: 46–8.

Steinberg, Samuel (2006), 'Franco's Kids: Geopolitics and Post-dictatorship in *¿Quién puede matar a un niño?*', *Journal of Spanish Cultural Studies*, 7(1): 23–36.

Suzy Sexi (2002), 'Borja Crespo: Perversiones a la carta', *2000maniacos*, 26: 13.

Syder, Andrew and Dolores Tierney (2005), 'Importation / Mexploitation, or, How a Crime-Fighting, Vampire-Slaying Mexican Wrestler Almost Found Himself in an Italian Sword-and-Sandals Epic', in Steven Jay Schneider and Tony Williams (eds), *Horror International*, Detroit: Wayne State University Press, pp. 33–55.

Tébar, Juan (1971), 'Juan Tébar lo ha visto así', *Terror Fantastic*, October, 1: 44–7.

— (1972a), 'La pantalla infernal: "à la recherche du fantastique (I)"', *Terror Fantastic*, March, 6: 40–3.

— (1972b), 'La pantalla infernal: "à la recherche du fantastique (II)"', *Terror Fantastic*, April, 7: 45–7.

— (1972c), 'La pantalla infernal: "à la recherche du fantastique (y III)"', *Terror Fantastic*, June, 9: 16–19.

Terror Fantastic (1971), '¿Qué pretende ser "Terror-Fantastic"?', October, 1: 5.

— (1972a), 'Erotismo en el terror', December, 15: 7.

— (1972b), 'Las que no veremos', April, 7: 7.

— (1973), '¿Cine español de exportación?', April, 19: 7.

The Hollywood Reporter (2011), '5 Spanish Filmmakers Ready to Crack the Global Market', 15 May, accessed 21 August 2011.

Thompson, Mike (2010), 'The Worst Horror Films Since 2000', metacritic.com, 16 October, accessed 14 May 2011.

Tierney, Dolores (2002), 'The Appeal of the Real in Snuff: Alejandro Amenábar's *Tesis*

(*Thesis*)', in 'Axes to Grind: Re-Imagining the Horrific in Visual Media and Culture', *Spectator*, Special Issue, Fall, 22(2): 45–55.

Tohill, Cathal and Pete Tombs (1995), *Immoral Tales. Sex and Horror Cinema in Europe 1956–1984*, London and New York: Titan.

Torreiro, M. (1995), 'Satán en la Gran Vía', *El país*, 27 October: 44.

— (1996), 'El alumno Amenábar', *El país*, 27 April: 43.

— (2006), 'Extraordinario y cruel', *El país*, 13 October: 44.

Torres, Sara (1999), 'Narciso Ibáñez Serrador, entrevista', in Carlos Aguilar (ed.), *Cine fantástico y de terror español: 1900–1983*, San Sebastián: Donostia Kultura, pp. 223–56.

Total Film (2006), 'Pan's Labyrinth', totalfilm.com, 24 November, accessed 12 December 2006.

Totaro, Donato (1997a), 'Nacho Cerda Interview', www.horschamp.qc.ca, 13 August, accessed 21 June 2002.

— (1997b), 'Necrophilic Art: *Kissed* and *Aftermath*', www.horschamp.qc.ca, 22 July, accessed 21 June 2002.

— (2001), 'Looking into the Crystal Ball of Horror: Interview with Nacho Cerdà', www.horschamp.qc.ca, 5 March, accessed 21 June 2002.

Triana-Toribio, Núria (2003), *Spanish National Cinema*, London: Routledge.

Triunfo (1971), 'Extra Terror', 27 March, 460.

Troppiano, Stephen (1997), 'Out of the Cinematic Closet: Homosexuality in the Films of Eloy de la Iglesia', in Marsha Kinder (ed.), *Reconfiguring Spain: Cinema / Media / Representation*, Durham, NC: Duke University Press, pp. 157–77.

Tudor, Andrew (2002), 'From Paranoia to Postmodernism? The Horror Movie in Late Modern Society', in Steve Neale (ed.), *Genre and Contemporary Hollywood*, London: BFI, pp. 105–16.

Turek, Ryan (2007), '*Pan's Labyrinth*. A Maze Thing', *Fangoria*, 259: 42–7.

V. A. (2000), *La novela popular en España*, Madrid: Robel.

Valencia, Manuel (1990), 'Editorial', *2000maniacos*, 2: 3.

— (1994), 'Editorial', *2000maniacos*, 15: 3.

— (1999a), '1989–1999. Toda una década de caspa y puterío', *2000maniacos*, 21.

— (1999b), 'México Loco Superespecial. Chilli Terror', *2000maniacos*, 22.

— (2002a), 'Bizarre Latino', *2000maniacos*, 26.

— (2002b), 'Cine 100% adolescente: *Kárate a muerte en Torremolinos*', *2000maniacos*, 25: 14–16.

— (2002c), 'Esto es lo que hay', *2000maniacos*, 25: 5.

— (2005), 'Pedro Temboury', *2000maniacos*, 33: 42–50.

— (2009), '20 años, 1989–2009', *2000maniacos*, 40: 28.

— (2010), 'Sangre y hachazos en el cine de tu barrio', *2000maniacos*, 41: 66–8.

Valencia, Manuel and Eduardo Guillot (1996), *Sangre, sudor y vísceras. Historia del cine gore*, Valencia: La Máscara.

Van Hoeij (2009), '[REC2]', variety.com, accessed 17 October 2009.

Vega (1981), 'El aparato (ideológico) de Eloy de la Iglesia', *Contracampo*, 25/26 November: 22–6.

Vié, Caroline (1994), 'Cronos, tiempo y sangre', *Fangoria*, 33: 48–51.

Vigil, Luis (1971), 'El señor Sci-Fi y su "Ackermansión"', *Terror Fantastic*, December, 3: 6–7.

— (1972a), 'Los monstruos más famosos son los de Forry', *Terror Fantastic*, January, 4: 6–7.

— (1972b), 'Mis amigos los monstruos, con la intervención personal del ackermonstruo', *Terror Fantastic*, February, 5: 4–5.

— (1975), 'Paul Naschy, el mito nacional', *Famosos Monsters del Cine*, April, 1: 24–30.

Vilella, Antonio (1971), '*El proceso de las brujas*', *Terror Fantastic*, December, 3: 54.

— (1972a), '*La ciudad sin hombres*', *Terror Fantastic*, May, 8: 51–2.

— (1972b), 'La noche del terror ciego', Terror Fantastic, November, 14: 60–1.
Villar, Carmen (2000), 'Terror de diseño', El Faro de Vigo, 21 April.
Vuckovic, Jovanka (2005), 'Traces of Death', Rue Morgue, July, 47: 16–19.
Weldon, Michael (1989), The Psychotronic Encyclopaedia of Film, London: Plexus.
Wheatley, Helen (2006), Gothic Television, Manchester: Manchester University Press.
Williams, Evan Calder (2011), 'To sit on a throne of teeth, graced with a crown of teeth: notes on opportunities blown and missed', http://socialismandorbarbarism.blogspot. com, 13 October, accessed 11 December 2011.
Willis, Andrew (2003), 'Spanish Horror and the Flight from Art Cinema', in Mark Jancovich et al. (eds), Defining Cult Movies: the Cultural Politics of Oppositional Taste, Manchester: Manchester University Press, pp. 71–83.
— (2004), 'From the Margins to the Mainstream: Trends in Recent Spanish Horror Cinema', in Antonio Lázaro-Reboll and Andrew Willis (eds), Spanish Popular Cinema, Manchester: Manchester University Press, pp. 237–49.
— (2005), 'La semana del asesino: Spanish Horror as Subversive Text', in Steven J. Schneider and Tony Williams (eds), Horror International, Detroit: Wayne State University Press, pp. 163–79.
— (2008), 'The Fantastic Factory: the Horror Genre and Contemporary Spanish Cinema', in Jay Beck and Vicente Rodríguez-Ortega (eds), Contemporary Spanish Cinema and Genre, Manchester: Manchester University Press, pp. 27–43.
Wood, Robin (1978), 'An Introduction to the American Horror Film: Part I: Repression, The Other, The Monster; Part II: Return of the Repressed; Part III; The Reactionary Wing', in Robin Wood and Richard Lippe (eds), The American Nightmare: Essays on the Horror Film, Toronto: Festival of Festivals, pp. 7–28.
— (1984), 'An Introduction to the American Horror Film', in Barry Grant (ed.), Planks of Reason: Essays on the Horror Film, Metuchen, NJ: Scarecrow, pp. 164–200.
— (1986), 'The American Nightmare: Horror in the 70s', in Hollywood from Vietnam to Reagan, New York: Columbia University Press.
Yaccarino, Michael (2000), 'La Residencia: A Classic of Spanish Horror Cinema Revisited', Filmfax, October–January, 75/76: 46–53.
Yoldi, Pedro (1971), 'Paul Naschy. Entrevista', Terror Fantastic, November, 2: 51.
— (1972) 'La mansión de la niebla', Terror Fantastic, March, 6: 47.
Zambrana, Manuel (2002), 'Darkness', Cinemanía, October, 85: 24–5.
Zinéfilo, Álex (2003), 'La "fama" mostrenca', 2000maniacos, 23: 63–5.

INDEX

Page numbers in *italics* refer to figures.

EU Authorised Representative:

Easy Access System Europe Mustamäe tee 50, 10621 Tallinn, Estonia

gpsr.requests@easproject.com

Printed and bound by CPI Group (UK) Ltd, Croydon, CR0 4YY

09/06/2025

01897302-0002